7/15/20
$29.99
AS-14
8/20

LOVING WISDOM

WITHDRAWN

Loving Wisdom

A Guide to Philosophy and Christian Faith

SECOND EDITION

Paul Copan

WILLIAM B. EERDMANS PUBLISHING COMPANY
GRAND RAPIDS, MICHIGAN

Wm. B. Eerdmans Publishing Co.
4035 Park East Court SE, Grand Rapids, Michigan 49546
www.eerdmans.com

Published 2020
First edition published by Chalice Press 2007
Printed in the United States of America

26 25 24 23 22 21 20   1 2 3 4 5 6 7

ISBN 978-0-8028-7547-1

Library of Congress Cataloging-in-Publication Data

Names: Copan, Paul, author.
Title: Loving wisdom : a guide to philosophy and Christian faith / Paul Copan.
Description: Second edition. | Grand Rapids, Michigan : William B. Eerdmans Publish-
    ing Company, 2020. | Includes bibliographical references and index. | Summary:
    "Presents a biblical philosophy of religion, addressing a wide range of topics and
    questions as they arise in scripture"—Provided by publisher.
Identifiers: LCCN 2019047949 | ISBN 9780802875471 (paperback)
Subjects: LCSH: Christianity—Philosophy. | Theology.
Classification: LCC BR100 .C77 2020 | DDC 230.01—dc23
LC record available at https://lccn.loc.gov/2019047949

*Christ . . . in whom are hidden all the treasures
of wisdom and knowledge (Col. 2:2b–3)*

*To Stuart C. Hackett—my first philosophy professor,
whose wisdom, intellect, and faithfulness to God
inspired me and so many others*

Contents

Preface

Despite the claim that philosophy of religion isn't really philosophy, such a view ignores the philosophy's actual history going back to ancient times.[1] What's more, the number of Christian philosophy of religion volumes has burgeoned over the past few decades and shows no signs of letting up. Many of them are well written and are characterized by rational coherence and clarity of expression, and they exhibit just how intellectually fruitful the Christian faith is. So why a new one then?

Well, it isn't quite new. This is a second edition, although very thoroughly revised and expanded. A lot has happened since the first edition in 2007.

ON PHILOSOPHY AND THE BIBLICAL METANARRATIVE

The book has certain key emphases. First, this book is a guide to Christian philosophy that engages with the biblical story or metanarrative and with texts of Scripture. I have a background in biblical studies and theology, and I find this quite helpful as I reflect and write on philosophical topics. Though many fine Christian-authored philosophy of religion books exist, I try to interact more with biblical texts and with scriptural themes as they have a bearing on philosophical topics and discussions.[2]

To reinforce this Scripture-philosophy combination, I've structured the book around the biblical "grand story" or "metanarrative"—beginning with the triune God and moving from creation and then the fall to redemption and re-creation in Christ. This is indeed "the story of reality." Various philosophical topics are incorporated into the structure of this book. For example, part III on the fall includes topics such as the problem of evil, primal sin, original sin, and hell.

Second, this book attempts to make important philosophical themes accessible to a popular audience and present them from a distinctively Christian perspective. Over the years as a Christian philosopher, I've engaged in the task of reading, reflecting on, distilling, and summarizing the work of other philosophers in order to reach a wider, more popular-level audience. One key subgroup is the church. I've attempted to show how ideas have consequences, how the academy influences the culture, and how Christians should be attuned to these realities in order to think through and live out their faith before a watching world.

As is evident in this book, I greatly appreciate the work of Christian philosopher Alvin Plantinga. He has observed that many academicians have a disdain for the term *popularizer*. However, he urges Christian philosophers not to leave their work "buried away in professional journals" but to make it available to the broader Christian community. If they don't connect their work to the life of the church, then they "neglect a crucial and central part of their task as believing philosophers."[3]

Third, this book offers insight on how to think Christianly about important philosophical matters in our day—and to live out their implications personally and existentially, in relationships, and in our spheres of influence. "Jesus is Lord" (see Rom. 10:9) was a very early Christian confession. The implications of this terse declaration are immense. Jesus is ruler over all things—from every choice we make in life and how we use our time to every discipline in the academy to every particle in the universe. The earth is the Lord's, and everything it contains (Ps. 24:1). Yet plenty of Christians engage in "sacred-secular" compartmentalizing: "Reading the Bible and praying are spiritual while painting houses or repairing cars isn't," or, "Being a pastor or missionary is sacred, but studying biology or being a politician is secular." This is a huge error. C. S. Lewis noted that while personal holiness and evangelism are important, they can't be cordoned off from the broader culture. If we do that, we'll just create a narrow, inferior, irrelevant subculture of our own. If Jesus is Lord over all things, we must bring him into the marketplace, the academy, and the political realm to show how in Christ all things hold together and are illuminated.

The wisdom of Christ, the foundation of his Word, and the power of the Spirit present us with robust resources to be world-engaging. Ours is a faith seeking understanding (*fides quaerens intellectum*), as the philosopher-theologian Anselm maintained. All creation belongs to God; we can appreciate and study this world, and God can reveal something of himself through even the birds of the air and the lilies of the field (Matt. 6:26–28). The hymn "This Is My Father's World" fittingly declares: "He speaks to me everywhere." Even the lessons a farmer learns about how to plant and harvest can be said to be the result of God's instruction and teaching (Isa. 28:23–29), whether the farmer is a believer or not.

The church father Augustine affirmed that all truth is God's truth. Yes, God has spoken to us through his incarnate Son (Heb. 1:3) and in his written Word (2 Tim. 3:16–17); this is *special* revelation. Here God reveals himself about his specific workings in history through national Israel and the Christ-event to reconcile hopelessly lost human beings to himself; along with this, he shows us how to live increasingly transformed lives shaped by the life, cross, and resurrection of Christ. But that's not all. God's revelation has an even wider reach through *general* revelation. God reveals his existence and something of his character and basic truths to us through the use of reason and drawing proper conclusions, a pricked conscience, the beauty and order of creation, and the depths of human experience across the ages (Ps. 19:1–2; Isa. 28:23–29; Amos 1–2; Rom. 1:19–21). We don't have to proclaim "The Bible says" to those who don't take it as authoritative, but we can speak biblical truth and use the means of natural revelation to remind unbelievers of a God who is there and is not silent,[4] as Paul did in Athens. Thus we hope to lead people to consider what this God has done to rescue us and support us as we live out our earthly lives as citizens of his kingdom.

Fourth, a better philosophical grasp of the biblical story will enhance our proclamation of the good news of Jesus. Statistics reveal that the number of Christians having conversations about their faith is shrinking. The reasons they give include not wanting to make conversations awkward, create tensions, or be considered weird.[5] But let's change that! To be more thoughtful about our faith will enable us to freely and engagingly affirm the truth wherever it is to be found. Truth can be found in a chemistry textbook or in an epic film like *The Lord of the Rings*. Again, like Paul at Athens, we can affirm wise insights from pagan philosophers across the ages and praise displays of heroism, self-sacrifice, forgiveness, and courage by non-Christians. But as we'll see, these truths and virtues scattered throughout the world and world history find their home and their ultimate basis in the cosmic Lord of history, Jesus of Nazareth.

Though we, like Paul, might be angered and dismayed by idolatry around us, the "unknown God" has made himself known (Acts 17:16–34). Through our common human experience, creation, conscience, beauty, and reason, God provides us with an abundance of connection points and conversation starters to engage those around us in the academy, in the marketplace, and in our communities. Along the way, this book offers suggestions for engagement.

Philosophizing as Christians shouldn't be shaped by passing fads in the academy or culture; we shouldn't focus our message on the identity politics of race, sexuality, class, nationalism, or other ideologies. Rather, our thinking is to be transformed by the reality that Jesus is Lord, and that we as subjects of King Jesus are to seek first God's kingdom and his priorities (Matt. 6:33).

Though being a thinking Christian can often involve theorizing and thought experiments and just plain imagination, a thoughtful Christian faith can't be reduced to mere abstractions and technical definitions. Those who truly love wisdom will consider what it means to live wisely: loving God and neighbor, trusting in the power of God, being charitable toward others, persevering in cultivating the use of our minds, and prayerfully and humbly telling others of the gospel hope we have within (1 Pet. 3:15).

Though I stand in the evangelical tradition,[6] I am attempting to write in the spirit of mere Christianity. The key creeds of the Christian church express this, being a distillation of what the Scriptures teach. Yet it is the triune God who unites believers to one another in Christ by his Spirit. One theologian expressed it this way: "In essentials, unity; in nonessentials, liberty; in all things, charity."[7]

ON TEXTUAL CRITICISM

As noted, this book is a second edition. And it fits the pattern textual critics have traditionally taken when it comes to scribal tendencies. When comparing variations in manuscripts, they have considered *the more difficult reading* (the *lectio difficilior*) and *the shorter reading* (*lectio brevior*) to be the more likely wording in the original autographs. We're told that scribes tend to smooth out difficult passages as well as to expand on a text that may need clarification. Well, as it turns out, *neither* of these guidelines is solid or foolproof. Both criteria have been questioned.[8]

This isn't a book about textual criticism, but it fits the traditional picture of scribal tendencies. This second edition is longer than the first: I've added new chapters (there are now thirty-two instead of twenty-one, although some have been subdivided). And the book clarifies and extends themes to make for a less difficult reading than the first edition. I've thoroughly revised nearly all of the chapters from the first edition, and I have added a good deal of new material and topics.

In addition to the "Further Reading" suggestions at the end of each chapter, study questions are included at the back of the book for those interested in using the book in discussion groups. One other upgrade: this new edition includes an index.

FURTHER READING

Copan, Paul, and Kenneth D. Litwak. *The Gospel in the Marketplace of Ideas: Paul's Mars Hill Experience for Our Pluralistic World.* Downers Grove, IL: IVP Academic, 2014.

Keller, Timothy. *The Reason for God: Belief in an Age of Skepticism.* New York: Penguin, 2009.

Acknowledgments

This book is gratefully and affectionately dedicated to the late Christian philosopher Stuart C. Hackett. His warm encouragement, daily prayers, faithful friendship, and philosophical rigor in his teaching, conversation, and writing instilled in me a love and appreciation for the task of philosophy.

Special thanks to my sister Lil Copan. She strongly urged me to consider Eerdmans while I was upgrading and revising *Loving Wisdom* for a second edition (it had been published by Chalice Press the first go-round).

As this book has evolved, I appreciate helpful comments from Chad Meister, Christopher Weaver, Charles Taliaferro, and Peter Frick—not to mention my philosophy of religion students, who have offered their own perspectives and questions along the way.

Thanks to my graduate assistant Liezl Bosch, who has read through and commented on the manuscript. She has also written the study questions to guide small group discussions, included at the back of the book.

I am grateful to Palm Beach Atlantic University for granting me a splendid sabbatical in 2017—and to Oxford University's Wycliffe Hall, where I was a visiting scholar ("academic visitor") during the Hilary and Trinity terms. There I began work on this second edition. I am grateful for the warm hospitality, friendships, and kindnesses experienced there.

I appreciate the editing suggestions of Jenny Hoffman at Eerdmans. Her comments have assisted in making this book clearer and smoother.

Robust thanks to my beloved wife, Jacqueline, for her sweet partnership and unstinting support in this and other book-writing and -editing endeavors.

PRELIMINARIES ON
PHILOSOPHY AND FAITH

1 | *The Blessings of Philosophy*

> See to it that no one takes you captive through hollow
> and deceptive philosophy, which depends on human
> tradition and the elemental spiritual forces of this world
> rather than on Christ.
>
> —Colossians 2:8 NIV

Thank God for philosophy! Some Christians may think this a strange, if not downright heretical, affirmation—especially in light of the Scripture verse above. Perhaps they—along with plenty of "freethinkers"—believe that "Christian philosophy" is an oxymoron. After all, isn't philosophy atheistic? Don't those who've grown up in church leave the faith once they've studied philosophy at university? And what's the need for philosophy? Isn't Jesus enough? And shouldn't we take Paul seriously when he calls philosophy "hollow and deceptive"?

We'll look at these questions shortly, but for now let us consider the blessings of being exposed to the study of philosophy and why we shouldn't be so suspicious of it.

THE BENEFITS OF STUDYING PHILOSOPHY

Philosophy Has Helped Us Articulate Biblical Doctrines

First, every key Christian doctrine drawn from Scripture has been formulated or expressed in philosophical language. Think of the Christian doctrines of the Trinity or incarnation. As early Christian theologians attempted to distill biblical language and express it in creeds, letters, and books, they used terms such as *being, substance, essence,* and *person* to clarify and distinguish these doctrines from one another. Christian philosopher Diogenes Allen has taught Princeton Seminary students about the importance of philosophy to more clearly understand biblical doctrines. He wrote: "Everyone needs to know some philosophy in order to understand the major doctrines of Christianity or to read a great theologian intelligently. . . . Philosophical knowledge enables one to appreciate more deeply the meaning of virtually every major doctrinal formulation and every major theologian."[1]

For example, when reading the theologian Augustine's *Confessions*, keep in mind the influence of Neoplatonic philosophy; this includes the idea that the soul has fallen away, wandered from God, and experiences a kind of homesickness. Yet by God's grace, the soul's odyssey (*perigrinatio animae*) can bring us back to our true home. Most people know that to read theologian Thomas Aquinas well, we should understand Aristotle's work. Even grasping the history of theology will require exploring important philosophical themes. When the Council of Nicaea (AD 325) used the philosophical term *homoousion*—Christ shares the *same nature* as the Father—it accurately expressed biblical teaching. As one biblical scholar observed, "In its own way, it expresses the Christological monotheism of the New Testament."[2]

We shouldn't be intimidated by philosophy's close connection to theology. We should simply acknowledge this fact and do our theological best as we forge ahead. The church has benefited from philosophy from the first century onward and still stands to benefit from it today.

"Everyone Is a Philosopher"

A second reason not to be suspicious of the notion of "philosophy" is this: you're a philosopher whether you like it or not! My first philosophy professor—Stuart Hackett—reminded his students: "Everyone is a philosopher." That is, each of us has a philosophy of life or "worldview." We have beliefs about what is real (metaphysics), about how and what we can know (epistemology), about right and wrong and living the good life (ethics). At the heart of our philosophy as Christians is the central reality of the triune God, and the topic of God is an important theme in "metaphysics." No, the Christian can't escape philosophy.

Some have desperately tried to dispose of philosophy. The late Cambridge physicist Stephen Hawking proclaimed that "philosophy is dead."[3] His solution? Physics must save us and furnish complete answers to who we are and where we've come from. That amateur philosopher Hawking was himself making a philosophical statement. Philosophy is unavoidable. After all, each of us belongs to the species *Homo sapiens*—or "thinking human."

You may be wondering: "Shouldn't we talk about *what philosophy is* before promoting its virtues?" Well, we've already indicated that philosophy's three major branches—metaphysics, epistemology, and ethics—are what we all inescapably think about at some level. We can't dismiss it or even be neutral about it. So we do have something of a clue about philosophy already.

As for definitions, some start with the literal meaning of philosophy (*philosophia*)—"the love of wisdom." Alvin Plantinga writes that philosophical reflection is "not much different from just thinking hard."[4] Another definition is simply "thinking about thinking." That is, we're engaging in the philosophical task if we try to clarify concepts, justify positions, offer arguments, and piece together or integrate ideas into a worldview that is coherent.

Philosophy Can Be a Helpful Tool

A third reason to appreciate philosophy is that, rightly used, it is your friend. The following statement has been falsely attributed to Socrates: "By all means marry. If you marry a good wife, you will be very happy. If you marry a bad wife, you will become a philosopher, and that is good for every man." Now, ancient rumor does suggest that Socrates's wife, Xanthippe, wasn't all that easy to get along with—a "shrew," some have called her. According the playwright Xenophon, Socrates claimed that if he could endure his own wife, he would have no difficulty in any other human relation. Of course, philosophers can and do have good wives (or husbands), but even if not, one can benefit from the resources of philosophy, if we'll allow it.

We ought to think of philosophy as a tool. People use hammers in home construction and repair, but some will misuse this fine tool. Before becoming a believer, one of my friends attempted to strike a lethal hammer blow on his father's head. Psychologist Abraham Maslow once wrote of what we could call "the temptation of the tool": "I suppose it is tempting, if the only tool you have is a hammer, to treat everything as if it were a nail."[5]

Likewise, philosophy can be put to proper use—or suboptimal use. Those who say that only science can give us knowledge haven't discovered this by scientific observation; it's a philosophical assumption. So if you only have the "hammer" of science, you're going to look for scientific explanations for everything. As we'll see, this is a misguided starting point on which to build our lives. As C. S. Lewis wrote, "Good philosophy must exist, if for no other reason, because bad philosophy needs to be answered."[6] We can't escape doing philosophy, but will we do it well or do it poorly?

Bad thinking—as well as being *un*thinking—is downright disastrous personally and hazardous to our spiritual and moral lives. This is why Paul exhorts us: "In your thinking be mature" (1 Cor. 14:20 ESV). Ignorance may be bliss, but it is not a virtue.[7] The point isn't for all Christians to get a PhD in philosophy but rather to become more thoughtful about their faith. For example, thinking more clearly and deeply about the triune God or the incarnation of Jesus can only enhance our worship in both "spirit" and "truth" (John 4:23–24). If we're muddle-headed about these doctrines, our worship will also be muddled. Whether we have had formal or informal exposure to philosophy or just become more reflective Christians, we'll be able to steer clear of fallacious reasoning, junk arguments, bad philosophies, and confused worship. So whoever finds a more thoughtful Christian faith finds a good thing and obtains favor from the Lord.

Proper Philosophizing about God Will Include Living Wisely

One comedian speaking at a Dartmouth College commencement told the parents in attendance: "If your child majored in fine arts or philosophy, you have good reason to be worried. The only place where they are now really qualified to get a job is ancient Greece. Good luck with that degree."[8] As it turns out, philosophy graduates often do well in a wide range of work settings—from teaching philosophy to working in law, politics, and business.

The more important point is that good philosophy—which includes reasoning about God (theology)—will always be connected to how we live, and this is our fourth reason for studying philosophy: it has implications for how we live—the choices we are to make, the character we should cultivate, what the good life looks like. Philosophy—if done properly—will not be detached from life.

The history of philosophy actually reveals that philosophy is concerned not only with the theoretical and the abstract but with the practical as well. Philosophy is a way of life, walking along the path of virtuous living; it is about *becoming* a certain person rather than simply *knowing*. The philosopher Plutarch wrote that "daily life gives us the opportunity to do philosophy."[9] The reality of our inevitable death turns us into philosophers as well. As Plato wrote in his *Phaedo*: "Those who really apply themselves in the right way to philosophy are directly and of their own accord preparing themselves for dying and death."[10]

We've seen that philosophy literally means the "love of wisdom." But what is wisdom? It is *the skill of living*. "The fear of the Lord is the beginning of wisdom" (Ps. 111:10; cf. Prov. 1:7): if we're going be true lovers of wisdom, it will begin with being rightly related to God ("the fear of the Lord"). That is, wisdom is fundamentally theological. After all, how can our very thought and life be properly directed unless we are God-oriented? God is the source of all reality outside himself, and he is the one who designed us to function and flourish when we live in accordance with that design (John 10:10). Even our eating and drinking can be carried out in light of that design (1 Cor. 10:31). Ultimately, we can't truly have wisdom without being rightly connected to God and his Word. We'll be out of touch with the human problem and its redemptive solution in Christ. That is, wisdom, at its heart, can't be "secular."[11]

Philosophy Can Guide Us in Our Doubting

Another reason for appreciating philosophy is that it can help us wisely and discerningly grapple with our doubts. Think about friends of yours who have walked away from the faith—perhaps due to doubts of various kinds. It's helpful to probe a bit here, though, as there are various types or "species" of doubt, not just one.

Intellectual doubt: For honest intellectual questions, we should seek out intellectual answers where possible. Sometimes we have to settle for the best possible or even partial answers. Sometimes we may be asking the wrong questions. "Why did God permit this particular evil?" is one such example. Why think we should expect an answer to this? Jesus himself offers general guidance about getting right with God ("repent") in the face of evils rather than trying to figure them out—something we're not well positioned to do (cf. Luke 13:1–5).

Emotional doubt: This springs from psychological insecurities—perhaps from not being able to trust earthly parents. No matter how plausible the answers given, the question "But what if . . . ?" always follows. Intellectual answers aren't the solution to emotional doubt, even though emotional doubters may give the impression that intellectual questions are at the root of their doubt.

Moral doubt: This emerges after someone crosses a moral line; he starts to have doubts about God's existence now that he's committed adultery or has started sleeping with his girlfriend. Doubts of this variety don't require intellectual answers but repentance.

Spiritual doubt: This version is the result of demonic assaults on us, which may come in various forms; demonic reminders of our inadequacy, failure, sin, and guilt leave us feeling condemned and in despair (Rev. 12:10), prompting us to doubt our standing before God. Martin Luther knew of this. In a letter to Jerome Weller (July 1530), he wrote: "When the devil throws our sins up to us and declares we deserve death and hell, we ought to speak thus: 'I admit that I deserve death and hell. What of it? Does this mean that I shall be sentenced to eternal damnation? By no means. For I know One who suffered and made a satisfaction in my behalf. His name is Jesus Christ, the Son of God. Where he is, there I shall be also.'"[12]

"Doubt wisely," the poet John Donne urged. Indeed, clear philosophical thinking can help us shake off certain kinds of doubt resulting from faulty thinking. For example, we can learn to doubt our doubts, as we often take our doubts too seriously and our beliefs not seriously enough.

Also, consider how some Christians fall prey to a false assumption many embrace—namely, that 100 percent certainty is required to believe anything. But that's a misguided, deeply flawed expectation: how can we know with 100 percent certainty that knowledge requires 100 percent certainty? While professional philosophers will disagree about many things, this complete-certainty criterion for knowledge isn't one of them. We know lots of things without being 100 percent certain.

Philosophy Can Assist Us as Witnesses for Christ

A sixth reason to appreciate philosophy is that it can enhance our Christian witness. Rutgers University philosopher Brian Leftow affirms that "it was Christianity that brought me to philosophy."[13] This shouldn't be surprising. Consider this: from the second half of the twentieth century onward, the philosophy of religion has experienced a remarkable renaissance and has become its own scholarly discipline. A growing number of very capable philosophers—many of them believers in God—have written philosophy of religion textbooks as well as journal articles and books dedicated to specific topics in this field: the nature and coherence of God's attributes, arguments for God's existence, the problem of evil, the plurality of religions, the God-science relationship, miracles, and so on.

In fact, "philosophical theology"—also called "the philosophy of theology" or "analytic theology"—has become a discipline of note. Formally trained Christian philosophers have done much rigorous work on the doctrines of the Trinity, incarnation, atonement, divine providence, and original sin. As a result, the discipline of Christian systematic theology has been strengthened through philosophical influence.

This is very encouraging as we proclaim the good news of Jesus in the marketplace of ideas. Many of us who engage in doing Christian philosophy have discovered that unbelievers often show a greater willingness to listen to the message of the gospel when they see how it makes sense of so many of life's big questions. Christian intellectual giants, on whose shoulders we stand, have helped create a broader cultural context that enhances the taking of the Christian faith more seriously. So we should join them in this endeavor wherever we can.

Jesus and Paul as Philosophers

Of course, Jesus—God in the flesh—was the most brilliant philosopher who ever lived. As the very wisdom of God (1 Cor. 1:24, 30; Col. 2:3), he was not only most truly human in faithfully carrying out his Father's will and embodying divine love. He was was rigorous in his thinking and also masterful in his use of logic. He spoke with clarity, coherence, and insight about the nature of reality (metaphysics), knowledge (epistemology), living virtuously (ethics and character), and the meaning of life, which is bound up with loving God and loving others.[14]

Another philosopher was the apostle Paul. He was a man of "great learning" (Acts 26:24; cf. 22:3). This cosmopolitan man was born in Tarsus, one of three leading philosophical centers in his day—the other two being Alexandria and Athens. Paul rightly called himself "a citizen of no insignificant city" (Acts 21:39). Paul was not only in the upper 1–2 percent of the educated people of his day.[15] According to New Testament scholar N. T. Wright, Paul would have been considered a "Jewish philosopher"; he would have been perceived as creating more a "new school of philosophy" than a "type of religion."[16] "Religion" in Paul's day would have been more a *private piety* that didn't threaten the public order or the stability of the Roman Empire. By contrast, a new "philosophy" *would* challenge the status quo. Socrates did this in Athens and would drink poison as his punishment.

Likewise, Paul's message—at whose heart was Jesus of Nazareth—presented an in-breaking of God's kingdom into human history through his agent, Jesus the Messiah. The implications were momentous: if Jesus is Lord, then Caesar isn't. This conviction gave rise to a dramatically different way of understanding the world (metaphysics); it also demanded a radical new ethic that created a new social identity that challenged conventional social and cultural boundaries like "slave and free." Paul was advocating that slaves and masters in Christ share meals together and "greet one another with a holy kiss" (Rom. 16:16; etc.)—the language of family in Christ. Turning upside down the Roman religious and social system was a threat (Acts 17:6), and Paul—like his philosophical predecessor Socrates—would be executed as a result.

Indeed, Luke actually presents Paul as the Christian Socrates coming to Athens (Acts 17).[17] He uses the very language of Plato's *Apology* to describe his teacher Socrates's activities: Socrates and Paul reasoned with people in the marketplace (*agora*), brought a "new" teaching, and were described as promoting "strange" or "foreign" deities. While at Athens, Paul talked with the Stoics and Epicureans—two notable schools of philosophy. He cited Stoics such as Epimenides ("in Him we live and move and exist" [Acts 17:28]) and Aratus ("we are his offspring" [Acts 17:28 NIV]).

Toward the end of his life, noted British philosopher Antony Flew—an atheist for decades—came to believe in the generic God of Deism. Even so, he considered the apostle Paul not only "a highly educated man" and a "first-class intellectual" but a man with "an outstanding philosophical mind."[18]

Some Christians who are suspicious of the life of the mind or a reflective faith may insist, "Just give me Jesus." But they should remember that this Jesus was a brilliant philosopher—the very wisdom of God incarnate—and so was his dedicated follower, Paul. To use our minds for God's glory and to understand our Master are part of our calling. To claim "the Bible is all I need" while repudiating the value of philosophy is to fail to realize just how philosophical books like Job and Ecclesiastes actually are. We need to remember that the cosmopolitan, intellectual giant Paul wrote a quarter of the New Testament, and he used his philosophical mind while doing so. Just read the carefully reasoned book of Romans!

We've seen that we have strong reason to appreciate philosophy. As a human being, you're a philosopher—a "thinking being." As a Christian, your faith has been informed by deeply philosophical minds, with Jesus and the apostle Paul as the greatest examples.

Further Reading

Copan, Paul. *A Little Book for New Philosophers: Why and How to Study Philosophy.* Downers Grove, IL: IVP Academic, 2016.

Copan, Paul, and Kenneth D. Litwak. *The Gospel in the Marketplace of Ideas.* Downers Grove, IL: IVP Academic, 2014.

Evans, C. Stephen. *A History of Western Philosophy: From the Pre-Socratics to Postmodernism.* Downers Grove, IL: IVP Academic, 2018.

Groothuis, Douglas. *On Jesus.* Wadsworth Philosophers Series. Belmont, CA: Wadsworth, 2003.

2 | *Philosophy and Scripture*

> The fear of the LORD is the beginning of wisdom.
>
> —Psalm 111:10

> In [Christ] are hidden all the treasures of wisdom and knowledge.
>
> —Colossians 2:3

"Faith is opposed to reason."
"Faith is just a leap in the dark."
"You'll lose your faith if you study philosophy. It's atheistic."

In our culture, we frequently encounter various dichotomies: faith versus reason, science versus theology, religion versus secularism, philosophy versus religion, empirical versus metaphysical. Yet pitting one against the other not only obscures the nuances between these categories; it can often—at least when it comes to the Christian faith—create wholly unnecessary, distracting conflicts. To clear up some of the confusion, let's explore terms like *philosophy, evidence, faith,* and *religion* in the next couple of chapters.[1]

A Quick Review

"What is your philosophy of life?"
"Well, my personal philosophy is . . . "

The word "philosophy" is bandied about in everyday conversations, which shouldn't be surprising. As we've observed, we're all philosophers, whether formally trained in philosophy or not.

We've talked about how philosophy is *hard thinking about things,* or that it's *thinking about thinking*—specifically, as this thinking relates to reality, knowledge, right and wrong, and the meaning of life. Plato said that thinking is "a dialogue within the soul" and that true philosophy entails a preparation for death. We've also noted that philosophizing cannot be detached from daily living and the formation of character.

Most importantly, we cannot truly love wisdom if we reject "the fear of the

LORD," the beginning and foundation of wisdom. And what is this fear? It is a deep awareness of our dependence on God and our need to attend and listen to our Creator. This fear that begins with a relationship with God ultimately leads to obedience. The angel of the LORD tells Abraham concerning his offering up of Isaac: "Now I know that you *fear* [me] . . . because you have *done* this . . . because you have *obeyed* me" (Gen. 22:12, 16–18).[2] Wisdom is inseparable from daily living before God and having our attitudes and habits transformed as a result. And not only does wisdom begin with rightly attending to God; it focuses in particular on paying heed to God's self-revelation in Jesus Christ, the very wisdom and power of God (1 Cor. 1:24) and the one "in whom are hidden all the treasures of wisdom and knowledge" (Col. 2:3).

Nevertheless, the average person will associate philosophy with words such as *irrelevance, confusion*, and *lofty abstractions*. The French Enlightenment thinker Voltaire said this: "When he who hears doesn't know what he who speaks means, and when he who speaks doesn't know what he himself means— that is philosophy."[3] Perhaps the best that could be said of philosophy is that it is an incredible waste of time.

Bring this question of philosophy to a church context and matters often get worse. Some Christians, including pastors and youth leaders, will tell you that philosophy is downright anti-biblical and dangerous. It's not merely "atheistic" and "skeptical," but they'll tell you that the Bible *itself* rejects philosophy, perhaps warning that philosophy inherently involves idolizing human reason rather than depending on the grace of God. But is this accurate?

PHILOSOPHY AS "ATHEISTIC"?

Those who believe this will feel justified when they read the words of agnostic philosopher Luc Ferry: "The quest for salvation without God is at the heart of every great philosophical system. . . . Philosophy also claims to save us—if not from death itself, then from the anxiety it causes, and to do so by the exercise of our own resources in our innate faculty of reason."[4] Philosophy frees us from the shackles of blind "faith."

This bold statement sounds impressive, but it is false and represents a presumptuous effort at self-salvation. Ferry's perspective doesn't actually reflect the history of philosophy itself. For one thing, if the tradition is true that the term *philosophy*—the love of wisdom—originated with Pythagoras (c. 570–495 BC), then Ferry is dead wrong from the outset! Pythagoras considered wisdom to be *divine* and believed that we mortals could aspire to divinity as we pursue the love of wisdom.

Second, the history of philosophy reveals many who believed in God; the Absolute or One; or a transcendent realm of truth, goodness, and beauty. They range from Plato to Plantinga and from Augustine to Alston.

Third, we'll see in the next chapter that "religion" itself is a vague, difficult-to-define term and that "philosophy" and "religion" mean something different today than they did in, say, the first century.

Finally, philosophy is inescapable for us as human beings, regardless of any traditional religious affiliation or worldview. "Everyone is a philosopher," we've noted. Every person will take a stance on "the big questions," even if she doesn't articulate the specifics of her views or her underlying assumptions. And not only does each of us *have* a philosophy, but we *practice* philosophy—we inevitably live out our philosophy day by day in the moral decisions we make, in the kind of character we cultivate. Welcome to the world of philosophy!

Furthermore, virtually every academic discipline has a "philosophy of" connected to it: "philosophy of science," "philosophy of history," "philosophy of mathematics," "philosophy of art," and, as we've seen, "philosophical theology."

Perhaps you have seen enthusiastic, serious-minded young Christians head off to university, only to have their faith rattled or even dismantled by atheistic or skeptical philosophy professors. The problem is not the discipline of philosophy, which has across the ages often been God-friendly. The problem is more how philosophy is taught. The *discipline of philosophy* doesn't oppose faith. Rather, those with *a philosophy of atheism or skepticism* often do.

PHILOSOPHY AS "ANTI-BIBLICAL"

Aside from the false notion that philosophy is atheistic, where would Christians get the idea that the study of philosophy undermines faith in Christ or belief in God in general? Perhaps experience leads them to conclude this: they've just heard many such stories or have even encountered hostile atheistic philosophy or science professors.

However, some Christians think that the Scriptures themselves oppose philosophy. Paul writes, "See to it that no one takes you captive through philosophy [*philosophia*] and empty deception" (Col. 2:8). And again: "Where is the philosopher [*sophos*]? Where is the scholar? Where is the debater of this age? Hasn't God made the world's wisdom foolish?" (1 Cor. 1:20 HCSB). And isn't the gospel "foolishness to those who are perishing" (1 Cor. 1:18)? Why bother with philosophy since the "natural man"—and woman—doesn't understand the things of God's Spirit (1 Cor. 2:14)?

Jesus himself tells Thomas the Doubter that those who *haven't* seen the nail-scarred, resurrection body of Jesus yet still believe are truly "blessed" (John 20:29). Surely, in the pursuit of evidence or reasons, we lose our capacity for "real faith." We're saved by grace, not by arguments, right?

Beyond this, some might appeal to theologians for support. After all, Martin Luther himself called reason a "whore"; he also chided "theologians of glory" whose "sophistic" methods opposed a "theology of the cross" (*theologia cruces*). Such scholars present abstract "proofs" for God; in so doing, they run the risk of veiling a suffering God dying in nakedness and shame on the cross. Salvation comes to those who humble themselves before the cross, not to those who trust in their self-supposed superior powers of reasoning. Did Luther think philosophizing implies a rejection of the cross? Is doing philosophy putting trust in human reason rather than the grace of God? Don't *experience*, *Scripture*, and *theologians* fairly warn us about philosophy's perils?

A RESPONSE TO THE "ANTI-BIBLICAL" CHARGE

Scriptural Responses

What then shall we say to these things? We've pointed out how philosophy has come to the aid of theology and how philosophy really is inescapable. We've also noted that Jesus would certainly qualify as a philosopher, as would Paul—a Christian Socrates in Athens. Now people want to use select passages from Paul to dispose of philosophy! How things have changed!

Let's now offer a response to Bible prooftexts used to support the opposition of faith to reason. As we look more closely, we see something fishy going on—namely, a good bit of Scripture twisting. For example, when Paul talks about being taken "captive through philosophy and empty deception" (Col. 2:8), he isn't talking about doing Christian philosophy ("according to Christ"); that would be the "good philosophy" C. S. Lewis talks about. Rather, Paul opposes the "bad philosophy" bound up with "the tradition of men" and "elementary principles"—with regulations such as "Do not handle, do not taste, do not touch!" (Col. 2:21) that imprison humans rather than set them free.

What of 1 Corinthians 1–2, in which the "word of the cross" is "foolishness" to the person without the Spirit? What Paul is *not* saying here is that the gospel opposes *philosophy* or *rationality*. After all, God is a rational being who created humans in his image and calls on them to "reason together" with him (Isa. 1:18). Rather, Paul's point is that the gospel stands as a challenge to human *pride* and *self-sufficiency*. The context refers to the arrogant dismissal of the gospel—that a publicly humiliated, naked, crucified Messiah is the means of reconciling humans to God. The cross strikes a blow to human self-confidence, self-salvation, and intellectual pretension.

Another problem with citing texts from 1 Corinthians 1–2 is that the anti-philosophers simply stop there and don't read to the end of the book. There Paul gives important evidence for Jesus's bodily resurrection, which includes a list of witnesses to the resurrected Jesus (1 Cor. 15:3–11). Paul shows that presenting evidence isn't opposed to preaching the anti-pride message of the cross to the "natural," Spiritless unbeliever.

The same is true of the Jesus-Thomas conversation in John 20—not seeing yet being blessed for still believing (John 20:29). Is this some blind-leap irrationality? Not at all. Immediately following this verse is an affirmation of the weighty, remarkable evidences that warrant believing in Jesus: "Therefore many other signs Jesus also performed in the presence of the disciples, which are not written in this book; but these have been written so that you may believe that Jesus is the Christ, the Son of God; and that believing you may have life in His name" (John 20:30–31). Instead of trusting his close friends who said, "We have seen the Lord," Thomas stubbornly insisted on viewing Jesus's wounds for himself (John 20:25).

Later, this same author writes as a fellow firsthand witness of Jesus, "the Word of life," concerning "what we have heard, what we have seen with our eyes, what we have looked at and touched with our hands" (1 John 1:1–3). In addition, biblical language—particularly in John and Acts—includes "evidence" and "reason" terms like "signs," "witnesses," "persuade," "dialogue," and "[make a] defense," and the Scriptures repeatedly attest to miracles as public evidence for the message of God's prophets and apostles.

In addition to Job's philosophical merits, we've noted that Ecclesiastes is a very philosophical book that contemplates life's meaning and its "futility," according to the cynical Teacher's "voice." There we have various philosophical views represented—fatalism, hedonism, nihilism, and more. Another voice, however, offers a corrective to that perspective, concluding that we must "fear God and keep his commandments" (Eccles. 12:13).

Theological Responses

What of Luther's remarks about the dangers of "reason"? Luther is simply talking about reasoning *without reference to God*. At his trial at the Diet of Worms, he insisted that his accusers show from Scripture or "from evident reason" that he was mistaken. Luther even spoke with great admiration for the pagan thinker Cicero: "Cicero is the best philosopher. . . . He wrote the best on natural, moral, and rational philosophy. . . . I hope God will forgive such men as Cicero their sins."[5] Even John Calvin, commenting on Colossians 2:8, observed: "Many have *mistakenly* imagined that Paul condemns philosophy."[6]

At bottom, the problem isn't philosophy. Rather, the problem is having a philosophy detached from Christ, philosophy that is adrift and without roots—ideas that are earthbound and rooted in mere human traditions and fashions. Justin Martyr was an early Christian philosopher who had been schooled in Platonism. Upon encountering Christ, he didn't abandon philosophy but rather came to understand that in Christ are hidden all the treasures of wisdom and knowledge (Col. 2:3). He proclaimed that he had found "this philosophy alone to be safe and profitable. Thus, and for this reason, I am a philosopher."[7]

FURTHER READING

Copan, Paul. *A Little Book for New Philosophers: Why and How to Study Philosophy.* Downers Grove, IL: IVP Academic, 2016.

Copan, Paul, and Kenneth Litwak. *The Gospel in the Marketplace of Ideas.* Downers Grove, IL: IVP Academic, 2014.

Moreland, J. P., and William Lane Craig. *Philosophical Foundations for a Christian Worldview.* 2nd ed. Downers Grove, IL: IVP Academic, 2017.

3 | Faith and Religion

And [Jesus] got up and rebuked the wind and said to
the sea, "Hush, be still." And the wind died down and it
became perfectly calm. And He said to them, "Why are
you afraid? Do you still have no faith?"

—Mark 4:39–40

Then the proconsul believed when he saw what had happened, being amazed at the teaching of the Lord.

—Acts 13:12

FAITH: WHAT IT IS(N'T)

"Believing What You Know Ain't So"?

Mark Twain's definition of *faith* was "believing what you know ain't so." Those
of kindred spirit today treat any notion of "faith" with disdain. "Faith" is for
Neanderthals, cave dwellers, and "unsophisticated" country folk. But the enlightened will live by "reason" and "evidence." For those of illuminated mind,
reason works and gets results; faith is the stuff of reality-denial, pretending,
or make-believe. Unsurprisingly, belief in God today is commonly lumped
together with belief in Santa Claus, the tooth fairy, and unicorns.

While some who believe in God may consider faith to be that irrational
leap in the dark, no Christian theologian would define faith this way; faith is
a matter of personal *commitment* (fidelity) to and *trust* (dependence) in Jesus's
sufficiency. Some would use the term *allegiance* (loyalty) to Jesus as king.[1] True,
some "religions" may promote "a blind leap in the dark" apart from reasons or
evidence; this arbitrary leap is called *fideism*. Claims like "I'm just choosing to
believe the Bible" prompt questions like "Why not just arbitrarily begin with
the Qur'an or Book of Mormon?"

By contrast, the biblical faith is regularly connected to reasons for considering it to be true. We've observed that Scripture makes clear that "faith" is completely compatible with public "signs and wonders" (Acts 4:30), "convincing
proofs" (Acts 1:3), "giving evidence" (Acts 17:3), "eyewitnesses" (Luke 1:2; 2 Pet.
1:16), "reasoning" (Acts 17:17; 18:4; etc.), and giving "a defense" (1 Pet. 3:15).

Evidence and publicly accessible supports can point us in the direction of where we ought to put our trust. When you pledge allegiance to a person in marriage, you want to have *good reasons* for marrying—compatible personalities and interests, a common direction in life, the same spiritual dedication.

Biblical faith is not only committed to truth-seeking and completely compatible with evidences and signs. It's also a position of the will—a volitional stance—that trusts God's personal character and promises rather than our own emotions and circumstances. Jesus tells Jairus, whose daughter has just died, "Do not be afraid any longer; only believe, and she will be made well" (Luke 8:50). Jairus knew of Jesus's track record, his character, and his authoritative word to go on—and that was enough.

Biblical faith isn't pretending; true faith opposes trusting in illusions and lies (e.g., Isa. 30:9–11; Jer. 20:1–6). Rather, we choose to "reckon" or "consider" certain realities, to trust that they are so (Rom. 6:11). We exercise our will in recognizing certain historical events that were "not done in a corner" (Acts 26:26).

But we do not stop there: we choose to live or act in light of their theological implications that help shape our identity and understanding of how we fit into the purposes of God in this world. "We died with Christ" and we were "raised with Christ"—that is, his death and resurrection aren't simply historical events dating to April of AD 30. We ourselves have been united with Christ through trust in him and his actions on our behalf so change our identity and destiny that we can say, "I was there at the cross. I died with Christ, was buried with him, and have been raised to newness of life" (Rom. 6:1–4). It's much like the Israelites who acknowledged at every Passover: "*We* were slaves to the Pharaoh in Egypt and the Lord our God brought *us* forth from thence with a strong and outstretched arm. If the most holy, blessed be He, had not brought our fathers from Egypt, then *we*, our children, and our children's children would have been slaves to the Pharaohs in Egypt."[2]

If certain events did not happen—the exodus from Egypt or the death and resurrection of Jesus, for instance—the Christian faith would collapse. We would be believing and proclaiming falsehoods and without hope in this world (1 Cor. 15:12–17, 32). As Yale theologian Jaroslav Pelikan stated: "If Christ is risen, then nothing else matters. And if Christ is not risen, then nothing else matters."[3]

Faith and Reason

So what does this look like as we think about the relationship of faith and reason? The philosopher Mortimer Adler illustrates the point nicely. For much of his life, he resisted personally trusting in God ("faith") even though he was fully convinced of the Christian faith's intellectual soundness ("reason"). He experienced a late-life conversion on a hospital bed, confessing that even philosophical reasoning in itself could not bring him into relationship with God: "I simply did not wish to exercise a will to believe." Again, faith is a volitional stance. He wrote:

> The soundest rational argument for God's existence could only carry us to the edge of the chasm that separated the philosophical affirmation of God's existence from the religious belief in God. What is usually called "a leap of faith" is needed to carry anyone across the chasm. But the leap of faith is usually misunderstood as having insufficient reasons for affirming God's existence to a state of greater certitude in that affirmation. That is not the case. The leap of faith consists in going from the conclusion of a merely philosophical theology to a religious belief in a God that has revealed himself as a loving, just and merciful Creator of the cosmos, a God to be loved, worshiped and prayed to.[4]

The Holy Spirit can use reason and evidence to awaken faith—just as he uses crises, chronic illness, the threat of death, and the failure of the substitute gods in which we have trusted.

Biblical faith is not truth-denying but rather truth-directed and evidence-affirming—or as the medieval theologian Anselm put it, a "faith seeking understanding [*fides quaerens intellectum*]." Faith in Christ actually opens our eyes to see new worlds open before us—new horizons for reasoning and philosophizing, for exploring how the natural world works, and for sending the imagination soaring as we work in the arts and literature. C. S. Lewis expressed the fruitfulness of the Christian faith this way: "I believe in Christianity as I believe that the sun has risen, not only because I see it, but because by it I see everything else."[5]

Faith and Freethinking

Critics of the Christian faith often consider it "restrictive"—a spiritual straitjacket or shackles that limit freedom of thought and exploration. Is this really so? Perhaps for some, sure. But behind this charge lurk some misunderstandings.

First, *every* philosophy of life will have limits as to what is true or acceptable and what is not. The atheist or naturalist therefore is not "free" to include God within his philosophical system. Rather than being a "freethinker" who can explore whether genuine miracles occur, he will exclude this possibility from the outset. Instead of being open to the existence of the soul or the possibility of life after death, he says that this is unthinkable or unlikely. He will seek alternative explanations of how the universe began, of strongly supported miracle claims, or of near-death experiences involving out-of-body experiences. A worldview by definition will exclude that with which it disagrees. That's just the nature of worldviews.

Second, the theist generally has more options than the one who disbelieves. The disbeliever trusts that natural, materialistic processes explain how everything in the universe works. By contrast, the theist certainly doesn't deny the reality of natural processes, but she sees God as the creator of these processes but also as one who can act in the world in special ways if he chooses. If the universe has been expanding for billions of years, leading to a biofriendly Earth, this whole process hardly conflicts with the existence of a God who set these processes in place with goals for human habitation and for relating to us.

For the naturalist, materialistic explanations are the only game in town. Ironically, many freethinkers have "broken the shackles of religion," only to bind themselves to the premise that they are just material beings and products of blind deterministic forces over which they have no control. Such "freethinking" sounds strikingly similar to the intellectual limitations they have denounced in "religion."

Those who pride themselves as "freethinkers" while condemning "faith" are often more narrow-minded than they realize. This is what one New Testament scholar and former atheist Michael Bird discovered: "Faith grew from seeds of doubt, and I came upon a whole new world that, for the first time, actually made sense to me. To this day, I do not find faith stifling or constricting. Rather, faith has been liberating and transformative for me. It has opened a constellation of meaning, beauty, hope, and life that I had been indoctrinated to deny. And so began a lifelong quest to know, study, and teach about the one whom Christians called Lord."[6]

Third, throughout history, the concept of God has been a very mind-expanding and fruitful one. Though an agnostic, the philosopher Sir Anthony Kenny acknowledges and makes this important point: "If there is no God, then God is incalculably the greatest single creation of the human imagination. No other creation of the imagination has been so fertile of ideas, so great an inspiration to philosophy, to literature, to painting, sculpture, architecture, and drama. Set beside the idea of God, the most original inventions of mathematicians and the most unforgettable characters in drama are minor products of the imagination: Hamlet and the square root of minus one [i.e., an imaginary number] pale into insignificance by comparison."[7]

Fourth, in our lives we'll *choose* to privilege certain beliefs and features of our experience over others. Charles Darwin's Christian faith faded over time. His daughter Annie's death (1851) was a severe blow. In a letter to Asa Gray dated May 22, 1860—the year after his *Origin of Species* was published—he wrote of his difficulties believing in a good God who allowed the ichneumon wasp to lay its eggs "within the living bodies of caterpillars" and the cat to "play with mice." And yet, Darwin admitted to Gray that "everything" being the result of "designed laws" with the details left to "chance" was not at all satisfying and that these matters are "too profound for the human intellect."[8]

Such an incident reminds us that everyone will choose to privilege something (e.g., an experience of evil, the abandonment of a parent, the loss of a child) over another consideration (e.g., the goodness of God). The stance we take will involve *choice* and *trust*. We will be either trusting or skeptical, but skepticism is itself a trust in our doubts over against our beliefs. This volitional stance of trust will shape our understanding of God, the world, purpose, and meaning. Yes, one may reject the goodness of God because of evil in the world, but in doing so, one abandons many resources available to him through the Christian faith: that the triune God is involved with humanity and steps into our evil and cruel world; that God endures suffering and humiliation on the cross for humanity's sake; that God guarantees that cosmic justice will be done; that God assures us that virtue and the deepest happiness will ultimately come together. We'll go into this matter in more detail when we discuss the problem of evil.

The key point is this: Christians have taken a different perspective on Scripture and Jesus because "they believe [it] to be a *better* focus than any other: *Look here rather than there*."[9] Or, as we cited C. S. Lewis before, we believe not only because we see the truth of the gospel but because by it we see everything else. Those who call themselves "freethinkers" have a faith or trust of their own. Their "faith" places new restrictions on them and doesn't give them "freedom" to include God, miracles, life after death, or salvation through Christ in their thinking.

RELIGION

This book offers a Christian philosophy of religion—a term coined by one of the Cambridge Platonists, the seventeenth-century philosopher Ralph Cudworth.[10] In our day, the "philosophy of religion" has come to be a discipline of its own in recent decades. This field is a now flourishing subdiscipline of philosophy, and scholars critical of belief in God are taking it seriously. For example, the NYU atheist philosopher Thomas Nagel admits that some of the most intelligent and well-informed people he knows are "religious" believers. He confesses he has a "cosmic authority problem" and acknowledges fearing God's existence: "I hope there is no God! I don't want there to be a God; I don't want a universe to be like that."[11] If "the fear of the LORD is the beginning of wisdom" (Ps. 111:10), Nagel serves as an illustration of how a remarkably intelligent person may still be without wisdom. Why? He is rejecting what gives all of reality its coherence and its ultimate explanation. No wonder the psalmist says, "I have more insight than all my teachers, For Your testimonies are my meditation" (Ps. 119:99).

What then *is* "religion"? In our day, people associate the term "religion" with "the sacred," "the holy," or "the transcendent" and the ways in which these furnish our lives with purpose and meaning. A common mistake moderns make is to pit "religion" against "the secular"; this is a post-Enlightenment creation. The assumption is that the nonreligious position is the rational, default one, which needs no justification; so if a burden of proof is to be borne, the "religious" person bears it, not the "secularist."

Since the September 11 attacks, a recent breed of rabid atheism has denounced not only Islam but all religions as delusional, toxic, and dangerous. This version proclaims that religion is the "root of all evil" or that it "poisons everything." This brand of atheism tends to ignore all manner of atrocities carried out in the name of atheism in the Soviet Union, Cambodia, China, and elsewhere that resulted in the deaths of scores of millions. A fair question to ask about wrongs done in the name of traditional religions is this: "Are these *consistent* with the teachings and practices of their founders or in opposition to them?" At any rate, we should explore this elusive concept of "religion" more carefully.

First, the term "religion" is vague and difficult, if not impossible, to define. Muslims believe in God, while Buddhists don't. Some religions emphasize the transcendent—that which is beyond our world; by contrast, Confucianism focuses more on the social order. Ninian Smart, who founded the first religious studies department in Britain, said that we should abandon all attempts to define religion.[12] Religion scholar Martin Marty tells us that at least seventeen different definitions of religion exist and that scholars will never agree on one of them.[13]

Second, the meaning of the terms "philosophy" and "religion" has not only overlapped throughout history, but "philosophy" used to mean what "religion" does today. As we've seen, religion in the first century was private piety—like a personal hobby—while philosophy would have been perceived as a threat to the public order—like Socrates in Athens. In the last chapter, we also saw that the Christian faith would have been considered a philosophy during this time in the Mediterranean world. Jesus was introducing what looked more like a "new school of philosophy than a type of religion,"[14] and Paul—who was from Tarsus, the birthplace of Stoic philosophy—would likewise have been considered a philosopher.

Another interesting twist is that philosophy's starting assumptions have varied widely. Plato downplayed the physical world and sense experience; the true source of knowledge is found in the eternal, unchanging realm—the forms (or "ideas") of beauty and justice, for instance. Following our five senses just isn't a stable source of knowledge. At the other extreme, David Hume (1711–1776) and the highly influential twentieth-century logical positivists grounded knowledge in sense experience. Given this wide spectrum, it would be unfairly dismissive to exclude God from the task of philosophy.

Finally, it may be more clarifying to use the term "worldview" or "philosophy of life" rather than the murkier term "religion." In an attempt to define "religion," one author suggests that it is "a form of life that seems to those who inhabit it to be comprehensive, incapable of abandonment, and of central importance."[15] A "form of life" is a pattern of activity whose practitioners believe has certain boundaries as well as particular actions bound up with it. "Religion" (literally, "a binding together") has three characteristics:

- *Comprehensive*: This form of life takes into account, and is relevant to, everything; a framework into which all the particularities of life can be placed, from how one dresses to the significance of marriage to moral actions.
- *Incapable of abandonment*: This form of life defines a person's identity—very much like a native English speaker who can't readily abandon his deeply embedded mother tongue, even if he could learn another language. "Conversion" to another form of life is possible—just as it's possible for a person to learn to speak in a language other than her mother tongue, say, if she moves to another country where a different language is spoken.
- *Of central importance*: One's form of life is no mere add-on or extra; it addresses issues of paramount importance: *What is real? What is to be valued? What is my purpose?*

But this description of a "form of life" sounds very much like a "worldview"—a philosophy of life that is rooted in deep heart commitments. As we've seen, everyone is a philosopher, which means that everyone has a worldview. We all take a stance on basic questions like "What is really real?" or "What are human beings?" or "Can we truly know?" or "Does his history have meaning?" or "Do right and wrong exist?" The philosopher Bertrand Russell said that behind every philosophy—or we could say "worldview"—is a "concealed metaphysic," an assumed view about reality, about what is ultimate.[16]

So it appears that what can be said about "religion" can be said of a "worldview." This means that the skeptic doesn't get a pass simply because she considers her views "nonreligious." What warrant or justification do I have for adhering to my philosophy of life—"secular" or otherwise? That is a question for all worldview-holders to answer.[17]

FURTHER READING

Chamberlain, Paul. *Why People Stop Believing*. Eugene, OR: Wipf & Stock, 2018.

Clark, Kelly James. *Philosophers Who Believe*. Downers Grove, IL: InterVarsity Press, 1997.

Copan, Paul. *A Little Book for New Philosophers: Why and How to Study Philosophy*. Downers Grove, IL: IVP Academic, 2016.

Moberly, R. W. L. *The Bible in a Disenchanted Age: The Enduring Possibility of Christian Faith*. Grand Rapids: Baker Academic, 2018.

Taliaferro, Charles. *Evidence and Faith: Philosophy and Religion Since the Seventeenth Century*. Cambridge: Cambridge University Press, 2005.

4 | *Kings and Priests*

You shall be to Me a kingdom of priests and a holy
nation.

—Exodus 19:6

You are a chosen race, a royal priesthood, a holy nation,
a people for God's own possession.

—1 Peter 2:9

A Story Fitting with Reality

We all like a good story, whether in a book or a movie. Liking a good story means liking its outcome. It's not that a story has to be of the sentimental, tidy, predictable, "happily ever after" variety. Yes, keep the stories realistic. But we typically gravitate to stories that have at least redemptive, morally satisfying endings. We find it troubling to encounter movies or books in which evil prevails and the "good guys" are destroyed. Movies that tend toward nihilism (meaninglessness) rightly disturb or unsettle us because we tend to operate as moral, purpose-directed beings.

Some are convinced that the universe has no point. The cosmos is indifferent, deaf to our cries and oblivious to our tears. Human beings are nothing more than molecules in motion—biological organisms trying to survive and reproduce but destined to eventual extinction along with all else in the universe. Is *that* the story we should believe?

The biblical story is quite different—illuminating, purposeful, and morally satisfying—and human beings play an important, meaningful part within it.

A True Story

The biblical story or "metanarrative" is *the story of reality*.[1] This "theodrama" can be roughly summarized as *God, creation, fall, redemption*, and *re-creation*. Our book explores these themes from a philosophical angle in hopes of showing how coherent, rich, and robust an account of reality it is. Stories can be coherent, fully of mystery and depth, stimulate the imagination, and teach wisdom without having actually happened. Think of Tolkien's Middle Earth,

Lewis's Narnia, or Rowling's Hogwarts. As the story of reality, the biblical story is anchored in history and reaches its climax in Jesus of Nazareth. This story matches up with—it corresponds to—the way things really are. It's like a socket wrench that fits perfectly on a bolt. This story isn't the stuff of "cleverly devised tales" (2 Pet. 1:16). If it were, then even its chief representatives would insist we abandon it: if, for instance, Jesus's body wasn't physically raised from the dead, then our faith is in vain (1 Cor. 15:14). But this is true about other key points of biblical history: if the walls of Jericho weren't razed (Josh. 6; Heb. 11:30–31), then our faith too would be vain.

An Illuminating Story

A story may be true, but rather dull and uninteresting. The biblical story, however, helps makes sense of things and shines light into darkness. We noticed how the Christian story helped C. S. Lewis "see everything else."[2] Another former skeptic, G. K. Chesterton, came to the Christian faith not because of "this argument or that argument" but "because it is an intelligible picture of the world." He compared this to putting on a coat that fits perfectly in every crease—or like putting on a theory like a "magic hat, and history becomes translucent like a house of glass."[3] Chesterton had read the atheists and skeptics. In doing so, he realized how materialistic explanations of the world—that matter is all the reality that there is—simply stripped us of our humanity. Personhood, goodness, beauty, wonder, mystery, purpose, meaning, nobility, and even good and evil were explained away or reduced to mere scientific explanations. The modern world had brought a kind of "disenchantment," and Chesterton saw the need for re-enchanting the world.

A True Fairy Tale

Tolkien observed that the Gospels in Scripture contain "all the essence of fairy-stories." The world's best legends, tales, and myths that begin "Once upon a time . . . " come together in the story of the historical Jesus of Nazareth—what C. S. Lewis called "myth became fact." Tolkien said that this "fairy story" has the "inner consistency of reality" without losing its deeper cosmic significance. The biblical story begins with joy and ends with it. In Jesus, *myth becomes historical fact*. The gospel hasn't done away with legends; "it has hallowed them, especially the 'happy ending.'"[4] No wonder many of our movies—visual fairy tales—emphasize redemption, forgiveness, and reconciliation as the story comes to an end.

Even so, the Christian faith—with all its sense, explanatory power, and philosophical soundness—is still a scandal. The philosopher Immanuel Kant (1724–1804) loathed the notion of bowing or kneeling in reverent worship before God—an act contrary to human dignity, he claimed. But while bowing before a fellow creature—human or angelic—is one thing (Rev. 19:10; 22:9), acknowledging divine worship-worthiness in humble adoration is another (Phil. 2:10). Creator and creature are not equal in dignity; our dignity derives from God, the supremely valuable being. Whether from finitude or—all the more—our sinfulness, it is fitting to bow before an all-good God, who, for our sakes, was willing to take on shame and humiliation and to die naked on an ancient instrument of torture. We Westerners are so familiar with the crucifixion that we are untouched by its horror and shame. In the ancient world, to follow a crucified Messiah was considered foolishness and shame (1 Cor. 1:18). He became "the author of [our] salvation through sufferings" (Heb. 2:10). God humbled himself to death on a cross; against Kant, bowing before God in humble response is certainly fitting.

WHO ARE WE?

Starting with God

Every philosophy of life will have an anthropology—a stance on what a human is. Do we interpret the human being through the grid of economics and class struggle (Marxism), biology and the struggle to survive (naturalistic Darwinism), or suffering produced by attachment to transitory things (Buddhism)? Are we bundles of experiences, streams of consciousness?

In the beginning of his *Institutes of the Christian Religion*, theologian John Calvin correctly wrote that in order to understand who humans are, we must first understand who God is—especially as he is revealed in the truest human, Jesus of Nazareth. He came as "Immanuel"—God with us. He lived among us getting his feet dirtied, his face sweaty, and his hands bloodied. He joined us in our suffering, encountering and overcoming injustice and evil in his resurrection, and now gives us hope and joy as we journey toward the fulfillment of God's creation and kingdom purposes.

Divinity and Dignity

Scripture affirms the dignity of God's human creation; unlike other creatures, humans were made as unique representations of God in the world—"in the image of God" (Gen. 1:26–27; 9:3; James 3:9). God bestows on us dignity and dignifying tasks, but he makes himself present to us and within us (1 Cor. 6:19; Rev. 3:12).

Consider two extremes—pantheism and Deism. These two views are represented in Athens—the pantheistic Stoics and deistic Epicureans (Acts 17:18). Pantheism affirms that everything is God, while Deism claims that God creates the world but remains detached from it. The biblical story cuts between these two perspectives: though God is distinct from his creation, he meets with and engages with his human creatures, starting in the primeval garden-temple. And throughout the Scriptures, God meets with humans at stone altars, at the portable tabernacle or permanent temple, or within human beings, who are God's temple (1 Cor. 6:19; Rev. 3:12)—or finally in the end when God will dwell in the midst of his people (Zech. 2:11; Rev. 21:3).

The Divine Image

What does the *image of God* mean? Kings in the ancient Near Eastern world set up statues or "images" of themselves throughout their domain; these represented regal power over a certain realm even where the king himself couldn't be physically present; the extent of the king's rule was wherever his image could be found.

Likewise, humans are made in the "likeness" or "image" of God to represent his authority and display his glory in the world—a distinctive not shared by other creatures. As his image-bearers, God bestowed on us the necessary capacities (e.g., rationality, relationality, spirituality, volition, self-awareness) to engage in a twofold task: to rule creation with God (Gen. 1:28; Ps. 8) and to relate to God or "walk with God" (Gen. 3:8; 5:22, 24; 6:9). That is, as co-regents with God over the creation, we work together with God, extending the knowledge and glory of God to the ends of the earth (cf. Hag. 2:4–5; 1 Cor. 3:4–9; 15:10; Phil. 2:12–13; Col. 1:29). This involves being fruitful and multiplying, naming animals, and tending to the garden (Gen. 1:29)—but also creating societies and cultures, making music, studying the world, and harnessing natural resources. As Tolkien observes, God's image-bearers are "sub-creators" who can use their imagination and create literature and art, and, in doing so, worship God.

As priests, we're designed to worship God—to work/serve (*'abad*) and guard (*shamar*) the temple-garden in Eden (Gen. 2:15); these terms could be translated "worship" and "obey"—terms used together elsewhere in the Book of Moses to refer to priestly/Levitical service and guarding the tabernacle/sanctuary (Num. 3:7–8; 8:25–26; 18:5–6; etc.). We aren't just "thinking humans" (*Homo sapiens*) or "rational animals" (Aristotle) but *Homo adorans*—designed by God to love and worship him and to be stewards over the earth. Put another way, God's image-bearers are designed to be lovers (loving God, loving others) and stewards with God over creation. We are like angled mirrors. From one angle, we are reflections or representatives of creation looking toward God, offering up praise and worship to him on behalf of all creation. From the other angle, as representatives of God looking toward creation, reflecting his glory to the entire creation by bringing his transforming presence of peace, joy, justice, love, and care to the rest of the world.[5]

JESUS: THE TRUEST HUMAN AND CHOSEN SON

The Jesus Story

This dual reflecting role is how humans ideally function. Yet humans fell away from this vocation, being alienated from God, others, the created world, and even within our own selves. Even so, God not only promised redemption through the woman's offspring (Gen. 3:16) but he also made a covenant promise to Abraham that his offspring will bring blessing to all the nations (Gen. 12:1–3). Hundreds of years later at Mt. Sinai, national Israel was to take up the mantle of being a kingdom of priests (Exod. 19:6). Like our earliest ancestors, they failed to live up to their calling—to be priest-kings and a light to the nations.

A second, new, and lasting covenant was anticipated and then inaugurated by Jesus of Nazareth—the true Israel and obedient Son that national Israel failed to be. This offspring of Abraham perfectly lived out Israel's story: the faithful Son Jesus was called "out of Egypt" (cf. Hos. 11:1 with Matt. 2:15); he was baptized in the Jordan River—a reenactment of the exodus; he was then tested in the wilderness for forty days; he chose twelve disciples, harking back to the twelve tribes of Israel; he ascended a mountain as the new Moses giving a "new law" for the restored community of Israel (Matt. 5–7). At his death, he "hangs on a tree," taking on the curse of Israel's exile (Gal. 3:13; cf. Deut. 21:23)—as well as the exile of all humanity (Eph. 2:12). The new, true Israel came to be formed through Jesus—complete with a new, redeemed "kingdom of priests" or "royal priesthood" (Rev. 1:6; 5:10; 20:6; cf. 1 Pet. 2:9).

A New Creation and a New Exodus

Through Jesus, both a new creation and new exodus are achieved. In the new creation, Jesus reveals himself to be the archetypal or truest human—the second Adam. He is the head of a new race, a redeemed humanity. As the "firstborn from the dead" (Col. 1:18; Rev. 1:5), his bodily resurrection from the dead signals the beginning of a restored creation (2 Cor. 5:17)—a promissory note guaranteeing our own bodily resurrection at the end of history as we know it. As the very "image of the invisible God" (Col. 1:15), Jesus lives out humanity's vocation and through his death and resurrection begins to burnish and restore that tarnished, obscured image. We leave the "old man" Adam behind and are being transformed into the likeness of Jesus Christ, the "new man" (Eph. 2:15; 4:20–24; Col. 3:8, 10–15).

In the new exodus, Jesus is the new Israel; the obedient, beloved Son that national Israel failed to be (Matt. 2:15; 3:17; cf. Hos. 11:1). Jesus fulfills Israel's covenant calling and creates a new community of Jews and gentiles in union with him. As a result, the transformed people of God spread his fame and glory to the ends of the earth through deeds of love and service, through being proclaimers of the good news of God's kingdom, and reconciling others to God. Ultimately, the final completion of this new creation will be fulfilled in the new heavens and earth.

Unlike Deism, God will dwell in the midst of his people and will "walk among [them]" (Lev. 26:11–12; cf. Exod. 29:45–6; Ezek. 37:27; Zech. 2:10–11). Unlike pantheism, God's people will maintain their distinct identity without being swallowed up or lost in divinity. Our present participation in the "eternal life" of the triune God (John 17:3) as "partakers of the divine nature" (2 Pet. 1:4) is a foretaste of enjoying the unshielded presence of God in the new heavens and earth.

FINAL THOUGHTS

The biblical story—the story of reality—concerns the triune God, creation, fall, redemption, and re-creation. We too are part of this ongoing story! We share in this unfolding of this story as we pray "your kingdom come" and as we work together with God to set back the powers of darkness, dehumanization, and death. We participate in spreading God's glory through renewing our minds and influencing the thought patterns of our own culture (Rom. 12:1–2; 2 Cor. 10:5), engaging in loving and just actions (Matt. 5:16), proclaiming the good news of Jesus and making disciples (Matt. 28:19–20), and keeping ourselves unstained by influences of darkness and even exposing them (Eph. 5:11; James 1:27).

This is the story of reality, and God calls us into it—to pledge allegiance to it, to embrace it, to step into it, to allow it to shape our thinking and identity that it may overflow to those around us. To do this is to live life according to the divine Designer's template. And as the book progresses, we'll explore the philosophical underpinnings and implications of this transformative, illuminating story.

FURTHER READING

Ganssle, Gregory E. *Our Deepest Desires: How the Christian Story Fulfills Human Aspirations*. Downers Grove, IL: IVP Academic, 2017.

Goetz, Stewart. *The Purpose of Life: A Theistic Perspective*. New York: Bloomsbury, 2012.

Goldsworthy, Graeme. *According to Plan: The Unfolding Revelation of God in the Bible*. Downers Grove, IL: IVP Academic, 2002.

Koukl, Greg. *The Story of Reality: How the World Began, How It Ends, and Everything Important That Happens in Between*. Grand Rapids: Zondervan, 2017.

McQuilkin, Robertson, and Paul Copan. Parts 1–4 of *An Introduction to Biblical Ethics: Walking in the Way of Wisdom*. Downers Grove, IL: IVP Academic, 2014.

Moreland, J. P. *Kingdom Triangle: Recover the Christian Mind, Renovate the Soul, Restore the Spirit's Power*. Grand Rapids: Zondervan, 2007.

5 | *The Need for God*

As the deer pants for the water brooks,
So my soul pants for You, O God.
My soul thirsts for God, for the living God.

—Psalm 42:1–2

GOD, LONGING, AND LIFE'S MEANING

A basic question in philosophy is, "What is the good life?" Jesus himself spoke about the abundant life (John 10:10), and he insisted that he was "the door" to that life of abundance (John 10:7, 9). The good, abundant life is not without trouble and even deep pain, but Jesus in his death and resurrection has overcome all of these things—and so we can take great courage (John 16:33). Coming to grips with the good life requires that we understand this christological fact—which means recognizing that this mortal life is not all the life there is; there is a life to come as well (1 Tim. 4:7–8). We must operate on a two-worlds model rather than a single-world model. Considering these factors will assist us as we consider our deepest longings and the meaning of life.

Considering Our Deepest Longings

N. T. Wright observes four basic yearnings that faith in God satisfies: "the longing for justice, the quest for spirituality, the hunger for relationships, and the delight in beauty."[1] Indeed, we humans have a number of deep longings—for close relationship, purpose, meaning, significance, forgiveness of guilt, the removal of shame, and overcoming the fear of death. These aren't mere superficial or occasional desires that humans experience now and then, such as the urge to climb a mountain or to live in a cabin in the woods at high altitudes. Many humans spanning the millennia and across civilizations attest to something more—to profound and sustained longings. And engaging with the best literature, poetry, music, and films helps us more deeply realize our own true humanity and more fully awakens those deep longings and desires.

So rather than simply asking about rational arguments for the Christian faith at this point, perhaps it's worth considering another angle: What if the Christian faith actually turns out to have the resources for us to live this good life? Some of us may be cutting ourselves off from the actual wellspring or source to fulfill our deepest of longings. And as we invite conversation with those outside the Christian faith, we can ask them, "How should we live as human beings, and how does your worldview help you carry this out in your everyday life?"

We long for deep relationships. What if there is a God who himself longs for humans to know and love him? And what if this God loves us despite our unloveliness and even sacrifices himself for those hostile to him (Rom. 5:6-10)? And we long to be valued. We appreciate when people remember our name and—all the more—when they accept and embrace us as significant, despite our failings and unloveliness. Why think an atheistic worldview could offer any promising leads for how creatures of great value and desiring to be valued could emerge from impersonal, unguided, valueless molecules in motion?

We are awed by the vast variety of beauty that surrounds us; in fact, it stares us in the face and confronts us. How do we make sense of this beauty if it's all mere molecular arrangements with no deeper meaning?

We value the importance of freedom to make morally significant, life-shaping choices. But if we're the products of blind deterministic forces, then genuine freedom is an illusion. All we think and do is shaped by prior physical processes over which we've had zero control. But if it turns out that a God exists who has made us as morally free creatures, this would rescue and make sense of that deep longing, and it would reassure us that our choices really matter.

Atheist (existentialist) thinker Albert Camus confessed, "I am searching for something the world is not giving me." This realization led him to take interest in the Christian faith and request baptism. Although this desire was not realized (he died in an auto accident in 1960), he recognized the need for outside assistance.[2]

This illustrates what Sir Roger Scruton noted: we moderns suffer from "metaphysical loneliness" brought on by a technological and narcissistic age. As one author put it, "I don't believe in God, but I miss Him."[3] To overcome this loneliness requires realizing that life is a gift that should fill us with "sacred awe." The failure to recognize that this world and our very lives are a gift bestowed on us has in fact led to the decline of belief in God; the decline hasn't actually come from the arguments of atheists.[4]

Recognizing Our Human Failure

One former atheist, Francis Spufford, wrote a book after his conversion, *Unapologetic*, on why the Christian faith makes much surprising emotional sense.[5] Spufford discovered that we humans are morally deficient and have a propensity to mess things up. In our default state, we are not at deep inner peace. We crowd out thoughts of our own deficiencies through technology, media, sports, and other distractions; we cannot sit quietly with ourselves. What's more, our lives are characterized by unsightly smudges, deep cracks, and profound brokenness. We carry guilt with us in the face of our moral failure—falling far short of the people we desire to be and the very standards we profess.

However, guilt and shame can also contribute to true self-discovery and prompt a move toward a solution to our failure if we will allow it, as Spufford did. In an interview, he spoke about why he left atheism:

> It turned out not to contain what my soul needed for nourishment in bad times. It was not any kind of philosophical process that led me out from disbelief. I had made a mess of things in my life, and I needed mercy, and to my astonishment, mercy was there. An experience of mercy, rather than an idea of it. And the rest followed from there. I felt my way back to Christianity, discovering through many surprises that the religion I remembered from my childhood looked different if you came to it as an adult with adult needs: not pretty, not small, not ridiculous, but tough and gigantic and marvellous.[6]

A "moral gap" exists between our performance and the virtuous ideals we recognize and praise. But if we are willing, our moral inadequacy be the start of a new quest to explore abundant spiritual storehouses found in the sufficiency of Christ instead of our pathetic personal pantry. After all, it is the "poor in spirit" who inherit the kingdom of heaven (Matt. 5:3).

Apatheism?

What about people who just don't care if God exists? They're not theists or atheists or even agnostics, but *apatheists*. Apatheism isn't a worldview or a belief system; it's an *attitude* of not caring about God's existence. It concerns *how* you believe, not *what*: it's a "disinclination to care all that much about one's own religion, and an even stronger disinclination to care about other people's"—and this position has been considered a "civilizational advance."[7] This attitude isn't new. The French Enlightenment philosopher Denis Diderot claimed that while it's important not to mistake poison hemlock for parsley, God's existence, by contrast, isn't important at all.

The problem with apatheism is that it's just an attitude; it's not an intellectual position that you can reason about or argue against. For the apatheist, it doesn't matter if there are good—even compelling—arguments for God's existence and character—these things of which we cannot now speak in detail. The apatheist doesn't care that the idea of God has been so culturally fruitful, as Anthony Kenny has observed, nor does it matter to the apatheist that faith in God—especially in the Protestant Christian tradition—has led to key moral reforms, human rights discourse, and the establishment of democracies.[8] Apatheism isn't a sophisticated intellectual position or some civilizational advance. From a spiritual, rational, and moral perspective, it's like not caring about having cancer. Or it's like a child who doesn't see the point of a good education.

If God exists, the implications are enormous. To their credit, various atheistic thinkers, like Thomas Nagel, recognize that the existence of a Cosmic Authority would be a game-changer for them. And what if the biblical warnings of judgment and the anguish of separation from God really are true? Shouldn't we care at least for extrinsic reasons?

Here's another consideration: in what other realm or discipline of life could one get away with not caring about the truth of things and their implications—for example, in much of science, engineering, medicine, and athletics? True enough, certain academics may promote unworkable, untested, outrageously impractical policies that are eventually implemented by lawmakers; when they fail spectacularly, and individuals' lives and businesses and even whole economies are ruined, no one in academia or in government is held accountable. When we don't care about ideas and their consequences, this isn't a civilizational advance; rather, it reflects a cultural immaturity and may reveal the need for psychological help.[9]

Even apatheists themselves have fears or inner conflicts that nag at them. They must deal with guilt, shame, insecurities, and the problem of evil or personal crises like all other human beings. And through their lives, loving, character, and the offer of friendship, the Christian messenger can be the personifying reality of God's presence to apatheists and their ilk.[10]

Considering Common Sense

C. S. Lewis was philosophically trained and even applied for a philosophy position at Oxford University. Well, he didn't get the position and so had to settle for an opening in English literature at Oxford instead—not a bad alternative!

One of the reasons Lewis's writings resonate with so many of us is that he was committed to commonsense notions that were being denied by many who claimed to be "following science." They insisted that beauty doesn't exist; that humans aren't free to make choices; that they have no intrinsic dignity; that there is no self but just a bundle of physical properties instead; that objective moral values don't exist; that there is no purpose or way things ought to be.

Lewis challenged this: the average human being knows better. Why reject what seems so obvious to us and embrace what seems so utterly contrary to our thinking and the way that we actually live? In fact, in our denying these things, we will often assume those commonsensical things that we deny. For example, a *self*—not just a bundle of properties—is presumably doing the denying. We believe we are freely claiming that we have no genuine freedom. If we call consciousness an illusion, we'll need to be conscious to experience that illusion. In rejecting God because of evil, we still assume a "way things ought to be." But why ought things to be different if nature is all there is?

While rational arguments and external evidences for God's existence are the typical philosopher of religion's stock-in-trade, we should not ignore inner existential reasons for belief in God rooted in these deep longings. The psalmists are often speaking of yearning or thirsting for God (e.g., Pss. 42:1–2; 63:1; 119:40, 174). Ecclesiastes 3:11 affirms that God has set eternity in our hearts. Augustine put it another way in his *Confessions*: "You have formed us for Yourself, and our hearts are restless till they find rest in You."[11] Similarly, C. S. Lewis spoke of *Sehnsucht*—a deep human longing for something we've never experienced, for a land we've never visited. He rightly claimed how strange it would be to have those deep longings without a source to fulfill these longings—much like being thirsty without water existing anywhere. The most fulfilling vacation or professional achievement, however exhilarating or fulfilling—can't sustain that emotional "high." We keep thinking, "There must be something more."

Such finite fulfillments are a far cry from deep union with the inexhaustible God in the life to come—something that no eye has seen, ear heard, or mind imagined (1 Cor. 2:9). Critics who portray the afterlife with God as boring and monotonous simply haven't reflected very deeply on what it means to be in the unshielded presence of the infinitely enthralling God. It's perfectly sensible to think that in the afterlife, God will grant redeemed humans the ever-deepening capacity to be enchanted, thrilled, and joyous in being with the maximally fascinating being.

Now it's true that having these deep longings doesn't guarantee that their fulfillment can be realized; however, they do serve as a pointer toward a Fulfiller. Consider Spufford's words above. Why do we have these deep longings to be free from guilt and to find forgiveness? We can commonsensically reason from our deepest longings to the fact that God makes the best sense of them:

I find that I have a profound, inescapable longing for forgiveness.

I also find that God in Christ provides this forgiveness—whereas atheism and other worldviews don't afford this.

Therefore, I would be justified in believing in God.

GOD, HAPPINESS, AND MEANING

We are meaning-seeking beings. We ask, "Why?" We often wonder what the purpose of this or that evil might be. We seek some kind of justification for it. We commonly hear people—even those who don't believe in God—confidently asserting, "Everything happens for a reason."

Believers rightly insist that God's nonexistence yields a certain absurdity or irrationality. If we're made for life with God—to become Godlike (Eph. 5:1)—our ultimate meaning cannot be achieved. This isn't to say that life has no meaning for the atheist. She can find much satisfaction in helping others, living virtuously, and "making the world a better place"—even without God on her radar. She might say, "There's no *cosmic* purpose, but *my* life is nevertheless quite satisfying. I have found purpose *in* life, even if there isn't purpose *to* life." So while there's no "global meaning," we could say that she still finds "local meaning."[12]

What are we to make of this popularly held view in the modern West? Here we offer a few brief comments.

First, meaning is connected to or derived from purpose. Why don't we use Monopoly money for financial transactions at a bank? Well, the purpose of Monopoly money is relevant only while playing the game itself—and nothing more. For the purpose of playing the game, Monopoly money has meaning, being useful to buy properties like Boardwalk and Park Place. Given the purpose of the game, the financial transactions have meaning. Again, this is merely a *local* meaning, not a *global* one. The money is worthless—without meaning—outside of that game. By contrast, dollars or pounds or euros have *meaning* because of an authoritative government's *purposeful* authoritative declarations. No purpose, no meaning. Likewise, in a universe that has no ultimate purpose, ultimate meaning does not exist.

Second, the purpose of life is bound up with happiness or pleasure—or, in biblical terms, "fullness of joy" (Ps. 16:11; cf. Acts 14:17). Augustine, Blaise Pascal, and C. S. Lewis alike affirmed that our deepest human desire is for eternal happiness. God has made us to enjoy complete happiness; each of us has been born for this. This happiness is intrinsically good—that is, it isn't a means to achieving or acquiring something else (i.e., an extrinsic good). Lewis said that God is a hedonist at heart; he is the inventor of pleasure, and at his right hand are pleasures forevermore (Ps. 16:11).[13] Lewis reasoned that pain, by contrast, is intrinsically bad.

We should make a few points clear here. For one thing, the pleasure involved in an immoral act (e.g., adultery) is still something good, but it is the *means* or the *action* that is wrong. It is action (or inaction) in violation of our duty to the moral law that renders an action wrong; it is not the pleasure of it; it is not the sweetness of an apple that is bad, but the stealing of it, Lewis insisted. People don't do cruel things because cruelty is wrong; they do so because the cruelty was pleasant (sadists) or useful (to gain money or power in the pursuit of happiness).[14]

In addition, though pleasure is good, it is not the only good. Justice, for example, is also good and cannot be reduced to pleasure. Goodness or value includes pleasure, but also much more than this—justice, beauty, rationality, duty, and acts that go beyond the call of duty (e.g., laying down your life for a stranger). And we could add this: since humans have been made in God's image, the pain and suffering they may experience is intrinsically distinct from—on a different level than—the pain experience of animals. So we must be careful not to transfer our own pain experience to that of animals. While we have a God-given stewardship responsibility not to bring unnecessary harm to animals, they don't bear God's image and thus are not intrinsically rights-bearing creatures.[15]

Finally, we can't make ourselves happy; rather, happiness *happens* to us. In other words, happiness or pleasure isn't a goal to be pursued but a gift to be received. Happiness is passive—done for me—not an action I do. The more we try to pursue happiness, the more it eludes us. In the biblical understanding, it is the result or the by-product of death to ourselves, our will, our agenda: "For whoever wishes to save his life will lose it, but whoever loses his life for My sake and the gospel's will save it" (Mark 8:35). As we find our contentment in God, then a deeper happiness or joy comes to us: "In Your presence is fullness of joy" (Ps. 16:11). So we may endure pain, not for its own sake, but for Christ's sake and finding a deeper pleasure or happiness in him. We do so in light of the gracious promise that we will experience ultimate happiness or joy in being Christlike (1 John 3:2). And even true love for *another* human is the pursuit of that person's happiness.

Third, the existence of God removes absurdity and irrationality by making room for a robust or complete view of purpose and meaning. We're attracted to stories in which people "live happily ever after"—where evil orcs, tyrants, and torturers meet their end and the people live in peace and harmony. We all desire perfect happiness, and when our greatest achievements—winning a Super Bowl or the World Cup finals—fail to produce it, we are let down.

If I desire perfect happiness but can't actually attain it, then this is an absurd condition. Think of Mother Teresa, who selflessly poured out her life for others in the slums of Calcutta (Kolkata), India. Her doing "little things with great love," as she liked to say, led to widespread admiration and even to her winning the Nobel Peace Prize. But this good life poured out for others was, from her perspective, quite different on the inside. Her frank and deeply vulnerable letters to her spiritual advisor revealed profound inner darkness and feelings of utter godforsakenness. She did, of course, pray early on in her work in Calcutta that God would allow her to share in the sufferings of Christ, and it seems she received an answer to this prayer.

At any rate, what does the moral atheist say to that? Perhaps something like this: "Mother Teresa did the right thing. Virtue is its own reward. We shouldn't be moral just because there's some reward for it." But it's a strange—indeed absurd and irrational—situation where being impeccably virtuous conflicts with my own self-interest at the most basic level. That is, I long for deep happiness but never experience it. What about "bad luck" or the misfortune of being born as an "untouchable" in India? What if one's "destiny" appears to be a lifetime of sweeping human excrement from India's streets? What if being a conscientious whistle-blower at my workplace leads to a lifetime of misery, social ostracism, and joblessness? Doing one's duty might mean sacrificing much, if not all, happiness.

Here's another absurdity: what about those who lived wickedly as Nazis and then spent quiet, undisturbed lives in Argentina, enjoying their families while eating steaks and drinking fine wines? Or maybe one isn't deeply wicked or horrific, but just takes a few strategic, non-horrific immoral shortcuts to avoid a life of imprisonment or social rejection. Isn't it irrational to live utterly without happiness if doing something shady or morally compromising might pave the way for at least a decent dose of happiness? Why not just drop out of the moral game if it conflicts with the last vestiges of my own self-interest? It's hard to make sense of "doing your duty" in utter opposition to happiness—permanently.

Of course, we should keep in mind that self-interest isn't the same as selfishness. When I'm hungry, I'll eat a meal because of a proper self-interest; this isn't selfish. While all selfishness is self-interest, not all self-interest is selfishness. The key point, however, seems clear: if this life is all there is, then it's not always irrational to act immorally.

The good news is that a maximally great God's existence—and thus cosmic purpose and ultimate meaning—removes a number of absurdities:

- *The absurdity of duty and dignity*: A world without a good God—but only valueless, nonconscious, nonrational, deterministic processes—can't account for objective moral duties and human dignity. A good God easily makes sense of these.
- *The absurdity of death's dishonors*: A world without a good God to bring justice means the wicked "get away with murder" and aren't called to account for their deeds—while all of the world's Mother Teresas don't see their sacrifices and virtue rewarded. A good God will bring cosmic justice for all.
- *The absurdity of dichotomies*: A world without God and thus without cosmic purpose can lead to a severe dichotomy—impeccable moral virtue and ultimate happiness may never meet. A highly moral person may be quite unhappy, and a morally compromised person may enjoy a reasonable dose of earthly happiness. But if God exists, we don't have to choose between morality or virtue over self-interest. A good God will guarantee that moral goodness and deepest happiness will be united in the life to come.

So the biblical God preserves moral duty and human dignity. The reality of God also eliminates the dishonors of injustice left unaddressed. Gone too is the dichotomy between moral goodness and ultimate happiness, which God guarantees will be united in the life to come.

To illustrate much of what we are saying here, consider the factory girl in Elizabeth Gaskell's novel *North and South*:

> I think if this should be the end of all, and if all I have been born for is just to work my heart and life away, and to sicken in this [dreary] place, with those mill-stones in my ears forever, until I could scream out for them to stop and let me have a little piece of quiet, and with the fluff filling my lungs, until I thirst to death for one long deep breath of the clear air, and my mother gone, and I never able to tell her again how I loved her, and of all my troubles—I think, if this life is the end, and that there is no God to wipe away all tears from all eyes, I could go mad![16]

We have deep longings; we were made for ultimate happiness; and God makes sense of both of their origin and fulfillment.

Before moving on, let's be clear: living a decent or moral life isn't our ultimate end or goal; it's not the meaning of life. Rather, it is to become Godlike, to become conformed to the image of Christ (Gal. 4:19), to become most fully real—truly human. This is made apparent by the fact that we won't have moral duties in the afterlife. As Lewis wrote, moral duties from our "school-days" on earth will have been forgotten in our final, transformed, and fully happy state with God, where there is no longer any "ought."[17]

FURTHER READING

Ganssle, Gregory E. *Our Deepest Desires: How the Christian Story Fulfills Human Aspirations.* Downers Grove, IL: IVP Academic, 2017.

Goetz, Stewart. *The Purpose of Life: A Theistic Perspective.* New York: Bloomsbury, 2012.

Puckett, Joe. *The Apologetics of Joy: A Case for the Existence of God from C. S. Lewis's Argument from Desire.* Cambridge, UK: Lutterworth Press, 2013.

Spufford, Francis. *Unapologetic: Why, Despite Everything, Christianity Can Still Make Surprising Emotional Sense.* New York: HarperOne, 2012.

6 | *Wired for God*

> Why should the nations say, "Where is their God?"
>
> —Psalm 79:10

> "Thus you shall say to Hezekiah king of Judah, 'Do not
> let your God in whom you trust deceive you. . . . Did
> the gods of [other] nations which my fathers destroyed
> deliver them . . . ?'"
>
> —2 Kings 19:10–13

Psychology and Biology: Friend or Foe of Faith?

Psychology and Belief in God

Many critics of belief in God consider "religion" to be for the weak-minded who can't handle life's challenges. Atheist Ludwig Feuerbach (1804-1872) wrote in his *Essence of Christianity*, "Religion is the dream of the human mind."[1] Karl Marx claimed that religion is like a drug for the oppressed—"the opium of the people." A century later, psychiatrist Sigmund Freud called religion an illusion, the result of human wishes and longings in the face of the superior crushing forces of nature. Because of these earthly fears and anxieties, we cling to a projection of loving Father God, which gives us a sense of security. Theology is nothing more than anthropology: humans create God in *their* image, not the other way around (cf. Gen. 1:26–27). We humans gave birth to God! So Freud and his ilk have claimed that theology can be fully psychologized.

Biology and Belief in God

In recent decades, criticism has come from within a developing science—the cognitive science of religion (CSR). CSR is an effort to "science up" religion, bringing together various scientific disciplines to discover why religious beliefs and practices develop as they do. Those involved in CSR include both critics and sympathizers. Critic Pascal Boyer claims that the latest "scientific" developments reveal that we humans have a "central metaphysical urge"—a strong "irredeemable" inclination toward "superstition, myth and faith, or a special emotion that only religion provides." This, he says, stands at the root of all religion.[2] Another critic says that belief in God is a "virus" of the mind and that there is a "built-in irrationality mechanism in the brain."[3]

For the critic, God doesn't exist; the idea of God is just a brain trick. Studies on young children around the world indicate that they are "intuitive theists"— that belief in God/gods seems a natural part of development—like walking and language learning.[4] We appear "wired" to detect agents like God or gods and to see design in the world. This is the result of a hyperactive agent detection device (HADD). You're more likely to survive if you're on the alert for potential agents out there—God/gods, spirits, demons, or haunted houses and ghost-inhabited forests—than if you just think natural forces alone are operational. Your HADD helps concoct agents that don't in fact exist, but this, happily, ensures that you'll straighten up and fly right in order to promote your own survival. Our *genetic* wiring shapes our minds (the *epigenetic*), whose ideas are eventually transmitted through *memetics*—the spread of religious ideas ("memes") through holy books, traditions, and religious leaders and institutions. This enhances survival and reproduction through cooperation and group-reinforced morality. For some, theology can be biologized. This has been called "neurotheology."

We've seen in brief that from both a psychological and biological perspective, the received view is this: adopting the default perspective of atheism or secularism reflects the healthy, non-deluded state of mind. The "religious" view, by contrast, is highly dubious and psychologically questionable; religionists are duped by the illusory tendencies of agency "detection." But despite such common dismissals of faith in God, these arguments not only make logical mistakes but can be turned on their head to favor belief in God.

GOD AND THE PSYCHOLOGY OF BELIEF

God, "the Fool," and the Psychoanalysts

Wisdom begins with knowing and honoring God: "The fear of the LORD is the beginning of wisdom" (Ps. 111:10; Prov. 9:10; cf. Prov. 1:7; 15:33). Yet Scripture calls a person a "fool" who insists that "there is no God" (Pss. 14:1; 53:1). Atheists will sometimes express indignation at this statement, as though the biblical authors think atheists are intellectually challenged.

Let's be clear. Plenty of intelligent atheists exist. The biblical writer, however, isn't claiming atheists have a low IQ. In fact, the "fool" isn't an atheist at all! Atheists wouldn't have existed in ancient Israel. Rather, the "fool," "scoundrel," "rogue," or "crass person" (*nabal*) acts as though God is removed, uninvolved, and unconcerned. The fool is thinking: "God is not here."[5] So this "scoundrel" thinks she can get away with committing injustice since God won't do anything about it. In Psalm 10, the very one who says, "There is no God" (v. 4), claims, "God has forgotten, he has hidden his face, he will never see it" (v. 11 ESV). For him, to "renounce God" is to *tell God*: "You will not call to account" (v. 13 ESV).

What about the atheist in our day? While one would have to be a fool to claim that intelligent atheists don't exist, we can say their fundamental orientation is misdirected, and so they are building on a false foundation. The atheist is averted from God and needs converting to God. Without the fear of God, he cannot ultimately live wisely—that is, he just won't have the proper skill for living as he ought. For one thing, he can't carry out the most fundamental duty—to love God with heart, soul, mind, and strength—and all that this entails. Instead of seeing God as the ultimate source of goodness and the fulfillment of our deepest desires, he seeks out contingent God-substitutes that cannot ultimately satisfy. God says this about his ancient people: "For my people have committed two evils: they have forsaken me, the fountain of living waters, and hewed out cisterns for themselves, broken cisterns that can hold no water" (Jer. 2:13 ESV). Even *good* things, such as a relationship, a career, or financial success can become *God* things—God-substitutes—that make for a flimsy foundation for life. The psalmist Asaph, who had for a time been thinking as a fool, came to realize that, besides God, he had nothing else in heaven and on earth—and that was enough: "God is the strength of my heart and my portion forever" (Ps. 73:25-26).

Getting Close to God

When we read about the presence of God in Scripture, we see something of a paradox. On the one hand, the psalmists take comfort in God's being near: "The nearness of God is my good" (Ps. 73:28). They don't want God to hide his face from them or to abandon them. Yet sometimes God's people also don't want the holy God to get *too close* to them: "Depart from me, for I am a sinful man, O Lord" (Luke 5:8 ESV). After Aaron's sons had been struck down for idolatry by offering "strange fire" in the tabernacle—Israel's portable tent-temple—God reminds Aaron: "By those who come near Me I will be treated as holy" (Lev. 10:3).

Earlier we read about atheist Thomas Nagel's "fear of religion." He admitted that he didn't want there to be a God. Ironically, the "fear" that Freud claimed drives people to fabricate the idea of God has its counterpart: an intelligent atheist might have a fear-driven belief—a kind of crutch or projection—to *escape* divine nearness and scrutiny. And we can concur with this terror, atheistic or otherwise: what mortal would *not* feel dread in a holy God's presence, apart from knowing God's grace, forgiveness, and fatherly heart (Ps. 103:10–14)?

Humans Are Made for God

These atheistic psychoanalysts have gotten it wrong: God isn't a crutch; he's a complete life-support system! But these psychoanalysts of religion haven't gone far enough in another way: the reason we have a longing for God is because God *designed* us to be satisfied in him alone. We've been created with a God-shaped hole that only he can fill, Blaise Pascal wrote. We've been *made for* God: "He has also set eternity in the human heart" (Eccles. 3:11 NIV). John Calvin called this the *sensus divinitatis*—the sense of the divine—within every human soul. However we understand this spiritual "sense," we have the capacity to relate to God, and the human heart cannot find true rest until it comes home to God, as Augustine declared.

This divinely placed longing for the transcendent—something beyond the this-worldly—has been formulated into an "argument from desire": God's existence makes sense of the yearning or "desire for something that has never actually happened."[6] The beauty of Bach's orchestral suites, the richness of Dostoyevsky's works, and the majesty of the Canadian Rockies point beyond themselves to something more beautiful, eternal, ultimate, and thus most deeply satisfying (John 4:13–14; 7:37–39). Experiencing these earthly goods reminds us of an everlasting good. We long for a country we haven't yet visited, for a deep joy we've never realized, for our truest home where we find the sweet rest and peace never attainable in this life. These are a foretaste of a greater "weight of glory." This path to God isn't an escape route. No, it is an alignment with reality that actually brings us to this destination—the location in which we "live happily ever after."[7]

The Cost of Following Christ

Being a faithful follower of Christ means an *entire revision* of priorities and use of time (e.g., gathering with believers, reading Scripture), greater intentionality concerning one's thought life and habits, and so much more. Belief in the biblical God isn't the escapist "easy way out."

What's more, a lot of believers readily recognize that they could often find greater social acceptability if they gave up belief in Christ. Christian intellectuals in the academy attest to the need for greater courage in following Christ given the immense peer pressure. The same can be said about life in high-ranking social circles. To be a faithful believer in such settings is hardly a cop-out. She is bucking the tide of presumed atheism and takes the narrow, less-traveled road (Matt. 7:13–14). Scripture attests to believers who have faced incredible hardships, torture, and death precisely *because of* their faith. This is hardly a picture of escapism (Heb. 11:32–40; cf. 2 Cor. 11:23–28). As Jesus told his followers, "In this world you will have trouble. But take heart! I have overcome the world" (John 16:33 NIV).

Freud and Fallacies

More fundamentally, the Freudian dismissal of belief in God rests on a fallacious line of reasoning. It attacks the person (ad hominem) rather than any arguments for God the believer may put forward. It is an example of the genetic fallacy—basing the truth or falsity of a belief based on its origin.

Consider how a broken clock in a store window may register 12:00 and, coincidentally, it turns out to be exactly 12:00! Now it would be false to say that, because the clock isn't working, it *can't be* 12:00 (it's 12:00 twice in a day). Conversely, it's incorrect to say it *must be* 12:00 because "that's what the clock says." Likewise, I may believe in God because my parents told me he exists, but the *origin* of my belief is a separate issue from the *truth* of that belief. Or consider that Jay may have bad motives for telling Kay something malicious— but true—about Em. But bad motives don't render false what Jay has said. Motivation is logically distinct from the truth or falsity of a belief.

So we should distinguish between the *psychology* of belief and the *rationality* of belief. No matter how much comfort belief in Jesus might bring, the Christian faith is false if Jesus's body rotted in the tomb (1 Cor. 15:17). And if that is so, then we ought to abandon the faith—and simply eat, drink, and be merry (v. 32)—since it gives a *false* sense of purpose and peace.

Interestingly, Freud's view that humans fabricate a comforting heavenly father figure reflects a biblical background, but not that of most other traditional religions. Islam rejects the idea of God as Father, and many Eastern religions hold to an impersonal Ultimate Reality—or none at all.

Also, Freud had no clinical support for his theory about religion and no clinical experience with genuine believers. Freud admitted in a 1927 letter to a pastor—Oskar Pfister—that his God-as-a-crutch theory had no empirical support. Rather, his theory merely reflected his personal views, which were influenced by Feuerbach.[8]

Also, Freud mistakenly assumed the universality of the Oedipus complex. That is, a young man has an intense, subconscious desire to kill his father and take (erotic) possession of his mother. In the original story, Oedipus killed his father Laius without knowing he was his father and married his biological mother Jocasta, thinking the woman who raised him, Merope, was his mother.

As noted, the Oedipus complex isn't at all universal. In fact, it's quite particular to Freud's own personal life, which gave shape to his own psychological theories. Freud hated his own father, who was a sexual pervert and caused his children much suffering. Freud tellingly claimed that psychoanalysis, which has taught us the intimate connection between the father complex and belief in God, has shown us that the personal God is logically nothing but an exalted father and daily demonstrates to us how youthful persons lose their religious belief as soon as the authority of their father breaks down.[9] If someone should be psychoanalyzed here, it's Freud!

So, if the skeptic wants to play the psychologizing game against the God-believer, we can, like the apostle Paul, "speak as if insane" (2 Cor. 11:23; cf. 1 Cor. 4:10). We can apply this line of argument to the world's leading hard-nosed atheists and hard-driving skeptics. These leading thinkers—from the seventeenth into the twenty-first centuries—had missing or negative father figures: David Hume, Baron D'Holbach, Ludwig Feuerbach, Karl Marx, Voltaire, Friedrich Nietzsche, Sigmund Freud, Albert Camus, Bertrand Russell, Jean-Paul Sartre, Madalyn Murray O'Hair, Daniel Dennett, Christopher Hitchens, and Richard Dawkins (who had been sexually abused as a boy by an Anglican clergyman). By contrast, leading theists with good fathers and father-substitutes during the same period include: Blaise Pascal, George Berkeley, Joseph Butler, Thomas Reid, Edmund Burke, Moses Mendelssohn, William Paley, William Wilberforce, François René de Chateaubriand, Friedrich Schleiermacher, John Henry Newman, Alexis de Tocqueville, Samuel Wilberforce, Søren Kierkegaard, Baron Friedrich von Hügel, G. K. Chesterton, Albert Schweitzer, Martin Buber, Karl Barth, Dietrich Bonhoeffer, and Abraham Heschel. So if someone plays the psychoanalysis game, it appears the believer in God is better positioned here. But, as we've seen, doing so commits the genetic fallacy.

That said, existential reasons for belief in God motivated by the desire for comfort, significance, security, forgiveness, meaning, and the like serve to complement rational reasons or arguments for God's existence. If God has made us for himself, it makes sense that this God-shaped hole we experience isn't a human invention.

GOD AND THE BIOLOGY OF BELIEF

The same line of argument used by the *psychologizers* of belief in God parallels the arguments used by the *biologizers* of belief. Not surprisingly, then, the same family of theistic responses is also available. Since we've, hopefully, gotten the hang of the "psychology" response, we can look at a briefer response to the similar "biology" side of the question.

First, we should distinguish between the biology of belief and the rationality of belief. Even if a tendency to believe in agency is hardwired *into* the brain, why think that it can't correspond to a reality *outside* the brain? To think otherwise would be to commit the genetic fallacy again. In this case, the critic would rule out God's existence—or the accurately perceived actions of other agents—because that inclination to believe in God (or other agents) is assisted by our biological hardwiring. But how does God's nonexistence follow from that? God may exist independent of the beliefs a brain generates about God.

Philosopher Peter van Inwagen makes this point:

> Suppose that God exists and wants supernaturalistic belief to be a human universal, and sees (he would see this, if it were true) that certain features that it would be useful for human beings to have—useful from an evolutionary point of view: conducive to survival and reproduction—would naturally have the consequence that supernaturalistic belief would in due course become a human universal. Why shouldn't he allow those features to be the cause of the thing he wants?—rather as the human designer of a vehicle might use the waste heat from its engine to keep its passengers warm?[10]

Furthermore, what if God has made belief in him much easier? As indicated earlier, studies have revealed that children grow up as "intuitive theists"; they have the propensity to believe in God or godlike beings.[11] Anthropologist (and atheist) Scott Atran notes: "Supernatural agency is the most culturally recurrent, cognitively relevant, and evolutionarily compelling concept in religion. The concept of the supernatural agent is culturally derived from an innate cognitive schema."[12] Maybe this inclination exists to create an easier pathway to belief in our Creator. Of course, we must be discerning rather than gullible, but we do the same with our sense perceptions: we generally trust them, but we nevertheless can discern that on a hot day the pavement ahead of us isn't really wet and that sticks don't actually bend in the water.

An application of the tendency to infer agency includes detecting or inferring design. No wonder we are often using design analogies to talk about things in nature: "cells are like factories" or "the brain is like a computer." Biologist Timothy Lenoir (not a theist) says that design-thinking "has been steadfastly resisted by modern biology. And yet, in nearly every area of research biologists are hard pressed to find language that does not impute purposiveness to living forms."[13] Geneticist and Nobel Prize–winner Francis Crick urged: "Biologists must constantly keep in mind that what they see was not designed, but rather [naturalistically] evolved."[14] Crick advocates suppressing what seems most apparent to us ("must constantly keep in mind")—which sounds a lot like the suppression of the truth noted in Romans 1:18.

In addition, the existence of God actually helps ground science to prevent it from being merely a naturalistic accident. For the moment, let's allow that belief in God is merely a by-product of blind, nonrational biological forces directed toward enhancing survival and reproduction. The same then would have to be true about scientific beliefs. Both would be the product of blind, deterministic processes. Why is belief in God a virus, as Richard Dawkins asserts, but scientific beliefs are not? Why are critics of faith in God so unself-critical about their own beliefs? After all, the same nonrational forces generated both sets of (dis)beliefs. Rather than leaving the emergence of scientific beliefs up to these impersonal, unguided mechanisms, we can anchor science in a rational being that creates reasoning, truth-directed minds capable of studying magnificently a designed, well-ordered world. This God is essential to a reliable belief-forming process. CSR reminds us that we can affirm a dovetailing of the biological tendency to believe in God with an actual God who has made us for relationship with himself.

Finally, we have independent reasons for holding that belief in God is not simply the product of overactive brains. As we'll soon see, these reasons include the beginning and fine-tuning of the universe—along with the existence of consciousness, rationality, volition, moral duties, and morally valuable beings. These features are highly probable if a personal God exists—but not if we're the products of impersonal, valueless, nonconscious, deterministic, nonrational processes.

Instead of saying that belief in God is a "useful fiction" to enhance survival, the actual existence of a personal God would better explain our inclination to believe in a transcendent realm. As sociologist Christian Smith pointedly asks: "Why in a spiritless and godless world would people ever conceive of spirits and gods in the first place? Why *voluntarily* sacrifice our lives for some intangible 'super-empirical' realm? The reason humans persist in looking beyond the finite realm in search of the source of coherence, order, morality, meaning, and guidance for life is because this realm doesn't contain it. Humans, though embodied, are moral, spiritual beings with the capacity for self-transcendence and reflection on our world and our condition; this in turn enables us to search for a world-transcending God."[15]

If God has designed us to flourish through personal knowledge of him (John 17:3), then natural processes that contribute to belief in God would make excellent sense. We're actually at our cognitive best when our minds are directed toward true belief in God. It simply doesn't follow that natural processes—psychological or biological—leading to belief in God aren't actually connected to the reality of God. In fact, the alternative looks deeply problematic: Why trust our cognitive or rational faculties if our beliefs have been produced by prior material processes over which we have no control?

FURTHER READING

Barrett, Justin. *Born Believers: The Science of Children's Religious Belief.* New York: The Free Press, 2012.

———. *Why Would Anyone Believe in God?* Walnut Creek, CA: AltaMira Press, 2004.

Ganssle, Gregory E. *Our Deepest Desires: How the Christian Story Fulfills Human Aspirations.* Downers Grove, IL: IVP Academic, 2017.

Puckett, Joe. *The Apologetics of Joy: A Case for the Existence of God from C. S. Lewis's Argument from Desire.* Cambridge: Lutterworth Press, 2013.

Spufford, Francis. *Unapologetic: Why, Despite Everything, Christianity Can Still Make Surprising Emotional Sense.* New York: HarperOne, 2012.

Vitz, Paul C. *Faith of the Fatherless: The Psychology of Atheism.* 2nd ed. San Francisco: Ignatius, 2013.

———. "The Psychology of Atheism: From Defective Fathers to Autism to Professional Socialization and Personal Convenience." In *The Naturalness of Belief: New Essays on Theism's Rationality,* edited by Paul Copan and Charles Taliaferro, 175–95. Lanham, MD: Lexington Books/Rowman & Littlefield, 2019.

Part I

GOD

Who is like the LORD our God?
—Psalm 113:5

7 | *The Triune God*

> The same Spirit . . . the same Lord . . . the same God.
>
> —1 Corinthians 12:4–6

"I Don't Believe in That God Either"

Just what do people associate with the term "God"? While at Oxford's Worcester College, the biblical scholar N. T. Wright would meet with each of his first-year students to get to know them in at least a preliminary fashion. Many of them would tell him: "You won't be seeing much of me; you see, I don't believe in God." Wright would reply to these students, "Oh, that's interesting; which god is it you don't believe in?" The students were surprised that their concept of God might be quite different from the biblical one. As Wright describes it, "they would stumble out a few phrases about the god they did not believe in: a being who lived up in the sky, looking down disapprovingly at the world, occasionally 'intervening' to do miracles, sending bad people to hell while allowing good people to share his heaven." Wright would startle them by proclaiming, "Well, I'm not surprised you don't believe in that god. I don't believe in that god either."[1] With increased fragmentation of belief and a kind of buffet-style selective spirituality, the lesson should be obvious: Don't take for granted that your concept of God is the same as that of those around you.

Despite diverse beliefs about the divine, some will press hard to create a greater sense of theological unity and downplay any belief that divides. So we hear, "Jews, Christians, and Muslims worship the same God." True, Arab Christians had used the term *Allah* to refer to the triune God long before Muhammad's time—and still do—and the theological similarities between Jews, Christians, and Muslims are closer to one another than to those of most Hindu concepts of the divine. That said, despite this important theological overlap between these three "Abrahamic faiths," Islam and traditional Judaism take a *unitarian* view of God: the one God is *a* person—not *three* divine persons in *one* being (Trinitarian). Indeed, Islam is emphatic that ascribing partners to Allah (*shirk*)—including the worship of Jesus—is blasphemous and most damnable. Indeed, the doctrines of the incarnation and the Trinity, which make the Christian faith so distinctive, prove to be a stumbling block to these other theistic visions.

God's Robust Relationality

As we observed in chapter 4, *theism* (from the Greek word *theos*—"God") is different from *Deism* (from the Latin word *deus*—"God")—a view dominant during the Enlightenment (1650–1800) that reached its zenith in the 1790s in England, its country of origin. Deism's deity creates the universe with immutable natural laws in place to keep all things working with clocklike precision. However, he is removed, detached from humanity, and doesn't get involved in the world's affairs through miracles—special divine acts in the world.

Theism is also unlike *pantheism* ("everything is God") at the other extreme. Theists, by contrast, affirm that a personal God creates the world as something distinct from himself, and in addition to sustaining the universe in being, God can freely act within it. The biblical faith emphasizes that God is "over all" (transcendent), but he is also "in all" (immanent) and "not far from each one of us" (Acts 17:27, 28). God rules and sustains his creation but is also deeply engaged with it.

Thus, at the heart of reality is personal relationship. The inter-relational triune God provides us with a rich, robust personal understanding of the Ultimate Reality. Relationships didn't arise when God created angelic or human persons. Rather, from eternity, the triune God existed in self-giving, loving mutual relationship. This mutual indwelling (Greek: *perichorēsis*) is intrinsic to this household or community of divine persons. Though distinct from one another, they are necessarily and inseparably united in this inter-penetrating, transparent, joyful love.

Trinity: Distinctions and Unity

Perhaps you've heard attempted analogies for the Trinity: "God is like the three states of water—solid, liquid, and gas. Or maybe it's more like an egg's shell, yolk, and white. Or maybe it's like a man who is simultaneously a father, husband, and son." Actually, these common pictures of the Trinity are fraught with error, and it reminds us to choose our analogies well—or perhaps to simply show there is no contradiction while avoiding analogies altogether. While all analogies will have their limits, some may offer insight, while others ought to be discarded from the outset.

The Scriptures inform us that God is somehow three and one. God is clearly one in *being* or "substance."[2] The Lord is "one" (Deut. 6:4; James 2:19), though not a solitary supreme "Person." Rather, God is *three distinct persons*:[3] Father, Son, and Spirit. They fully, inseparably share in that one divine *nature* and *being* of God. We see indications of this threeness at Jesus's baptism—a reenactment of the exodus (Matt. 3:16–17); in the Great Commission (Matt. 28:19: baptism "in the name [not 'names']" of Father, Son, and Spirit); in the Upper Room Discourse, where Jesus makes mention of two other divine persons: "I will ask the Father, and He will give you another Helper [the Holy Spirit], that He may be with you forever" (John 14:16; cf. 14:26; 15:26); in Paul's benediction: "May the grace of the *Lord Jesus Christ*, and the love of *God*, and the fellowship of the *Holy Spirit* be with you all" (2 Cor. 13:14; cf. 1 Cor. 12:4–6). Even in the Old Testament, we have hints or foreshadowings of Trinitarian doctrine with its use of "Spirit," "Word," and "Wisdom" (Gen. 1:2; 6:3; Num. 11:29; Ps. 33:6, 9; Prov. 8:22–31). Notice that these aren't three different manifestations or modes of one person, much like three different states of water as ice, steam, and liquid or a man who is a father, husband, and son. (This is the heresy of *modalism*—God as a person appearing in different modes or forms.) Nor do they comprise three equal parts of God like a three-leafed clover (the heresy of *partialism*). The Father, Son, and Spirit are *united*, but they shouldn't be *equated* ("the Father is the Son"). And they are *persons*, which means that the Spirit is not some impersonal "it"—like a force or influence.

Think of a triangle. We're not here aiming to offer another flawed Trinity analogy; we're only noting how helpful it is to keep three Trinitarian "corners" in balance or tension: *threeness, oneness,* and *equality. Threeness* pertains to persons sharing divine being, but this threeness avoids *tritheism* (polytheism). *Oneness* pertains to the divine being, or even the divine nature. There aren't three divine beings or divine natures. This emphasis seeks to avoid the heresy of *modalism*—a divine person reveals himself in different "modes" at different times such as Father, Son, or Spirit.

Equality stresses the full equality of rank within the Godhead, thus rejecting an inherent, eternal subordinationism. The divine persons are "equal in glory and coeternal in majesty" (Athanasian Creed, fifth century). The way God acts in the world (*ad extra*—known as the "economic Trinity") can be distinguished from God as he is in himself (*a se*—known as the "immanent Trinity"). There are many possible worlds that don't include an incarnation or redemption. There are possible worlds in which the Father or Spirit could have become incarnate, as Thomas Aquinas suggested. In the actual world, Jesus submits to his Father's will as human being, but this special activity doesn't cut across all possible worlds.[4]

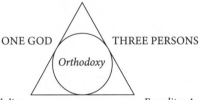

Oneness: Avoiding Tritheism/Polytheism

ONE GOD   THREE PERSONS

Orthodoxy

Threeness: Avoiding Modalism   EQUALITY   Equality: Avoiding Subordination

Rather than being some isolated self or solitary ego, God is supremely relational in his self-giving, other-oriented nature. Within God is intimate *union* as well as *distinction*—an unbreakable communion of persons. The persons of the Godhead can be *distinguished* but not *separated*. God is both *community* and *unity*.[5]

Because a relational God exists and chooses to create humans in his image, relationality is central to our identity as humans. No wonder the Ten Commandments divide into two tables—our relationship to God and to fellow human beings. Jesus himself summarizes our twofold duty: "love the Lord your God" and "love your neighbor" (Mark 12:28–31). We have been made for communion with God first and foremost, but how we regard fellow human beings reflects our spiritual condition (1 John 4:20). We recognize what love is by the model of the self-giving God in Christ (1 John 3:16).

Yet despite this rich doctrinal treasure, many Christians are functionally unitarians, viewing God as *a person* rather than as a God in community. So let's explore this further.

Understanding the Trinity without Demystifying It

The Trinity, Logic, and Mystery

Theologian Thomas Aquinas famously said that the doctrine of the Trinity is specially revealed through Scripture. God reveals something of his power, intelligence, goodness, and other features of his divine character through *general* revelation: nature, conscience, reason, and human experience. But we just wouldn't come up with the doctrine of the Trinity based on general revelation alone. We need the resources of *special* revelation to begin thinking about and formulating the doctrine of the Trinity. But just because we can't naturally reason *to* the doctrine of the Trinity doesn't mean we can't reason *about* it.

Even so, the "rationality" or "logic" of the Trinity doesn't minimize the wonder and awe at a God whose mysterious greatness is beyond comprehension and whose ways are unsearchable (Rom. 11:33).

Eastern and Western Emphases

The Eastern Christian tradition has emphasized God's threeness—namely, the distinctiveness of each divine person. This emphasis has been called "social Trinitarianism," which highlights what is known as the doctrine of *perichorē-sis*—a deep, interpersonal communion between Father, Son, and Spirit, with each indwelling the other. As Jesus put it, "the Father is in Me, and I in the Father" (John 10:38; cf. 10:30; 17:21). By contrast, Western Christianity (Roman Catholicism and Protestantism) has traditionally placed a greater stress on God's oneness, though this has shifted in recent decades.

Considering Some Analogies

Jehovah's Witnesses, Mormons, and Muslims will claim that this doctrine is a contradiction—that $1 + 1 + 1 = 3$! While the Trinity is a mystery, it is a logically coherent one. After all, threeness pertains to *persons* while oneness pertains to *substance* or *being*. Some Christians will stop here, content with the affirmation that this important doctrine contains no formal contradiction. And we can appreciate their care in being doctrinally cautious. But we can go beyond this to offer some suggestive analogies that may prove illuminating.

Here is one analogy that emphasizes the oneness while trying to avoid a part-whole relationship: one might suggest a carved piece of solid marble that is pillar, statue, and fountain all in one column. So while God is not a material being, God in his nature is "formed" in a manifold way; the divine nature is constituted by Father, Son, and Spirit rather than each person possessing the divine nature.[6]

Social Trinitarians will emphasize that some type of part-whole relation is inescapable. They emphasize that the members of the Trinity are three centers of divine personal awareness and will. Thus they may use another kind of analogy: the mythological three-headed dog Cerberus that guards Hades's gates. Cerberus is a single organism (substance)—one dog, not three dogs—but has three distinct centers of awareness. Each possesses the same canine nature but is inseparably united in one being. In the natural world we have comparable analogies in, say, two-headed snakes or turtles; in such cases we have distinct centers of awareness within one unified, indivisible organism. Likewise, God is one immaterial soul (substance) with three distinct centers of consciousness, rationality, and will (persons); these are deeply and necessarily interconnected, sharing the same unique divine nature and acting with united will in creation, redemption, resurrection, and new creation.

Another analogy might be that of the notes of a chord—say, C, E, and G. Each note alone fills the whole of the "heard" space, but when the other two notes are added, we have an integrated sound within the same space with distinctive, mutually enhancing notes.[7]

Whichever type of analogy is used, we have threeness and oneness without contradiction.

Elaborations on and Clarifications of the Trinity

The triune God is one intrinsically relational being consisting of three eternal mutually indwelling persons who are necessarily and inseparably united as a divine community. That's a packed sentence that requires some expansion.

First, God is three persons in one being, as we have pointed out. Jesus's first followers were Jews—orthodox monotheists, passionately committed to God's unique *oneness*: "The LORD is our God. The LORD is one," they proclaimed (Deut. 6:4; cf. Mark 12:29). Yet Jesus is affirmed as the "one Lord" in an early Christian creed (ca. AD 55); that is, he shares the divine identity. This is evident in Revelation 1:8, where the "Almighty" is called the "Alpha and Omega," yet Jesus himself—who will "come quickly"—also calls himself "the Alpha and the Omega" (Rev. 22:12–13). There can't be two Alphas and Omegas. Trinitarian doctrine helps us make sense of such claims and removes any apparent conflicts.

Second, each of the three persons possesses the divine nature. Not only is God one spirit-being with three centers of awareness in that being, but each person is also divine in nature. A *nature* is what makes a thing (or person) what it is. God possesses certain qualities, without which he wouldn't be God. For example, God is necessarily self-existent; he cannot *not* exist. As a maximally great being, God is also necessarily good and thus cannot do or command what is intrinsically evil. These characteristics make him what he is, and each divine person necessarily possesses these qualities. So God is one in *being* and in *nature*. Father, Son, and Spirit—three *persons*—share in this one *being* and possess the same divine *nature*. Again, *threeness* pertains to persons; *oneness* pertains to God's being and nature.

Third, in distinguishing between (a) person and (b) nature and being, we must keep in mind two ways to use "is." Mark Twain is the pen name for

Samuel Langhorne Clemens, the author of *The Adventures of Tom Sawyer* who smoked twenty-two cigars a day.[8] In this use of "is," we can say that Twain and Clemens share the identical qualities; what can be said of one can be said of the other. We can easily reverse the names without changing the meaning: "Samuel Langhorne Clemens is Mark Twain" and "Mark Twain is Samuel Langhorne Clemens." The "is" in each of those statements indicates identity: Mark Twain = Samuel Langhorne Clemens (and vice versa). The names, which refer to the same person, are interchangeable and thus identical.

When it comes to divine persons, we must think of the "is" of *predication*. The statement "Jesus is God" (which is theologically correct) *isn't* identical to "God is Jesus" (which isn't theologically correct). Unlike the Mark Twain example, "Jesus" doesn't exhaust what it means to speak of "God." Jesus and God are not identical. According to the Bible, Father and Spirit are called divine—just as Jesus is.[9] In the statement "Jesus is God," we use "is" to describe or predicate—not identify or equate: Jesus is God in that he shares in the nature that only two other persons share; so there isn't just one person who can properly be called God.

Fourth, the triune persons are deeply interrelated or mutually indwell one another, sharing a necessary, unbreakable oneness. You and I possess a common human nature, which makes us what we are. Yet you and I contingently exist. But God necessarily exists—and necessarily exists in deep, mutually indwelling relationship. Like three angles of a triangle are necessary for it to qualify as a triangle, so each member of the Trinity necessarily exists in an unbreakable life together. Just as body and soul are distinct yet engage in a deep interactive unity, all the more do the members of the Trinity, who share a deeper, mutually engaging unity.

Fifth, the unity of this mutually indwelling divine family means they act as one rather than in isolation from one another. Whether creating, revealing, or redeeming, the three persons of the Trinity necessarily act as one:

in creation (e.g., Gen. 1:1–2; John 1:1–3);
in redemption (2 Cor. 5:17; Gal. 2:20; Titus 3:5);
in Jesus's resurrection from the dead: raised by the *Father* (Gal. 1:1; cf. Acts 2:24, 32); the *Spirit* (Rom. 1:4); and *Jesus* himself (John 10:18; cf. 2:19: "I will raise it up"); and
in the indwelling of believers (John 14:16, 18, 23; Rom. 8:9).

Unlike the feuding, plotting, independent-minded deities of Greece, Rome, or India, the triune God acts in harmony and without opposition.

The Relevance of the Trinity

Why is the doctrine of the Trinity so vital for our day? Here are some areas to consider.

The public square: Many Westerners assume God is a single, unitary person—a Cosmic Monarch who merely rules and commands—rather than seeing him first as an intrinsically relational loving, triune God who desires friendship with humans. Also, this relational God better helps ground human dignity, human rights, and the need for community and cooperation with one another in this world.

Interreligious dialogue: The relational triune God serves as the basis for deep human relationships but also as a richer foundation for relational virtues such as compassion, kindness, love, and generosity—quite unlike most Eastern philosophies and religions, in which the Ultimate Reality is impersonal or nonexistent.

Feminist philosophy and theology: One objection to the biblical God has to do with the perception of a powerful, hierarchical, "male" deity, even though God is a sexless being (cf. Gen. 1:26–28). Also, though God reveals himself as a personal Father (emphasizing both authority and intimacy), God is also mother-*like* (Deut. 32:18; Isa. 42:4; Ps. 131:2; Hos. 13:8). If we begin with the deeply interpersonal relationality of the triune God, we find that many of these concerns are diminished or fall away altogether.

Philosophy: Philosopher William James called "the problem of the One and the Many" philosophy's most central problem going back to the pre-Socratic philosophers: Heraclitus claimed that ultimate reality is *many* and *changing* (*no unity*) while his counterpart Parmenides claimed that reality is *one* and *unchanging* (*no plurality*). In the Trinity, unity and plurality come together and find their foundation. We live not in a *multiverse* but a *universe* sustained and held together by the one triune God.[10]

FURTHER READING

McCall, Thomas H. *Which Trinity? Whose Monotheism?* Grand Rapids: Eerdmans, 2010.

Moreland, J. P., and William Lane Craig. *Philosophical Foundations for a Christian Worldview*. 2nd ed. Downers Grove, IL: IVP Academic, 2018. Chapter 31.

Sanders, Fred, and Klaus Issler, eds. *Jesus in Trinitarian Perspective*. Nashville: B&H Academic, 2007.

Torrance, Thomas F. *The Christian Doctrine of God: One Being, Three Persons*. Edinburgh: T&T Clark, 1996.

8 | *Talking about God and Knowing God*

He made known His ways to Moses,
His acts to the sons of Israel.

—Psalm 103:7

For as the heavens are higher than the earth,
So are My ways higher than your ways
And My thoughts than your thoughts.

—Isaiah 55:9

Is God Like Harvey?

Perhaps you've heard of the movie called *Harvey*, in which Elwood P. Dowd (James Stewart) is convinced that he has a giant six-foot, three-and-a-half-inch rabbit friend named Harvey. Harvey is invisible and makes himself apparent only to outcasts like Dowd.[1] Despite all of the conversations Dowd appears to have with his friend Harvey, onlookers get the strong impression that Dowd is out of touch with reality.

Let's bring things a bit closer to home. What if I told you that I had a dear friend named Scott, who is a high-quality person who cares about me? Then you'd tell me you'd like to meet him. I'd then inform you that you can't actually see him. He doesn't have a body. But it's still possible to have a personal, deeply meaningful relationship with him. Now you would probably think that this is quite odd. Yet we speak of our "friend" Jesus or of having a "personal relationship with God," which may sound strange to the outsider.

Likewise, various philosophers have claimed that it's not even coherent to talk about a "disembodied person." To them, the idea of God sounds like my invisible friend Scott.

A further problem is that even if God does exist, can we speak of God accurately, metaphorically, or somewhere in between?

Is the Idea of God Intelligible?

A Word from Our Critics

Charles Dodgson—Lewis Carroll—wrote a bit of nonsense that philosophy of religion books sometimes quote when discussing the intelligibility of God:

> 'Twas brillig, and the slithy toves
> Did gyre and gimble in the wabe:
> All mimsy were the borogoves,
> And the mome raths outgrabe.[2]

Various critics have claimed that statements such as "God loves us" and "God created the world" are much like Carroll's poem. It's like saying "drogulus" (A. J. Ayer) or "teavy" and "toovy" (Rudolf Carnap) made the universe. It's just gibberish. Another philosopher (D. Z. Phillips) claims that "God" arises in the context of religious communities as well as practices such as prayer but has no meaning outside of these circles. How could a being without ears "hear" our prayers? To talk about God as real outside of these religious communal practices is just linguistic and conceptual confusion.

We should understand that the "problem of religious language" is typically a problem for those who think that such theological affirmations should be scientifically (empirically) verifiable to be meaningful. What empirical evidence can we give that God is love? Given the vast amount of evil in the world, how much evil would suffice to show that God doesn't really exist? Can the claim "God is love" ever be falsified? According to Scottish skeptic David Hume, if a claim can't be experienced by the senses or empirically proven, then it is only "sophistry and illusion." He advises: "Commit it then to the flames."[3]

Atheists have claimed that "God" just doesn't fit into our everyday understanding of "a person" or "a personal being." A "disembodied personal being"— like the immaterial rabbit Harvey—makes no sense. How could a spirit-being make a physical world? And why think that an eternal, necessary being exists when all the beings we encounter are finite and contingent?

Science and Sensibility

Theists have presented the following responses to such criticisms. For one thing, *not all nontheists seem to have this problem*. Various intelligent critics of theism have a basic idea of what is meant by God. J. L. Mackie, for instance, claimed that he just didn't find the concept of, say, an immaterial person to be unintelligible: "There is really no problem about this." True, he acknowledged, we're acquainted with embodied persons, but we can readily conceive of an omnipresent spirit who can create a material world from nothing.[4]

Furthermore, many skeptics who criticize the concept of God seem to have a decent idea of what they're criticizing. They believe they are offering a coherent criticism of divine attributes—God as spirit, all-knowing, all-powerful, and all-good—which they seem to grasp quite well.

An additional problem is that if we're making science our court of appeals, then this is a nonstarter. After all, the task of science isn't properly positioned to make such judgments about God's reality. If science is all about studying and understanding the natural world, why think that's somehow a criticism of the concept of God? It's like having a fishing net that can catch only large fish; all the minnows slip through, since the netting is too wide. So, scientists can make plenty of interesting and legitimate observations about the physical world, but they're not able to capture all the reality there is. The "netting" of science is only going to "catch" physical things with microscopes and telescopes—not nonphysical ones like God, angels, or souls.

We now face two additional problems—namely, those of *arbitrariness* and *self-contradiction*. As we'll explore in more detail, why think science *alone*—and no other discipline like philosophy or theology—can tell us all that we can know? And how can one scientifically prove that all knowledge must be scientifically provable? This is a philosophical assumption rather than a scientific conclusion or observation. So when atheist astronomer Carl Sagan claimed, "The cosmos is all that is or ever was or ever will be,"[5] he was stepping outside science to make this claim. After all, scientists assume logical laws, the trustworthiness of the human mind, and many other things philosophical. This isn't to deny that empirical verification has a place—a point Paul strongly emphasizes when it comes to the available evidence for Jesus's publicly checkable bodily resurrection (1 Cor. 15:3–11). It's just not the only reason to believe something to be true.

Finally, certain implications of scientific discovery help support belief in God. The late philosopher Antony Flew spent most of his professional career espousing atheism and even the meaninglessness of religious language. However, it was the theistic implications of scientific discoveries that led him to believe that God exists after all: the beginning of the universe (the big bang and the universe's expansion), the remarkable precision tuning of the universe to produce and sustain life, and the complexity of biological life.[6] He concluded that naturalism lacked the explanatory resources to account for these obvious empirical facts.

We've briefly noted that we can speak intelligibly about God. But what about our descriptions of God? Given the limitations of human minds and language, how can we *refer to* or *describe* God? Is God simply *ineffable*—beyond any accurate human description?

CAN OUR DESCRIPTIONS OF GOD BE ACCURATE?

Speaking with Athenians

When speaking to an Athenian audience, Paul referred to "an unknown God" whose altar he had seen (Acts 17:23). However vague this deity seemed to the Athenians, Paul took the occasion to clarify the nature of this God about whom they were ignorant.

If God's ways are higher than ours (Isa. 55:9) and we can't truly know his mind (Rom. 11:34), then perhaps we can't speak about or refer to God accurately. Just how much description is sufficient to refer accurately to God? What if we use the term "God," but the object to which we're referring is inaccurately named God? Christians maintain that God is all-knowing. Some will claim (and I would disagree here) that God knows all truths past and present but that it's logically impossible that God knows the truth of future human choices. Are we referring to the same God or a different one?

Now if we had to be absolutely, unmistakably precise in our descriptions of God, we could never claim that we are actually referring to him—only to the descriptions of a person's devising. But surely a child of tender age can recognize his own mother's voice and appearance, even if his descriptions about her are vague and imprecise. In fact, we may find ourselves having a somewhat basic grasp of terms—"black holes," the "big bang," "history," "science," "sociology," and so forth—but what we can describe is often sketchy and inexact. Of course, definitions are important and helpful, especially as we discuss philosophy or Christian doctrines like the Trinity. But to insist on a "rule" or "criterion" of perfectly describing something in order to converse about it isn't how we typically operate. If we need to perfectly define or describe God before he can be evaluated, then we'll have to use *words* constantly, which *also* must be analyzed or defined perfectly—ad infinitum.

We often find ourselves in the thick of particular conversations and basic exchanges of information without having laid out rules and criteria to get them going. Similarly, when we are speaking with modern-day Athenians, we can communicate to varying degrees what "God" means and basically describe him (i.e., the eternal Creator of the universe who has manifested himself in

Jesus of Nazareth to redeem human beings). Certainly many of our theological descriptions will never be exhaustive; they will be imprecise to some degree and may simply serve as pointers in the direction of God.[7]

Adherents to the "Abrahamic religions"—Judaism, Christianity, Islam—will refer to "God" or "Allah" as possessing the various "omni-" attributes, and this can be coherently understood in this cross-religious dialogue. But further clarification is needed as the discussion goes deeper and differences become more apparent. Yet these differences don't require us to come up with new names for the divine or that we can't meaningfully use the term "God" to refer to the maximally great being.

Cataphatic or Apophatic?

When we say "God is good" or "God is just," what exactly do we mean? According to thinkers like Thomas Aquinas, we can't speak *positively* about what God is like. (This is called *cataphatic* theology.) Rather, we can say only what God is not like, which is called *apophatic* theology. As Thomas said, "Now we cannot know what God is, but only what he is not."[8] So we use words beginning with *un-*, *in-*, or *im-*: God is *un*created, *in*corporeal (having no physical body), *im*passible (not able to suffer), *im*mutable (not changeable). Rather than saying "God is good," we use the "way of negation" (*via negativa*) and say instead, "God is not evil." No word ("name" [*nomen*]) can be used literally of God.

Aquinas used the method of analogy for referring to God. When our language refers to God, it is somewhere between the *univocal* (precise, exact) sense and the *equivocal* (imprecise, inexact). God is in a category all of his own. This is much like using "good" in the following two statements: "Jim is a good man" versus "Fido is a good dog."

Christian apophatic ("negative") theologians are right to remind us of God's unsurpassable greatness and "otherness." It is fitting that we be "lost in wonder, love, and praise"[9] before the mysterious, untamable, infinite triune God. The Scriptures themselves speak of God's ways as *un*searchable and *un*fathomable or *in*scrutable (Rom. 11:33). Humility is a fitting response to a God who shatters our human categories, and we must frequently remind ourselves about the dangers of idolatry by creating false conceptions of God to domesticate him and to suit our self-centeredness.

However, as we read the Scriptures, does the apophatic emphasis clearly stand out? It seems not. By way of backdrop, it appears that certain Greek conceptions of God—from Plato, Plotinus's Neoplatonism, and Pseudo-Dionysius—have strongly influenced some forms of negative theology.[10]

How so? The typical Greek gods—think of Zeus, Poseidon, and Hercules—possessed special powers, but they were flawed and dysfunctional. None of these humanlike (anthropomorphized) deities would qualify as "the greatest conceivable being."

So, various Greek philosophers tried to improve on the concept of deity or "God." We shouldn't be surprised that this revised understanding yielded something less dynamic and less personal. In fact, the divine in Greek philosophy tends to be *impersonal, abstract,* and *lifeless.* By contrast, the Scriptures emphasize a God who is holy, personal, covenant-making, willing, dynamic, and history-engaging. This triune, intrinsically relational God creates his image-bearing priest-kings that they might rule with him and relate to him. God's making us in his image creates the very possibility of God's revealing himself to us that we might think and speak more clearly about him.

It appears that the modesty that apophatic theology attempts to practice actually leads to an unintentional resistance to God's self-revelation. Jesus said that the one who has seen him has seen the Father (John 14:9). Though we are weak and flawed, God still speaks to us in the thus-and-so-ness of human language and culture. No, not exhaustively, but adequately and accurately. God's Spirit ensures that we experience the personal knowledge of God, and the incarnation is a reminder of the profound divine-human connection. Jesus—"the one and only Son"—has "exegeted" or explained the Father to us (John 1:18 NIV). God has a deep desire to communicate himself to us, and, if we respond to his grace, we can know God's extraordinary love, which surpasses ordinary human knowledge (Eph. 3:14–19).

When we consider divine love and Christian love described in 1 John 3–4, we can have a general grasp of this: we know what love is because of God's love for us in Christ, who laid down his life for us (3:16). As a result, we can "*love* one another, for *love* is from God; and everyone who *loves* is born of God and knows God" (4:7, my emphasis). The text adds, "If God so *loved* us, we also ought to *love* one another" (4:11, my emphasis). Though our love pales in comparison to God's, it's still love, and we know God's own love by his revealing it (4:13).

Here is another thought: if we assume that we should take the way of analogy in referring to God, how could anyone be accused of idolatry? After all, if someone engages in false worship, it seems that we would have to have the same (univocal) understanding of divine nature and that which is worship-worthy in order to properly identify a theological point of departure: "The divine Zeus is worthy of worship" versus "the divine Trinity is worthy of worship." For a genuine contradiction to exist between true and false worship, the same sense of the term *God* would have to be grasped and applied by both the orthodox believer and the deviant one.[11]

The Bible bends over backwards to tell us that we can genuinely *know* God! The knowledge of God revealed to us, though limited, is true. We can know something of God as he really is through his historical acts and biblical revelation; what's more, his incarnate Son Jesus has (con)descended to us and has accurately interpreted him for us (John 1:14, 18). To see Jesus is to see the Father (John 14:9).

FURTHER READING

Flew, Antony, with Roy Abraham Varghese. *There Is a God: How the World's Most Notorious Atheist Changed His Mind.* New York: Harper, 2007.

Gunton, Colin. *Act and Being: Towards a Theology of the Divine Attributes.* Grand Rapids: Eerdmans, 2003.

Taliaferro, Charles. *Philosophy of Religion.* Oxford: Blackwell, 2009.

9 | The Divine Attributes (I):
Perfection, Necessity, and Self-Sufficiency

> For great is the LORD and greatly to be praised;
> He is to be feared above all gods.
> For all the gods of the peoples are idols,
> But the LORD made the heavens.
>
> —Psalm 96:4–5

NONE LIKE GOD

"Who is like You?" the awestruck biblical poets rhetorically ask (Exod. 15:11; Pss. 35:10; 71:19; 89:6, 8). Jeremiah puts it plainly: "There is none like You" (Jer. 10:6, 7). Biblical writers regularly express wonder at God's magnificent greatness. The New Testament affirms that Jesus reveals what God is really like (John 1:14, 18; 14:9; Heb. 1:1–2). As we look at Christ, we see God's greatness revealed in humility, condescension, love, and grace. However, we shouldn't forget that God as revealed in Christ is not only kind but also severe (Rom. 11:22), loving as well as wrathful (John 3:16, 36; cf. Jude 5; Rev. 2:16, 20–23).

So as we turn to God's attributes, we don't begin with impersonal Greek philosophical abstractions about what "the Absolute" or the "divine perfections" look like. As Jaroslav Pelikan has observed, the idea of "an entirely static God" was a Greek philosophical concept adopted by a number of Christian theologians—though without much biblical support.[1] Nevertheless, we can affirm that sometimes Greek philosophical categories have helped provide clarifying terms and concepts to articulate doctrines like the Trinity and incarnation (e.g., *person, substance, nature*). Given that Christian doctrine has been developed and refined over the centuries, we should seek to be excellent students of the Christian tradition and the unfolding of doctrine. Even more fundamentally, we must be students of the Scriptures.

Consider the example of the earliest Christians looking to the Scriptures as the final authority. The Bereans conferred with the Scriptures to validate or confirm that what Paul was teaching them about Jesus was true (Acts 17:11). The church council in Jerusalem (Acts 15) anchored its final decision concerning gentile Christians in the Old Testament Scriptures, even though it was rooted in a broad consensus of apostles, elders, and the church: "It seemed good to the apostles and the elders, with the whole church" (v. 22).

It is an important undertaking to engage philosophically with Christian doctrines to more precisely define and clarify them. In doing so, we should be well-anchored in the biblical text as well as the history of doctrine. Yet philosophical discussion of the divine attributes need not be—and should not be—an intellectualizing of faith. Christian philosophers and theologians alike run the risk of cognitive idolatry—making God an object of fine-toothed examination while ignoring submission to him as worship-worthy, personal, and mysterious.

While thinking rigorously about God's self-revelation in Scripture, may our hearts be "strangely warmed" in doing so. Philosophically minded theologians and theologically minded philosophers from Augustine and Anselm to Jonathan Edwards and Alvin Plantinga have exhibited both spiritual warmth and mental rigor in the pursuit and worship of God.[2] Let us follow in their footsteps as we consider the divine attributes of perfection, necessity, and self-sufficiency, among others.

"Perfect-Being Theology"?

Eleventh-century theologian Anselm said that God is the greatest conceivable being or a maximally great being—the being "than which nothing greater can be conceived." That is, God has the superlative attributes (eternal, infinite, unchanging, etc.), including the "omni" attributes: omnibenevolence (all-good), omniscience (all-knowing), omnipotence (all-powerful), and omnipresence.

This "perfect-being theology" is sometimes resisted by theologians, who may consider this a Greek philosophical concept rather than a biblical one. They may further claim that human intuitions are fallen and not always reliable. Of course, we shouldn't impose foreign concepts onto the biblical text, however well-meaning we may be. But what do the Scriptures say?

They speak of a God who is incomparable to anything else: "To whom will you liken me?" (Isa. 46:5 ESV). The biblical writers wonder, "Who is like the Lord our God?" (Ps. 113:5). When making an oath with Abraham, God has nothing greater to swear by than himself (Heb. 6:13–14). Anselm is only echoing what he read in the Scriptures. And what is the *alternative* to "perfect-being theology"—some kind of "imperfect-being theology"? That obviously can't be right.

Some claim that because humans are tainted by sin, this includes our intuitions about God. But isn't the recognition of our profound sinfulness an *accurate* theological realization, with the help of the Lord? If this can be accurate, why not accurate intuitions about a maximally great, worship-worthy being that are confirmed by Scripture? Surely we're not off the mark if we grasp that a being worthy of the title "God" must be perfect in every way (cf. Deut. 32:4).[3] In fact, intuitions are inescapable and important for all manner of reasoning and decision-making. We have *moral* intuitions (Amos 1–2; Rom. 1:20; 3:19), and we often find these reliable ("I ought to stop that toddler from heading toward the swimming pool").[4] Why think these pervasive intuitions must necessarily conflict with divine revelation? Rather, they can reveal that we are functioning properly, according to our design.

To speak of God as *infinite* is the basic idea behind what contemporary theistic philosophers say about God: he is without bounds or limits, being "maximally great," "supremely excellent," and the "most perfect" or "absolutely perfect" being.

As we unpack various attributes of God in this and the next couple of chapters, we'll look into questions raised by critics: Is a *necessarily existent being* incoherent? Can God make a stone so big that he can't lift it? If God knows what we're going to do, do we have freedom? Do our prayers really do anything if God has already planned everything out?

Theologians and philosophers have weighed in on how to understand the divine attributes, offering a range of views. This can be a great help. While skeptics—or believers themselves—may critique the merits of one particular view of, say, omniscience, three or four other views may be left to examine. Unfortunately, we can't survey the different approaches and then weigh the merits of each, but we can look some important points and insights.

GOD'S NECESSITY AND SELF-SUFFICIENCY

> Of old You founded the earth,
> And the heavens are the work of Your hands.
> Even they will perish, but You endure;
> And all of them will wear out like a garment;
> Like clothing You will change them and they will be changed.
>
> (Ps. 102:25–26)

> You alone are God. (Ps. 86:10)

The universe's existence depends on something outside itself. Not so with God, who exists necessarily and self-sufficiently. Theologians call this divine *aseity* (*a se* = [being] by itself). So great is this God that he cannot *not* exist!

Just because something is *everlasting*, that by itself doesn't mean it is *necessary*. Various medieval theologians like Aquinas thought it logically possible that the universe could have been created out of nothing from eternity by God and thus everlastingly dependent on God. Though such a possibility may seem odd or even incoherent to us, such thinkers insisted that just because something is everlasting, that doesn't mean it exists necessarily. It can exist but only in dependence on something else—namely, God's sustaining power. What is necessary, though, has an existence in and of itself, and it exists in every conceivable or possible world.

Philosopher Immanuel Kant believed the idea of "necessary existence" was a contradiction in terms. "Existence" isn't included in the definition of anything, including God. After all, plenty of people don't find the statement "God does not exist" to be self-contradictory. So why think "God exists" is a logically necessary statement?

Such an objection doesn't have much power to it, though. Some philosophers have responded to Kant by utilizing the language of possible worlds (modal logic). By *possible worlds*, we don't mean "logically possible *physical* universes," but simply states of affairs or configurations of reality. So a possible world could be utterly "empty," except that God exists within it; or in another possible world angels might exist with God—and nothing else.

By definition, necessary truths or basic logical laws exist in all possible worlds—for example, the law of noncontradiction ("a statement and its opposite can't both be true"). There's no possible configuration of reality in which such laws wouldn't be true. (These laws, of course, are themselves rooted in the mind of God.) So if it's no problem that logical laws exist in all possible worlds, then it's certainly not incoherent to say "God exists" is true in all possible worlds. Just as basic logical laws by definition would exist or apply in all possible worlds, it's hardly incoherent that God by definition would exist in any of them. There can be no God-less possible world. So it's simply question-begging—assuming what one wants to prove—to say that a necessary being can't exist.[5]

As we look at the "Who made God?" objection later in the book, we'll note that prior to the twentieth-century discovery that the universe is finite, plenty of atheists had believed that the universe existed eternally—even necessarily—and thus didn't need any explanation. Unlike the universe, which doesn't *need* to exist, God's nature requires that he exist in every possible world.

Furthermore, God's self-sufficiency speaks to the question of why God created human beings. God wasn't lacking anything such that he felt compelled to create out of some inner need. He freely created out of his full and perfect love. Also, the doctrine of the Trinity strengthens the concept of God's self-sufficiency—that he is perfectly complete, content, and joyful in himself, as Father, Son, and Spirit. He didn't have to create, "as though He needed anything" (Acts 17:25). God, the source of all things (Rom. 11:35–36), freely and graciously creating us out of his goodness so that we might be partakers in the very life of the triune God's love and joy (2 Pet. 1:4). God wants as many people as possible to get in on what the three-in-one God has enjoyed all along.

Process theology or traditional panentheism—"God in the world"— declares that God somehow needs the world.[6] As a soul has a body, so the world is God's body; they are eternally and necessarily dependent on one another. This view, though, isn't well rooted in Scripture, which sees the universe (heavens and earth) as capable of perishing or enduring (Ps. 102:25–26). God alone endures from everlasting to everlasting (Ps. 90:2). To its credit, panentheism emphasizes God's relationality and his interaction with creation, but the doctrine of the Trinity already suggests this. Also, such interdependence models of God and creation dramatically conflict with the consensus of science—that the universe had a beginning a finite time ago: the universe is expanding, and it is winding down (the second law of thermodynamics), which suggests that it has been wound up.

Physicist Paul Davies sees the clear implications of the question, What caused the big bang? "One might consider some supernatural force, some agency beyond space and time as being responsible for the big bang, or one might prefer to regard the big bang as an event without a cause." However, "we don't have too much choice": it's either "something outside of the physical world" or "an event without a cause."[7] The universe hasn't always been around, and it isn't God's "body."

Divine necessity and self-sufficiency powerfully suggest the doctrine of creation out of nothing (ex nihilo)—God simply wills it ("speaks") and it comes to be (Ps. 33:6)—and that God sustains all things in being. As with classical panentheists, the Latter-day Saints (Mormons) assert that God can neither create nor annihilate matter. He's merely the Organizer, not the "Originator," of these primal elements. This conception of God falls short, however.

As noted, such a view flies in the face of contemporary scientific discovery; the universe came into existence without preexisting matter, energy, space, and time. It is also theologically problematic: it diminishes God's self-sufficiency, power, and freedom. That is, if God wanted to create a cosmos but had no preexisting materials "lying around," then he wouldn't be able to create a universe. This means creation would just be a fluke—a lucky chance—that

God happened to have the right materials handy, waiting to be used! Not so! God's freedom, self-sufficiency, and all-powerful nature are most adequately reflected in the doctrine of creation out of nothing.[8]

FURTHER READING

Copan, Paul, and William Lane Craig. *Creation out of Nothing: A Biblical, Philosophical, and Scientific Exploration.* Grand Rapids: Baker Academic, 2004.

McCall, Thomas H. *An Invitation to Analytic Christian Philosophy.* Downers Grove, IL: IVP Academic, 2015.

Taliaferro, Charles. *Philosophy of Religion.* Oxford: Wiley-Blackwell, 2009.

10 | *The Divine Attributes (II):*
God and Time, Omniscience, and Human Freedom

GOD AND TIME

From everlasting to everlasting, You are God. (Ps. 90:2)

"God is outside of time," Christians commonly affirm. "God sees past, present, and future all at once—in the 'eternal now.'" Various prominent theologians have affirmed this as well. In his *On the Consolation of Philosophy*, medieval theologian Boethius (c. 480–524) refers to God's eternity as the "simultaneous and complete [*totum simul*] possession of infinite life." God completely grasps past, present, and future all at once. Is this *really* so? Is God *outside* time (timeless) or *in* time (temporal)? What *is* time? While the variations and details would bog us down,[1] here's a brief attempt to discuss the topic.

Augustine confessed: "What, then, is time? If no one ask of me, I know; if I wish to explain to him who asks, I know not."[2] Augustine had a better grasp of time than he let on. Time is, another has remarked, what keeps everything from happening all at once. Time is the succession of events or happenings, and it is characterized by "before-ness" and "after-ness." So without the *change* of events, time wouldn't exist.

Some have distinguished between "lived time" and "measured/clock time." Though time continues to move along apart from our perceiving it (it is objective), "lived time" reflects our experiencing time, not simply measuring it. So when we think of the "present," we don't view it as balanced on a knife's edge between past and future—that's more a feature of measured time—but rather in terms of moments or experiential happenings.

What is God's relationship to time, though? Though Scripture uses words such as *forever*, *everlasting*, or *eternal*, such words by themselves don't tell us whether God is *in* time (temporal) or *outside of* time (eternally timeless).[3] We have to look at some philosophical considerations to discern what is the case.

Tensed versus Tenseless Views of Time

For starters, the *tensed* or *dynamic* view is called the A-theory of time, while the *tenseless* or *static* view is called the B-theory of time. God's being omniscient (all-knowing) involves his knowing all truths—including tensed facts such as "I *am* (now) *typing* these words on August 26, 2019," "Julius Caesar *was killed*," or, "Jesus *will return*." It would be counterintuitive that God would know all truths but not be able to distinguish between past, present, and future (e.g., "X occurred," "X is *now* occurring," "X will occur"). But if God is in the "eternal now" and "sees all events at once" then he can't distinguish between tenses. All that God can know is tense-less truths such as, "Jesus is born in 5 BC," or, "The American Revolution begins on April 19, 1775."

If all events are simultaneous to God, as some claim, then God couldn't know *when* an event is actually occurring. If he is outside of time, it's hard to see how God would be able to differentiate between past, present, and future. How could he know something *at this time* that will *no longer* be true as a *present*-tense statement tomorrow? Yet for God to be omniscient, he would have to be *in* time to know *tensed* facts.

On the "eternal now" view, God's creating out of nothing or becoming incarnate in Christ wouldn't make sense. After all, this perspective suggests that God and the universe coexist statically or tenselessly—and that leaves us wondering: Why does the universe exist rather than nothing at all? Creation out of nothing entails a shift from God's not being Creator to his acquiring the property of being Creator.

Imagine you're looking at a mural—like Atlanta's *Cyclorama*—portraying a sequence of Civil War events (1861–1865): the pre–Civil War raid on Harper's Ferry by John Brown, Lincoln's being elected as the sixteenth president, the attack on Ft. Sumter, the First Battle of Bull Run, then Antietam, Gettysburg, Sherman's "March to the Sea," and Lee's surrender to Grant at Appomattox Court House. Now imagine that the Civil War is *actually* raging beyond the walls of our mural in the round. You can see the sequence of events on the mural before you, but you can't know which ones have already taken place, which are taking place now, and which will take place in the future.

This illustrates the sort of problem that emerges if God is "outside of time." In the "eternal now" view, God knows the (static) sequence of all events across history (*Paul Copan is typing on August 26, 2019*), but not the (dynamic) awareness of what events are past, present, or future (e.g., *Paul Copan is now typing*) since present events ("is now") are constantly becoming past ("was then"). For God to know all things, he would have to be aware of when the present changes into the past and the future changes into the present.

Time and Change

Some philosophers claim such a dynamic view doesn't square with God's unchanging nature (immutability). Why not? Because change must be from perfection to imperfection or vice versa. God's omniscience and immutability are therefore incompatible. However, this view of immutability is problematic: it incorrectly assumes that *change* entails something *negative*. We can readily think of *neutral* changes—like the South Pole's temperature fluctuation or a chameleon's color alteration. God's awareness of changing events seems inescapable if we're to preserve the notion of omniscience.

Also, this dynamic change in God's temporal awareness isn't an *intrinsic* change—namely, in God's nature, which is fixed and stable—but a change in God's *relationship* to creation. It seems that denying God's omniscience itself is more problematic than denying that God's knowledge changes as time progresses. God's knowledge isn't *necessarily* unchanging. Consider this: through creation, God has come to know us as his creatures—this is something he didn't know apart from creating. If God had freely refrained from creating, then he wouldn't have had this knowledge that we are his creatures. That is, if the creation is contingent, then God's knowledge of his creation—once he actually creates—is also contingent. By creating, God comes to know the tensed truth, "My creation *now* exists."[4]

So the timeless triune God, at creation, enters into time because he is truly related to happenings within creation. The beginning of the universe is the beginning of God's time. So Christ's return is still in God's future, whereas Christ's death is in God's past. The view we're suggesting is that God is *timeless*—and changeless—*without* or apart from the universe, but *in time*—and changing in tensed awareness—*with* the universe. But some lingering questions remain.

Questions about God and Time

To unpack the God-time relationship a bit more, let's explore a variety of common questions on this topic.

#1: Doesn't God's being "in time" limit or "trap" him?

Not at all. Though God is *in time*, he still perfectly knows all events, including future ones. He knows all events without the universe; his creating the universe—and thus time—does not mean he suddenly forgets them. The divine attributes remain constant—omniscience, goodness, and so on. If anything, eternal timelessness would limit God since he couldn't know what is happening at present; all he could know is which event precedes or follows another. There's no theological need to say that God must be outside of time. His being temporal (with the creation-event)—along with his possessing complete fore-knowledge of all that will transpire and his dynamically interacting with his creation—offers us a biblically robust approach to God's relationship to time.

#2: Isn't there a "before" creation and "after" creation, which suggests time prior to creation?

Time is the succession of events—the series of happenings; so technically there isn't any (physical) time *without* the universe's existence.[5] To talk of God's being timeless "before" creation is a mistake. This is like saying it's physically impossible for temperatures to go "below" absolute zero (0 Kelvin or −273.15 degrees Celsius), even though we use the term *below* as a manner of speaking. So we should reject the temporal language of "before" and "after" creation. It's clearer to speak of God existing timelessly or atemporally *without* the universe and temporally *with* the universe. That is, God is *causally* prior to creation, not *temporally* prior to it. From eternity, God timelessly willed to freely create and redeem. (Think of a person sitting from eternity who freely chooses to stand up.)

The same applies to the matter of the triune God's existence without the universe: just as we should reject the langage of "before" creation, so we should reject the language of the creation being "future" to God. There is *no literal future* in God's existing without the universe since time doesn't exist in such a scenario. Without creation, there just is no time, and without time, there can be no future-tensed events.[6] (Think back to the example of not being able to go "below" absolute zero.)

#3: How can God, without the universe, exist in a changeless state?

Critics have argued that a being can't be both timeless *and* personal; they claim that *personhood* presupposes *time*. But why think personal beings must have a succession of thoughts or that knowing something necessarily involves an earlier and a later time? Must all knowledge—or awareness in general—involve time?

Philosopher of mind Daniel Dennett—hardly sympathetic to belief in God—has laid out various "conditions of personhood": being rational and being capable of verbal communication and self-consciousness, among several other features.[7] What's significant for us is that temporal succession in thought doesn't figure into this definition: that is, it's just not intuitively obvious that personhood *necessarily* involves temporal mental succession, even if this is how human thinking generally operates. So we should be careful about how we define personhood lest we distort or diminish it. For example, while we typically say that the capability of consciousness is a condition of personhood, we don't say that personhood ceases while we're in a dreamless sleep or are unconscious.

Admittedly, since we associate personal consciousness with sequences of events, thinking about God's own timeless awareness without the creation is difficult to grasp. Yet timeless personal existence is hardly incoherent. Without the universe, the mutually indwelling persons of the triune God delight in the sublime, eternal exchange of love in a kind of transfixed gaze of pure joy. It is like lovers who, simply by looking deeply at each other, communicate mutual concern, joy, and contentment—quite unlike the impersonal, detached "God" of certain Eastern philosophies. So we can think of the infinite, perfect, interpersonal, and transparent love of the Trinity as being mutually and telepathically communicated—all without any need for change.

DIVINE OMNISCIENCE

> Even before there is a word on my tongue,
> Behold, O LORD, You know it all. (Ps. 139:4)

God is omniscient (Latin: *omnis* = "all"; "*sciens*" = "knowing"); he "knows all things" (1 John 3:20) and is "the only wise God" (Rom. 16:27). God knows the details of our lives better than we do (Ps. 139:1–18)—even down to the very number of hairs on our heads (Matt. 10:30); he is aware when the humble sparrow is sold or falls to the ground (Matt. 10:29; Luke 12:6). God knows everything within the universe: "I know every bird of the mountains"; indeed, "everything that moves in the field is Mine" (Ps. 50:11). He knows both the momentum and location of every subatomic particle in existence. God's omniscience means that if something is true, God knows it. If something happens, he is aware.

But some skeptics claim that God's omniscience entails more than just knowing truths. He must also *experience* what we experience, including lust or envy, in order to know fully.[8] After all, doesn't it seem odd and counterintuitive that humans would know what it's like to lust or envy but that God doesn't? But wouldn't God's *not* knowing this mean that he's not omniscient? But if God *does* know these things, then he can't truly be God since he's not all-good.

Here's one such argument: "Since God has all of men's knowledge and more, He must know lust and envy. But to say God has known lust and envy is to say that God has had the feelings of lust and envy. But this is incompatible with God's moral goodness. Hence God does not exist."[9]

Or we shift from immoral experience to first-person ("I") experience. Let's say that when spilling a bag of sugar at the grocery store, I can knowingly say, "*I* made a mess." Now God can know *that* "Paul Copan made a mess," but only *I* can know—from a first-person perspective—that "*I* made a mess." So God couldn't say, "*I* made a mess," in which case God is lacking knowledge.[10]

These criticisms don't have as much bite to them as first may appear. For one thing, Scripture itself lays out important parameters regarding God's omniscience. God's knowledge doesn't mean *having the experience of* envy or lust. Yes, God knows humans perfectly and how sin operates, but being all-knowing just doesn't require having *experiential* knowledge of sin.

The biblical God is morally perfect; he doesn't need to *be* immoral to know what is immoral and what immorality can do to a person. God's being all-knowing means that God knows all truths. Because God's omniscience can't be separated from his goodness, neither can it be reduced to sheer information storage. Of course, God knows much more than all truths: he knows us as persons; he experientially knows what it's like to be God—and neither of these can be reduced to a set of true propositions.

In addition, God's maximal greatness means he knows or grasps all truths *immediately*—not to mention having deep and immediate access to the experiences and thoughts of his creatures. Say that a non-divine person comes to know a vast sum of truths and human experiences, but he comes to know them only circuitously or indirectly—perhaps through lots of study, learning by trial and error, and so on. That kind of knowing isn't ideal when it comes to knowing accurately and directly. So an important aspect of God's knowing everything is not just *what* God knows (the content) but *how* he knows it (the means).

Some skeptics insist that for God to be omniscient, he must know

- all truths (*propositional* knowledge);
- how things are done (*procedural* or *skilled* knowledge); and
- all things by direct acquaintance (*experiential* knowledge).

Now we've seen that God's supremely good knowledge excludes immoral experiences such as envy or lust. Here the critic makes philosophically problematic demands that result in metaphysical (real) contradictions. If, say, an omniscient God must know exactly what you know in the exact way you know it, this leads to metaphysical confusion. Why? You alone—and no one else—have a private ("first-person") perspective; only you can know or have that "inner feel" of what it's like to be you. True, God knows what goes on in your mind far better than you do yourself. But what he knows is as an "outsider," while you know it as an "insider." This is a simple metaphysical fact: God doesn't know these things: "I am Alexander the Great," or, "I wrote *The Scarlet Letter*." If so, that would mean that God would believe he is someone else—a serious problem indeed! It's metaphysical silliness to demand that God have direct acquaintance of what it's like to experience life as you.

Again, God is "intimately acquainted" with all our ways, knowing our thoughts "from afar" and our words before they're on our tongue (Ps. 139:2–4); though God doesn't have *my* experiences, feelings, and thoughts, he has immediate and deep access to them. God's understanding is much richer than knowing all truths. All that is needed to secure divine omniscience in this case is that God knows everything you and I and everyone else know about anything.

Beyond this, God perfectly and completely empathizes *with us*: "Just as a father has compassion on his children, so the LORD has compassion on those who fear Him. For He Himself knows our frame; He is mindful that we are but dust" (Ps. 103:13–14). This is what one philosopher calls "omnisubjectivity."[11] But it's a phony challenge to say God has to know (a) *everything* that (b) *any* person knows (c) *in an identical way*. Yes, if something is true, God knows it intimately. However, insisting that "God must know all that humans know in the way that they know" is nonsensical—metaphysically absurd. God distances himself from the abominable idea of infant sacrifice—"a thing which I never commanded or spoke of, nor did it ever enter My mind" (Jer. 19:5). If we're going to criticize what the Scripture claims qualifies as divine omniscience, we should work with biblical definitions rather than fabricated definitions we impose on Scripture.

As we'll see with other attributes, we shouldn't separate or isolate one attribute from another—like God's knowledge from his goodness; the very integration of all of God's great-making attributes is essential for a proper understanding of maximal excellence.

DIVINE FOREKNOWLEDGE AND HUMAN FREEDOM

> None of the rulers of this age has understood; for if they had understood it they would not have crucified the Lord of glory. (1 Cor. 2:8)

Some theologians and philosophers of more recent vintage have questioned whether God can know the future free acts of human beings—an idea that has been called "open theism." If he knows what they'll do, are they really free? And if those acts are truly free, and if it's up to humans to choose, how can God know these choices in advance? Maybe God just has complete knowledge of all necessary truths as well as truths about the past and present but just can't know future human choices since they don't yet exist. Such a view, however, is problematic for a number of reasons.

First, Scripture indicates that God, by his very nature, knows the future free choices of human beings. He knows what we'll say even before we speak (Ps. 139:4, 16). Jesus was aware that the religious authorities would kill him (Mark 8:31), that Judas would betray him (Mark 14:18), that someone would make his colt available for Jesus's triumphal entry (Mark 11:1-6), that another would provide a room for Jesus's Passover celebration with his disciples (Mark 14:12–16), and that Peter would deny him not just once—but three times—before the rooster's crowing (Mark 14:30). God knew humans would freely sin before they actually did; that's why Jesus's atoning sacrifice was "foreknown before the foundation of the world" (1 Pet. 1:19–20): God knew humans would go wrong of their own free will. Even texts where God seems surprised or claims "now I know" (e.g., Gen. 22:12) should be qualified. Open theists claim that God knows all truths up to the present, just not future choices. But when God goes down to Sodom and Gomorrah to "investigate" its wickedness, he says, "I will go down now, and see if they have done entirely according to its outcry, which has come to Me; and if not, I will know" (Gen. 18:21). Or what about when God asks of Adam, "Where are you?" (Gen. 3:9). If we read this text like the open theists read these other "surprise" texts, then God doesn't even know the present, let alone the future.

Consider when the angel of the Lord says to Abraham, "Now I know that you fear God" (Gen. 22:19). Was God surprised? No, we simply have concrete or visible evidence of Abraham's readiness to trust the promise of God. Abraham all along had expressed confidence that God would somehow rescue Isaac. He told his servants that he and Isaac would go and worship and "*we will return*" (Gen. 22:5 NIV). No wonder the author of Hebrews says that Abraham believed that God could raise the dead (Heb. 11:19). God *already* knew of Abraham's confidence without Abraham's having to raise the knife.

God even knows hypothetical situations of what human beings would do if placed in certain circumstances. In 1 Samuel 23:6–10, God knows that if David were to stay at Keilah, King Saul would pursue him. If that were the case, Keilah's inhabitants would hand David over to Saul. Based on God's knowledge of future hypotheticals and his revealing this, David and his men actually leave and are safe from danger.

Likewise, Jeremiah gives King Zedekiah of Judah the Lord's message: he knows that if Zedekiah would surrender to the king of Babylon, his entire family would be spared, and Jerusalem wouldn't be burned with fire. But if Zedekiah doesn't surrender, he won't escape and the city will be burned (Jer. 38:17–18), which is what indeed happened. Or consider the crucifixion of Jesus, which revealed the hidden wisdom of God, "which none of the rulers of this age has understood; for *if they had* understood it they would not have crucified the Lord of glory" (1 Cor. 2:7–8). Other such examples appear in Scripture.[12]

How then does God know human future free choices if it's truly up to human beings to do the choosing? Of course, knowledge of all events—past, present, and future—is essential or innate to God; without it, he wouldn't be a maximally great being. In Isaiah 42–44, God challenges Babylon's gods (idols) to make known what will take place in the future—something only Yahweh can do; that's what makes God God—even if we don't know how he knows. We may not be able to explain *how* God is all-powerful or omnipresent, though it's essential to God. Likewise, we may not be able to tell how God knows future human choices, though this, too, is innate to God.

Some thinkers refer to God's knowledge of future human choices using a *perceptual* model. Aquinas refers to God's "divine sight," seeing the whole sequence of future events at once: "Just as he who goes along the road does not see those who come after him; whereas he who sees the whole road from a height sees at once all those traveling on it."[13] This model raises the question of how God could "see" past, present, and future events taking place all at once since they don't all *now* exist. Perhaps a more accurate portrayal—a *rational* model—is this: Since God by his nature innately knows all truths, including truths about the future, God must know what will take place.[14]

Second, we should distinguish between what *will* happen and what *must* happen, between what is *certain* and what is *necessary*. If God knows that my wife and I will go out to the Breakers Hotel for an anniversary brunch, then it *will* happen. Now it doesn't logically follow that this *must* happen. If we had freely chosen to go another time or to a different place, then God would have known *that*. So if God knows what we'll freely choose, then it's *true* that the event *will* happen—that it's *certain*. But it's *false* that it therefore *must* happen—that it's *necessary*.

Third, God's knowledge of future actions doesn't by itself hinder human freedom since knowledge doesn't actually *cause* anything. God's foreknowing what we freely choose to do is caused by or grounded in what we'll freely choose to do. God's knowledge of a future event doesn't cause this event. A psychic may have an accurate intuition of a future event—say, a murder tomorrow that will take place just down the street.[15] Someone is murdered, but the psychic's knowledge didn't actually *do* anything. The psychic's awareness doesn't mean the murder *necessarily* occurred—nor that the awareness *caused* it to take place. The murderer acted freely. It would seem strange to claim that simply knowing something will take place actually causes it to happen. Why should things change if God is the knower? His knowing a murder will occur doesn't mean he caused it.

What grounds God's knowledge of what we would freely choose to do is that we will freely choose to do it in the actual world. Of course, we're talking about more than divine foreknowledge here. After all, God's knowledge of creaturely choices includes all possible worlds, not merely the world God chooses to create or actualize. God's knowledge of creaturely choices goes beyond what we *would do* in the actual world. After all, God intrinsically knows all kinds of possible persons in possible worlds who would make possible choices, but these are never realized since God didn't create these alternative worlds.

Fourth, God not only knows what *we* will do in the future, but he also knows what *he* will do in the future. But does this mean that God isn't free? The triune God isn't hemmed in or constrained by outside forces; he is free to act as he wisely chooses. From eternity, the triune God decided to freely create humans and graciously rescue them from their desperate plight. But if God knew what he would do, was he determined to act as he did simply because he knew his own future actions? In one of his earlier writings, *On the Free Choice of the Will*, Augustine addressed this: "Don't you see that you will have to be careful lest someone say to you that, if all things of which God has foreknowledge are done by necessity and not voluntarily, his own future acts will be done not voluntarily but by necessity?"[16] God's foreknowledge of his own actions doesn't cause him to do them; rather, he does them freely. So God's simply knowing what I'll do in the future doesn't *cause* me to do something either.

The subject of prayer is relevant here: Why pray if God knows what's going to happen anyway? Does prayer really accomplish anything? The biblical picture suggests that God, who knows that we will pray, may bring about certain events that wouldn't have taken place had we not prayed (cf. James 5:16–18). James 4:2 indicates that we "do not have" because we "do not ask."

Reflect on this scenario: For the moment, set aside the matter of God's ability to raise the dead. At any rate, you hear a friend of yours is in an auto accident, but you don't yet know whether he's alive or not. What good will prayer do since he's in fact either alive or dead? Well, God knows how you'll freely pray in response to hearing the news of this accident; so, in his foreknowledge, he may well have already worked out his purposes so that your friend would live in direct response to the prayer you offered up—but die if you hadn't.[17] The prayer of a righteous person can accomplish much (James 5:16)!

Fifth, God knows the array of possible worlds and ones he could feasibly create, and he knows what free creatures would do in particular circumstances. He thus chooses to create this (actual) world to bring about his wise purposes without undermining human freedom. God arranges the details of the actual world in light of his knowledge of what human creatures would freely do in whatever world they would happen to exist. So God arranges the details of the actual world without eliminating or undermining our freedom. And as we've seen, certain Scriptures portray God as surprised or gaining knowledge about something—and we could add that he appears to be regretful or changing his mind. We shouldn't assume that God didn't know what would happen; rather, such narratives nicely illustrate the divine-human interaction and God's engaging humans on the stage of history.

A related question is God's foreknowledge as it relates to the question of the saved, the lost, and the unevangelized. In keeping with his goodness, God created a world in which as many persons as possible are saved and as few persons as possible are lost. In light of God's desire to save any and all who would freely respond to him, perhaps it's the case that anyone who is lost would have been lost through his own free rejection of God's initiating grace in *any* world in which he would have existed. As we'll see later, one is separated from God's glorious presence not because he was born at the wrong place and at the wrong time but because he freely rejected God's initiating grace.[18]

Further Reading

Craig, William Lane. *The Only Wise God: The Compatibility of Divine Foreknowledge and Human Freedom.* Eugene, OR: Wipf & Stock, 2000.

———. *Time and Eternity: Exploring God's Relationship to Time.* Wheaton, IL: Crossway, 2001.

Flint, Thomas P. "Molinism." *Philosophy/Philosophy of Religion*, Oxford Handbooks Online, February 2015, doi: 10.1093/oxfordhb/9780199935314.013.29.

Taliaferro, Charles. *Contemporary Philosophy of Religion.* Oxford: Blackwell, 1998. (Note: this book offers a more detailed discussion than his *Philosophy of Religion.*)

———. *Philosophy of Religion.* Oxford: Wiley-Blackwell, 2009.

| *The Attributes of God (III):*
Omnipresence, Incorporeality, Beauty, Omnipotence

OMNIPRESENCE

> Where can I flee from Your presence? (Ps. 139:7)

After Hagar, Sarah's handmaiden, was obviously expecting her (and Abraham's) child, Ishmael, Sarah oppressed her so that she fled into the wilderness. God met this desperate woman there, assuring her that he had not abandoned her and offering promises regarding her son. She replied by "naming" God: "You are a God who sees" (Gen. 16:13).

God is omnipresent (Latin: *omnis* = "all"; *praesens* = "being before/at hand"); everything is present to him. The psalmist mused: "Where can I go from your Spirit?" (Ps. 139:7). In his dedicatory prayer at the newly built temple, Solomon declared that God's presence is unbounded: "Behold, heaven and the highest heaven cannot contain You" (1 Kings 8:27). Paul would later tell the Athenians: "The God who made the world and all things in it, since He is Lord of heaven and earth, does not dwell in temples made with hands" (Acts 17:24). God is intimately aware of all that takes place—and is able to act anywhere—in the universe or in created realms beyond.

God's omnipresence reminds us that the cosmos isn't cold and hostile; "the Father of lights" fills it with his personal, glorious presence (James 1:17), which brings great comfort to the believer (Ps. 139:6). The pervasive divine command throughout Scripture is "Do not fear." The reason? "For I am with you" (e.g., Isa. 41:10). On the other hand, God's omnipresence can also trouble those who don't want him to have access to or charge of their lives.

Now, God's being "present everywhere" isn't like some ether gas that permeates the entire universe. (Many scientists of yesteryear held this ether view.) It's not as though his presence physically expands with the universe! Space has to do with in-betweenness, and the existence of space depends on physical objects. Space came into being with the creation of these physical objects. Without them, there would be no space. Without them, God—the creator of all these objects—existed spacelessly.

In essence, God's omnipresence includes these two features: (a) God's perfect *knowledge or awareness* of every object within his creation (this would include the spiritual realm of creation, which angelic beings inhabit); and (b) his capacity to *act* on these objects he created and sustains in being. Everything everywhere is known to God's mind, is upheld by his power (Col. 1:17; Heb. 1:3), and can be causally affected by God's actions on them.

In light of Albert Einstein's work on the special theory of relativity (STR), some might wonder whether there *can* be any privileged access. Can there be an objective vantage point for judging whether two events are simultaneous or whether an object is in motion or at rest? Contrary to popular belief, Einstein didn't do away with Isaac Newton's claim that an absolute frame of reference existed—namely, a divine one. STR doesn't reduce God to just another observer *within* the universe. All created things are simultaneously "present" to him; each spatial object is immediately accessible to him.

Einstein rightly spoke of our limited frame of reference as finite observers. So we may not be able to tell which events are simultaneous and which aren't—especially since all objects in space are in motion. What is "now" to us (e.g., witnessing a supernova—a star explosion—through our telescopes) may have actually occurred millions of years ago. Or when a clock is traveling at the speed of light, the time on a clock actually slows down or stretches out (this is known as "time dilation") in comparison to a stationary clock or one traveling at less than 186,000 miles per second.

God, however, isn't locked into a finite (relative) framework; all events throughout the universe are immediately accessible to him. The immediacy of these events to God can be compared to the universe's cosmic background radiation—the hissing after-effect of the big bang—that permeates the universe. That's the static noise we hear when fiddling with our radio dial. This example serves as an analogy of God's objective privileged access to every point of the universe; that is, God has a cosmic perspective over everything in the universe, which he sustains in its very being, and can readily act on them as he chooses.[1] This is what we mean by "omnipresence."

INCORPOREALITY

> God is spirit, and those who worship Him must worship in spirit and in truth. (John 4:24)

The Scriptures affirm that, though the Son of God could become incarnate, the triune God is spirit. The "King eternal" is "invisible" (1 Tim. 1:17), dwelling in "unapproachable light," whom no one "has seen or can see" (1 Tim.

6:16). Christ himself is the image of "the invisible God" (Col. 1:15). Being spirit means more than just "disembodied" or "immaterial." The point here is that God isn't confined to one sphere of existence—say, the physical universe—but transcends such limits and fully penetrates every dimension of reality: visible and invisible, earthly and heavenly (Col. 1:16).

The late philosopher John Hick claimed that being a person without finite (bodily) boundaries makes no sense. An infinite (unbounded) person is "a self-contradiction. God cannot be both a person and infinite."[2] Another philosopher, Jaegwon Kim, finds it incredible that an "immaterial substance" without any material characteristics could influence and be influenced by the motions of material bodies strictly governed by physical law.[3] Or how does it make sense that an unobservable, eyeless, earless being can observe the world and listen to prayers? How can this being act justly, lovingly, or forgivingly without a body?

Orthodox believers, however, assume that God's seeing or hearing simply refers to his *awareness of* activity in the world and that he doesn't need physical organs to detect it. Think about the claim that a person can't act lovingly or forgivingly without a body. While we typically recognize human forgiveness or love through bodily actions—hugs, spoken words of affirmation—we also know people can act one way with their bodies but think or feel the opposite within. Someone may pretend to forgive another—complete with bodily actions—but still remain bitter and unforgiving in her soul.

Persons are more than their bodies or bodily actions. While bodily actions often prove helpful in communicating what a person is thinking or feeling, they don't *necessarily* give us direct access to love or forgiveness.

Some may wonder whether a spirit-being can act on physical objects, whether large planets or subatomic particles. But if all matter, energy, space, and physical time began to exist a finite time ago, we have very legitimate reason for thinking that an immaterial or spirit-being brought them into existence. Physicality had a beginning, which means that something nonphysical must be behind it. So even though God is spirit, he leaves indicators or traces of his existence throughout his physical creation.

Divine Beauty

> One thing I have asked from the LORD, that I shall seek:
> That I may dwell in the house of the LORD all the days of my life,
> To behold the beauty of the LORD
> And to meditate in His temple. (Ps. 27:4)

Philosopher Roger Scruton points out the connection of beauty in art to the transcendent or "religious." These appropriately fit together. When the aesthetic is cut off from its divine roots, he says, it loses all coherence and intelligibility.[4] No wonder that "it is in our feeling for beauty that the content, and even the truth, of religious doctrine is strangely and untranslatably intimated to us."[5]

In a similar vein, J. R. R. Tolkien wrote, "We find it difficult to conceive of evil and beauty together." While it seems easy to think of an ogre living in a hideous castle, we can't imagine a house with a noble purpose—an inn for travelers or a hall for a virtuous king—that is "sickeningly ugly."[6] Fine-tuning this a bit, we can readily imagine a connection between beauty and a most perfect being.

We take for granted the reality of beauty. For example, people study and critique art and devote their lives to discerning between good and bad or kitschy art. Clearly, a vast qualitative difference exists between Rembrandt's masterpieces and a four-year-old's doodlings or stick figures. To deny the objectivity of beauty is to affirm that evaluating art is fundamentally a waste of time. Even mathematical theorems or scientific theories are considered beautiful by atheist and theist alike. These theorems have a harmony, a concord, and an elegance to them. As we'll note later, the reality of beauty in the universe makes excellent sense if a God of beauty exists.

Various theologians have written on the beauty of God—and for good reason! The Scriptures depict God as the source of beautiful things, like the lilies of the field that surpass even Solomon's regal garments (Matt. 6:28-30), or as the one who commands the tabernacle and temple to be places of beauty (Exod. 31:1-11; 35:34; etc.). The beautiful heavens declare God's glory (Ps. 19:1). As Gerard Manley Hopkins wrote, "The world is charged with the grandeur of God," who is beauty itself.[7]

The Puritan theologian Jonathan Edwards wrote much about the beauty and excellence of God's being. Beauty is the very essence of divinity. For Edwards, God's holiness and beauty are fairly interchangeable. The spiritual beauty of God is the source of all lesser, created beauties in the world.

Likewise, the mysteries of the perichoretic love within the Trinity and the self-emptying of the incarnation, the self-sacrifice of Christ on the cross, and the "higher" ways of God (Isa. 55:9) all depict divine beauty in various forms. No wonder that in the Eastern Orthodox tradition, the "love of beauty" is the beginning of theology.[8] One believer with a Muslim background, who would eventually die for his faith, said, "The more I study the world's religions, the more beautiful Jesus appears to me."[9]

More could be said about the attribute of God's beauty, but we should at least note how God is beautiful in his being and that he is the wellspring of finite beauties.

OMNIPOTENCE

> Is anything too difficult for the LORD? (Gen. 18:14)

Scripture portrays God as "the Almighty," who does what humans can't, who accomplishes the impossible: "Behold, I am the LORD, the God of all flesh; is anything too difficult for Me?" (Jer. 32:27). The angel Gabriel informs Mary about her miraculous virginal conception, adding that "nothing will be impossible with God" (Luke 1:37). After Job's overwhelming encounter with God, Job affirms, "I know that You can do all things" (Job 42:2).

What does it mean that God can "do all things" or is "omnipotent" (Latin: *omnis* = "all"; *potens* = "powerful")? Can he undo the past—say, Napoleon's death or Julius Caesar's crossing the Rubicon—as though it never happened? Can he make square circles? Can he cease to exist? French philosopher René Descartes believed that the Almighty, if he wants, has the power to make 2 + 2 = 5, change laws of logic, or alter the basic structure of morality.

When people discuss God's power, they commonly raise the "stone paradox": Can God make a stone so big that he can't lift it? After all, he can do *anything*, right? And if he *couldn't* make such a stone, he must not be all-powerful after all. Yet even if God *could* make such a stone, he's still not all-powerful since he couldn't lift it! This apparent dilemma, however interesting, is flawed. No being, great or not, can do something self-contradictory or nonsensical. Can God, for whom no stone is too great to lift, make a stone too great to lift? The question answers itself. C. S. Lewis said: "I know very well that if it is self-contradictory it is absolutely impossible. . . . His Omnipotence means power to do all that is intrinsically possible, not to do the intrinsically impossible. You may attribute miracles to Him, but not nonsense. . . . It remains true that all *things* are possible with God: the intrinsic impossibilities are not things but nonentities. . . . Nonsense remains nonsense even when we talk it about God."[10]

Just as there's no possible world in which God doesn't exist, there can be, by definition, no God-defying rocks. The stone question is meaningless. The same applies to other impossibilities like changing the past. It would be possible to delete all evidence of an event: God could remove all the physical indicators of a meteor that struck the earth—and even delete the memories of people who may have witnessed it. But no power can undo what happened, making it *un*-happen. How could an event that *has* actually occurred *not* have occurred?

Another consideration: Does God have power to do wrong—even if he chooses not to use it? In addition to our intuitions about intrinsic goodness, which can't be marred by evil, the Scriptures also suggest that God by his very nature can't do what is evil—it's not simply that he *won't* or *chooses not to* do evil. For example, it's impossible for him to lie (Titus 1:2), to be pulled down by sin (James 1:13), to break his promises (Heb. 6:17–18), or to change in his good, holy character (Hab. 1:13; Mal. 3:6; Heb. 13:8). There are some things that God could not command (Jer. 7:31).

Now if God can't sin, he may be perfectly good; but is he truly all-powerful or even free? Here's the apparent dilemma: (a) If he could potentially sin, then he appears not to be perfectly good; but (b) if God couldn't sin, then it seems that he is not really free or all-powerful, since there's at least one thing God couldn't do. How do we begin to resolve this matter?

First, we can't separate God's *goodness* from God's *power*—or any of his other attributes, because this supremely great being possesses these great-making qualities together. An immensely powerful—but evil—being might prompt fear in us, but that being wouldn't be worthy of our worship. God, however, is by definition a worship-worthy, perfect being. Just as God's omniscience is more than sheer information-storage, God's omnipotence is more than brute power. Sheer might itself doesn't make its possessor supremely excellent. Rather, goodness is a kind of hub that connects and holds together the "spokes" of the various divine attributes.

Second, the "power to sin" turns out to be powerlessness. Anselm argued that if God were able to sin, this would be a deficiency since "[God's] powerlessness puts him in another's power."[11] The ability to sin reveals a deficiency in God's character, making him less than necessarily good. It would also undermine God's full power. How? To say of the world-conquering Alexander the Great, "He *cannot* lose in battle," reveals a deficiency not in *him* but rather in his *enemies*. As Anselm put it, "Thus when I say that I can be carried off or conquered against my will, this is not my power, but my necessity and another's power. For to say, 'I can be carried off or conquered,' is the same thing as to say, 'Someone is able to carry off or conquer me.'"[12] Said Aquinas, "To sin is to fall short of a perfect action; hence to be able to sin is to be able to fall short in action, which is repugnant to omnipotence."[13] God's inability to sin—a metaphysical impossibility—doesn't undermine his omnipotence any more that a general's inability to lose a battle should be seen as a lack of power or ability.

Third, God's power doesn't undermine human freedom but rather works with it. As we'll see in the chapters on evil, God takes human freedom seriously and works out his purposes without undermining personal agency and responsibility. He doesn't trample on creaturely freedom.

Fourth, skeptics may make faulty assumptions about, or artificial demands of, divine omnipotence. Michael Martin wrote something odd about this divine attribute—namely, that God's being all-powerful entails his doing something that wasn't done by God. God's being omnipotent means that he could, say, create a certain state of affairs—namely, the flooding of Hidden Valley that is brought about directly or indirectly by a *non-*omnipotent being.[14] But this turns out to be confused—a misplaced focus. Rather than focusing on the actor, Martin's scenario raises problems with who the agent actually is—God or a non-omnipotent being—rather than the act itself or the states of affairs produced. The latter is the relevant issue; the former creates metaphysical confusion. God can flood a valley, and we know that human agents can also flood valleys, but both can't flood the same valley at the same time. Focusing on the state of affairs produced rather than on the actors dissolves this omnipotence puzzle.[15]

Finally, omnipotence involves God's having the greatest possible scope of power—"maximal power." Perhaps the following set of descriptions will help us form a coherent understanding of omnipotence:[16]

- *Bringing about certain states of affairs that are logically possible*: Such power isn't simply "the ability to do anything at all": God's making himself cease to exist or creating square circles would be metaphysical nonsense. No power, however great, can produce something self-contradictory.

- *Being bound up with divine goodness*: Not *every* ability to do something should be considered worthy of divine power.[17] As we've seen, it would be wrong to worship a being with raw power but who is horrifically evil. Worshiping the supreme, intrinsically good God, who is also omnipotent, is a different story.

- *Taking into consideration the world God has freely chosen to create from among other possible worlds that God chose not to create*: God has both chosen *to* create and chosen a *particular* world to create. The actual world is one in which God weaves the free choices of human beings into the intricate tapestry of his overarching, glorious, and often-mysterious purposes. Because of the wisdom and power God exerted in creating the actual world, it would be an inappropriate expectation that God change course and shift from the actual world to bringing about another world that God could have created but, in his wisdom, chose not to.

- *Not including altering the past* (a metaphysical impossibility): God's omnipotence doesn't require changing events that have already occurred—

for example, the assassination of Abraham Lincoln or the Hundred Years' War (1337–1453). Erasing all evidence of an event is not undoing the fact that the event took place. That said, God does have the power to bring about some present or future states of affairs. That means he would also have foreknown them and thus would have brought about certain states of affairs that preceded them. This scenario has a bearing on whether God really answers prayer. As we've noted, prayer makes a difference: "You do not have because you do not ask" (James 4:2). God, knowing the various states of affairs and human choices in the possible worlds he could have created, creates a world in which he responds to certain prayers he knows will be prayed. God, knowing what we would freely pray in advance, configures a world so that our prayers can have a genuine impact on the world.

God is certainly free to act—say, to create a world rather than not—and to exert his power within it. But we must take care to understand what God's being all-powerful truly means and that the power to do the metaphysically impossible isn't power at all.

FURTHER READING

Moreland, J. P., and William Lane Craig. *Philosophical Foundations of a Christian Worldview*. 2nd ed. Downers Grove, IL: IVP Academic, 2017.

Morris, Thomas V. *Our Idea of God: An Introduction to Philosophical Theology*. Downers Grove, IL: InterVarsity Press, 1991.

Taliaferro, Charles. *Philosophy of Religion*. Oxford: Wiley-Blackwell, 2009. For more detailed discussion, see Charles Taliaferro, *Contemporary Philosophy of Religion*. Oxford: Blackwell, 1998.

Taliaferro, Charles, Paul Draper, and Philip L. Quinn, eds. *A Companion to Philosophy of Religion*. 2nd ed. Oxford: Wiley-Blackwell, 2010.

The Attributes of God (IV): Immutability, Impassibility, Simplicity (?), Humility

IMMUTABILITY

> I, the LORD, do not change. (Mal. 3:6)

Aristotle called God the "Unmoved Mover." Theologian Paul Tillich called God "the Ground of all being." Throughout church history, theologians have often portrayed God as absolutely changeless. *Any* change is presumably negative; so if God experienced any change whatsoever, this would entail—it is argued—that God would have to become either more perfect or less perfect.

Such portrayals of God, though, sound more like a static, impersonal, abstract, or mathematical principle rather than the dynamic, living, acting, history-engaging personal being of Scripture. Theologian Colin Gunton has reminded us not to remove utterly God's *act* from his *being*.[1] God's action reveals something of who he is. God has acted in creating and engaging with the world and thus is not *absolutely* changeless.

We've seen that change on God's part wouldn't involve moving from perfection to imperfection; neutral changes that don't impinge on God's character are unproblematic. So God can change from *not* being Creator to *becoming* Creator without diminishing his greatness. God shifts from *not being* incarnate to *becoming* incarnate in Jesus of Nazareth—a fairly decisive change! God's necessary goodness, power, and knowledge aren't affected at all by his acquiring these new characteristics—ones he didn't have in the prior state.

An absolute immutability doesn't describe the biblical God. God comes to experience what it's like to be Creator. On having created, God experiences an awareness of tense or the passage of time. God's knowledge of present events changes with the passage of time. So even if God had freely chosen not to create a world, it would still be the case that absolute changelessness isn't an essential feature in God. It's still possible that God, if he chose to, could experience change.[2]

Historical theologian Jaroslav Pelikan points out that God's immutability in Scripture refers—contrary to certain theological portrayals—to his promise-keeping, covenant faithfulness, and reliable character.[3] God is unchanging in his goodness and can't do evil (James 1:13). And unlike fallen humans, God isn't fickle—that is, he won't "repent" or "change His mind" (1 Sam. 15:29; cf. Mal. 3:6).

Why then does the Bible elsewhere tell us that God *does* "change His mind" or "repent"?[4] Or why is God "grieved" or "sorry" (*nacham*) that he made humans (Gen. 6:7)? For one thing, this isn't a change in God's nature or character. Also, the words for "repent" or "be sorry" in the Old Testament have a range of meanings depending on the context. They can refer to the experience of emotional pain or regret, suggesting God's dynamic relationality. While God isn't being fickle, he is intimately engaged with his creation, not aloof from it.

Here is another use of "repent": Moses pleads with God not to destroy Israel (Exod. 32:12, 14), and God relents. Or, God sends Jonah to Nineveh, threatening to judge it, but God "changes his mind" or "repents" by sparing the city. In this context (Jon. 3:9–10), "repent" (*nacham*) refers to relenting or changing from a stated course of action because of the recipient's change of heart. Repenting means "retracting blessing or judgment" based on human conduct. A change within the recipients after a threat renders blessing or judgment no longer appropriate.[5] Although Jonah confidently proclaimed, "Yet forty days and Nineveh will be overthrown" (Jon. 3:4), he already knew that God, being gracious and compassionate, was capable of showing mercy (Jon. 4:2)—if there was repentance. That's why he didn't want to warn Israel's enemies! David, while fasting and weeping in hopes that his son would live, reckoned, "Who knows, the LORD may be gracious to me" (2 Sam. 12:22).

There's often an underlying conditionality behind God's warnings: judgment *will* come *unless* we repent: "At one moment I [God] might speak concerning a nation or concerning a kingdom to uproot, to pull down, or to destroy it; if that nation against which I have spoken turns from its evil, I will relent concerning the calamity I planned to bring on it. Or at another moment I might speak concerning a nation or concerning a kingdom to build up or to plant it; if it does evil in My sight by not obeying My voice, then I will think better of the good with which I had promised to bless it" (Jer. 18:7–10).

During the time of Noah, Moses, and Jonah, God already knew exactly what he was going to do—though this meant "relenting" or "repenting" in response to how humans acted. When biblical narratives portray God changing his mind, they appear to ignore the question of whether God knew this change would take place. God even seems surprised at times. Why? The biblical authors use a literary means and conventions to depict an interactive God who takes the dynamic divine-human drama seriously.

So while God's faithful character and promise-keeping don't change, he still experiences changes. The triune God isn't the static, untouchable deity commonly associated with traditional Greek philosophy. He's a prayer-answering, history-engaging God.

IMPASSIBILITY

How often they . . . grieved Him in the desert. (Ps. 78:40)

Related to the question, "Can God change?" is the question, "Can God suffer?" Traditional Christian theology has held that God can't suffer (he is impassible): he can't be acted on by his creation. The Scriptures, though, present a God who is able to suffer. God can be "grieved in His heart" (Gen. 6:6). His Spirit can be quenched (1 Thess. 5:19) and resisted (Acts 7:51). God movingly declares about unfaithful Israel: "How I have been hurt by their adulterous hearts which turned away from Me" (Ezek. 6:9). Biblical scholar D. A. Carson asks, if God doesn't suffer, "Why does the Bible spend so much time depicting him as if he does?" Indeed, the "biblical evidence, in both Testaments, pictures God as a being who can suffer."[6] Here's Jaroslav Pelikan again: "It is significant that Christian theologians customarily set down the doctrine of the impassibility of God without bothering to provide very much biblical support or theological proof." This concept came into Christian doctrine from Greek philosophy.[7]

God's sovereignty and unchanging nature imply that God isn't at the mercy of his creatures' actions, nor does he lack control of his emotions. Advocates of God's absolute impassibility are right to protect this emphasis. On the other hand, God isn't indifferent to creaturely attitudes and actions—which is an indication of divine perfection (i.e., perfect love). Perhaps it's more helpful to distinguish between God's being emotionally *touched* by human suffering, repentance, and grief and his being emotionally *crushed* by human experiences and actions. Of course, God is perfectly joyful within himself and contented in the knowledge of his good creation and in his directing history to its completion (cf. Ps. 50:7–15).[8] But God truly does suffer—particularly in the incarnate Christ on the cross. The Scriptures portray a God who can, to some degree, be *exasperated* with his creatures, including ancient Israel (e.g., Neh. 9:28–30; Ps. 81:10–16; Isa. 5:4). God also suffers with his creatures, especially with his own redeemed people (Acts 9:4–5: "Why are you persecuting Me?"). As Alvin Plantinga observes, "Some theologians claim that God cannot suffer. I believe they are wrong. God's capacity for suffering, I believe, is proportional to his greatness."[9]

Is God play-acting in his suffering, since he knows what is going to happen anyway? Not at all! Consider how we may know that a loved one is going to die in the near future, but that doesn't eliminate the experience of pain and sorrow once she actually dies. Furthermore, suffering isn't imposed on God from outside. God suffers because of his sovereign decision—something that comes from within the triune God, something God determines to accept.[10]

DIVINE SIMPLICITY

> God said to Moses, "I AM WHO I AM." And he said, "Say this to the people
> of Israel, 'I AM has sent me to you.'" (Exod. 3:14 ESV)

The doctrine of divine simplicity tends to be one of the more obscure and
debated aspects of the divine nature. Many Christian theologian-philosophers
across the ages have held this doctrine; others have found it curious, elusive,
incoherent, and even unbiblical! Simplicity (or "simpleness") hasn't been uni-
formly defined in the history of Christian theology. Given its notable lineage,
we want to mention it and offer a few thoughts for those with ears to hear.

Many theologians, including Anselm and Aquinas, have considered God's
simplicity to be his defining feature—what sets him apart from his creation.
This concept of simplicity has at least *eight* different senses, some of them
being more general—or, on the other hand, more restrictive—than others.[11]
According to some interpretations of simplicity, God literally has *no* distinct
attributes or characteristics. So, unlike God, we're *compound* beings: we have
(a) *essential* qualities, which make us what we are—such as the capability to
think and choose; and (b) *accidental* ones—qualities or properties that could
have been different, like being snub-nosed or brown-eyed.

Simplicity entails that God doesn't *have* properties; he just *is* those properties. His attributes are one: for God, *wisdom = love = holiness = justice = omnipresence = omnipotence*. God's *existence* is identical to his *essence* or *nature*.
That is, God's nature *requires* that he exist, whereas any creature's essence or
nature is *contingent* (that is, it's logically possible that no creature exist). Everything about God is essential to him; there's nothing nonessential or "accidental."
In my Aquinas philosophy class at Marquette University, one student joked:
"Why does God have low insurance rates? Because he has no accidents!"

Also, while creatures can *actualize* or realize their *potentiality*—like an
acorn having the potentiality to become an oak—there's no potentiality in
God. God is "pure act(uality)" (*actus purus*). That's the brief overview, and
what follows is a brief response.

We can agree with what some versions of simplicity are trying to preserve—
that God's nature demands that he exist necessarily and that there's no world
in which he doesn't exist. We can also affirm that God isn't a being who just
happens to have all the right attributes that make him supremely excellent. He
doesn't have "generic deity" characteristics, as though another being could be
omniscient or omnipotent but not be God.

However, some versions of divine simplicity look to be more an exercise in

Greek metaphysics than a description of Scripture's robust, history-engaging triune God. Not only does it seem really hard to derive certain notions of simplicity from Scripture; they also seem philosophically problematic, for the following reasons.

- God's love, holiness, and omnipresence are distinct properties, even if they're possessed by the same being. Being a husband and being a father are clearly distinct, though the same man can have both characteristics. Or, some properties may always go together in all possible worlds (they are "coextensive")—a triangle's trilaterality and triangularity, say—but these properties aren't identical. Likewise, God's omniscience or goodness always coexist in any possible world, but they're not identical.
- If God is simple, then, in some versions of simplicity, God really doesn't seem to be a personal agent. If God *is* his properties of omnipresence and wisdom and love, then he appears to be more like an abstract object—like *triangularity* or *evenness*—but abstract objects can't act or do anything.[12]
- If everything about God is absolutely essential to him, not accidental or contingent, then God apparently can't know things he *could* and *should* know—like possible worlds he could have created. It seems that whatever God does, he *had* to do. His choices and actions are necessary, not free. However, it's because of the free exercise of God's will or eternal determinations that certain contingent characteristics come to exist in God—God as Creator or Redeemer. There is *some* potentiality in God:[13] God is free, and he can bring about a contingent state of affairs—such as creation—if he so chooses.
- Aquinas claimed God isn't really related to his creatures; rather, his creatures are related to him. This is an attempt to preserve God's perfect similarity across all logically possible worlds. But this seems to push matters too far. God very clearly has the quality of being the Creator. Yet, without the universe, the triune God didn't have the quality of being Creator. So we have two distinct states in the divine life—one in which God knows, "I exist alone," and another in which God knows, "I have created creatures."[14] It seems strange to insist that God's act of power ("pure act") is the same in all possible worlds, if, say, human creatures exist in some worlds but not others. Isn't God's free choice the very reason he created something contingent? If God chooses to create, then contingency is introduced into God. Through creation, God acquired an accidental (or non-necessary) characteristic of being Creator and

then Savior. We could also add that by creating, God becomes temporal. Even though God doesn't change in his nature, non-necessary change is introduced. So perhaps those insurance rates *should* be raised!

- The doctrine of the Trinity seems problematic for certain versions of simplicity since there are distinctions within God. The Father, Son, and Spirit have their respective person-defining relationships and characteristics that distinguish each divine person from the other. The Father's relation to the Son is really different from the Son's relation to the Spirit. And there's something about the Father that makes him the Father and not the Son or Spirit. All attributes within the Godhead aren't equivalent.

HUMILITY

> I dwell on a high and holy place,
> And also with the contrite and lowly of spirit. (Isa. 57:15)

Some people charge that God seems so egotistical and attention-seeking. Atheist Bede Rundle puts it this way: "If you are going to make your god in the image of man, you might at least filter out some of the less desirable human traits. God should be above any sort of attention-seeking behaviour, for instance, and an insistence on being told how unsurpassably wonderful one is does not rate highly."[15]

Is this what Scripture reveals? Is God vain? Why then the demand for us creatures to be humble? Scripture reveals an exalted God who is also humble. This attribute isn't often noted; so we devote some space to it here.[16]

Humility and Realism

Humility involves an appropriate acknowledgment and realistic assessment of oneself. Pride, on the other hand, is an inflated view of one's self or accomplishments. So "pride" or "vanity" doesn't accurately describe God, who has a realistic—rather than inflated—view of himself. Vanity is an overblown self-perception. Yes, God knows himself to be maximally great. Denying this would be a denial of reality—like a world-famous concert pianist saying, "I don't play piano all that well." But God doesn't take credit where credit isn't due: he doesn't take credit for making humans freely choose this or that, since it's up to humans to do the choosing. And contrary to what some theologians assume, God isn't so "sovereign" that he wants to take credit for evil (James 1:17). God accurately knows the extent of his greatness and his rightful place in the order of things; however, that doesn't spill over into reality-denial. His concern for his "glory"—due honor, credit, and acknowledgment—stems from his being in touch with reality. Our diminishing the credit this maximally great God deserves—not to honor him—is to enter the realm of reality-denial (Rom. 1:21).

Divine Other-Centeredness

The triune God is intrinsically other-centered within himself. Because many people don't think of God as essentially triune, they more easily fall prey to the notion that God is vain. No, God is by nature other-centered in the self-giving love within the Trinity. Within God, no vanity exists, only mutual, other-oriented love.

The Divine Image and Worship

God's making us in his image isn't a mark of inappropriate divine pride—like a vain toy maker creating objects to look just like him. As with our salvation, our being God's image-bearers is a gift he bestows on us to rule creation with him and to share in the life of the divine triune family. God lovingly bestows his image on us—with the Creator's high compliments, having been made "a little lower than God" (Ps. 8:5). God gives opportunity for us to enter into life—"eternal life"—with the triune God (John 17:3; 1 John 5:2). This means that not only is the name of Jesus to be "glorified" in us, but we too are "glorified in" him (2 Thess. 1:12)—much like the moon reflects and shares in the sun's glory. We too receive glory and praise from God himself (Rom. 2:29)—yet another expression of divine humility.

The divine image means we're created to worship God. God doesn't diminish our humanity, but rather helps us realize our purpose of relating deeply to God. Such worship realistically reflects our place in the universe: that we are creatures/sinners and God is Creator/Savior. To worship God is to acknowledge his "worth-ship"—a mind-set of self-forgetfulness as we remember and acknowledge God.[17] Worship not only humbles but also exalts and transforms us: "For a human being to seek such universal and eternal fame would be to aspire to divinity, but God must be desired to be known to be God. The good of God's human creatures requires that he be known to them as God. There is no vanity, only revelation of truth, in God's demonstrating his deity to the nations."[18]

Divine Jealousy

Associated with the charge of divine vanity is petty jealousy. Contrary to caricature, God's jealousy is right and just—as when a third party encroaches on a marriage. This jealousy springs from divine *pain*—not from an inferiority complex that makes prideful, selfish demands. After all, it is a response to the denial that God is God and that knowing God is central to our human flourishing. No wonder Scripture's references to divine "jealousy" are predominantly in the context of idolatry and false worship.[19] Choosing this-worldly pursuits or various God-substitutes over against a relationship with God is a reality-denial, which only harms us.

Seeking Praise?

When the Scriptures call us to praise God, isn't this the picture of divine vanity—of God fishing for compliments or seeking flattery? Actually, God isn't commanding praise, but rather creatures are spontaneously urging one another to recognize God's greatness, goodness, and worth-ship. Naturally flowing praise simply completes and expresses the creature's enjoyment of God. God doesn't need our praise for an ego boost: "If I were hungry, I would not tell you, For the world is Mine, and all it contains" (Ps. 50:12).

Creatures who are caught up with the enjoyment of God fittingly erupt in praise, spontaneously beckoning the rest of us to do the same: "praise is becoming" (Ps. 147:1), which C. S. Lewis learned well: "But the most obvious fact about praise—whether of God or anything—strangely escaped me. I thought of it in terms of compliment, approval, or the giving of honor. I had never noticed that all enjoyment spontaneously overflows into praise. . . . The world rings with praise—lovers praising their mistresses, readers their favorite poet, walkers praising the countryside, players praising their game. . . . I think we delight to praise what we enjoy because the praise not merely expresses but completes the enjoyment; it is appointed consummation."[20]

Divine Self-Humbling

In Scripture, God regularly reveals his humility and service as he engages with humanity. God not only is "high above the nations" but he also "humbles Himself to behold" things in heaven and on earth (Ps. 113:4–6). Indeed, "the high and exalted One" also dwells "with the contrite and lowly of spirit" (Isa. 57:15). This is evident especially in the example of Jesus of Nazareth. Jesus describes himself as "gentle and humble in heart"—in the very same context as his declaring of being the unique revealer of the Father and as the one who can give the weary soul rest (Matt. 11:27–29). Though "Lord" and "Teacher," Jesus takes the role of a slave who serves his disciples (John 13:1–20; cf. Luke 12:37: Jesus "the master" will "gird himself . . . and wait on them"). He is "among you as the one who serves" (Luke 22:27); he came to "serve" and "give His life a ransom for many" (Mark 10:45).

Though "equal with God," the Son of God didn't clutch this glorified status but humbled ("emptied") himself (Phil. 2:6–8). He not only "became flesh, and dwelt among us" (John 1:14) and dined with society's undesirables and outcasts. He also died a slave's death on a cross—a shameful, degrading, naked, public, and cursed humiliation. This is how low God was willing to go for our salvation.

John's Gospel powerfully depicts this. Jesus's being "lifted up" on the cross (John 12:32; cf. 3:14–15; 8:28) is both literal (physically raised up onto a cross) and figurative (spiritual exaltation and honor from God). Yet this humiliating death is precisely when he is "glorified" (John 12:23–24; 13:31–32). In other words, *God's great moment of glory is when he experiences the greatest humiliation and shame.* The depths to which God was willing to go for our salvation reveals his amazing greatness.

Theologian Colin Gunton correctly observed: "It is as truly godlike to be humble as it is to be exalted."[21] The triune God's other-centered character within himself and self-sacrificial love toward us reveal great humility and love, which call for our worship, devotion, and praise.

FURTHER READING

Copan, Paul. "Divine Narcissism? A Further Defense of God's Humility." *Philosophia Christi* 8, no. 2 (Winter 2006): 336–46.

Meister, Chad, and Paul Copan, eds. *The Routledge Companion to Philosophy of Religion.* 2nd ed. London: Routledge, 2012.

Moreland, J. P., and William Lane Craig. *Philosophical Foundations of a Christian Worldview.* 2nd ed. Downers Grove, IL: IVP Academic, 2017.

Taliaferro, Charles, Paul Draper, and Philip L. Quinn, eds. *A Companion to Philosophy of Religion.* 2nd ed. Oxford: Wiley-Blackwell, 2010.

13 | *The God of Truth (I): Truth on the Decline*

> Only fear the LORD and serve Him in truth with all
> your heart; for consider what great things He has done
> for you.
>
> —1 Samuel 12:24

> Jesus said to him, "I am the way, and the truth, and the
> life; no one comes to the Father but through Me."
>
> —John 14:6

> Sanctify them in the truth; Your word is truth.
>
> —John 17:17

JESUS AS THE TRUTH IN A POST-TRUTH SOCIETY

We're told that we live not only in a post-Christian era but in a post-truth age as well. Dedication to truth, it appears, is on the decline—this is a time of "truth decay." So you would think that if truth were passé, then the true-for-you-but-not-for-me sorts wouldn't get upset with other people's truth-claims. Why do relativists bother getting angry—unless they believe their view is true for *every* person? Relativism is often passive-aggressive—tolerant and easy-going *until* you challenge relativism's inconsistencies. No wonder Pope John Paul II spoke of the "dictatorship of relativism."

In the biblical texts above, we see that the faithful triune God is the anchor for truth—the Father's "word is truth"; Jesus is "the truth" who faithfully reveals God's character; and "the Spirit of truth" has come as "another Helper" in Jesus's stead. Jesus calls himself "the *true* vine" (John 15:1). That is, he is genuine and very much unlike ancient Israel—the faithless, fruitless vine (Isa. 5:1–7; cf. Ps. 80:8, 14); yet as we disciples—branches—are dependent on ("abide in") him and as he sustains ("abides in") us, we bring forth the authentic fruit of love as the new Israel of God. Our producing true fruit by depending on the true vine—without whom we can do nothing—reflects a life anchored in reality.

True faith in Christ is gritty. It doesn't shield us from reality but is fundamentally a vision *of* reality.[1] Christ possesses all the treasures of wisdom and knowledge, and he holds all things together (Col. 2:3; 1:15). So truth isn't mere factual knowledge of theological truths, which demons possess (James 2:19). Personal—in fact, "filial"— knowledge of God is the heart of eternal life (John 17:3), which increasingly sets us free from the reality-distorting powers of sin and Satan and God-substitutes (John 8:32, 44; 1 John 5:21).

In this and the next chapters, we'll explore the postmodern and secular scenes. We'll try to get some perspective and offer some responses to some of the present cultural moods and mind-sets.

POSTMODERNISM AND SECULARISM

> Justice is turned back
> And righteousness stands far away;
> For truth has stumbled in the street,
> And uprightness cannot enter.
> Yes, truth is lacking;
> And he who turns aside from evil makes himself a prey.
>
> (Isa. 59:14–15)

We find ourselves in a postmodern world that is paralyzed by uncertainty and skepticism and suspicion toward the truth. We're told that truth and morality are what we humans have invented or constructed. Not only this, our world has also been described as increasingly "secular" and that we are living off the fumes of a fading "Christendom." These shifting tides and turbulent waters can leave us feeling unsettled and even fearful. But we have a soul anchor (Heb. 6:19), and despite change and despair, the hope of the gospel can still shine forth. Yet it is still important to grasp how we actually got here in the first place.

Postmodernism and How We Got Here

Prior to the 1600s, the *premodern* Western world was largely shaped by the biblical story or metanarrative of God, creation, fall, redemption, and re-creation. God made sense of the world and of how humans fit in to it all. The existence and design of the universe along with the reality of human dignity and rights, moral responsibility and duties, and beauty and reason were anchored in the reality of this good, truthful triune God.

The emergence of the *modern* world ("modernism") has come to be associated with the Roman Catholic philosopher René Descartes (1596–1650)—the "father of modern philosophy." He was deeply concerned about a rising skepticism in the academy as well as a perceived fragmentation of Christianity that had arisen because of Protestantism—a further fragmentation after "the Great Schism" of 1054, when the Eastern Church and the Roman Church divided. Of course, the printing press had been invented before the rise of the Protestant Reformation, and so the handwriting was already on the wall: the proliferation of all manner of ideas—both reformational, deformational, and informational—was only a matter of time.[2] Though Descartes was a Catholic, it is widely agreed that his quest for certain knowledge unwittingly gave birth to a plurality of new ideas, philosophical fragmentation, and a new way of looking at the world (i.e., the inadvertent de-centering of God in the quest for knowledge).[3]

Descartes embarked on a "skeptical voyage," putting everything he believed to the test of severe doubt: maybe his beliefs were an illusion, or perhaps an evil demon was systematically deceiving him. But at least he couldn't doubt his doubting, and since doubting itself is a form of thinking, he couldn't doubt his own existence, since one has to exist in order to think. He concluded: *I think; therefore, I am ("cogito; ergo sum").*

Descartes sought to anchor his certainty in God's existence. But observers—both sympathetic and hostile—have pointed out that his epistemological undertaking led to the modern project: God came to be displaced as the starting point for knowledge; now, the individual human knower took center stage. Despite his own Roman Catholic frame of reference, Descartes unwittingly sowed the seeds for the proliferation of modernist thinking.

Modernism gave rise to various "systems" or metanarratives (French: *grands récits*), which adhered to many of the same ideals of the premodern world—rights, freedom, beauty, moral duties. But God was no longer deemed a necessary foundation to explain them. Rationalism emphasized reason; Romanticism, feelings; Marxism/Communism, economics and opposition to economic classes; Nazism, racial purity and power; and scientism, science as the only basis for knowledge. However, the atrocities and wholesale slaughter under Nazism and Communism in the blood-soaked twentieth century—the systematic killing of over one hundred million persons—called into question the very idea of metanarratives. Such systems were considered by many to be inherently oppressive; they proved to be total, dehumanizing failures.

According to some, it appears that all we're left with are fragmented, limited perspectives—without anything universal or humanity-embracing. This is the *postmodern* era—a mood or mind-set that emerged in the latter half of the twentieth century. Anything claiming to be universally true as well as unbiased and objective was increasingly treated with suspicion. Reason isn't neutral and can't be trusted; it is finite, historically limited, and colored by biases and agendas. What's more, reality is *constructed*, since there is no mind-independent reality to which our thinking must conform. We can't speak of "the way things really are," and none of us has access to reality. Finite, biased humans fabricate their own reality and personal identity. "Truth" and "reason" and "knowledge" are nothing more than tools to coerce and domineer.

In terms of historical symbols, the storming of the Bastille during the French Revolution (1789), inspired by opposition to the established church and the monarchy bound up with it, represents the shift from *premodernism* to *modernism*. And exactly two hundred years later, the fall of the Berlin Wall (1989), which divided free West Germany and Communist East Germany, represents the shift from *modernism* to *postmodernism*.

One writer has described postmodernism in a nutshell as suspicion or "incredulity toward metanarratives."[4] In the absence of metanarratives, what is left? Postmodernists tell us that metanarratives, which claim to be universally true pictures of the world, inevitably lead to oppression. They create an insider-outsider division and leave no room for "the Other." Even so, some postmodern thinkers like Michel Foucault did remain quite sympathetic with Marxism.

Postmodernists tell us that all we're left with are "mini-narratives"—finite, culturally limited perspectives or the viewpoint of one's own identity group. So we have further fragmentation—a constellation of viewpoints with nothing to hold them together. They are "incommensurable"; that is, we have no neutral way of measuring or comparing one perspective with another. In conversation, we simply can't determine whether we are even referring to the same thing: "That's just your perspective!"

So with postmodernism, not only is any God-established foundation called into question; so are universal truths, morality, human dignity, and reason.

Secularism

Our era has been also called "secular." In the past, this term has meant non-religious or religiously neutral. However, the more fundamental idea about our era is that belief in God is *contestable*; it's one option among many. In the Middle Ages, virtually everyone claimed to be a Christian, and belief in anything *but* God seemed outlandish and outrageous. Things have changed dramatically. Today, God isn't simply being excluded from the public square and the marketplace of ideas; rather, God is increasingly *marginalized* and viewed as *irrelevant*. That is, God doesn't fit within the "plausibility structure" of the secular-minded.

No longer does faith in God—a strictly private matter—inform public life and shape its thinking. In the wake of Charles Darwin, it's now possible to be an intellectually fulfilled atheist, as Richard Dawkins put it. The "enchanted" premodern world has now become "disenchanted"—science has removed all mystery, wonder, and personhood. Unbelief or disbelief is now the default position, and the "religious" person bears the burden of proof to make her case. Paul Elie summarizes the state of things in this way:

> We are all skeptics now, believer and unbeliever alike. There is no one true faith, evident at all times and places. Every religion is one among many. The clear lines of any orthodoxy are made crooked by our experience, are complicated by our lives. Believer and unbeliever are in the same predicament, thrown back onto themselves in complex circumstances, looking for a sign. As ever, religious belief makes its claim somewhere between revelation and projection, between holiness and human frailty; but the burden of proof, indeed the burden of belief, for so long upheld by society, is now back on the believer, where it belongs.[5]

This secular approach to reality—or interpretation of reality—essentially ignores the reality of God from the business of life. In our contemporary era of science, technology, automation, and control, the world has become increasingly depersonalized. That is, even as "believers," we can easily live as *practical atheists*, going through our day without giving much thought to our need for God. It's possible to ignore the reality of God's personal, gracious presence within the world.[6]

In the next chapter, we examine themes of truth, reality, and the place of faith in God in a postmodern, secularized, and disenchanted culture. While affirming truth and the reality of God is still vital, we must learn to creatively and wisely engage with a society that is increasingly rootless and cut off from the realm that can help restore our humanity.

FURTHER READING

Copan, Paul. *"True for You, but Not for Me": Overcoming Objections to Christian Faith*. 2nd ed. Minneapolis: Bethany House, 2009.

Everts, Don, and Doug Schaupp. *I Once Was Lost: What Postmodern Skeptics Taught Us about Their Path to Jesus.* Downers Grove, IL: InterVarsity Press, 2008.

Hicks, Stephen R. C. *Explaining Postmodernism: Skepticism and Socialism from Rousseau to Foucault.* Expanded ed. Roscoe, IL: Ockham's Razor Publishing, 2017.

Moberly, R. W. L. *The Bible in a Disenchanted Age.* Grand Rapids: Baker Academic, 2018.

Moreland, J. P. *Scientism and Secularism.* Wheaton, IL: Crossway, 2018.

Sweetman, Brendan, ed. *The Failure of Modernism: The Cartesian Legacy and Contemporary Pluralism.* Mishawaka, IN: American Maritain Association, 1999.

> For they are a rebellious people,
>   lying children,
> children unwilling to hear
>   the instruction of the LORD;
> who say to the seers, "Do not see,"
>   and to the prophets, "Do not prophesy to us what
>   is right;
> speak to us smooth things,
>   prophesy illusions,
> leave the way, turn aside from the path,
>   let us hear no more about the Holy One of Israel."
>   —Isaiah 30:9–11 ESV

THE TRUTH ABOUT POSTMODERNISM

We live in a world that is becoming increasingly familiar with fake news and historical revisionism. Yet notions of *error*, *lying*, and *illusion* presuppose truth. In fact, truth is turns out to be inescapable: if we deny the truth, we affirm the truth. If someone says, "There is no such thing as truth," she is nevertheless assuming that *it's true that there is no truth*.

Postmodernism's skepticism about—or rejection of—reason's legitimacy will ultimately use reason to draw this conclusion. To deny there can be any meta-narrative is to affirm a metanarrative of one's own: the only true metanarrative is that of limited, cultural, or individual perspectives. The postmodernist ends up replacing one metanarrative with another. The postmodernist claim that we can't have access to reality itself presupposes access to reality; it's a claim to know at least something about reality—namely, that we can't have access to it.

The postmodern posture questions any authoritative stance, but that is to take an authoritative stance. Authority is inescapable: *someone* will have to be the ultimate authority—God, someone else, or I myself. At the end of the day, it's fundamentally a theological issue. We're still left with the question: why *this* authority rather than *that* one? Indeed, why should I fully trust any finite, biased, historically limited person like myself—or you or another? A supremely good and wise God is the only being who doesn't suffer from these limitations.

"For now we see in a mirror dimly . . . ; now I know in part" (1 Cor. 13:12). We agree that humans are limited, finite, and biased. We don't have to be postmodern to know this. The statement assumes that even limited humans can truly know something, even if not exhaustively so. It just doesn't follow that bias or limitation necessitates false beliefs. In fact, claiming that we have biases is itself a statement of knowledge. We can be finite knowers even if we don't have a God's-eye view of things. To deny knowledge is to affirm it.

THE TRUTH ABOUT KNOWLEDGE

What is *knowledge*? It can be summed up as *warranted true belief*. If I *know* something, I must *believe* it, and it must be *true*. But that's not enough. I could believe something that's true—but completely by accident. Remember that stopped clock that just happens to be correct twice a day? If I conclude the correct time when observing a stopped clock, it's only an *accidentally* true belief. A third component—*warrant*—is necessary for a true belief to be categorized as "knowledge"; in the case of the clock, perhaps I look more closely and see that the clock is unplugged or that the second hand isn't moving and then look at more reliable sources for time-telling.

Must knowledge be certain? Paul writes, "For this you know with certainty" (Eph. 5:5). He assumes we can have knowledge even *without* certainty. In fact, very few things can be known with absolute certainty, although we can have *confident* knowledge (Luke 1:4; Acts 1:3). Certainty is just a psychological state, which doesn't guarantee knowledge at all. How many times have we been "absolutely certain" about something, only to discover we were dead wrong? We can have confident knowledge that other minds exist and that the universe is older than fifteen minutes even if we don't have absolute certainty. It's logically possible that the world is illusory, but so what? Even given that utterly remote possibility, it just doesn't follow that we should be skeptical about the external world. We can have knowledge—warranted true belief—without 100 percent certainty. And for those who insist that knowledge requires 100 percent certainty, how do they know this with 100 percent certainty? They don't. And no philosopher today takes absolute certainty as the criterion for knowledge.

THE TRUTH ABOUT SKEPTICISM

Many will dismiss truth-claims because of suspicious motives ("the senator was just being political"). But, whatever the motives, are the claims actually *true*? Motives don't prove or disprove a position. But for the total or global skeptic, we may wonder what what may be driving that skeptical enterprise. Even so, the one thing the skeptic doesn't doubt at all is the operation of her mental faculties and the reality of logical laws. Philosopher Dallas Willard noted that a comprehensive skepticism is an affliction of the mind for which treatment is appropriate, but it can't be advanced as a *rational* ground for anything.[1]

Furthermore, contrary to what some may suppose, we don't need to pit *skepticism* against iron-clad *knowledge*, as though we're left in the mire of doubt unless we have airtight, irrefutable beliefs. Rather, think in terms of a spectrum: we can know rock-solid truths like 2 + 2 = 4 and highly probable truths that the universe is expanding, beliefs that are plausible or beyond reasonable doubt—and, at the other end, there are beliefs that are unlikely or even nonsensical.

Is skepticism ever appropriate? Temperamentally, some of us may be more skeptical than others. Regardless, not all skepticism is bad. A *healthy* skepticism and discerning judgment are what wisdom calls for; gullibility and naivete aren't intellectual virtues (Eph. 4:14). Scripture takes a commonsense view on these matters—a "critical realism." While a world exists independently of human minds (realism), we must still engage in sifting, judging, and discerning (critical). For example, in John 7:24, Jesus tells his critics not to judge by mere appearances (naive realism) but to make right and sound judgments (critical realism).

While skepticism may be justified in particular or limited ways (*local* skepticism)—like Jesus's skepticism toward many of the religious leaders of his day (Matt. 23)—a full-blown version (*global* skepticism) is corrosive and destructive to daily life, to a growing faith, and to stable relationships. As with relativists, skeptics still follow inescapable logical laws and trust that their minds are properly functioning—and so aren't fully consistent if they're global skeptics.

THREE COUNTER-SKEPTICAL PRINCIPLES: CHARITABILITY, FIDELITY, CREDULITY

If skepticism shouldn't characterize our lives as Christians, what should? Three principles are helpful here: the principles of *charitability, fidelity*, and *credulity*.

Charitability

Charitability interprets a person's perspective in the most favorable and rational light, all things being equal. Instead of a spirit of dismissiveness, we give others the benefit of the doubt and try to frame their positions with a generous spirit.

Fidelity

The principle of *fidelity* affirms that, despite earthly disappointments, it is utterly fitting to trust our faithful heavenly Father, who did not withhold his only Son in order to redeem us (Rom. 8:32). As supremely good, God is concerned about our spiritual well-being, not our spiritual harm (Matt. 7:8–11), even if we are persecuted for the sake of righteousness. And we can thus be of good cheer, even if we have troubles in this world, because Christ has overcome the world (John 16:33).

Whether one is a full-blown skeptic, simply questions belief in God, or is a fully devoted follower of Christ, each one's *will* is inescapably involved, and each person will choose to privilege *something* over another thing. Where there's a will, there's a way of looking at the world. For example, an agnostic may focus on a particular "defining experience"—perhaps the abandonment of a parent, the loss of a child, or a disturbing encounter with evil. But a skeptical stance will shape or—in this case—distort our experience of God. The experience of evil is not self-interpreting. We can choose to focus differently—on something far more sound and stable than the limitations of our own vantage point. We can concentrate our attention here: on God's revelation in Scripture and in Christ; the more powerful, wide-ranging explanation and resolution to the human problem that they offer; God's deep love for us in sending his Son into a broken world to rescue us and bring us into his family; and assuring us that, through his resurrection victory and a final new creation, God will set all matters right in the end.

So for the believer and unbeliever alike, truth is not merely intellectual. At some point, we must align our wills with a particular vantage point that presupposes our own authority or trust in someone else's. No wonder Jesus said, "My teaching is not Mine, but His who sent Me. If anyone is willing to do His will, he will know of the teaching, whether it is of God or whether I speak from Myself" (John 7:16–17).[2] We can ask: who would be the most authoritative and reliable person to trust—I myself, someone of my own choosing, or Jesus of Nazareth? As we look around at the available, recognized authorities, Jesus readily surpasses the competitors.

Credulity

The commonsense principle of *credulity* affirms that *the everyday world is generally how we experience it to be.* We shouldn't assume our sense experience and day-to-day engagement with the world is an illusion, as some Eastern schools of thought claim. Nor should we reject basic moral intuitions that strike us as obvious and seem so bedrock-solid—like "Torturing babies for fun is wrong" or "Kindness is a virtue rather than a vice." To reject such moral intuitions will mean a complete dismantling of what it means to be human and how we ought to live. In the absence of weighty reasons to do otherwise, we should stick with what is most obviously true.

So we should take such basic experiences as innocent unless proven guilty. Now in some instances, our sense experience could be proven guilty. Perhaps we're taking prescription drugs, but the doctor tells us that these medications will at times impair our judgments, affect our moods, or even cause hallucinations. In such exceptional cases, we shouldn't live according to the principle of credulity. Yet to reject this general guiding principle means that the only alternative is, as William Alston put it, "complete skepticism about experience."[3]

Truly, even the most skeptical will typically follow this realistic principle of common sense without constantly questioning the stuff of everyday life. After all, there's no reason to reject what seems so obvious to us in favor of non-commonsensical alternatives. While it's logically possible we could be wrong, as one philosopher argues, "[How] can I be irresponsible in believing what seems obviously true, even after extensive reflection?"[4]

THE TRUTH ABOUT SECULARISM

We've already seen how "secularism" is its own philosophical outlook. Secularists make assumptions about reality (metaphysics), right and wrong (ethics), and knowledge (epistemology)—the three fundamental pillars of philosophy. That is, "secularism" is a worldview or philosophy of life, which involves a *volitional* stance.

Also, the "secular" isn't some neutral, default realm that's obviously distinct from the "religious." No, it advocates a way of life and thinking, just like any other worldview—and is just as "contestable" or challengeable. Secularists bear a burden of proof because they make all kinds of truth-claims on a vast spectrum of conflicting beliefs: one version of secularism ("humanism") takes for granted human dignity, human rights, objective moral duties, free will, consciousness, and so on; other secularists (e.g., strict or rigid naturalists) will deny all of these. Why one version of secularism and not some other? The bare assertion that the secularist view is true and unassailable is readily challengeable.

Many who claim to be secularists advocate following objective "science" rather than the murkiness of "religion." Yet the person who lives by science alone must ultimately die by science alone. While science is of great value and benefit to humanity, living by science *alone*—"scientism"—kills the human being. Indeed, scientism dismisses all things fundamental to human existence: *design* (purpose and meaning), *discernment* (consciousness, intentionality), *duties* (morality), *dignity* (human worth/personhood), *determination* (free will/moral responsibility), and "*divinity*" (spiritual awareness and the capacity to relate to God). While science has its place, reducing everything to the scientific and the scientifically verifiable leads to a mechanistic, depersonalized, valueless, material view of the world. That is, the world becomes disenchanted. All mystery and meaning are lost; everything we take to be "human" has been stripped away.

Thinkers such as G. K. Chesterton, J. R. R. Tolkien, and C. S. Lewis sought to *re*-enchant the world, to bring back charm and awe and mystery, human dignity, goodness, and beauty. They saw the triune God as holding all things together and making sense of what we know is true about humanity and human experience. In chapter 4, we noted how Chesterton and others came back to the Christian faith because it presented "an intelligible picture of the world" and that with the Christian faith, the disparate pieces of the puzzle came together remarkably well. As we continue to observe, the existence of the triune God proves to be an excellent way to make sense of the way things are.

THE TRUTH ABOUT TRUTH

Relativism, which is at home in a postmodern world, claims that truth is relative to one's own cultural, historical, or individual perspective or preferences. That is, truth isn't *universal* (true for all), and it isn't *objective* (true independent of what people happen to believe). By contrast, the gospel of Jesus reminds us that we can't flourish as human beings if we deny the truth, since it is the truth that sets us free (John 8:32). The truth is that we are sinners in need of redemption, and redemption demands repentance. But relativism denies the existence of any moral standard, of which we have fallen short (Rom. 3:23). This means that redemption is impossible for the relativist so long as she believes there's no sin from which she must be rescued.

How should we define truth? *Truth is a match-up with reality*—a kind of corresponding relationship (truth as *correspondence*). Think of a key perfectly fitting into a lock. If the key is "true," the match-up makes locking and unlocking a door possible. If a story or statement is true, it corresponds or matches up with the way things really are. So *reality is the truth-maker*.

One philosopher compares truth to betting on a horse: the success or failure of one's bet depends on whether the horse wins or not. Winning is independent of one betting. Likewise, a true statement is faithful to reality. Reality confers truth or falsity on a statement. To say that the moon is made of cheese is false because it doesn't match up with reality.

Alternative theories of truth exist in addition to this correspondence view—for example, the *coherence* and *pragmatic* views of truth. In the first case, some might claim that internal coherence guarantees the truth of a belief system (the *coherence* view of truth). Yet it is possible to have two or more coherent systems or worldviews that are completely opposite each other. (This is called the "plurality objection.")

The coherence view is onto something: coherence is crucial for any worldview. But it is more a *criterion* for truth—a possible truth-*indicator*—rather than what *constitutes* truth. If a belief system is not coherent, the beliefs cannot be true, but just because a belief system is coherent, this doesn't guarantee its truth. That is, while belief system X must be coherent to be true, it must have the additional feature of matching up with reality.

Others might claim that truth is what works or produces well-being and human flourishing (the *pragmatic* view of truth). While many things that work are true, some claims are true—say, concerning the present temperatures at the North and South Poles—but these statements don't really "work" or "do" anything to contribute to human flourishing. At bottom, they're true because they match up with reality. A "noble lie" or other falsehoods might be useful for preserving societal order and human flourishing. However, something more than "workability" is needed.

While the truth will always be coherent and will often "work" by leading to human flourishing and happiness, we can't say that whatever worldview is coherent or "works" must be true. Any theory of truth on offer will ultimately be grounded in the way things are, which points us to a correspondence view of truth.

THE TRUTH ABOUT RELATIVISM

By definition, truth is exclusive. It excludes error. But the "true for me but not for you" relativist insists that no one is wrong (unless you disagree with the relativist). The writer Plutarch distinguished between *flatterers* and *friends*. A flatterer will be like a shadow to me—a "yes-man" who changes when I change and complies with everything I say and do. A faithful friend, however, will be impartial in his commitment to the truth and assist me in aligning myself with it. Likewise, the relativist treats truth as a flatterer to shadow or imitate him rather than a friend to assist and correct him as necessary.

Relativists fundamentally deny their own position by their assertions: They insist that it's *wrong* to impose morality on others, that you *ought* to be tolerant, that you *shouldn't* judge, that it's culturally *insensitive* to be ethnocentric. If truth is just a matter of perspective, the relativist is either saying something *trivial* (his own view is a matter of perspective; so why pay attention to it?) or *self-contradictory* (if you disagree with his perspective, you're wrong). In fact, since no one can live consistently as a relativist, the relativist will often slip in moral assertions or rules to make his view sound less radical: "You can do whatever you want, just as long as it doesn't hurt anyone" or "just as long as it's between two consenting adults." Why tack on an absolute rule to a relativistic maxim? The relativist has to borrow moral rules from outside his self-refuting system. Roger Scruton writes: "A writer who says that there are no truths, or that all truth is 'merely relative,' is asking you not to believe him. So don't."[5]

Also, there's no difference between truth-telling and lying for the relativist, since, according to him, what I say is just "my truth" while he has "his truth." And there's no difference between *reality* and *illusion* or a *dream state* for the relativist. Nor is there any difference between *sanity* and *insanity*: the person in a padded cell who thinks he is Napoleon Bonaparte—well, isn't that true for him but not for me? Relativism undercuts the obvious distinction between being in touch with reality and out of touch with it—a serious problem.

To get along, relativists will have to be *selective*: they tend to be relativists about God and ethics—but nothing else. They're not relativists about whether Paris is the capital of France or who was the winner of the last World Cup championship. They don't say that the active ingredients in a medical prescription are "true for the pharmacist but not for me." And when it comes to ethics, if people think that torturing babies for fun or rape is morally neutral, they haven't reflected very deeply on morality. *They don't need an argument; they need help.*

Also, don't ignore the personal reasons why people opt to be relativists. Atheist philosopher John Searle points out: "I have to confess . . . that I think there is a much deeper reason for the persistent appeal of all forms of anti-realism [e.g., relativism] and this has become obvious in the twentieth century: it satisfies a basic urge to power. It just seems too disgusting, somehow, that we should have to be at the mercy of the 'real world.'"[6]

Relativists don't really arrive at their conclusions because they have *reasoned* their way to a relativistic position, and, as Jonathan Swift of *Gulliver's Travels* famously wrote, it's pointless to argue a person out of a position not reasoned into. What's more, relativists will engage in reasoning up to a point, but this task requires the use of fixed logical laws independent of our minds, and it requires trust that our minds are not systematically deceiving us. These two factors serve to undermine relativism.

Motives don't prove or disprove a position, but they can shape a person's position and also give insight about how to approach a person who dismisses objective truth. Perhaps the relativist has a difficult time with *authority* and *trust*. So she just trusts herself and is her own authority. For the Christian, helping the relativist or postmodernist move from distrust to trust will be critical. This requires faithful friendship and being a safe place for the relativist to process honest questions.[7] This is the first barrier to overcome before a post-modernist is properly positioned to consider God's own loving authority and how God has our best interests in mind (Deut. 4:40; 6:24; 10:13; cf. 8:16; 30:9).

To a point, we can sympathize with some of postmodernism's reaction to a certain arrogance and presumed unbiased neutrality in modernistic systems. The twentieth century revealed the great human havoc that was wrought through Nazi concentration camps, Communist gulags (labor camps), and killing fields. We can also appreciate postmodernism's emphasis on human limitation and bias—and that we are never completely free from our own historical context. Yet the foundations of postmodernism and relativism sit on shifting philosophical and theological sands. These viewpoints deny the realities founded on an unshakable kingdom built not by human hands, and in end, these viewpoints turn out to be self-refuting and unlivable. The gospel provides an obvious corrective to truth-denial as well as false authority-claims.

FURTHER READING

Copan, Paul. *"True for You, but Not for Me": Overcoming Objections to Christian Faith*. 2nd ed. Minneapolis: Bethany House, 2009.

Everts, Don, and Doug Schaupp. *I Once Was Lost: What Postmodern Skeptics Taught Us about Their Path to Jesus*. Downers Grove, IL: InterVarsity Press, 2008.

Hicks, Stephen R. C. *Explaining Postmodernism: Skepticism and Socialism from Rousseau to Foucault*. Expanded ed. Roscoe, IL: Ockham's Razor Publishing, 2017.

Moberly, R. W. L. *The Bible in a Disenchanted Age*. Grand Rapids: Baker Academic, 2018.

Moreland, J. P. *Scientism and Secularism*. Wheaton, IL: Crossway, 2018.

Part II

CREATION

O LORD, how manifold are your works!
In wisdom have you made them all;
the earth is full of your creatures.
—Psalm 104:24 ESV

For since the creation of the world His invisible attributes, His eternal power
and divine nature, have been clearly seen.
—Romans 1:20

15 | *Moving toward God:*
   Reasoning, Imagining, Seeking

> The heavens are telling of the glory of God.
>
> —Psalm 19:1

The philosopher Immanuel Kant was struck by "the starry heavens above" and "the moral law within" as pointers to God. Yet the late philosopher of religion John Hick insisted that the universe is "religiously ambiguous." So much for any attempt to "prove" the existence of God![1] Even Kant argued that, despite the seemingly persuasive arguments *for* God, equally compelling opposing arguments are available—what he called "antinomies." And aren't there philosophers who insist that, if God exists, he hides himself quite well? Why isn't he more obvious?

In this chapter, we consider not only God's hiddenness but also the role of arguments for God's existence, prayer, the will, and other such matters.

Divine Hiddenness, the Will, and "Spectator Knowledge"

Evidence and Divine Obviousness

Why is God hidden? Why doesn't he make himself more obvious, revealing himself to everyone with signs and wonders? Perhaps God should have stamped "Made by Yahweh" on every cell and atom, on every tree leaf, and on every heavenly body. After all, doesn't God want everyone to be saved and none to perish (1 Tim. 2:4; 2 Pet. 3:9)?

We mentioned earlier that if God exists and has designed human beings for relationship with himself, then we would expect that indicators of God would be widely available or accessible. Perhaps divinely placed evidences *around* us and our *inner* hardwiring make it easier for us to believe in God. This has been called the *wide accessibility principle*.

But given that a loving divine-human relationship must be uncoerced, "forced love" is a contradiction in terms. We could understand that evidence for God could be easily reinterpreted or resisted. Call this the *easy resistibility principle*.[2]

Blaise Pascal—of "Pascal's Wager" fame—encapsulates both of these two principles in his book *Pensées* (*Thoughts*). God is willing to reveal himself to those who seek him with all their heart, but he remains hidden from those who flee him with all their heart: "He so regulates the knowledge of Himself that He has given signs of Himself, visible to those who seek Him, and not to those who seek Him not. There is enough light for those who only desire to see, and enough obscurity for those who have a contrary disposition."[3]

Think of a radio dial: when it's not properly tuned in to receive frequency transmissions, all we get is static. Likewise, failure to seek God intentionally—with all our heart (Jer. 29:13)—will render us more susceptible to the static and distortion; this will obscure our accurately perceiving God. As the late singer Keith Green put it, "You're so proud of saying you're a seeker, but why are you searching in the dark? You won't find a thing until you soften your heart."[4]

Think about it: Why should God reveal himself to those utterly unwilling to taste and see his goodness? Why should God waste powerful or even perfectly adequate evidence on those who refuse to submit to him as the Cosmic Authority? Even in his own hometown of Nazareth, Jesus refused to do miracles because of the locals' unbelief (Matt. 13:58). Why entertain them with divine pyrotechnics when they don't even care about the direction in which those signs point? No wonder Jesus refused to perform a miracle for the curious Herod, who then "treated him with contempt and mocked him" (Luke 23:7–11). Those who demand signs set themselves up as the authority, demanding that God perform while they sit back and evaluate whether they should respond to the show God has just put on for them. Even if we had amassed mountains of evidence for God, that wouldn't guarantee that we would love and trust him.

When it comes to trust in God, miracles can be a means of encouraging faith: "these [signs have been] written [down] so that you may believe that Jesus is the Christ . . . and . . . have life through his name" (John 20:31). But when it comes to God, evidence can be overrated—as though this guarantees trust in God. The demons have plenty of evidence for God's existence, but they hate God (James 2:19). After Jesus raised Lazarus from the dead (John 11), Jesus's opponents sought to kill not only Jesus but also his resuscitated friend (John 12:10). No wonder Jesus affirmed that even if someone comes back from the dead, the obstinate person won't be convinced (Luke 16:31).

Personal Knowledge

Simply observing evidence without a willingness to appropriate it and to realign one's life accordingly reveals that the problem is moral and personal, not evidential. In fact, it's possible that the more apparent God's presence may be, the more one may come to hate God. Agnostic philosopher of science Michael

Ruse commented: "What I dread is that God might give me what I need rather than what I want."[5]

As we saw earlier about Mortimer Adler, to simply stockpile evidence for God's existence is incomplete without a willingness to embrace God as *my* Lord and *my* God (John 20:28). Evidence without a readiness of will only removes God further from us (John 7:17).

The kind of knowledge God is interested in isn't detached knowledge but rather personal knowledge—an *I-You* kind of knowledge. Detached knowledge is not personal knowledge, which goes beyond "spectator evidence"—believing that "God is"—to actually trusting him as one who "rewards those who seek him" (Heb. 11:6 ESV).[6] The Christian philosopher Paul Moser rightly warns that arguments for God's existence "often leave their inquirers without an authoritative volitional challenge."[7]

Our dedication to seeking God or being willing to see with new eyes can fade as we age. There is something to that saying about not being able to teach an old dog new tricks. As psychiatrist M. Scott Peck observed: "By the end of middle age most people have given up the effort. They feel certain that their maps are complete and their Weltanschauung [worldview] is correct (indeed even sacrosanct), and they are no longer interested in new information. . . . Only a relative and fortunate few continue until the moment of death exploring the mystery of reality, ever enlarging and refining and redefining their understanding of the world and what is true."[8]

It's not too late to call out to God at any stage of life. In fact, according to agnostic philosopher Anthony Kenny, "One thing seems clear. There is no reason why someone who is in doubt about the existence of God should not pray for help and guidance on this topic as in other matters." It's like calling out if you're lost in a cave or stranded on a mountainside, even though you may not be heard. But you *may* be heard. Likewise, calling out to God is a rational act even if you're not sure he exists.[9]

THEISTIC "PROOFS" VERSUS GOOD REASONS OR POINTERS

Consistency and the Demand for Proof

After I had spoken to the Philomathean Society—a debate club at Union College (NY)—a young man came up to me with a challenge: "Prove to me that God exists." I responded, "Well, what would you take as an acceptable level of proof?" The question seemed to throw him off-balance a bit. After a long pause, he admitted, "I'm not sure. I guess I've never thought about that before."

In our day, the word *prove* is certainly overused and abused. For many, "proof" means "absolute"—without the possibility of alternative explanations or possibilities. It means *mathematical certainty* of the 2 + 2 = 4 variety—no wiggle room permitted. But so often those taking this approach don't live up to their own standards. How many beliefs do *they* claim to know with that same level of absoluteness? No doubt they are holding the Christian to a higher standard of provability than they themselves follow for their own beliefs.

In conversations, it can be helpful to keep this in mind. Are critics more charitable with their views but more stingy with yours? Do they say, "Well, it's remotely possible," for themselves but, "Give me absolute proof," for you? Urge them to apply the golden rule of skepticism to their own methods: "Apply the same level of skepticism to your own beliefs as you do to another's." Or we could make it the golden rule of charitability: "Cut slack for another's beliefs the way you cut slack for your own." Otherwise, the situation would look more like a case of "heads I win, tails you lose."

As we've seen, we take a lot of commonsense beliefs for granted that can't be proven the way many insist they should. These bedrock beliefs are properly basic; they arise out of our everyday experiences. Why deny what seems so obvious to us—especially if the alternative doesn't seem even remotely plausible? We should treat those kinds of beliefs as innocent until proven guilty.

As we've seen, reasons for belief in God are available both through rational arguments and our deepest longings (freedom from guilt, the longing for significance). We can think of them in terms of *clues, pointers, signposts, indicators*, and *echoes* of God's voice (Ps. 19:2)—evidences that are available to those who seek. But, as we've seen, this requires an engaged will and a humble heart.

God's Two Books

God has specially, savingly revealed himself in his written Word and in his incarnate Word, Jesus Christ. Yet God has another "book"—not just his *Word* of special revelation but also his book of *works*, his general revelation. God's publicly available self-revelation of his existence and nature ("natural revelation") is found in *creation, conscience, cognition (reason)*, and *commonsense experience*—and even in various *coincidences* in our lives. These can be turned into pointers to God's existence and nature ("natural theology"). The goal of these arguments is to show that their conclusions are more plausible or reasonable than their denials; these reasons for God offer the better or best explanations for important features of our universe or human experience.[10]

The heavens declare God's glory (Ps. 19:1–2), and the creation reveals God's "invisible attributes"—namely, "His eternal power and divine nature," and this renders people "without excuse" (Rom. 1:20). The Creator "did not leave Himself without witness," doing good and giving "rains from heaven and fruitful seasons, satisfying your hearts with food and gladness" (Acts 14:17). Mere intellectual acknowledgment of God's existence is inadequate. Rather we are to "honor Him as God" and "give [him] thanks" (Rom. 1:21). Also, Paul told the Athenians that God is "not far from each one of us" and that all without exception are commanded to repent. This suggests that God's initiating grace has been provided for every person to actually fulfill God's command (Acts 17:27–30).

"Thick" and "Thin" Theism

So where do we take this fact of God's general revelation? When we talk about arguments for God's existence, critics might reply, "This doesn't prove the God of the Bible," or, "This doesn't show that God is *all*-powerful or *all*-knowing." We can readily agree.

In the famous 1947 BBC debate between atheist Bertrand Russell and Christian philosopher Frederick Copleston, the discussion began with a provisional definition of God rather than a full-blown one, and they started to work from there:

> COPLESTON: As we are going to discuss the existence of God, it might perhaps be as well to come to some provisional agreement as to what we understand by the term "God." I presume that we mean a supreme personal being—distinct from the world and creator of the world. Would you agree—provisionally at least—to accept this statement as the meaning of the term "God"?
>
> RUSSELL: Yes, I accept this definition.[11]

Speaking from a Christianized context, Thomas Aquinas's arguments for God—"the Five Ways"—end with conclusions such as "this all men speak of as God" or "this we call God."[12]

We can begin with generalities about God's existence and move to specifics about how he has more specifically revealed himself. So this is something of a two-step process. The general paves the way for the special or particular; some may wonder what makes Jesus so special, but if they first have reason to think God exists, then it is natural to build on this realization. So we don't rest content with a kind of "thin theism"—that a God exists. God's existence is just the first part of the gospel. We must go beyond to a "thick theism"—Trinitarian theism—that is richer, more specific and savingly significant. We should begin with the thin and move toward the thick and fully embracing the gospel.

Consider the face that the universe began to exist and that we have excellent philosophical as well as scientific reasons for thinking so.[13] This points to "something out there" that started and arranged a biofriendly universe; we live in a metaphysically haunted universe that cries out for a God-type explanation.[14] From this thin theism, we press forward and ask: "Has this being 'out there' done anything to help us in our brokenness, moral failure, misery, and suffering?" The most likely candidate here is Jesus of Nazareth, whom so many religions hold in such high regard as a spiritual leader and many "secularists" respect as a moral authority. Why not begin here since so many want to claim or appeal to Jesus in some fashion? What if the Gospels got Jesus right? What if he truly claimed to be the full revelation of God (John 14:9), who came to mend that brokenness, to offer forgiveness, and to restore us to the God from whom we have been alienated? This is indeed good news!

"He Speaks to Me Everywhere"

Yet there's more good news. As one hymn writer put it, "And everywhere that man can be, Thou, God, art present there." Another one wrote, "He speaks to me everywhere." God has already gone ahead of us to make his presence available or apparent to people, even if they aren't familiar with Scripture (Acts 17:27). So when speaking with unbelievers, remember that they *already* have "God experiences." You have a shared awareness of these glimmers of divine light. God's self-revelation can be detected through creation, cognition, conscience, commonsense experience, and "coincidences," and many people can readily identify with these realities:

> *Creation*: We are awed by the amazing, beautiful world around us—from mountainous landscapes to starry skies, from roaring oceans to exquisite flowers and birds that are both colorful in feather and beautiful in song.
>
> *Cognition*: We assume our minds are trustworthy and that the laws of logic are binding on us. We have good reason to trust our minds rather than constantly doubt our memory beliefs ("I had eggs and coffee for breakfast"). Why such confidence if our beliefs are products of nonrational, material forces?
>
> *Conscience*: Even people who seem morally desensitized or calloused (1 Tim. 4:2; cf. Eph. 4:19) likely weren't always that way. We can explore

what it was like for them when they first deeply violated their conscience, before they suppressed their guilt and shame. All of us have an
awareness of falling short of our own standards.

Commonsense Experience: We can be immediately aware that we are thinking selves, that we are morally responsible, that we—as well as other
humans—have dignity.

"Coincidences": How frequently have we escaped death or had other close
calls and near misses, even from serious injury? In large measure, many
of us—through no conscious decision of our own—live a "charmed" life,
which can serve as something of a wake-up call. Psychiatrist Scott Peck
spoke of his own experience, including

> times I just missed being hit by cars while on foot, on a bicycle or
> driving; times when I was driving a car and almost struck pedestri-
> ans or barely missed bike riders in the dark; times when I jammed
> on the brakes, coming to a stop no more than an inch or two away
> from another vehicle; times when I narrowly missed skiing into trees,
> almost fell out of windows; times when a swinging golf club brushed
> through my hair, and so on. What is this?
>
> I suspect the majority will find in their own personal experiences
> similar patterns of narrowly averted disasters, a number of accidents
> that almost happened that is many times greater than the number
> of accidents that actually did happen. Could it be that most of us do
> lead "charmed lives"? Could it really be that the line in the song is
> true: "'Tis grace hath brought me safe thus far"?[15]

It seems that such matters are worth considering as we look at the details of
our own lives. Given these "coincidental" manifestations of grace, small and large,
perhaps there is something "out there" seeking to get our attention, receive our
gratitude, and remind us that our times are not in our own hands (Rom. 1:21).

A Modest Proposal

So we need not fret if specific arguments don't entail the direct conclusion
that the "God of the Bible" exists. They're not intended to conclude this since
we're still reasoning from general revelation—not yet from special revelation.

For example, the cosmological argument for God as the cause of the
universe tells us that an immensely powerful being that we call God, exists.
This argument doesn't inform us that this being is good and worship-worthy,

though. That's the work of the moral argument. Indeed, most of the arguments point to one or a small cluster of features or qualities of God—but not to the full array of them.

However, if it can be shown that these qualities don't contradict each other, then they can be plausibly referring to the *same* being. But why not suggest, as David Hume did, that perhaps a committee of gods created the universe? In reply, we can say that if one God will do, why affirm a bunch of gods? There's no need to multiply entities beyond necessity, as suggested by "Ockham's razor"—the principle of simplicity or economy.

Some might reply that that if the options are "the universe" and "the universe plus God," then we should just settle on "the universe" as the simpler view. But *simple* is one thing; *too simple* is another: yes, it's "simpler" to say the universe just popped into existence out of nothing, but something from nothing is metaphysically impossible—*too* simple. Being can't come from nonbeing. Simpler? Yes. Possible? Not at all. Spontaneous generation—life bursting into existence from nonliving matter—is fantastically fun, but it runs counter to reality and to possibility. The chances of a universe coming from nothing are exactly zero. So to get rid of God in the name of simplicity is to get rid of the very explanatory power required to account for the universe's beginning.

Celestial Teapots, Flying Spaghetti Monsters, and the One True God

Let's apply some of these points to some silly suggestions as an alternative to the traditional God. Bertrand Russell suggested a very British alternative: Why not think a "celestial teapot" is the creator? Richard Dawkins suggested a "flying spaghetti monster." Atheist philosopher Daniel Dennett proposed "Supermanism": maybe it's Superman—not God—who's behind it all.

Such proposals aren't all that impressive. For one thing, physical objects like teapots or spaghetti monsters or even Superman would be part of the physical universe—unlike the one true God who transcends and is distinct from the space-time world.[16] Second, this objection proves nothing; it just reminds us that we can't comprehensively specify the nature of the universe's Creator. The universe came into existence apart from previously existing matter, energy, space, and time; so we can still legitimately conclude that its cause must be personal, powerful, and immaterial—so not a teapot or pasta monster. Third, this objection doesn't undermine the conclusion that the finely tuned universe was designed by a remarkably powerful and intelligent being. Fourth, why think a flying spaghetti monster is a necessary being (one that necessarily exists in all possible worlds)? Something is either necessary (it exists by its very nature without relying on something outside of it) or contingent (it depends on something else for its existence and does not exist by its very nature). Does the flying spaghetti monster's nature require that it necessarily exist? We have no reason to think so.

What about Superman? Well, he was once Super*boy*, who grew up in Kansas in the 1930s, and happens to be weakened by kryptonite. Why think that Superman is an improvement over Captain Marvel, let alone a necessarily existent God who exists in all possible worlds? As Alvin Plantinga points out, "Superman may be faster than a speeding bullet and more powerful than a locomotive, but he is pretty small potatoes when compared with God."[17]

But wait! What if we beef up Superman into Super-dee-duper-man, who is eternal, all-knowing, and all-good, and who exists in all possible worlds? Well, now what we're talking about is a lot less like Superman—or a spaghetti monster or a celestial teapot—and more like the maximally great being of traditional theism.[18]

While successful theistic arguments don't give as many specifics about God, they shouldn't be dismissed as irrelevant or insufficient given what they're designed to do. Rather, they at least present a reasonable basis for believing in the existence of a transcendent being (a) with whom we have to deal, (b) to whom we should be rightly related, and (c) who has a rightful claim on our lives.

ENGAGING THE WHOLE PERSON

As we converse and engage with unbelievers, we should engage the whole person, not simply the intellect. This includes a person's *will*. Since the metanarrative one follows is rooted in a *heart* commitment, it is insufficient to stop with the mere rearrangement of intellectual furniture in a person's mind. The *will* must be engaged as well (John 7:17). We must be willing to come to God and Christ so that we might find life (John 5:40).

When a person's will is unmoved and intellectual arguments seem unpersuasive and irrelevant, sometimes engaging the imagination opens a new pathway to encountering spiritual realities. Consider how Nathan confronted David's sin by telling a powerful, arresting parable that caught him off guard and lowered his defenses (2 Sam. 12:1–7). Jesus likewise told stories, often containing arresting, shocking elements—like a father who runs to embrace his son (cf. Luke 15:11–32). These stories could awaken the imagination and help his hearers rethink their pre-set ideas of God's kingdom: "Could God really be like that?"

Literature professor Louise Cowan became a Christian through reading the classics—Dostoyevsky, Tolstoy, and Shakespeare. She had found that intellectual arguments for the Christian faith didn't connect with her:

Not until a literary work of art awakened my imaginative faculties could the possibility of a larger context than reason alone engage my mind. I had been expecting logical proof of something one was intended to recognize. What was needed was a way of seeing. I had to be transformed in the way that literature transforms by story, image, symbol before I could see the simple truths of the gospel. Above all else this seems to me the chief value of what we call the classics: they summon us to belief. They seize our imaginations and make us commit ourselves to the self-evident, which we have forgotten how to recognize. . . . Even for the things ordinarily considered certain, we moderns require proof. In this state of abstraction, we are cut off from the fullness of reality. Something has to reach into our hearts and impel us toward recognition.[19]

In his *Chronicles of Narnia*, C. S. Lewis intended to use stories to engage the imagination. He wanted to get past the "watchful dragons" of intellectual resistance in order to help people see the world differently. The imagination asks: *What if the world really is this way? What if a loving God really exists and has revealed himself in Jesus after all? Could it be that in Christ all the pieces fall into place?*

As Lewis was coming out of atheism, he was persuaded by his Inkling friends to reimagine how the Jesus of history could be "myth became fact"; Lewis came to see that the fragmentary myths in various religions, cultures, and great literature depicting grace, cleansing, forgiveness, redemption, goodness, and beauty pointed to their historical realization in Jesus of Nazareth.

Personal stories and thoughtful discussions of thought-provoking films and literature may open up new horizons as we engage the contemporary mind. As Louise Cowan discovered, by using the *imagination* to see the world with new eyes, *reason* can then be reengaged to revisit the Christian faith to see how it more clearly addresses our most profound questions and deepest longings than do alternative philosophies of life. Once reason can reevaluate and make judgments about the sense of these answers, finally the *will* is better positioned to respond.[20]

PRAYING AND TRUSTING IN THE LORD

Engaging in the task of giving a reason for the hope that lies within us (1 Pet. 3:15) includes challenging the will, inspiring the imagination, and engaging the intellect.[21] Beyond this, resisting ideas that oppose the gospel and the true knowledge of God require a spirit of prayer and trust in God's power rather than in our own intellectual strength (2 Cor. 10:4–5). To awaken people to the reality of God and their need for him, he can use arguments and evidence just as he can personal crises, calamities, personal relationships, the arts and literature, the fear of death, or the weight of guilt and shame. To present unbelievers with reasons and evidence for faith without trust in God is to work at cross-purposes with the gospel (1 Cor. 2:3–4). We would be engaging in a kind of "cognitive idolatry." No wonder Alvin Plantinga exhorts Christian philosophers, who can easily fall into this trap, with these words: "We Christian philosophers must display more faith, more trust in the Lord; we must put on the whole armor of God."[22]

FURTHER READING

Copan, Paul, and William Lane Craig, eds. *Contending with Christianity's Critics: Answering New Atheists and Other Objectors.* Nashville: B&H Academic, 2009.

Gould, Paul. *Cultural Apologetics: Renewing the Christian Voice, Conscience, and Imagination in a Disenchanted World.* Grand Rapids: Zondervan, 2019.

Plantinga, Alvin. *Knowledge and Christian Belief.* Grand Rapids: Eerdmans, 2015. (Note: This volume summarizes key themes from Plantinga's *Warranted Christian Belief* [New York: Oxford University Press, 2000.])

Walls, Jerry L., and Trent Dougherty. *Two Dozen (or So) Arguments for God: The Plantinga Project.* New York: Oxford University Press, 2018.

Willard, Dallas, ed. *A Place for Truth: Leading Thinkers Explore Life's Hardest Questions: Highlights from the Veritas Forum.* Downers Grove, IL: IVP Books, 2010.

16 | *God—the Best Explanation (I):*
The Problems with Naturalism

> In the beginning God created the heavens and the earth.
>
> —Genesis 1:1

> The earth is full of Your lovingkindness, O LORD.
>
> —Psalm 119:64

"With enemies like that, who needs friends?" Did I write that correctly? Actually, yes—though with some qualifications. What I mean is that, often without knowing it, the believer actually has a lot of allies in the unbelieving world—just as Paul did while in Athens when he called Stoic thinkers to his aid. Of course, these intellectual opponents strongly disagree with us about whether God exists, but they prove to be allies by giving us much good material to make the case for God. As the Beatles sang, "I get by with a little help from my friends."

For one thing, a number of them affirm their respect for the rigorous thinking and intellectual competence of their Christian counterparts. Atheist philosopher Thomas Nagel acknowledged that "some of the most intelligent and well-informed people I know are religious believers."[1] Another atheist philosopher, Quentin Smith, likewise noted the upsurge of theistic—and primarily Christian—philosophers in the second half of the twentieth century: "Realist theists were not outmatched by naturalists in terms of the most valued standards of analytic philosophy: conceptual precision, rigor of argumentation, technical erudition, and an in-depth defense of an original world-view."[2] Second, as we'll see in the next chapter, naturalists often present strong reinforcement to theists, suggesting that the world appears a lot more theistic than naturalistic. But let's first examine naturalism—the leading competitor to the Christian faith in the academy. Then we'll see how God's existence makes better sense of what we know about the universe and our own human experience. This is what has been called "the inference to the best explanation"—a view that provides the greater explanatory scope and power and plausibility and offers the best overall fit. Finally, we'll point out what naturalists themselves say about the shortcomings of their own worldview.

Naturalism's Creed

Three Tenets

Theists affirm that a necessarily existent, maximally great being exists, has created a world distinct from himself, and has made human beings to reflect him and to relate to him. By contrast, the metanarrative of naturalism has three central tenets. Regarding the nature of reality (metaphysics), matter is all that exists—that is, *materialism*. Regarding causation (etiology), all events are physically determined by prior physical events going all the way back to the big bang—that is, *determinism*. Harvard biologist E. O. Wilson illustrates this: "All tangible phenomena, from the birth of the stars to the workings of social institutions, are based on material processes that are ultimately reducible, however long and torturous the sequences, to the laws of physics."[3] Regarding knowledge (epistemology), the scientific method is the *only* source of knowledge—that is, *scientism*. (Some soften the standard by saying that science is the *best* way of knowing; this would be *weak* rather than *strong* scientism.) In the words of Bertrand Russell, "what science cannot discover, mankind cannot know."[4] The implications are deep and dramatic. Naturalism "denies that there are any spiritual or supernatural realities," and it affirms that "anything that exists is ultimately composed of physical components."[5]

As an aside, the term *supernatural* in certain contexts can be rather unhelpful—a term of distraction. It's often a catch-all term that includes all manner of paranormal events or agents like ghosts or witches. This may give the impression of mere superstition and fantasy, and "God" is just tossed into this mix of confusion and misrepresentation.[6]

That said, naturalism essentially rules out the spiritual realm (God, angels), signs and wonders (miracles), the soul, self-determination (free will), survival after death, the significance of humans, a solution to the problem of evil, and salvation for humankind. As one naturalist grimly puts it, naturalism demands "full coverage" and "exacts a terribly high [metaphysical] price."[7]

Naturalism's Two Versions

Naturalist philosopher John Searle embraces this grim picture, and he points out the problem: "There is exactly one overriding question in contemporary philosophy. . . . How do we fit in? . . . How can we square this self-conception of ourselves as mindful, meaning-creating, free, rational, etc., agents with a universe that consists entirely of mindless, meaningless, unfree, non-rational, brute physical particles?"[8]

Another naturalist, Huw Price, points out what exactly is under threat: "Like coastal cities in the third millennium, important areas of human discourse seem threatened by the rise of modern science. . . . The regions under threat are some of the most central in human life—the four Ms, for example: Morality, Modality, Meaning, and Mental."[9]

Perhaps we should unpack these four Ms under assault by strict naturalism.

Naturalistic Illusions

Morality: Human dignity, moral duties, right and wrong, virtuous character.

Modality: Free will, moral responsibility (as opposed to determinism—no modalities or alternative possibilities).

Meaning: Objective meaning rooted in a purpose to life, as opposed to nihilism (meaninglessness).

Mental: The soul or self, (self-)consciousness, inner (first-person) awareness, intentionality, life after death.

It seems that naturalism ultimately denies what is so obvious and fundamental to us as humans. And even if we intellectually deny the four Ms, we tend to live our day-to-day lives as though they do. At any rate, this stark form of naturalism shreds to bits what we humans have taken for granted about our very humanity.

Some naturalists say that maybe we don't have to go that far with such a strict, grim naturalism. As it turns out, there are two major versions of naturalism on offer. One philosopher, Wilfrid Sellars (1912–1989), distinguished between what he called the "scientific image" and the "the manifest image." The "scientific image" refers to this more rigid—and bleak—naturalism. The "manifest image," however, is a broader naturalism that is much more humanity-affirming; it includes human dignity, personal moral responsibility, purpose, duties, beauty, consciousness, and so on. This "manifest" version is what seems most obvious or commonsensical to us—a view that doesn't require us to throw out what seems central to our humanity.

We'll come back to concerns with strict naturalism. But what do strict naturalists think of broad naturalism? Though not often articulated, they assume that some metaphysical cheating or inappropriate borrowing is going on here: the broad naturalists have gone soft. They're latching on to something that looks more like theism. Morality, consciousness, and personal responsibility are just an illusion to enhance survival and reproduction. Soft naturalists aren't being "scientific" enough. They have detached themselves from the deep metaphysical roots of naturalism.

Strict naturalist John Searle tells it straight: if you think that you got married because you were consciously in love with your partner or that you spoke up at a meeting because you consciously disagreed with the presenter, "you are mistaken in every case. In each case the effect was a physical event and therefore must have an entirely physical explanation."[10] So Searle, who suggests that he himself can't help believing what he does, informs us that free choice is just an illusion.

For the strict naturalist, the same goes for moral duties, free will (personal responsibility), beauty, and purpose:

More Naturalistic Illusions

Morality: This is a "corporate illusion" that has been "fobbed off on us by our genes to get us to cooperate" (philosopher Michael Ruse).[11]

Free will: "Your sense of personal identity and free will" is nothing but "the behavior of a vast assembly of nerve cells and their associated molecules" (what geneticist Francis Crick calls "the astonishing hypothesis").[12]

Beauty: It suggests a "deeper reality" and points to a "religious resolution, were it not to be an illusion" (philosopher Anthony O'Hear).[13]

Purpose: Naturalistic Darwinian evolution produces "the illusion of purpose which so strikes all who contemplate nature" (zoologist Richard Dawkins, who himself switches positions when it comes to everyday life: he's "a passionate anti-Darwinian when it comes to politics and how we should conduct our human affairs").[14]

Concerns with Naturalism Proper

Strict naturalism—or naturalism proper—isn't without its problems. They are related to *creedalism*, to *commonsensicalism*, and to *self-exceptionalism*.

Creedalism

Strict naturalists stick with their creed, and they attempt to follow it to the letter. But basic questions arise when we examine the threefold creed of naturalism—*materialism*, *determinism*, and *scientism*.

Regarding *materialism*, how can one show that matter or nature is all there is? To insist that only matter exists is a position of arbitrary trust. Harvard biologist Richard Lewontin insists that our starting point is that all causes are physical or material ones, and this materialism is absolute, no matter how irrational it may sound to others. If you don't accept this materialistic worldview, perhaps you will "allow a Divine Foot in the door"—something that can ruin the practice of science.[15] But the assumption that the physical is all the reality there is is arbitrary and without evidence, and it wrongheadedly excludes God from consideration—including the possibility of God as the originator of the physical universe ("I don't know what caused the universe's existence, but it wasn't God").

As for *determinism*, isn't the naturalist's conclusion about the reality of naturalism produced in him by past events and forces over which he has no control? One can't actually *know* that determinism is true. Even if it is true, one believes it by the sheer luck of prior physical causes that produced this belief. How can we confidently draw rational conclusions from beliefs caused by nonrational forces?

In terms of *scientism*, to say that only science can give us knowledge is itself a *philosophical* assumption, not the conclusion of scientific observation. How can one scientifically prove that all knowledge must be scientifically provable?

Commonsensicalism

What about the problem of *commonsensicalism* and naturalism? In the words of Alvin Plantinga, Hume the skeptic "thought there is something *wrong* in believing the things we ordinarily do."[16] But why should we deny them? Why repudiate the fundamentals of our humanity and our experience that seem so utterly inescapable to us? Shouldn't we give the benefit of the doubt to common sense—unless we have overpowering reasons to deny it?

So the four Ms we've discussed shouldn't be rejected in the absence of the strongest reasons to the contrary. Let's take the M of Morality. If a worldview demands that I deny the reality of evil, well, so much the worse for that worldview. If we must choose between the reality of evil and a worldview that denies it, the worldview (or at least that part of it) has to go.

Consider another M—the Mental. Broad naturalist Thomas Nagel has put forth a blistering criticism of strict naturalist Daniel Dennett. Why? Because Dennett calls consciousness an "illusion." Nagel considers this utterly confused, because one must be *conscious* in order to experience an *illusion*! Dennett's view requires us to "turn our backs on what is glaringly obvious." It's like the question in the 1933 Marx brothers film, *Duck Soup*: "Who you gonna believe—me or your lyin' eyes?"[17]

Self-Exceptionalism

We are rightly suspicious of people who arbitrarily make themselves the exceptions to the rules they demand everyone else to follow. We repeatedly see the self-exceptionalism problem under naturalism—a theme related to commonsensicalism: How does the strict naturalist detect "illusion" and mere "appearance" so clearly while everyone else is ongoingly duped into thinking morality, consciousness, beauty, and free will are real? Why aren't strict naturalists under the same "illusion" as the rest of us? How would they even know the difference between illusion and reality? How have they been able to rise above the physical forces that keep the rest of us hoodwinked by illusions?

Actually, these self-excepting claims of strict naturalists nicely illustrate how humans can make free decisions or draw rational conclusions that aren't determined by mindless physical forces. All too often, strict naturalists act like insider-information Gnostics: they claim to have an insight made known to only a select few but kept hidden from the rest of us commoners. They consider themselves "above the law" in the natural world.

MISCELLANEOUS QUESTIONS ABOUT AND CONCERNS WITH BROAD NATURALISM

Let's circle back around to broad naturalism. Though we can commend its affirmation of the inescapability of our humanity, it turns out to be too *theistic*, too *transcendent*, and too *tightfisted* to be sustained as naturalism.

Too Theistic

This broad version isn't the naturalism of Searle and Dennett. But it looks suspiciously like theism—minus God. It wants to hang on to the four Ms that are far more readily explained by God's existence—features naturally at home in a theistic world but not in a naturalistic one. Broad naturalists help themselves to the features of our humanity that make great sense if a personal God—particularly the triune God—exists. That they want to hang on to these is understandable since they too bear the image of God. So they find various commonsense features of our humanity inescapable: personhood, duties, choice, morality, consciousness, personal responsibility, and awareness of beauty. Yet these things don't square well with the valueless, impersonal, unguided, deterministic material processes from which these things supposedly came.

Naturalists of both stripes will regularly appeal to science and the physical to dismiss the idea of an immaterial being like God. The only persons that exist are physical, they claim. So God is ruled out based on "scientific observation." We should follow the hard sciences rather than resort to "spooky" explanations like God or the soul. But this is to get things exactly backwards. *Scientific knowledge requires the nonphysical—the mental or inner subjective experience—to get study of the physical off the ground.* It's because we are minds or selves or souls, which enables us to actually understand the physical world. As the philosopher Richard Fumerton writes, "Scientific knowledge . . . ultimately rests on the kind of knowledge about which the naturalist is suspicious."[18] To understand the physical, we need the nonphysical mind—the mental.

Too Transcendent

Another concern with broad naturalism is this: as it moves away from the stark implications of naturalism, it moves in the direction of the transcendent—to a *non*natural realm "above" or beyond nature. Atheist philosopher Erik Wielenberg recognizes that a moral realm doesn't fit within the natural realm but must exist beyond it. Moral facts can't be explained naturalistically. These eternally existing moral facts are *non*natural, but he makes the curious claim that God has nothing to do with them.

Notice that Wielenberg has to go *beyond* the natural world to account for them.[19] This is looking a lot like Plato's transcendent realm of "forms"—particularly, "the Good." These forms are distinct from the physical world. But to move in a transcendent ("nonnatural") direction means we're on our way to theism. We'll come back to Wielenberg later, but it is worth noting for now this philosophical balancing act: he finds himself in a Platonic-like transcendent realm while trying to avoid two extremes: the harsh implications of naturalism on the one hand and the connection between God and morality on the other. The existence of God greatly helps us to avoid this kind of metaphysical dancing.

Too Tightfisted

Finally, broad naturalism is tightfisted: it won't allow God to do any explanatory work, however natural the fit is between God and the phenomena we take for granted. For example, it's not hard to see a connection between creaturely consciousness and a supremely conscious being—or between human dignity and a supremely valuable being. Yet we're told that *only* nature can—or is permitted to—account for morality, beauty, purpose and meaning, personhood, consciousness, agency (choice), and rationality.

That's way too stingy. For one thing, God's existence actually helps explain what naturalism fails to—such as the universe's beginning and fine-tuning for life and the production of life from nonliving matter. Nature can't be ultimate since *nature itself* had a beginning. What's more, the natural order is governed by mathematically and physically precise conditions that make the *existence* of scientists and their *efforts* possible.

Second, why must we be forced to choose between natural processes and God's existence, as many broad naturalists insist? Why couldn't God use the evolutionary process to bring about moral beings with capacities to reason and make moral choices that correspond to a preexisting moral realm, which is rooted in God's very good character?

Behold, I tell you a mystery: an atheist like Wielenberg tries to grasp an exceedingly thin reed to hold his system together. He trusts absolutely that an astonishing cosmic accident took place, which helps ground his moral system: Over billions of years, *morally valuable* creatures would eventually evolve from *valueless* processes, and their moral understanding and evident duties would match up precisely with eternally preexisting *moral facts*, which seemed to have anticipated their arrival! Why not the simpler, more elegant route—namely, that a supremely valuable, personal being has created valuable, morally responsible, finite agents?

FURTHER READING

Copan, Paul, and Charles Taliaferro. *The Naturalness of Belief: New Essays on Theism's Rationality*. Lanham, MD: Lexington Books, 2018.

Goetz, Stewart, and Charles Taliaferro. *Naturalism*. Grand Rapids: Eerdmans, 2008.

Taliaferro, Charles. *Philosophy of Religion*. Oxford: Blackwell, 2009.

Trigg, Roger. *Beyond Matter: Why Science Needs Metaphysics*. West Conshohocken, PA: Templeton, 2015.

17 | *God—the Best Explanation (II):*
The Naturalists Are Declaring the Glory of God

> The heavens are telling of the glory of God;
> And their expanse is declaring the work of His hands.
> Day to day pours forth speech,
> And night to night reveals knowledge.
> There is no speech, nor are there words;
> Their voice is not heard.
> Their line has gone out through all the earth,
> And their utterances to the end of the world.
>
> —Psalm 19:1–4

The psalmist wrote, "Let the righteous smite me in kindness and reprove me; / It is oil upon the head; / Do not let my head refuse it" (Ps. 141:5). For our purposes, the smitings of the naturalist can serve to sharpen the believer's thinking about God and other matters. But in some of their claims, naturalists also lend support to belief in God, as we shall soon see. To a helpful degree, they are "telling the glory of God" and "declaring the work of His hands." But before proceeding, we should consider what makes for a more satisfactory explanation as we compare naturalism and theism.

ASSESSING OUTLOOKS

The grand story of naturalism rejects God and the rest of the biblical story—humanity's fall into sin, Christ's saving work, his bodily resurrection, and life beyond the grave. But how do we fairly assess competing theories like naturalism and theism? We would suggest that the worldview likely to be true is the one more *natural, unifying,* and *basic* than the alternatives (think "nub"). We've already gotten some hints, but perhaps we should focus a bit more on this.

More Natural

By *natural,* we don't mean "explicable by natural processes alone." For one thing, the beginning of the universe couldn't be explained by natural processes, since natural processes came about through the universe's beginning. The origin of the universe means the beginning of matter, energy, space, and time. Given naturalism and theism, which features of the universe and human experience will more naturally, least surprisingly, more probably emerge?

By *more natural*, we mean least surprising, most easily fitting, or most at home within a particular worldview. Atheist Erik Wielenberg optimistically asserts: "From valuelessness, value sometimes comes."[1] But to assert is one thing; to justify is another. On what basis does he make this wishful claim? The answer seems to be that Wielenberg *hopes* that this is somehow the case. But why think that value—including personhood, dignity, moral agency, free will, and moral duties—could emerge from valueless material processes? This is highly unlikely in a godless universe but highly probable if a good God exists. And why think *morally valuable* creatures should emerge? Why not say that morally indifferent creatures could more likely emerge instead?

A further problem remains: if we are the products of deterministic physical processes, as Wielenberg believes, then why should we even trust our minds if our very thoughts have been produced by physical forces over which we have no control? As it turns out, morally valuable creatures, moral duties, and even trustworthy minds *aren't* at home in Wielenberg's world. They are very much at home in a theistic world, however.

More Unifying

By *more unifying*, we mean that a theory or worldview brings greater coherence, interconnection, and unity. We can ask: which story—naturalism or theism—brings together a range of phenomena like the beginning and fine-tuning of the universe, consciousness, rationality, beauty, free will, human dignity, and moral duties?

Now these features of reality are really quite different from each other: consciousness has very distinct properties from moral value or beauty or rationality. What brings all of these features together? On top of these features is the question of how this fits together with the production and fine-tuning of a universe. The existence of a maximally great being readily accounts for the anchor for all of these distinct features in the world. The (broad) naturalist, by contrast, will have to anchor morality, meaning, modality, and the mental (the four Ms) in nonmoral, meaningless, deterministic, nonconscious, physical stuff. Of course, no physics textbook describing the properties of matter will include value, meaning, or consciousness. Beyond all of this, we still need further explanation of how a universe could originate from nothing and be so biofriendly.

More Basic

A final criterion is *basicality*: Is the feature in question "just there" (a brute fact), or can one worldview offer a deeper explanation than others? In the aforementioned Russell-Copleston BBC debate, Russell was asked about the cause of the finite universe, to which he replied: "I should say that the universe is just there, and that's all."[2] But surely a deeper explanation is necessary. The universe is *contingent*; it didn't have to exist. If the universe—matter, energy, space, and time—began to exist a finite time ago, then some *more basic*, independent cause brought it into being.

ASSESSING PHILOSOPHIES: FIVE-POINT CALCULUS OF WORLDVIEWS

We've just looked at criteria for assessing the greater plausibility of two competing theories or worldviews—in this case, theism versus naturalism. The more likely one is *the more natural, unifying, and basic* ("nub"). Of course, this applies to other worldviews as well.

In this section, however, we can expand on this question. To assess which worldview is more likely true, perhaps we can reform things a bit by offering a more specific five-point calculus. This is another kind of TULIP acrostic: Truth, Usefulness, Logic, Integrity, and Productivity. Another way of putting it would be to ask if the worldview is *factual, practical, logical, moral*, and *fertile*.

This "calculus" isn't some mathematical algorithm or formula guaranteed to produce a certain belief-outcome. After all, our trust is in the Lord. Yet keep in mind that all kinds of personal considerations, experiences, and judgments will be included in one's approach to the God question (e.g., how much decisive weight we give the problem of evil). But these criteria are a helpful, nonarbitrary guide to think through the consistency of our philosophy of life.

A little reflection reveals that these categories don't carry equal weight. Coherence and logic are more fundamental and decisive than practicality or livability: if a worldview or story is to have a hope of being true, it must be logical and coherent—although, ideally, logic and livability would come together. Assuming a worldview is coherent, if we can't live out that worldview, perhaps we need to rethink the truthfulness of that worldview. As world religions scholar Huston Smith suggested, we humans seem to require "eco-niches"—a grid or worldview that enables us to make sense of reality and human experience. This kind of fit makes sense if we've been made in God's image: being human, we'll seek a sense of place and meaning rather than feeling isolated and anxious—likely signs of a poor fit between our minds and reality. A good fit will be evidenced by the world's making sense.³

So here is something of a working list to offer some general guidance for any worldview.

- **Truth: Is it *factual*?** Does the worldview take seriously empirical facts from history and science? On this score, the Christian faith is certainly checkable, emphasizing the importance of signs, eyewitnesses, and historical truth—things that were "not done in a corner" (Acts 26:26). For example, it insists that if Jesus's tomb was not empty, we ought to abandon the faith (1 Cor. 15:32).
- **Usefulness: Is it *practical*?** Does it take *commonsense* or *everyday experience* seriously? Can it be consistently lived out, or do the practicalities of life defy it? If I claim that the physical world is an illusion, for instance, I still must live as though it is not. Or is it like Richard Dawkins's naturalistic Darwinism, which he admits can't be lived out when it comes to politics, ethics, and getting along in society?
- **Logic: Is it *logical*?** Does the worldview take *reason* seriously? Does it value coherence? Or is it self-contradictory—like relativism, which presumes to be absolutely true for everyone? Presumably, postmodernists who insist that "coherence" is merely a human construction will nevertheless attempt to give a coherent reason for thinking this! And with strict naturalism, we've seen the problem with Daniel Dennett's calling consciousness an illusion: to experience an illusion *requires* consciousness. Some will ask about the Christian faith: what of the presumed contradiction between a good God and the problem of evil? We'll look at this more closely in part 3.
- **Integrity: Is it *moral*?** Does the worldview take seriously right and wrong as well as good and evil? Does the worldview consider Hitler's, Stalin's, and Mao Tse-tung's regimes to be evils? Or does the worldview deny the reality-status of moral truths like *Torturing babies for fun is wrong*? If it denies the reality of such evils as well as moral duties and virtues, they haven't probed deeply enough into the nature of reality and their own humanity. Now a theory may claim to be "just following science," but science can't tell us whether humans have dignity and worth and moral oblgations. That's not the domain of science.
- **Productivity: Is it *fertile*?** Does the worldview expand our horizons to offer robust and fruitful explanations for a broad range of phenomena? Like C. S. Lewis said, does it help us to "see everything else"? Does it

illuminate and make sense of key features of the universe and human experience, including our deepest longings for freedom from guilt and shame, for justice and beauty, for significance and security? Does it help address the deep moral gap between the virtuous ideal and our failure to live up to it?

CHARTING THE DIFFERENCES

The following chart focuses on key features of the universe and of human experience against the metaphysical backdrop or "furniture" of theism and naturalism. As we can see, theism affords the best or most natural fit with these phenomena. For example, is it more probable that consciousness emerged from nonconscious matter or from consciousness? As we go down the list, the phenomena in question fit beautifully into a theistic framework; a naturalistic context is far less probable.

Theism versus Naturalism

Phenomena We Observe, Assume, or Recognize	Theistic Context	Naturalistic Context
Things exist. (Yet why does anything exist at all?)	God's very nature requires his existence. God necessarily exists and is the cause of all other reality.	The physical universe's parts are all contingent and thus cannot be self-existent.
(Self-)consciousness exists.	God is supremely self-aware/self-conscious.	Consciousness was produced by mindless, nonconscious processes.
Personal beings exist.	God is a personal being.	The universe was produced by impersonal processes.
We believe we make free personal decisions/choices, assuming humans are accountable for their actions.	God is spirit and a free being who can freely choose to act (e.g., to create or not).	We have emerged from materialistic, deterministic processes beyond our control.

Phenomena We Observe, Assume, or Recognize	Theistic Context	Naturalistic Context
Secondary qualities (colors, smells, sounds, tastes, textures) exist throughout the world.	God is the ultimate source of pleasure who gives capacities to his creatures to enjoy or take pleasure in experiencing the world around us.	The universe was produced from colorless, odorless, soundless, tasteless, textureless particles and processes.
We trust our senses and rational faculties as generally reliable in producing true beliefs. The world is knowable.	A God of truth and rationality exists.	Naturalistic evolution is only interested in survival and reproduction, not truth. So, many beliefs would help us survive (e.g., the belief that humans have dignity and worth) but be completely false.
Human beings have intrinsic value/dignity and rights.	God is the supremely valuable being.	Human beings were produced by valueless processes.
Objective moral values/duties exist.	God's character is the source of goodness/moral values, and his commands constitute human duties ("ought").	The universe was produced by nonmoral processes. Things just are what they are.
The universe began to exist a finite time ago—without previously existing matter, energy, space, or time.	A powerful, previously existing God brought the universe into being without any preexisting material. (Here, something emerges from something.)	The universe came into existence from nothing by nothing. (Here, something comes from nothing.)
First life emerged.	God is a living, active being.	Life somehow emerged from nonliving matter.

Phenomena We Observe, Assume, or Recognize	Theistic Context	Naturalistic Context
The universe is finely tuned for human life (known as "the Goldilocks effect"—the universe is "just right" for life).	God is a wise, intelligent Designer.	All the cosmic constants just happened to be right; given enough time and/or many possible worlds, a finely tuned world eventually emerged.
We (tend to) believe that life has purpose and meaning. For most of us, life is worth living.	God has created/designed us for certain purposes (to love him, others, etc.); when we live them out, our lives find their true meaning and greater enrichment.	There is no cosmic purpose, blueprint, or goal for human existence.
Real evils—both moral and natural—exist and take place in the world.	Evil's definition assumes a design plan (how things ought to be but are not) or standard of goodness by which we judge something to be evil. God is a good Designer; his existence supplies the crucial moral context to make sense of evil.	Atrocities, pain, and suffering just happen. This is just how things are—with no plan or standard of goodness to which things ought to conform.
We have deep longings for security (relationship), significance (purpose), forgiveness and relief from guilt, and freedom from fear of death.	God has created us to find our satisfaction in him.	These longings are merely biological, being hardwired into us by naturalistic processes to enhance survival and reproduction.

We've seen here that God's existence—particularly, that of the God of Scripture—offers a better fit to what we know than does naturalism. It also offers a better fit than Eastern philosophies and traditional religions that generally promote an impersonal Ultimate Reality—or even none at all. A good, powerful, wise God better helps us to "see everything else."

A Little Help from Our Naturalistic Friends

We've seen how the existence of consciousness, beauty, free will, personhood, rationality, moral duties, and human value—not to mention the beginning and fine-tuning of the universe—is hardly surprising if a good, personal, rational, creative, powerful, and wise God exists. However, these phenomena are quite startling and outrageously improbable if they are the result of deterministic, valueless, nonconscious, nonrational, material processes.

But there's more: many naturalists themselves contribute to the case for God's existence by acknowledging the disconnect between a naturalistic universe and these phenomena under discussion. That is, they acknowledge the unnaturalness of naturalism and thus help make a good case for God's existence. The naturalists are declaring the glory of God!

I've written elsewhere about this topic,[4] but we'll briefly review what certain naturalistic thinkers have to say about a range of phenomena.

The World's Existence

The German philosopher Gottfried Leibniz posed the question: "Why is there something rather than nothing at all?" Here, the issue isn't the beginning of the universe but rather the *fact* of existence—why anything exists at all. Naturalists have gone on record to note their astonishment. Oxford philosopher Ludwig Wittgenstein would periodically be awestruck by the fact that something exists: "*I wonder at the existence of the world.*" Indeed, he would remark, "How extraordinary that anything should exist!" or, "How extraordinary that the world should exist!"[5]

Another naturalist, Michael Ruse, says the existence of planets, suns, organisms, and humans is "a pretty remarkable state of affairs." He asks, "Why is there any of it? . . . One doesn't expect something like this, with its astounding interdependency and innumerable complex parts functioning in service of the whole, to just happen."[6]

The universe is completely comprised of contingent or dependent things. Why do they exist? We are forced to consider something independent of the universe, something on which all these contingent things depend.

The Beginning of the Universe

The big bang is an event that takes us back 13.8 billion years, to the universe's beginning. Astrophysicists John Barrow and Joseph Silk confess that this looks like "the traditional metaphysical picture of creation out of nothing, for it predicts a definite beginning to events in time, indeed a definite beginning to time itself."[7] Because they reject the existence of God, their only option is to confess that something came from nothing: "What preceded the event called the 'Big Bang'? . . . The answer to our question is simple: nothing."[8] Of course, this last point is problematic since being can't come into existence from nonbeing.

The late atheist William Rowe acknowledged something similar. He said that "the emergence of the Big Bang theory of the origin of the universe has given new weight to an argument for the existence of some sort of creator."[9]

Fine-Tuning and Design

Stephen Hawking and Leonard Mlodinow have pointed out the "tailor-made" universe that leaves little room for alteration. We are alive by virtue of "a series of startling coincidences in the precise details of physical law." Indeed, the "extremely fine-tuned" laws of nature and most of the universe's fundamental constants, if only modestly altered, would render the universe inhospitable to life.[10]

Even when it comes to biological organisms, the language of design seems to be inescapable. Stanford naturalistic philosopher of science Timothy Lenoir: "Teleological [design/purposive] thinking has been steadfastly resisted by modern biology. And yet, in nearly every area of research biologists are hard pressed to find language that does not impute purposiveness to living forms."[11] For example, Richard Dawkins asserts: "The machine code of the genes is uncannily computer-like."[12] Nobel Prize–winning biologist Francis Crick acknowledged that, given many necessary conditions for biological life, "the origin of life appears at the moment to be almost a miracle."[13] Other biologists acknowledge that it is "virtually impossible to imagine how a cell's machines could have formed spontaneously as life first arose."[14]

Consciousness

The reality of consciousness or awareness is commonsensical and undeniable; the very act of rejecting it would require a conscious agent. We've observed that a naturalistic universe doesn't have the resources to produce consciousness—what naturalist Colin McGinn calls "a radical novelty in the universe"— something utterly unpredictable given all that preceded it.[15] The existence of a supremely aware being, however, makes this highly likely. Philosopher Geoffrey Maddell points out that "the emergence of consciousness, then is a mystery, and one to which materialism signally fails to provide an answer."[16]

Another naturalist, Michael Lockwood, says he is a "materialist"—that consciousness simply reduces to—is nothing more than—brain activity. Yet he admits that "no description of brain activity of the relevant kind . . . is remotely capable of capturing what is distinctive about consciousness. So glaring, indeed, are the shortcomings of all the reductive programmes currently on offer, that I cannot believe that anyone with a philosophical training, looking dispassionately at these programmes, would take any of them seriously for a moment, were it not for a deep-seated conviction that current physical science has essentially got reality taped, and accordingly, *something* along the lines of what the reductionists are offering *must* be correct."[17] He admits that consciousness reveals the limits of what science can explain, that our understanding of matter appears to be woefully deficient, and the consciousness appears to be "an occult power" that lies beyond our grasp to explain.[18]

Rationality and Free Will/Agency

We take moral responsibility for granted—our penal and judicial systems assume it. So the excuse of "My genes made me do it, your honor!" wouldn't cut it in a court of law. This presumed responsibility stands in contradiction to the determinism of many naturalists. They have acknowledged that, as presently understood, natural processes couldn't "produce a being that is truly free to make choices" (the late Cornell biologist William Provine).[19] Given naturalism, it's hard not to conclude that we're "helpless" and "not responsible" for our actions (Thomas Nagel).[20]

What's true about our will is also true about rationality. Linguist Noam Chomsky claims that it's "just blind luck"—a "lucky accident"—that our beliefs happen to be true (i.e., conforming more or less to the way the world actually works).[21] Likewise, Stanford philosopher Richard Rorty insisted that naturalism requires that "every sound or inscription which will ever be uttered" by humans is utterly predictable based on the physical micro-processes at work within them.[22] This would mean that Chomsky's and Rorty's assertions of these truths are "just blind luck" and the result of physical processes rather than the workings of properly functioning rational minds aimed at the truth.

Beauty

When we discussed the attributes of God, we briefly touched on the topic of beauty. Let's expand a bit here.

Some claim that "beauty is in the eye of the beholder." We could call this the beauty-as-*feel* view. My insistence that "the forest is beautiful" only means "the forest inspires me and fills me with awe." Beauty isn't a characteristic of the object itself; it is simply a reflection of my feelings—my emotional response to that object (aesthetic nonrealism).

However, there is the beauty-as-*real* view (aesthetic realism). Beauty is a true property or characteristic of the object—whether a tropical sunset or a particular building, work of art, or piece of literature. Niagara Falls or the paintings of Rembrandt van Rijn and Vincent van Gogh can be called beautiful, whereas a junkyard or a garbage dump is not.

Real beauty exists. Why think this? First, *we have disagreements* about whether a certain piece of art is beautiful or tacky—or somewhere in between. This very fact indicates that beauty is objective and that artistic standards exist; these aren't a matter of our feelings. Real disagreement implies real beauty. After all, what's the point of disagreeing about our feelings? Second, real beauty makes sense of *aesthetic training and expertise*. What a huge waste of time it would be to get training in art criticism if beauty is merely a matter of feelings. This goes against common sense. Third, real beauty makes the best sense of *commonly agreed-upon or even universal claims* concerning the beauty of certain objects. Consider the seven wonders of the natural world like the Grand Canyon—or human-created wonders of the world like the Taj Mahal. The reality of beauty includes consideration of the universal attestation of literature or film as *humorous*, *poignant*, *terrifying*, or *enchanting*. Yes, these describe reader or audience responses, but they also describe characteristics of the literature or films themselves.[23] Science takes seriously not only order but also beauty. Scientists recognize that certain theories are beautiful or elegant—and thus to be preferred over clunky or inelegant ones.

Various naturalists recognize not only the reality of beauty but also that it doesn't easily fit within a naturalist universe. Nobel Prize–winning physicist Steven Weinberg acknowledges: "Sometimes nature seems more beautiful than strictly necessary."[24] Naturalistic philosopher Anthony O'Hear points out: "In experiencing beauty we feel ourselves to be in contact with a deeper reality than the everyday."[25] In fact, he notes in theistic tones, "Art can seem revelatory."[26] Paul Draper, an agnostic philosopher, recognizes that "theism is supported by the fact that the universe contains an abundance of beauty. . . . A beautiful universe, especially one containing beings that can appreciate that beauty, is clearly more likely on theism than on naturalism and so is evidence favoring theism over naturalism."[27]

Objective Moral Values

Philosopher Joel Marks tried valiantly to be moral atheist (a "broad naturalist"). However, it dawned on him that, to be consistent, he would have to give up on morality because "atheism implies amorality." No God means no morality.[28] Oxford philosopher J. L. Mackie similarly acknowledged the "oddness" of morality in a natural world; it's highly improbable that moral properties could have "arisen in the ordinary course of events"—unless there was a God to bring this about.[29]

When it comes to the value of human beings and how they contrast with other biological creatures, even naturalists will note how humans stand apart. Dawkins acknowledges that humans "have the power to defy the selfish genes of our birth. . . . We, alone on earth, can rebel against the tyranny of the selfish replicators."[30] Dennett sings a similar tune: "Like other animals, we have built-in desires to reproduce and to do pretty much whatever it takes to achieve this goal. . . . But we also have creeds, and the ability to transcend our genetic imperatives. This fact makes us different."[31] We could add other items that illustrate the naturalness of belief in God and cite naturalists who lend support to theism as well as indicate just how unnatural naturalism is in accounting for these features of reality.

Just as Moses was "educated in all the learning of the Egyptians" (Acts 7:22) and as Daniel and his three friends had shown "intelligence in every branch of wisdom" in Babylon (Dan. 1:4), we can benefit from the learning of naturalists in the academy, who often help supply surprisingly helpful resources of theism. And as we've seen, rather than pitting natural processes against the idea of God, we recognize that God uses natural processes in the accomplishment of his purposes.

FURTHER READING

Copan, Paul, and Charles Taliaferro. *The Naturalness of Belief: New Essays on Theism's Rationality*. Lanham, MD: Lexington Books, 2018.

Goetz, Stewart, and Charles Taliaferro. *Naturalism*. Grand Rapids: Eerdmans, 2008.

Taliaferro, Charles. *Philosophy of Religion*. Oxford: Blackwell, 2009.

Trigg, Roger. *Beyond Matter: Why Science Needs Metaphysics*. West Conshohoken, PA: Templeton, 2015.

Werther, David, and Mark D. Linville. *Philosophy and the Christian Worldview: Analysis, Assessment, Development*. New York: Continuum, 2012.

18 | *The Reasons for God (I):*
God as the Cause of the Universe

> The earth is full of the lovingkindness of the LORD.
> —Psalm 33:5

> The whole earth is full of His glory.
> —Isaiah 6:3

> In the beginning God created the heavens and the earth.
> —Genesis 1:1

TRAVELERS OR BALCONEERS?

In his classic *Knowing God*, the British theologian J. I. Packer mentions two sorts of people with an interest in God—some are like travelers, while others are like balconeers. The travelers are taking a difficult journey on the hot, dusty road; they have doubts, struggle with sin, and wrestle with what it means to honor God in their daily lives. The others, though, sit high above the road on their balconies, sipping their drinks, observing the travelers, and commenting on how the journey appears to be going for all of these weary walkers.

Though they are interested in what goes on below, the balconeers are armchair theologians—detached theoreticians who aren't truly engaged as disciples of Jesus Christ or interested in seeking after God. For them, God is more of an abstraction than a personal reality whose existence demands wholehearted seeking.[1]

We are called to be travelers, not merely balconeers—or as Danish philosopher Søren Kierkegaard put it, actors rather than spectators, followers rather than admirers of Jesus. As we've said, settling for sound theistic arguments without seeking God and humbling ourselves before the Cosmic Authority falls short of true, saving belief. Trust in God as Lord and *my* Lord is personal and no detached abstraction. As "the Hound of Heaven" (Francis Thompson) and "the Transcendental Interferer" (C. S. Lewis), the reality of God requires removing the "No Admittance" sign that has hitherto kept God at a safe distance from the door of our souls.

Keep in mind too that, no matter how widely available the evidence may be, some will persist in their resistance to God. When pressed, Oxford scientist

Peter Atkins admitted in an interview, "You're probably right" that there is no evidence that would persuade him out of his atheism.[2] Evidence has serious limitations for a will set against belief in God.

If God exists, the proper posture is *humility*—not demanding God perform signs and jump through our evidential hoops. And we should be grateful for whatever glimmers of divine light are available to us and allow God to have access to us through more than intellectual means. God can speak to us through an experience of beauty, through guilt and shame, through crisis and loss. The still-important rational arguments may be less relevant than personal and spiritual issues. So we shouldn't cordon off God from areas where he may speak most loudly to us.

By the power of God's Spirit, a range of factors can help point people to God. And we shouldn't rest content with people having justified true belief in God. This can be a start, but we point people further—to the good news of Jesus Christ, who has come to befriend us and to remind us of a loving Father who offers us acceptance through his beloved Son (John 14:9).

THE COSMOLOGICAL ARGUMENT: THE UNIVERSE'S CONTINGENCY, GOD'S NECESSITY

Existence, Illusion, and Difference

Gottfried Leibniz's question—"Why is there something rather than nothing at all?"—is a fundamental one, as we've seen. Why does anything—from planets to porpoises to persons—exist at all? We've noted how some atheists have been awestruck by the fact that something exists. Philosopher Richard Taylor—who believed in the detached God of the Aristotelian variety—pointed out that it's easy to be deluded into presumption by the steady, seemingly unchanging existence of something: "It is strange indeed . . . that a world such as ours should exist; yet few people are very often struck by this strangeness but simply take it for granted."[3]

Of course, we're assuming that the universe or the created order isn't an illusion. *Maya* (illusion) is found within the Advaita Vedanta Hindu tradition, whose notable ancient philosopher is Shankara (d. AD 820). This tradition is *monistic*; that is, there is *one* undifferentiated reality (*nirguna*)—namely, the pure consciousness of Brahman ("God" or the Ultimate). Any differences—between good and evil or subject and object or even the various Hindu deities—are only apparent, much like a wrinkle in a carpet. If you believe in difference, this is a manifestation of ignorance.

By contrast, the philosopher Ramanuja (d. AD 1137) said that we can't think logically, know anything, or make sense of reality unless difference (*saguna*) exists. Yet all these different things are part of Brahman. This is the doctrine of pantheism—that all (*pan*) is God/divine (*theos*).

This is, of course, quite different from biblical theism, in which God is distinct from his non-divine creation. The argument we're discussing takes for granted the reality of the external world and that God is distinct from his continent creation.

"[The Universe] Is Just There, and That's All"

The cosmological argument (Greek: *kosmos* = "world, universe") moves from a series of causes to some ultimate cause or sufficient reason for the existence of the world. This argument presupposes the validity of the principle of sufficient reason (PSR)—namely, for everything that exists, there is a sufficient reason for its existence. For example, if we hear a loud noise and ask what caused it, an explanation of "Nothing caused it; it just happened" wouldn't be a sufficient explanation.

The cosmological argument has three basic versions. The *Thomistic* version (from Thomas Aquinas) argues to a Sustainer (sustaining Ground) of the universe's existence. The *kalām* argument (from medieval times) points to a personal Creator (Cause) of the universe's beginning; the series of past events cannot be infinite but rather began to exist. Our focus here will be the *Leibnizian* version (after the philosopher Leibniz): God is the sufficient reason for the universe's existence, thus answering the question, "Why is there something rather than nothing?" We'll also see how evidence for the universe's beginning strongly supports this argument.

Critics like Bertrand Russell, we've seen, assume the universe is "just there, and that's all." Others like Michael Martin have challenged the idea that the universe had a cause: "This beginning [of the universe] may be uncaused," and this is "being taken seriously by scientists."[4] This is a strange phenomenon: appealing to science to challenge God's existence even though it's highly unscientific that something could come into existence from literally nothing.

Some say that "something" coming from "nothing" happens with subatomic particles, which allegedly "pop in and out of existence" in a quantum vacuum. But not even in the murky world of subatomic particles do entities literally come from nothing. As physicist John Polkinghorne put it, a quantum vacuum isn't nothing but rather is a low-energy state that is a "humming hive of activity."[5] And while it may *appear* that something comes from nothing, this merely reflects our ignorance of the quantum world. The way something appears isn't to say that it *actually is* the case. We shouldn't confuse (lack of) *knowing* with *being*.

The skeptic David Hume, whom atheists are fond of citing, called the idea of something arising without a cause an "absurd Proposition."[6] Richard Taylor reminds us of Hume's good sense on this point: "The idea that [the world] might have come from nothing at all, that it might exist without there being any explanation of its existence, is one that few people would consider worthy of entertaining."[7]

Apart from the universe's beginning, we have to ask how *the whole series of events* exists. We can't simply appeal to one contingent event by saying another contingent event caused it. This is like check-kiting: even though I have no money in my bank account, I'll write a check anyway, and then I'll write another check to cover the first, and so on. The problem is that there's still no money in the bank. The "contingent" checks need an "ultimate" basis for writing them.

"Who Made God?"

In Bertrand Russell's essay "Why I Am Not a Christian" (1927), he quoted philosopher John Stuart Mill's autobiography: "My father taught me that the question 'Who made me?' cannot be answered, since it immediately suggests the further question, 'Who made God?'" By such reasoning, Russell concluded: "If everything must have a cause, then God must have a cause."[8] Atheists of more recent vintage make the same argument. For example, Daniel Dennett asks: "If God created and designed all these wonderful things, who created God? Supergod? And who created Supergod? Superdupergod?"[9]

This "Who made God?" question, though, actually looks pretty fishy. Why? It quietly assumes an atheistic viewpoint. This is the tactic of question-begging, assuming what one wants to prove. So *what* is the assumption? It's this: "Everything has a cause." But that assumption isn't a *necessary* truth, like $2 + 2 = 4$. The very idea that God *began* to exist is nonsensical. What makes God God is that he can't not exist; this is one of his characteristics that sets him apart as God. No wonder various early church fathers referred to the triune God as the only "unbegotten" being; everything else was created—and thus "begotten." Since God is by definition uncaused and uncreated—the cause of all reality outside himself—to ask "Who made God?" is a category confusion. It demands that something necessary be contingent. It's like asking "Who made the Unmakeable?" or "What color is middle C?"

The second reply here is that no orthodox theist will affirm that "everything has a cause." To say this means that this would then apply to God. Rather, the theist affirms that *whatever begins to exist has a cause.* God didn't begin to exist. God is uncaused.

Some will respond: "That's absurd. How can something just *be*?" Though we may not be able to take in the idea that something can exist from eternity, we can't escape this conclusion, as we'll soon see. But it's of interest to note that many atheists and skeptics two hundred years ago assumed that the universe was "just there" and didn't need a cause. It was self-sufficient and self-explanatory. How things have changed! Now that we know the universe began to exist, some people are assuming that all things had a beginning.

How do we know, though, that the universe began to exist a finite time ago? There are various reasons.

First, the universe is expanding, and as we trace it back, it comes to a starting point. Second, we can actually detect the hissing noise of the universe's beginning. This "cosmic microwave background radiation" of the universe was discovered in 1964 by Arno Penzias and Robert Wilson of Bell Labs. That annoying static on our untuned radios is actually the noise from the early universe. This proved to be a further indicator of the universe's beginning. Third, the second law of thermodynamics indicates that the universe's energy (which is convertible to mass) is spreading out or dissipating. The winding down of the universe suggests that it has been wound up. If the universe were beginningless, then its energy would have been fully "spent."

Thus, the physicist Paul Davies asks, "What caused the big bang?" His reply is: "One might consider some supernatural force, some agency beyond space and time as being responsible for the big bang, or one might prefer to regard the big bang as an event without a cause. It seems to me that we don't have too much choice." Either "something outside of the physical world" caused the universe, or it was "an event without a cause."[10]

In addition to those atheists of yesteryear who assumed the universe could be eternally existent and self-explanatory, we could add Greek philosophers like Plato and Aristotle. To them, necessarily existent things aren't counterintuitive. Some things (e.g., Platonic "forms" of Goodness and Justice) by their very nature just don't need a cause; it's philosophically acceptable—indeed, inescapable—to have a stopping point to the string of contingent things. The self-*existent* isn't the self-*contradictory*.

This brings us to another point. Nothing ("*no thing*") cannot produce *some*thing. Being can't come from nonbeing, since no potentiality even exists for anything to arise. In other words, *unless something can pop into existence uncaused out of nothing (which we've seen is impossible), then you'll have to acknowledge that something has always existed.* This, however, couldn't be the universe, which is comprised of contingent or dependent parts. The universe didn't have to exist; it could have not existed.

CONTINGENCY AND NECESSITY

This brings us to the distinction between necessary and contingent existence—between ultimate and intermediate explanations. A *contingent* being is caused; that is, its reason for existence is found outside of itself. By contrast, a *necessary* being is *uncaused*. Its reason for existing is found in its very nature. It cannot not exist. It is eternal, uncaused, and self-sufficient rather than finite, caused, and dependent.

Contingent Being	Necessary Being
1. Caused (actualized)	1. Uncaused
2. Sustained	2. Self-sustaining
3. Finite	3. Eternal
4. Intermediate explanation	4. Ultimate explanation

Some might concede that the universe somehow came into existence a finite time ago. However, they might press the following point: "Well, isn't it rather *convenient* that the God you believe in has all the 'right properties' or 'great-making properties' to be the greatest possible being?"

We could reply that God exists by necessity. His maximal greatness is bound up with his nature; the reason for his existence is found in who God is by definition—like 2 + 2 = 4 by definition. But we can go further. We can ask some things about the contingent universe, which *didn't have to exist*: Isn't it likewise "convenient" that the universe not only came into existence a finite time ago without any preexisting matter or energy, but it also happens to be exquisitely finely tuned to be (a) life-*permitting*, (b) life-*producing*, and (c) life-*sustaining*—all the way from a single-celled organism to the eventual appearance of human beings? Isn't it astonishing that all the parameters required for this are astonishingly "just right"? Why is such a precision-tuned contingent universe that is "just there" permitted or taken for granted but not a necessary God who by his nature "just has" all of the right great-making properties?

David Hume once asked why the universe couldn't simply be a necessary being. The problem is that, unlike God, nothing about the universe renders it necessary by definition. Every part of it is contingent and winding down, and there's no reason that it had to exist. Philosopher Charles Peirce pointed out that universes aren't as numerous as blackberries. So we can't study how other possible universes—if they exist—originate, function, and compare with our own.

That's true, but metaphysics is metaphysics, and we can confidently say that something cannot come into existence uncaused out of nothing, blackberries notwithstanding. We can also say that if a universe is contingent in *all* its parts, then the universe is *completely* contingent. It's truly a meaningful fact about the universe that *none of its members is necessary*. This suggests that the universe is not a necessary being, and there's nothing strange about saying this philosophically or scientifically. So something independent of the universe and noncontingent must explain its existence.

Theistic Question-Begging?

Some might accuse *us* of question-begging: "You're just assuming God's existence to account for a beginning." Actually, we're not. We're only saying that the universe began to exist (empirical observation) and that nothing begins to exist without a cause (metaphysical truth). In light of these two points, we can explore what the nature of that cause is.

They might further charge us with question-begging about the principle of sufficient reason (PSR): "Why think that this principle is obvious and ought to be followed?" But the very question answers itself: it presupposes the demand for a sufficient reason!

Yes, the PSR is intuitively obvious, and even naturalistic scientists like Stephen Hawking have assumed it in seeking their own holy grail—a naturalistic "theory of everything" or a "grand unified theory."[11] They want a comprehensive and sufficient explanation for everything, though without appealing to God. Rather than seeking the *best* explanation, they seek only the best *naturalistic* explanation. Yet this pursuit is futile: their God is scientism, their glory is in their naturalistic explanations, and they set their minds on contingent things.

Even nontheistic scientists lend a hand in giving reasons for God here. Tufts University cosmologist Alexander Vilenkin asks, "Did the universe have a beginning?" His response is: "It probably did." He adds, "We have no viable models of an eternal universe."[12] Though Vilenkin says its cause is a mystery, the status of a finite universe leaves open a Creator God as a highly plausible explanation. Again, we're certainly not assuming that God exists, but we find that God certainly presents a suitable explanation for the universe's existence.[13]

Closing Reflections

The question of why something exists rather than nothing at all matters for those in nontheistic religions as well. British Buddhism scholar Paul Williams became a Christian after twenty years as a dedicated Buddhist. He found he couldn't answer the fundamental question of why the contingent universe exists at all. He concluded that only a necessary being—something classical Buddhism rejects—could serve as an adequate explanation to that question: "I have come to believe that there is a gap in the Buddhist explanation of things which for me can only be filled by God, the sort of God spoken of in a Christian tradition such as that of St. Thomas Aquinas."[14]

Williams kept on bumping up against implications of this question, and this worried him. He worried about things like the doctrine of rebirth (e.g., being reborn as a cockroach in South America in the next life and thus losing personal dignity) or having no hope. Eventually this nagging thought prompted him to consider a different perspective—a different vision of the world. Williams came to see that the existence of God answers these key *why* questions.[15]

Williams discovered that the existence of God is more than an intellectual question. It answered a host of other related questions about hope, dignity, value, and purpose. The gift of our very being and the remarkable world in which we find ourselves calls for honoring God and giving him thanks (Rom. 1:21). As the prophet Daniel pointed out to the proud Babylonian ruler Belshazzar: "But the God in whose hand is your breath, and whose are all your ways, you have not honored" (Dan. 5:23 ESV).

The argument from contingency reminds us that our origins and our continued existence are the gracious bestowal of a God who desires that we "should seek God, and perhaps feel [our] way toward him and find him. Yet he is actually not far from each one of us" (Acts 17:27 ESV).

FURTHER READING

Moreland, J. P., and William Lane Craig. *Philosophical Foundations for a Christian Worldview.* 2nd ed. Downers Grove, IL: IVP Academic, 2017. Chapter 25.

Pruss, Alexander, and Joshua Rasmussen. *Necessary Existence.* Oxford: Oxford University Press, 2018. (Note: this book is a densely argued defense of God's necessary existence; Taliaferro's book is a more accessible introduction.)

Taliaferro, Charles. *Philosophy of Religion: A Beginner's Guide.* Oxford: Blackwell, 2009.

19 | The Reasons for God (II): God as the Designer of the Universe

> Lift up your eyes on high and see who has created
> these stars,
> The One who leads forth their host by number,
> He calls them all by name;
> Because of the greatness of His might and the strength
> of His power,
> Not one of them is missing.
>
> —Isaiah 40:26

In Charlotte Brontë's *Jane Eyre*, the heroine, Jane, walks out into the night to pray for Mr. Rochester and reflects as she gazes at the stars above: "We know that God is everywhere; but certainly we feel His presence most when His works are on the grandest scale spread before us; and it is in the unclouded night-sky, where His worlds wheel their silent course, that we read clearest His infinitude, His omnipotence, His omnipresence. . . . Looking up, I, with tear-dimmed eyes, saw the mighty Milky-way. Remembering what it was—what countless systems there swept space like a soft trace of light—I felt the might and strength of God."[1]

It's not just theists who see design in the universe. The ancient Stoics did as well. In *On Providence*, Seneca—who died by Nero's order (AD 65)—spoke of the structure of the universe and the movements of its heavenly bodies—that they do "not persist without some caretaker"; they don't "move at random," nor do the particles of which they are made arrange themselves by chance.

All of this sounds very much like Romans 1:20—that the visible creation reveals God's "invisible attributes"—namely, "His eternal power and nature." In this case, divine wisdom or intelligence is evident.

Brontë and Seneca point us in the direction of teleological arguments (Greek: *telos* = "goal, end"). Features of and in the universe or of biological organisms appear to be *specifically*, *complexly*, and *interrelatedly* arranged or ordered in such a way that suggests some personal directing intelligence or mind behind these arrangements. Human conception, gestation, birth, and beyond are the outworking of natural processes God has put into place; we can look at the entire process and still say that we have been "fearfully and wonderfully made" (Ps. 139:14).

NECESSITY, CHANCE, OR DESIGN

Furthermore, it would seem that attributing these remarkable outcomes to either *necessity* or *chance* is unsatisfactory. To say that the natural laws of the universe and its development *had* to be this way (necessity) isn't true. For one thing, there's no reason to think that the finite universe—and thus the physical laws accompanying it—had to exist at all. Things could have been otherwise. Physicist Paul Davies reminds us, though, that nature's laws are "contingent": "It seems, then, that the physical universe does not have to be the way it is: it could have been otherwise."[2]

The *chance* explanation is unsatisfactory as well; after all, chance doesn't actually *do* anything. This notion simply informs us of statistical (im)probabilities. To blithely say "it could have happened" that a life-permitting, life-producing, and life-sustaining universe is the product of chance is naive. It fails to take seriously all that is required to get from "zero" to a single-celled organism to *Homo sapiens*. The God hypothesis, by contrast, renders this outcome highly probable.

"Darwin Did Away with Design"

Some scientists will insist that seeing divine design in the world is for the already-convinced. It just isn't obvious to the unbeliever. Enter Charles Darwin (1809–1882), whose work promoted two concepts: *common descent* (all organisms are related) and *natural selection* (biological variations that enhance survival and reproduction endure into succeeding generations while those that don't tend to fall away). Darwin didn't incorporate genetics—the laws and processes of biological inheritance discovered by Gregor Mendel (1822–1884)—which left Darwin's system incomplete.

As we've seen, Darwin found certain things theologically troubling: not only his young daughter Annie's death, but also the ichneumon wasp that laid its eggs "within the living bodies of caterpillars," and the cat that "should play with mice." Darwin noted that while we go for pleasant walks in the peaceful woods, hidden from our view is the warfare that takes place between organisms all around us. Thus Darwin considered intellectually unsatisfying the idea that God permitted these things. Darwin came to believe that the "works of nature"—which involve extinctions, predation, "cruelty," wastefulness, and anatomical clumsiness—couldn't be the result of a designer.

In Darwin's wake have come thinkers like Richard Dawkins, who said that Darwin made it possible to be an intellectually fulfilled atheist. He acknowledges that before Darwin, it would have been difficult to deny divine design. Then, God appeared to be the best explanation of things. Indeed, many will claim that Darwin's discovery now *undermines* the notion of design. Philosopher James Rachels claimed that "Darwin's great contribution was the final demolition of the idea that nature is the product of intelligent design."[3] Even the Christian thinker John Henry Newman declared, "I have been unable to see the logical force of the argument myself. I believe in design because I believe in God; not in a God because I see design."[4]

A Few Responses to the Critics

So where does this leave the arguments from design?

First, design is secondary to the actual origination of the finite universe; we have good reason to think that something preexisting and independent of the universe was responsible for its beginning. Some personal being like God would qualify, bringing into existence something without preexisting matter or energy and, from a state of changelessness, introducing a universe teeming with activity.

Second, Darwin's emphasis on biological evolution leaves untouched the universe's remarkably precise fine-tuning for life. This startling biofriendliness has been called "the Goldilocks effect": the conditions for life aren't "too hot" or "too cold" but "just right." If the balance of the universe's four forces—gravity, strong and weak nuclear forces, and electromagnetism—was even minutely altered, life would be impossible.

The many conditions of the universe are elegantly balanced, as it were, on a razor's edge—with infinitesimal to no variation allowed. When it comes to the universe's rate of expansion—which is only one of those conditions—the late Cambridge physicist Stephen Hawking describes just one fragile scenario: "If the rate of the [universe's] expansion had been smaller by even one part in a hundred thousand million million, the universe would have recollapsed before it ever reached its present size."[5] Sir Fred Hoyle, the agnostic astronomer, observed the need for an explanation for these remarkable, exquisite, life-permitting conditions: "Such properties seem to run through the fabric of the natural world like a thread of happy coincidences. But there are so many odd coincidences essential to life that some explanation seems required to account for them."[6] That is, to say "we just happened to get lucky" is inadequate.

Furthermore, we should distinguish three stages that shed further light on the requirements for life: the universe is not only life-*permitting*, but also life-*producing*, and then life-*sustaining*. The astonishingly improbable odds of life emerging and developing in a naturalistic world disappear if theism is true; in this case, the existence of moral creatures capable of relating to God becomes highly likely. The problem isn't "evolution versus creation" but "God versus no God" or "guided versus unguided evolution."

The naturalist should consider: just because the universe is life-*permitting* doesn't guarantee that it will in fact produce life. But even if life could be *produced* from nonliving materials, this would have to be under highly specified, very precise conditions. Indeed, scientists are still baffled at how life could emerge from nonlife. Even if they could replicate these initial conditions for life—and they're still having a go at it—this would just go to show that this takes a lot of intelligent planning. Getting life from nonliving matter is a kind of biological big bang.

Beyond this, even if we could get a single-celled organism from nonliving matter, this doesn't guarantee that life could be *sustained* to get us to *Homo sapiens*. At each level, we add massive improbability to massive improbability. According to naturalist Daniel Dennett, in light of the long, torturous sequence of events required for humans to appear on the scene, we "almost didn't make it"![7]

The Increasing Unlikelihood of Naturalism

Stages to Consider	Calculated Odds
1. A Universe (or, Producing Something from Nothing in the Big Bang)	Exactly 0. (Something cannot come into existence from literally nothing; there isn't even the *potentiality* to produce anything.)
2. A Life-*Permitting* Universe	Roger Penrose (agnostic physicist/mathematician) notes the odds of a life-permitting universe—a figure requiring more zeroes than there are atoms in the universe: "The Creator's aim must have been [precise] to an accuracy of one part in $10^{10(123)}$."[8] What number are we talking about? It "would be 1 followed by 10/123 successive '0's! Even if we were to write a '0' on each separate proton and on each separate neutron in the entire universe—and we could throw in all the other particles as well for good measure—we should fall far short of writing down the figure needed. [This is] the precision needed to set the universe on its course."[9]

3. A Life-*Producing* Universe (Life from Nonlife)	Stephen Meyer calculates the odds for the necessary 250 proteins to sustain life coming about by change as being 1 in $10^{41,000}$.[10]
4. A Life-*Sustaining* Universe (Moving from the Bacterium to *Homo Sapiens*)	Astrophysicists Frank Tipler and John Barrow calculated that the chances of moving from a bacterium to *Homo sapiens* in 10 billion years or less is $10^{-24,000,000}$ (a decimal with 24 million zeroes).[11] Francisco Ayala (evolutionary biologist) independently calculated the odds of humans arising just once in the universe to be $10^{-1,000,000}$.[12]

Third, we need not assign purpose to every specific natural event or process. For example, cats playing with mice is part of a larger structure in the created order that is worth considering.

For one thing, God created the predatory animals and the food chain from the outset (cf. Job 38:39–40; 39:28–29, 39–40; 41:1, 10, 14; Ps. 147:9). Psalm 104:20–28 is part of a creation psalm, and here the psalmist considers such activity to be God's provision and calls it "good [*tob*]"—the same word found in Genesis 1.

We can speak of a *broader* design or teleology with God's higher goals in mind; thus we don't have to justify all the particulars of such natural events. As we'll see in our discussion of evil, the "messiness" of predation and animal death has a higher goal in mind. This includes the fact that God endows his creation with certain causal powers—much like seeds that germinate, grow into plants, and bear fruit (cf. Gen. 1:11–12).

Fourth, however Christians may view the matter of evolution, the process hardly undermines divine design. Consider the necessary cooperation and interdependence that develop as life becomes more complex. As we move from the building blocks of life all the way up to humankind, we see progress at work. This involves transitions from cells to genes that form into chromosomes; and beyond this, simple ("prokaryotic") cells cluster to form more complex cells with compartments ("eukaryotic"); individual cells aggregate to form multicellular organisms; asexual reproduction develops into sexual reproduction; solitary individuals form colonies; primates develop into human societies that require building on shared memory and cultural cooperation, which enables them to exercise stewardship over the earth.

In the unfolding of life forms, autonomy gives way to greater cooperation: "Cooperation is now seen as a primary creative force behind greater levels of complexity and organization in biology . . . [and it is] easy to agree on the basic role played by cooperation in the diversification of life."[13]

While this process may involve seeming "wastefulness," it is this kind of process that is required for genuine, loving relationships to be possible—in both human relationships as well as in the divine-human engagement. This developing hierarchy involves a certain messiness to arrive at this outcome. As the noted philosopher of science Michael Polanyi observed: "But if we accept, as I do, the view that living beings form a hierarchy in which each higher level represents a distinctive principle that harnesses the level below it (while being itself irreducible to its lower principles), then the evolutionary sequence gains a new and deeper significance. We can recognize then a strictly defined progression, rising from the inanimate level to ever higher additional principles of life."[14]

Though Christians disagree about "evolutionary creation," my point is to keep the main thing the main thing. Again, the fundamental issue isn't evolution versus creation; it's God versus no God. Did the natural world come into being on its own, and does it continue to operate on its own? Or did it originate from a nonnatural Source, and is it being directed by that Source toward certain ends?

Fifth, a God-designed world does not entail utter completeness and utopian perfectionistic function. No, God didn't create us with immortal bodies, and God created the food chain—"Nature red in tooth and claw." While God created a "very good [*tôb meʾōd*]" world (Gen. 1:31), it wasn't intended to be absolutely perfect. What's more, Numbers 14:7—a post-fall text—uses even more positive language than Genesis 1 to refer to the promised land: it was an "exceedingly good land [*tôbāh hāʾāretz meʾōd meʾōd*]." And even early on, it was "not good" that man was alone (Gen. 2:18). Furthermore, the command to subdue (*kabāsh*) the earth (Gen. 1:28) suggests some *resistance*—and that resistance would persist as long as humans inhabit the old creation (Rom. 8:22).

As N. T. Wright comments, "Creation, it seems, was not a tableau, a static scene. It was designed as a *project*, created in order to go somewhere. . . . The point of the project is that the garden be extended, colonizing the rest of creation; and Human is the creature put in charge of that plan."[15] And, he adds, "if Human was going to do this [to reflect God's image into the new world God was making], Human was going to have to keep in tune with God."[16] So those who wonder about seeming "inefficiencies" in creation should take the broader view. God's higher purposes often include struggle and refining.

Some may even wonder why God "wasted" so much space in the universe. Why not create a universe teeming with life throughout?

Actually, the universe's parameters are meticulously calibrated. For us to get life in one far-flung corner of the universe, *we need a universe just this size.* In the universe's very beginning, God began with the building blocks of matter (protons and neutrons), then fused the lightest element (hydrogen) with the next heavier elements of helium and lithium. The amount of these heavier elements would then determine the necessary elements for planets and life itself that would be produced within stars. Without a perfect balancing of proton and neutron mass density, the creation of our planet and life on it would have been impossible: "For life to be possible, the universe must be no more or less massive than it is."[17]

It takes billions of years to produce life in an expanding universe, and the God of Scripture isn't in a hurry to accomplish his purposes. Those who consider God's ways inefficient probably don't care about what purposes God may have in mind. If God has overriding reasons for fixing his redemptive attention on our comparatively small planet inhabited by human creatures, and if this ends up leaving much of space empty, so what? Why think that God should be a maximally efficient God? That deity looks more Germanic or Scandanavian than biblical. The priority of efficiency should be judged according the overarching goal in mind. The God of Scripture is relational, extravagant, and willing to delay for his own reasons (cf. 2 Pet. 3:9, 13).

Sixth, naturalists often arbitrarily dismiss design despite admitting the "appearance" of design. Richard Dawkins defines biology as "the study of complicated things that give the appearance of having been designed for a purpose."[18] Elsewhere, he writes: "So powerful is the illusion of design, it took humanity until the mid-19th century to realise that it is an illusion."[19]

But how does one determine whether something merely *appears* designed or is *actually* designed? This determination goes beyond the domain of science: it's a philosophical and theological question. Dawkins simply *asserts* non-design, but how does he *know* this? If something appears designed, what if that's the case because biological processes really *are* guided rather than unguided?

Furthermore, when naturalists get upset with a God who allows predation and wastefulness and extinction, they're assuming a kind of standard for the way things ought to be. But within an unguided system of nature, there is no way things *ought* to be. So the arguments from Darwin and others that apparent evils exist in nature *don't even make sense* without a norm or standard by which to determine that there has been a departure from the way things ought to be.

Seventh, scientists depend on notions of elegance, beauty, and mathematical precision, which are better suited to a theistic perspective than a naturalistic one.

Why do scientists affirm the truth of James Clerk Maxwell's electromagnetic equations? In part, because they have a beauty or elegance to them. Scientists will opt for an elegant theory over an inelegant, clunky one. Nontheistic scientists and philosophers point to remarkable, mind-pleasing patterns in the universe, which make excellent sense in a theistic universe. The physicist Eugene Wigner referred to the "uncanny usefulness of mathematical concepts" in the natural sciences; it "is something bordering on the mysterious" and "there is no rational explanation for it."[20] Bertrand Russell likewise spoke of the "supreme beauty of mathematics . . . like that of a sculpture"; it is "sublimely pure" and, like poetry, inspires the "true spirit of delight" and "exaltation" within us.[21]

Eighth, the notion of being an "intellectually fulfilled atheist" suggests the concept of purpose or design. Dawkins's declaration that "Darwin made it possible to be an intellectually fulfilled atheist"[22] presumes that we have certain capacities that ought to be cultivated and a goal toward which we must strive. If intellectual fulfillment is a goal we ought to pursue, and if it would be wasteful for us not to live up to our potential, how can a purposeless, material world make sense of such a notion?

As we've seen, the late former atheist Antony Flew became a believer in God because he was persuaded by the many pointers to God through scientific discovery: the universe's beginning and fine-tuning for life as well as the remarkable complexities of biological life. When it comes to first life, Flew wrote: "It has become inordinately difficult even to begin to think about constructing a naturalistic theory of the evolution of that first reproducing organism."[23] He insisted on following the evidence wherever it led, and the indications of design didn't appear so elusive after all.[24]

MULTIPLE WORLDS AND DESIGN

Some suggest that ours is just one of a vast number of parallel existing universes. This is called the many worlds hypothesis (MWH). Given the vast number of worlds—a potentially infinite number—surely *some* of them would produce life. And, it turns out, we happen to be in one of those particular universes that are life-permitting.

Should we be threatened by such a scenario? Does it exclude God from consideration? A few comments are in order.

For one thing, the MWH hardly rules out God, who could have created a host of universes, not just one. In fact, God is necessary to account for any contingent universe—whether one or many.

Second, we know of no mechanism to generate universes. What gets them going in first place? We would still need to bring God into the picture to account for the emergence of multiple universes as a capable universe generator. The more basic question here is: How did *any* of these purported finite universes begin to exist?

Third, all of these universes—if they exist—would be winding down. We know that, according to the second law of thermodynamics, our own universe is finite. Its energy is dissipating, suggesting it has been wound up. This would apply across the board to any existing universes—again, if they exist.

So the MWH doesn't actually advance the critic's argument; that is, it bypasses the more basic question of how universes could come into existence from nothing. On this question, theism offers a robust, explanatory context: a personal, powerful, and intelligent Source brought about this universe with its delicately balanced, life-producing conditions.

Another big problem is that we just don't have any evidence for these alleged universes. The MWH is merely speculative and without any scientific support. This hypothesis is just as metaphysical a view as the idea that God exists and created the universe. Those who put forward the MWH scenario to bypass God appear to be sealing God off from consideration; they are creating conditions in which no amount of evidence—however intricate and vast—could ever count as evidence for actual design. For this reason alone, we ought to be suspicious. For all of the critics' appeal to scientific evidence, it looks like the MWH is merely speculative and even metaphysical. The fact is, these critics are stuck with just one universe—an observation that *does* have scientific support—and it just happens to have all of the amazing, life-permitting, life-producing, and life-sustaining conditions built into it!

Firing Squads, Royal Flushes, and Cosmic Surprise

Our naturalist friends may shrug all of this off. They tell us: "If the universe weren't so biofriendly, then we wouldn't be here to wonder about its amazing biofriendliness. So we shouldn't be surprised that the universe is the way it is." But this is a truism—a rather uninteresting, unilluminating fact.

Philosopher John Leslie offers this example: "If you faced a firing squad with fifty guns trained on you [and they missed], you should not be surprised to find that you were alive after they had fired. After all, that is the only outcome you could possibly have observed—if one bullet had hit you, you would be dead."[25] But it would be ludicrous to merely shrug this off: "However, you might still feel that there is something which very much needs explanation: namely why did they all miss? Was it by deliberate design? For there is no inconsistency *in not being surprised that you do not observe that you are dead,* and *being surprised to observe that you are still alive."*[26]

In other words, it's one thing to say we shouldn't be surprised that we don't witness conditions *incompatible* with our existence, since we do, after all, exist. But it doesn't logically follow that we shouldn't be surprised that we *do* witness conditions to the universe that *are* compatible with our existence. The fitting response to surviving the shooting can be nothing else but utter amazement. Why? Because you would suspect that your still being alive was the result of a purposeful plan.

It's much like a card dealer who keeps on getting royal flushes hand after hand. You wouldn't accept the dealer's response to your suspicious questioning if he says, "You shouldn't be surprised at these consecutive royal flushes since we wouldn't be discussing the matter had I not gotten all of these royal flushes in a row."

FURTHER DESIGN-RELATED QUESTIONS

"Who Designed the Designer?"

Richard Dawkins claims that this question is the key anti-theistic argument in his book *The God Delusion*.[27] That is, if God is responsible for the universe's design, then he must have been designed too. Now this line of reasoning is similar to the "Who made God?" argument—and just as misguided. The reason that this is a worthless argument is that it leads to an infinite regress of explanations—in this case, designers: Who was the designer of the designer of the designer of the designer—you get the idea—of the world's designer? If we used Dawkins's line of reasoning, we couldn't rationally justify *anything*. There can be no sufficient reason for anything.

However, we *do* have a sufficient reason to explain the world by one designer, who needs no further explanation. A Model T Ford or a painting like *Starry Night* clearly had a designer. We don't have to go back any farther than Henry Ford or Vincent van Gogh to explain the existence of these creations. Like the "Who made God?" objection, why does the (presumably intelligent) designer need to be designed? A designer is a sufficient explanatory stopping point.

But what if we don't know the reason or intention behind the design? It seems clear that we can detect design even if we don't know what the designer's intentions are. For example, in the mid-1800s, John Gorrie—a Florida medical doctor—invented the ice machine to keep his patients with yellow fever cool.

By just looking at this device with its cannisters, piping, and wooden frame, one wouldn't readily know the reason for its creation. But *that* it was designed is obvious enough.

"Is Design Opposed to Science?"

Ironically, many who declare design to be "unscientific" readily offer "empirical evidence" or "naturalistic explanations" for apparent design. But how scientific is that? As we noted earlier, distinguishing between *apparent* design and *actual* design is a theological or philosophical matter—not something science can help us determine. If something *appears* designed, well, why not consider that it actually *was*? According to various representatives of science we've quoted, at least in principle, we can detect "apparent" design, but it still may be the case that a designer is actually behind it. It's a whopping non sequitur to say that *apparent* design *can only be* apparent design and that it's somehow illegitimate to infer *actual* design.

Let's say that life emerged on Earth through the intelligent planning of Martians rather than God. Would this be a scientific explanation? If God did exactly the same thing as Martians—initiating life on this planet—based on the identical evidence, why would this, even if true, be bad science or even no science at all?[28] Why should we exclude God from having this role?

To a significant degree, science actually *presupposes* design: the universe is *comprehensible*; its patterns and processes can be studied and understood by human minds (Ps. 111:2). Physicist Paul Davies reminds us: "Science began as an outgrowth of theology, and all scientists, whether atheists or theists . . . accept an essentially theological worldview."[29] Kant himself affirmed that science can't get underway without certain (largely) theistic assumptions such as the world's knowability and orderliness. The world has been placed in an "artfully arranged structure," having a "determinative purpose, carried out with great wisdom," and created by a "sublime and wise cause."[30]

As we've seen, even naturalists acknowledge the reality of beauty in the natural world. Beyond this, they observe the brilliant mathematical precision behind the workings of the universe, both grand and small. Naturalistic scientists use beauty or elegance as a standard by which to assess scientific theories and formulate scientific laws. At many intersecting points, naturalistic scientists seem able to detect something quite akin to design. Indeed, naturalists will compare the working of nature to factories with assembly lines, computers, cameras, and the like.

Theism happily accommodates this realization. What would otherwise be staggering coincidences multiplied in excelsis are well situated and highly probable in a theistic world. By contrast, they are quite baffling given a naturalistic world. The heavens indeed declare the glory of God (Ps. 19:1), and the earth is full of his lovingkindness (Ps. 33:5).

Paul Davies describes his own experience: "Some of my colleagues embrace the same scientific facts as I, but deny any deeper significance. They shrug aside the breathtaking ingenuity of the laws of physics, the extraordinary felicity of the physical world, and the surprising intelligibility of the physical world, accepting these things as a package of marvels that just happens to be. But I cannot do this."[31]

If we're looking in the universe for indications of a Designer, we can readily find them. And despite naturalism's inability to account for beauty and the mathematical intricacies of natural laws, perhaps the fact that naturalists assume, detect, and talk about the reality of beauty and that they readily use design analogies continues to provide a pathway for engagement.

Even so, it is misguided to rest content with the mere fact of a personal, powerful, intelligent Creator's existence (cf. James 2:19). Though it's a start, believing the mere fact of God's existence is inadequate. We must move beyond this to earnestly seeking God as well (Heb. 11:6). What are the Designer's designs *for me*? What demands does this being place on my life so that I might fulfill my God-given purpose in this world? Is there a way of finding out this being's purposes for humanity?

Aristotle said that, unlike other animals, only human beings can go against their nature and defy the purpose for which they exist.[32] The various pointers to a Designer serve as available clues to help awaken and motivate us to understand our design and fulfill the reason for which we have been made—although we can resist such gracious influences (Acts 7:51).

FURTHER READING

Murray, Michael, ed. *Reason for the Hope Within*. Grand Rapids: Eerdmans, 1999.

Plantinga, Alvin. *Where the Conflict Really Lies: Science, Religion, and Naturalism*. Oxford: Oxford University Press, 2011.

Ratzsch, Del. *Nature, Design and Science*. Albany: SUNY Press, 2001.

Taliaferro, Charles. *Philosophy of Religion: A Beginner's Guide*. Oxford: Blackwell, 2009.

20 | The Reasons for God (III): God as the Source of Goodness

> You . . . are of purer eyes than to see evil and cannot look at wrong.
>
> —Habakkuk 1:13 ESV

> All have turned aside; together they have become worthless; no one does good, not even one.
>
> —Romans 3:12 ESV

We have looked at two key arguments for God's existence (cosmological and teleological), and in this chapter we offer a third (moral). We could examine other arguments: an argument from beauty, an argument from reason, an argument from consciousness, an argument from religious experience. We've touched on some of these in other chapters, but space doesn't allow us to elaborate beyond this point.

However, the moral argument is a very important argument both intellectually and personally. If we're honest and reasonably self-aware, we recognize that we are inescapably moral creatures: we must wrestle with choices that shape or destroy character, and we must contend with guilt and shame because we can readily see the moral gap between the ideal and our own miserable performance. This moral reality is thrust on us, and we must wrestle with it intellectually and personally. Here is the good news: not only does the triune God ground moral reality, but he also provides forgiveness and gracious help for us in our moral and spiritual need (Heb. 4:16; Jude 24).

OUR MORAL AWARENESS

That Includes "Pagans" Too

"Everybody Knows" is a haunting song sung by the late iconic Canadian songwriter Leonard Cohen. With his deep, resonant voice, he calls out those who think they've gotten away with adultery and more. Everybody knows that the fast-moving plague is coming soon and that you're in big trouble: "there's gonna be a meter on your bed that will disclose what everybody knows."[1]

Cohen was on to something. Francis Schaeffer used the image of a recording device that perpetually hangs around our neck from birth onward. It records everything you say and tracks your activities day and night—and even thoughts and attitudes. If our lives were put on replay, how would we measure up to even *our own* professed standards and "thousands and thousands of moral judgments" made against others?[2] We are inescapably moral beings, but when we compare our performance to the moral ideal, this "moral gap" shows us all to be miserable failures. Repeatedly, biblical texts indicate that "the whole world" is morally accountable to God; every mouth will be silenced (Rom. 3:19).

This includes people who know the Bible well and those who have not read even a shred of it. Since they are God's image-bearers, they can get a lot right about God's moral demands on humanity. How so? Because we come into the world as intrinsically valuable beings with the capacity for moral awareness, contemplation, and action. Though our conscience can be suppressed and seared as with a hot iron (Rom. 1:18; 1 Tim. 4:2), we can also pay attention to it. Our moral understanding can be refined and cultivated through moral reflection and action.

Of course, the conscience can be blunted through cultural influence, family upbringing, or choices that lead to a hardened heart. But as Augustine said in his *Confessions*, he met many people who would deceive, but no one who would want to be deceived. We humans find ourselves quick to judge others for the same offenses we commit (for example, when we're driving). We tend to be harder on others than we are on ourselves. Indeed, all of us—whether Christians or "pagans"—can recognize moral truth. Something of God's moral nature will shine through even in cultures less influenced by the Christian faith. C. S. Lewis's *Abolition of Man* catalogs the same moral codes from vastly different civilizations and cultures—Babylonian, Egyptian, Hebrew, Greek: *Don't murder; honor your parents; don't take what isn't yours; tell the truth.* In that spirit, Amos 1–2 speaks of gentile nations that will be judged by God ("I will send fire"); the implication is that these nations should have known better than to rip open pregnant women, break treaties, act treacherously, and stifle compassion.

The Proper Basicality of Our Fundamental Moral Intuitions

Torturing babies for fun is something we know immediately to be abhorrent (a "pre-philosophical intuition"). We don't have to think about it or try to prove it. We immediately grasp it—much like our sense perceptions. Those who deny the fundamentals of morality are simply in error. A person who says gang-raping a woman isn't morally wrong needs *help*, not a philosophical *argument*. Atheist Kai Nielsen affirms that we know that wife-beating and child abuse are utterly wrong; we should believe this rather than any skeptical theory that denies it: "I firmly believe that this is bedrock and right and that anyone who does not believe it cannot have probed deeply enough into the grounds of his moral beliefs."[3]

Such moral beliefs are "properly basic." That is, we find such beliefs arising out of our experience—independent of age or education—and we have no good reason to deny such commonsensical beliefs. If we somehow overthrew or seriously called into question these deeply held, nonnegotiable rational and moral convictions about wife-beating or gang rape, it would cause the fabric of our very humanity to unravel.

This doesn't mean that our basic beliefs can't be overturned, but the "principle of credulity," which we discussed earlier, is applicable here: *Treat basic moral intuitions as innocent unless proven guilty.*

Of course, we might make mistakes about what we perceive. What appears to be a dead bug on the floor turns out on closer inspection to be a raisin, for instance. But we don't call into question the reliability of our senses. Likewise, people disagree about morality—those moral "gray areas"—but this doesn't mean we can't get a lot right if we pay attention to our conscience or engage in rational discussion. It's like what the lexicographer Dr. Samuel Johnson said: "The fact that there is such a thing as twilight does not mean that we cannot distinguish between day and night."

Scottish "commonsense realist" Christian philosopher Thomas Reid put it this way: these sorts of basic beliefs are not the result of our manufacturing them, but, like the production of coins, such inescapable beliefs were stamped onto us by "the mint of Nature." We take it "upon trust, and without suspicion" that our minds aren't systematically deceived. Reason and perception "came both out of the same shop, and were made by the same artist," and we have no reason to cast serious doubt on reason or perception.[4]

Indeed, from early on, we recognize moral duties that somehow seem to be imposed on us. As children on the playground during recess we've heard or made statements such as these:

> "How'd you like it if anyone did the same to you?"—"That's my seat, I was there first"—"Leave him alone, he isn't doing you any harm"—"Why should you shove in first?" . . . "Come on, you promised."[5]

Though we are inescapably moral beings, a moral realm exists independent of us. The Holocaust was evil not just because we *feel* it was evil. The fact that morality is "outside of us" means we don't *invent* morality. We *discover* it. This moral realm makes sense of reforms like the abolition of slavery or the Civil Rights Act: obviously blacks had value independent of these events; the legislation merely confirmed and made legal what was already known. We don't "make" something good or evil.

Morality as a Clue to the Universe's Meaning

The first part of C. S. Lewis's book *Mere Christianity* argues that basic moral beliefs actually give us a clue to the meaning of the universe. We have no reason to overturn or dispense with our commonsense understanding of morality. And if a worldview rejects the reality of goodness and evil, then so much the worse for that theory. These moral values point us in the direction of a moral being and lawgiver.

Although broad naturalists will put forth various arguments for objective moral values without God, as we'll see, they aren't robust, deep, or comprehensive enough. Their reasons only "nibble around the edges." They don't actually provide us with a proper moral framework, a solid moral structure. Without a good God, it's hard to account for the profoundly moral world in which we find ourselves, including human dignity, personal responsibility, and so on. A more promising argument looks like this:

> If God does not exist, objective moral values and duties do not exist.
> Objective moral values and duties do exist.
> Therefore, God exists.

Some will claim that moral beliefs merely enhance survival and reproduction (more on this below). We don't deny the influence of culture or genetics on our moral thinking. But to claim that morality reduces to culture or genetics is actually a very shallow or superficial account of moral reality. Fundamental moral instincts or intuitions aren't the *basis* of morality; rather they *reflect* a moral realm that we can access and understand.

A fuller, clearer understanding of morality is available to us if a good God exists. Indeed, we've noted how naturalists like J. L. Mackie and Joel Marks emphasized that objective moral values would actually provide a reason for God's existence, though these naturalists reject the reality of those moral values.

The God-Morality Connection

We've seen that objective moral values do exist, and atheists who have a decently functioning conscience can get a lot of moral things right without consulting the Bible. Human dignity makes sense given the existence of a good God who has made us in his image (Gen. 1:26–27). Now this isn't true about all versions of theism. For example, according to Islam, the idea that humans are made in God's image is blasphemy and an insult to Allah. And this makes it all the more difficult for Muslims to grasp the incarnation. But we can't elaborate here.

As we've noted, the moral argument maintains objective moral values exist and are deeply connected to God. Naturalism or other nontheistic alternatives may try to ground value, but they tend to lack richness, robustness, and depth.

We've all heard decent, respectable atheists say things like "I don't need God to be good" or "I know right from wrong without belief in God to inform me." The late atheist philosopher Michael Martin said much the same thing—namely, that both theists and nontheists will give the same reason for why rape is wrong: it violates the victim's rights, traumatizes the victim, and tears apart the fabric of society.[6] So the existence of God doesn't actually contribute anything more to the discussion.

Actually, this reasoning doesn't dig down far enough. Notice what Martin is taking for granted: *human beings have intrinsic dignity and rights.* But where do rights and dignity come from in a universe of impersonal, nonconscious, unguided, valueless, deterministic material processes? In addition to rights and dignity, *rationality* and *free will* are required for humans to be held morally responsible for their actions—still more items borrowed from the pantry of theism. This is the problem with "the manifest image" of naturalism. As we've seen, a personal, self-aware, purposeful, good God provides the needed metaphysical context to make sense of such dignity, rights, rationality, and agency.[7]

For atheists to claim that they have genuine moral *knowledge* misses the point of the moral argument. Atheists bear God's image and thus can know moral truths without belief in God. The problem is *being*, not *knowing*: How did we come to be intrinsically valuable, morally responsible *beings*? Since we possess this dignity, we can therefore *know* our moral duties and exert our will to make moral choices. A metaphysic of valueless, deterministic, nonrational, nonconscious processes can't account for moral, valuable beings.

This is the problem with many "secularized" ethical theories on offer today—they simply *assume* human dignity and moral responsibility. These include certain versions of Kantianism (duty), utilitarianism (consequences), social contract theory (agreement), or virtue ethics (character).[8] No wonder naturalists who strive to be consistent with their worldview acknowledge its stark implications—no *meaning* (nihilism), no *value*, no *freedom*. As Alex Rosenberg observes, even though we have evolutionarily produced feelings that keep us cooperative and nice, still "there are no facts of the matter about what is morally right or wrong, good or bad."[9]

Naturalists who are moral realists are metaphysically borrowing from theism; they cannot avoid moving in a transcendent, Godward direction. As the agnostic Paul Draper affirms, "A moral world is . . . very probable on theism."[10] Moral values are rooted in personhood and ultimately in the divine, tripersonal Trinity. This kind of context—not naturalism—leads us to expect outcomes like human dignity, rights, and the demand for universal benevolence.[11]

Morality as an Illusion

Illusions, East and West

We've seen that the biblical God offers a rich explanation for our moral nature, for moral duties, and for the moral standard by which we judge something to be evil. We've also noted that some philosophies dismiss morality altogether, even calling it an illusion. To assume differentiation—good-evil, right-wrong—is faulty Western "either-or" thinking. But were the atrocities authorized by Hitler, Stalin, Pol Pot, and Mao Tse-tung illusory? Why accept this view?

Robert Pirsig, author of *Zen and the Art of Motorcycle Maintenance*, described a lecture he attended in India. The professor discussed how the world was an illusion. Pirsig asked if the bombs dropped on Hiroshima and Nagasaki were illusory. In reply, "the professor smiled and said yes." Thus Pirsig "left the classroom, left India and gave up."[12]

For a different reason, plenty of naturalists in the West also claim that morality is an illusion: we strongly *feel* we have moral duties, but we don't actually *have* them. We only *think* morality is objective, but that is an illusion. Philosopher of science Michael Ruse claims we've developed this "awareness of morality—a sense of right and wrong and a feeling of obligation to be thus governed"—because it has "biological worth."[13] Without this strong moral impulse, we would disregard morality.[14] He says, "If you think about it, you will see that the very essence of an ethical claim, like 'Love little children,' is that, whatever its truth status may be, we think it binding upon us *because we think it has an objective status*."[15] Morality is merely a "corporate illusion" that has been "fobbed off on us by our genes to get us to cooperate."[16] But naturalistic (i.e., unguided) evolution doesn't require that we *follow* the feelings of morality, since actual duties are nonexistent.

Problems with the Illusory Morality View

We encounter several problems if we accept this view of morality as an illusion. The first thing is the denial of the obvious. Why reject what seems so commonsensical and inescapable to us? Such moral beliefs are as evident to us as seeing trees or flowers or cars when looking out the window. It's no wonder many naturalists embrace "the manifest image"; they refuse to give up human dignity, duties, and other moral values because they are unavoidable.

Second, the *biological* doesn't exclude the *theological*. Let's say that biological evolution had a role in creating or shaping our moral feelings. So what? How does it follow that an independent moral realm doesn't exist? In fact, the existence of these deep moral feelings could actually reflect the existence and engineering of a good God—an objective moral realm beyond ourselves. We saw this with Freud's argument against God: if we have a deep longing for God, then God doesn't exist but is only a human construction or projection. In that same chapter, we also observed something similar about the mind's tendency to detect agency (the cognitive science of religion), which doesn't at all exclude the reality of God.

Third, the naturalist has a further problem—namely, how unguided, nonrational processes can lead to reliable, rational thought. How do nonrational physical processes produce logical reasoning and knowledge? How can matter have beliefs? Why should we even trust our minds if they are nothing more than the products of unguided, naturalistic evolution? If our beliefs have been formed by prior nonrational, nonconscious, physical forces—forces beyond our control—then why trust any of our beliefs? Yes, those beliefs may help us to fight, feed, flee, and reproduce, but truth is irrelevant. If naturalism *were* true, a lot of false beliefs would enhance survival and reproduction. For example, "Humans have dignity and worth" or "Humans have moral duties" would be false but facilitate survival. In fact, believing the *truth*—that we have no dignity or duties—could actually *hinder* our survival. Naturalistic evolution isn't concerned about truth, only survival.

If naturalism is true, each of our beliefs is produced by physicality, not rationality. If a belief is true, it's just by accident; it's not rational thinking or following logical laws that guided us to those conclusions. So we can't help believing what we do. There is no way I ought to think, only the way I do think. No wonder Charles Darwin had "the horrid doubt" that the convictions in any person's mind are no more trustworthy than those of a monkey's.[17] Given naturalism, the cause of my belief that naturalism is true is simply due to my brain chemistry. Why consider any beliefs produced by such processes reliable? After all, my brain chemistry could just as readily produce the belief that naturalism is false.

Yet "illusionists" like Ruse nevertheless trust their own reasoning process as reliable. As we've said, they exempt themselves from the illusion everyone else is under. They are somehow able to rise above the masses, trusting their own reasoning process about moral beliefs while informing the rest of us that we can't trust our moral reasoning process.

In his *On the Soul* (*De Anima*), Aristotle maintained that rationality is what makes humans distinct from other animals. Now, various atheists will argue that the ability to reason gives us value, and so we don't need to appeal to God.[18] But this position is problematic. As we've seen, it assumes that reasoning beings somehow emerged from nonrational processes—not exactly a natural fit. Also, does this mean that philosophers like Aristotle or Alvin Plantinga have greater value because of their reasoning powers than a two-year-old or your average plumber or electrician?

By contrast, being made in the image of a truthful, rational being removes these problems—as well as various rationalizations and loopholes of self-exclusion and self-contradiction. A reliable, rational God helps ground our general trust in our senses and moral intuitions.

THE NATURALISTIC FALLACY: MOVING FROM IS TO OUGHT

As we've seen, naturalists like Ruse claim that we don't have any duties in a naturalistic world. We only *think* we do. Yet some thinkers will claim that duties eventually emerge once our brains and nervous systems have sufficiently evolved. But we run into a problem: How do we move from *is* to *ought*? How do we shift from scientific *description* to moral *prescription*? Unless we already have value from the start (e.g., human beings having dignity and duties by a supremely valuable Being), we have no good reason to think value should emerge from valuelessness.

One naturalist who believes that we humans can "rise above" our biological origins says that asking "Why should we be moral?" is like asking "Why should we be hungry?" Being moral is as much a part of human nature as being hungry or having other biological urges hardwired into us by evolution.[19]

Is this so? C. S. Lewis observed, given such conditions, moral impulses are no more true (or false) "than a vomit or a yawn."[20] Thinking "I ought" is on the same level of "I itch." Indeed, "my impulse to serve posterity is just the same sort of thing as my fondness for cheese" or preferring mild or bitter beer.[21] To describe how humans do behave is one thing, but science can't prescribe how we *ought* to behave. It's an illegitimate logical leap from *is* to *ought*, from valuelessness to value—unless, of course, humans already possess value to begin with—and that is something a good God's existence readily explains.

We have not only the *is-ought* problem but the *self-sacrifice* problem as well: we have no rational reason for certain important moral values like deep self-giving. The heroic act of giving one's life for another—perhaps for a stranger—is one we applaud as noble and good. Yet this act makes no rational sense if the natural world is all there is. Why should I give up my brief existence on earth—the only existence I'll ever know—for others? Self-sacrifice appears idiotic.

The philosopher John Hick uses the illustration of an ant endowed with rational capacities and free will so that he can resist committing suicide for the sake of the ant colony:

> Suppose him to be called upon to immolate himself for the sake of the ant-hill. He feels the powerful pressure of instinct pushing him towards self-destruction. But he asks himself why he should voluntarily embrace this fact. There is a cause that may lead him to do so, namely the force of instinct. But is there any *reason* why, having the freedom to choose, he should deliberately carry out the suicidal programme to which instinct prompts him? Why should he regard the future existence of a million million other ants as more important to him than his own continued existence? After all, they are all ants, all but fleeting moments of animation produced and then annihilated by mindless and meaningless forces. . . . Since all that he is and has or ever can have is his own present existence, surely in so far as he is free from the domination of blind force of instinct he will opt for life—his own life.[22]

But self-sacrifice makes excellent sense in a theistic world—to lay down our lives for our friends or even strangers (cf. John 15:13; Rom. 5:7). After all, this earthly life is not the only one there is; so we don't have to clutch it desperately and take all measures to stay alive or survive as long as possible.

DIFFERENT MORALITIES?

If naturalists like Ruse are correct, then survivalist morality is arbitrary and could have developed in opposite directions. Ruse gives this example: instead of evolving from "savannah-dwelling primates," we, like termites, could have evolved needing "to dwell in darkness, eat each other's [waste], and cannibalise the dead." If we had developed *termite* morality ("termite makes right"!), then we would "extol such acts as beautiful and moral" and "find it morally disgusting to live in the open air, dispose of body waste and bury the dead."[23]

Our awareness of morality—"a sense of right and wrong and a feeling of obligation to be thus governed"—is only of "biological worth," serves as "an aid to survival," and "has no being beyond this."[24] Whether morality is primate- or termite-based is irrelevant—what matters is only what enhances survival and reproduction. Some authors have even suggested that rape can be explained biologically: when a male cannot find a mate, his subconscious drive to reproduce his own species pushes him to force himself on a female.[25] Nonhuman animals engage in rape-like acts; why not human males if it enhances survival and reproduction? To oppose what is "natural" requires appealing to a standard beyond nature, a *non*natural realm; that is, moral duties are truly binding regardless of whether or not they enhance survival and reproduction. This rising above natural urges—a move into the transcendent—once again looks like serious borrowing from a worldview like theism.

THE MORAL GAP

The moral argument is, in my estimation, the strongest and most powerful argument for God's existence. Our deep moral awareness not only serves as a clue to the meaning of the universe; it also can help us seek moral and spiritual help in light of our profound personal failures, guilt, and shame. Resisting the reality of a moral standard will prevent us from finding redemption.

We are aware of the moral gap that exists between our *performance* and the *ideal* we've failed to reach. If we are willing to see it, this moral gap reminds us that we need outside assistance—grace from a source beyond ourselves. We need help to live as we ought.

The philosopher Immanuel Kant insisted that "ought implies can." That is, if we have a duty to do something, then we ought to be able to carry it out. For example, consider the classic comedy *Dirty Rotten Scoundrels* (1998), a movie involving three con artists. It appears a cruel joke to Janet Colgate for the pretending psychiatrist Dr. Emil Schaffhausen III to tell the (also pretending) wheelchair-bound Freddie Benson that he ought to get up and dance. Comedy aside, we understand that duty requires ability.

The fact is, we have failed in what we ought to do, and now we're left wondering how we could ever bridge the moral gap in order to overcome guilt and shame to find forgiveness. Awareness of this gap, though, can lead us to cast ourselves on God's mercy and to trust in Christ, who bridged the gap that we ourselves could not. It is this God who "is able to keep [us] from stumbling, and to make [us] stand in the presence of His glory blameless with great joy" (Jude 24). So we could modify Kant somewhat: ought implies can—though with divine assistance.[26]

Philosopher John Rist finds that there is "widely admitted to be a crisis in contemporary Western debate about ethical foundations."[27] Taking seriously a personal God and Creator, the infinite Good and Source of all finite goods—including human dignity—helps provide the needed robust metaphysical foundation for human rights and objective moral values.

Furthermore, a successful moral argument, while enhanced by the doctrine of the mutually loving Trinity, can point us to the need for divine grace and forgiveness through Christ; it can prompt us to ponder our moral and spiritual plight and prayerfully seek assistance through more specific revelation from God.

That said, the moral argument does point us to a supreme personal, moral being (1) who is worthy of worship, (2) who has made us with dignity and worth, (3) to whom we are personally accountable, and (4) who may reasonably be called "God." Ultimately, the moral argument can be a stepping stone to the gospel, which even more vividly points us to our moral failure and the need for forgiveness, which has been secured for us in Christ.

AND WHAT ABOUT THE EUTHYPHRO "DILEMMA"?

Young children will frequently ask their parents about the permissibility of certain actions: "Why can't I do that?" They often receive the disappointing and arbitrary (or at least abitrary-sounding) reply, "Because I said so."

Likewise, various critics of theism have claimed that God's commands are just as arbitrary as the capricious parent's. God, we're told, engages in his own "Because I said so" assertions. And maybe God could have commanded the opposite—simply because he said so. And don't the Scriptures remind us that we are in no position to question the Cosmic Authority? Writes Paul, "Who are you . . . who answers back to God?" (Rom. 9:20). The point isn't that God's justice is capricious. No, the point is that God's wisdom and judgments are often beyond our own grasp (Isa. 55:9; Rom. 11:33–34; 1 Cor. 1:25). While God has reasons for what he does, we often don't have access to those reasons. And perhaps if we did, we still wouldn't understand them. This is different from God's being capricious.

In Plato's *Euthyphro* dialogue, Socrates raises another question about morality: could there be a standard of morality that's independent of the gods? He asks: "Is what is holy holy because the gods approve it, or do they approve it because it is holy?"[28] Socrates is referring to the capricious, immoral, humanoid deities of the Greek pantheon. These fallible deities are hardly the standard of goodness; they're far removed from the maximally great being of Scripture: "LORD, who is like You?" (Ps. 35:10).

Perhaps we can adjust Socrates's question for a theistic context, as critics do: "Is something good because God commands it (arbitrariness), or does God command it because it's good (i.e., God abides by some external standard of goodness)? In either case, the connection between God and morality apparently has a problem. Goodness is either *arbitrary* or *autonomous*.

Lots of atheists—and perhaps some theists too—call this "the Euthyphro dilemma," treating the matter as though arbitrariness and autonomy were the only two options. In quite a dramatic fashion, atheist philosopher Louise Antony calls this an "explicit and vivid" dilemma from which there is no escape.[29] Actually, *it's no dilemma at all*. The real problem is that the moral naturalist *doesn't like the alternative*!

Why are the arbitrariness-autonomy alternatives not a dilemma? Among other things, we have more than two options. Also, the dilemma advocates use mistaken categories and assume too much.

A Third Option: God's Intrinsic Goodness (Aretaic Option)

For one thing, we have a third option: God's commands spring from his intrinsically good nature or character. The horns of the Euthyphro "dilemma" aren't exhaustive. God doesn't command something because it is good (or vice versa); rather, God's commands flow from his necessarily good, worship-worthy character. We could call this the *aretaic* alternative (Greek: *aretē* = "excellence, virtue"). So we evade the *arbitrariness* and *autonomous standard* alternatives altogether by speaking of God's excellent character as the source of divine commands. There's no dilemma, and the literature on this is abundant.[30]

Divine Evil Commands?

Critics like philosopher Wes Morriston may ask, "What if God commanded something terrible?"[31] But an intrinsically good God simply couldn't command something intrinsically evil—like torturing babies for fun. To ask, "What if God were to command rape or baby torture?" is like asking, "Can you create a square circle or be a married bachelor?" That would be a contradiction in terms. If God commanded something evil, he would not be worthy of worship.

For those who ask, "What if God's character is evil?" our reply is: "Then we're not talking about *God*—the Greatest Conceivable Being. If our creator happened to be evil, we wouldn't be obligated to worship him." Only an intrinsically good being is worship-worthy. It's because this being is the standard of goodness that we worship him. We could add that God, as the Cosmic Authority, will issue commands that may be jarring or morally difficult, although he will do so for morally sufficient reasons.[32] God can't issue *intrinsically evil* commands (Jer. 19:5).

Furthermore, the "dilemma" proponents get something else wrong as well. To say that "what God commands" makes something "good" is a problem. In this case, God would be bound by his own command. He could only do what is good if he commanded something first. Did God first need to command *himself* about the manner in which he ought to create? No, God has no duties. He *does* what is good because of his very *nature*. God doesn't need to check himself or his commands against a standard outside himself; he simply acts, and it is good.

Infinite Regress

The critic might push back once more: "What if there's a moral standard independent of God?" We can simply say: We don't need to appeal to one, since a worship-worthy God serves as the sufficient and necessary standard of goodness. And if one claims that a standard exists independently of God, then we can ask: "And what makes *that* the standard and not *another* one beyond that one—or one beyond that one, ad infinitum?" We're left with an infinite regress—and a moral standard that ever eludes us. It's like the infinite-regress question we saw in the last chapter: "Who designed the Designer?"

We can ask the naturalist of a parallel dilemma, which would also lead to an infinite regress: "Are these moral facts good simply because they are good, or is there an independent standard of goodness to which they conform?" The Euthyphro argument doesn't offer any advantage or improvement over theism. It's unnecessary to insist on a standard outside of God's character. Why go beyond when the supreme Good—God—will suffice? The principle of sufficient reason applies to the moral argument. And so does the principle of economy (Ockham's razor): Why multiply additional standards of goodness unnecessarily?

Category Confusion

Another problem with the Euthyphro "dilemma" argument is its category confusion: critics confuse the *good* (value) and the *right* (duty). It's *good* to donate your kidney to a stranger (this act is called "supererogatory"—going beyond the call of duty). But this magnanimous act isn't *duty* or obligation. Goodness is a much broader category. Think of goodness (value) as a huge circle, inside of which are beauty, character, rationality, acts of supererogation, and *duties* (the right). Duties or moral obligations are only one category of value.

Goodness or value can't be reduced to God's commands (which are our duties). There is more to goodness than mere duties (what is *right*). As we've seen, God is intrinsically good and supremely valuable. A good, worship-worthy God has no duties, as we have seen. The point is that, contrary to the assumption behind the "dilemma," "good" doesn't equal "commanded by God."

The Presumption of Human Dignity

Even if the Euthyphro-friendly critic were successful in showing that a moral standard independent of God exists, we're still left with a number of big gaps that naturalism doesn't (or can't) easily fill. This critic of theism still engages in worldview-borrowing. She still takes for granted the kinds of things God readily supplies: human dignity and worth, free will, moral duties, rationality, and consciousness.

How does this work? God's personhood is connected to ours: without persons—divine or human—there would be no value. By contrast, our moral naturalist believes the following: (a) a preexisting moral standard exists; (b) valuable, rights-bearing, rational human beings evolved over hundreds of millions of years from nonvaluable, nonrational, nonconscious matter; and (c) humans are somehow connected to that eternal independent moral standard. This is a stunning cosmic coincidence of utterly disconnected phenomena. The existence of God dissolves the coincidence by providing a thoroughly organic connection between them.

A Christianized Euthyphro?

Defenders of Euthyphro will point out that some Christian philosophers hold that an objective moral standard can exist even if God doesn't.[33] We won't go into a detailed response here, but it's worth noting that these thinkers tend not to believe that God exists in every possible world, but—interestingly—they hold that objective moral values (e.g., "gang rape is wrong") cut across all possible worlds.

But why would these *values* be necessary, but not *God*? After all, humans don't exist in all possible worlds; only a necessary being like God does. Why are these values necessary when humans are contingent beings? It's odd that these theistic thinkers favor necessary moral values that are allegedly *independent* of God but that have such *deep connection* to finite humans and their duties. This is strange, because if God didn't exist, no humans would exist. Why connect necessary morality to contingent humans rather than the noncontingent God?

And what does it mean to say that the moral value "justice" simply exists disconnected from persons? How does an abstract "justice" or "love" exist independent of personhood? These abstract values just hang there without explanation—like mere brute facts in a Platonic world. A more natural connection is that these moral values that exist in all possible worlds are grounded in a personal, good God who exists in all possible worlds.[34] We could say the same about consciousness: it necessarily exists because God, a supremely conscious being, exists in all possible worlds.[35]

The existence of a good, supremely valuable being makes excellent sense of deep moral realities. While the naturalistic moral realist can make forays into justifying morality without God, her position isn't very robust. It is a more surface defense of objective moral values that leaves us with metaphysical gaps—holes that this supreme being readily fills.

FURTHER READING

Baggett, David, and Marybeth Baggett. *The Morals of the Story: Good News about a Good God.* Downers Grove, IL: IVP Academic, 2018.

Baggett, David, and Jerry L. Walls. *God and Cosmos: Moral Truth and Meaning.* New York: Oxford University Press, 2016.

———. *Good God: The Theistic Foundations of Morality.* New York: Oxford University Press, 2011.

Lewis, C. S. *Mere Christianity.* Part 1. Various editions.

Moreland, J. P., and William Lane Craig. Chapter 25 of *Philosophical Foundations for a Christian Worldview.* 2nd ed. Downers Grove, IL: IVP Academic, 2017.

21 | *Science, Nature, and God*

> The earth is the LORD's, and all it contains,
> The world, and those who dwell in it.
>
> —Psalm 24:1–2

> How great are His signs,
> And how mighty are His wonders!
>
> —Daniel 4:3

> How great are Your works, O LORD!
> Your thoughts are very deep.
>
> —Psalm 92:5

The triune God has created a world that humans—his priestly and kingly image-bearers—could study with diligence and rigor, with sweet pleasure, and with humble gratitude toward their Maker. We're able to understand many of creation's marvelous workings: "Great are the works of the LORD; / They are studied by all who delight in them" (Ps. 111:2). Since God created the world and how it operates, he isn't bound or limited by nature, as though its processes were necessary and inviolable.

God's self-revelation—his power, his wisdom, his creativity—can be detected through the world he has made—one of God's two "books," as we have seen. Yet God reveals himself through the miraculous as well. In this chapter and the next, we explore the interrelationship of God and creation and also the place of the miraculous in the world.

We'll see that we don't have to choose between false alternatives: the ordinary—though still amazing—divinely established workings of the natural world and God's special action in the world. God graciously displays himself through both—if we have eyes to see it.

GOD-SCIENCE MODELS

While the *Word* of God is the basis for doing theology, the *world* of God is the basis of doing science. Both theology and science are human endeavors, and we must keep going back to the sources as we revise our not only our theology but our scientific theories, too. A word to the wise: for all of the appeal to "scientific proof" in our day, it's good to keep in mind that discarded scientific theories abound.[1] So the idea that "science will eventually figure it out" is a bit too overconfident.

So, what does the National Institute for Standards and Technology have to do with Jerusalem, or the Brookhaven National Laboratory with the Portico of Solomon? How do scientific theorizing and experimentation connect to a biblical outlook? Various understandings of this relationship have been proposed. A commonly used classification is the fourfold model of Ian Barbour, with minor variations from others.[2]

> *Conflict*: One view considers faith in God and the operations of science to be opposed to each other. If both can't be true, this typically means faith in God must be false, not science ("irreconciliation").
> *Independence*: This perspective holds that the two are separate, nonoverlapping realms. As the late Harvard biologist Stephen Jay Gould claimed (following Galileo and others), science teaches us how the heavens go while faith in God teaches us how to go to heaven; science teaches us about the ages of rocks while faith in God teaches us about the Rock of Ages.[3] These two realms, however, have nothing to do with each other.
> *Dialogue*: This view sees science and faith in God in conversation with each other—as mutual partners that can learn from and show ongoing respect to each other.
> *Integration*: This approach sees science and faith in God forming a more complete whole or a fuller picture of reality.

Our emphasis here will take both the dialogue and integration views seriously.

What Is Science?

Harvard biologist Richard Lewontin, we've seen, claims that science must begin with materialism: all reality is comprised of matter. Science itself is "the only begetter of truth."[4] The geneticist J. B. S. Haldane insists that scientific practice must be "atheistic." That is, "when I set up an experiment I assume that no god, angel or devil is going to interfere with its course; and this assumption has been justified by such success as I have achieved in my professional career. I should therefore be intellectually dishonest if I were not also atheistic in the affairs of the world."[5]

As for Lewontin, we can say that science is one possible begetter of truth, but not the only one: presumably, Lewontin didn't draw this conclusion from scientific observation. As for Haldane, Alvin Plantinga offers this point: "There is an enormous difference between atheism and assuming that God won't interfere with my experiments."[6] The founders of modern science—mostly Christians—assumed that natural processes will operate according to certain fixed regularities *unless* God acted directly in the world. These scientists assumed that explanations for physical events (e.g., chemical reactions) don't *normally* depart from the physical or natural world. But God can act in the world and turn water into wine, if he so chooses.

New Testament scholar Craig Keener—a personal friend and an academic known for his meticulous and careful research—has documented many cases of healing in Jesus's name both across church history and throughout the world today; these can be found in his hefty two-volume defense of miracles. So how would Haldane treat the following story recounted by Keener? Vietnam veteran Carl Cocherell broke his ankle in Branson, Missouri, in 2006. During a vision of Jesus that night, Carl was told that his ankle was healed. He had another x-ray taken by his hometown doctor in Michigan a couple of days later; Carl was told that he never had a broken ankle since there was no evidence of even tissue damage. But when Carl showed his first x-ray, the doctor acknowledged that the ankle had indeed been broken.[7] If God's existence is possible, then science can't limit all physical events to only one kind of cause—materialistic and natural. Miracles don't have to disrupt scientific endeavor.

At the end of this chapter, we'll look at the details of "methodological naturalism." But for now, let's look at what science is.

First, when it comes to defining (natural) science, here is a good start, in my estimation: *the attempted objective study of the natural world whose theories rationally connect to specific empirical phenomena and whose concepts and explanations do not normally depart from the natural realm.* What does all of this mean? Let's focus on three words to anchor our discussion: *empirical, rational,* and *objective.*

Empirical: Human minds can study the empirical world by way of the senses—or by sensory extenders such as telescopes or microscopes. We don't conclude how many teeth a horse has by contemplating this in an armchair; rather, we go to the barn, open the horse's mouth, and start counting.

Rational: The world that natural science studies is predictable and orderly, thanks to the wise God who created it. We can expect it to be generally understandable. This means we can count on its uniformity. It's safe to assume that natural laws detectable within our solar system won't be different in other, far-flung portions of the universe. Also, we can detect patterns and regularities in the world, and these help guide us as we look at the past and also predict how natural processes will continue to operate in the future.

Objectivity: Science looks beyond the individual scientist and experimenter to others who study the same phenomena and who can analyze the same processes in order to confirm or correct.

This is a brief overview of key aspects of science. By contrast, we come to *scientism*, which is philosophically problematic.

SCIENTISM

Strong and Weak

Science is one of many disciplines that give us knowledge. *Scientism*, by contrast, is a bold and audacious stance that severely limits knowledge. We've seen that it's one of the pillars of naturalism: knowledge comes through science. However, it actually has two versions, both of which have serious problems.

The strong version affirms that *only* science can give us knowledge. It's like the kangaroo in Dr. Seuss's *Horton Hears a Who*. She insists that Horton the elephant is wrong about life existing on a tiny speck of dust: "If you can't see, hear, or feel something, it doesn't exist!" Likewise, the physicist Stephen Hawking declared that science can help us answer "why we are here and where we came from. . . . And the goal is nothing less than a complete description of the universe we live in."[8]

The second is like unto it. The weak version claims that science is the *best or surest* path to knowledge. This has even affected theology. Increasingly, Christians are taking science as the greater authority than Scripture. But if, say, neuroscience challenges the idea of the soul, then we have to reject that idea. Whatever science says, then theology had better hop to it and adjust accordingly. If "science" concludes that the only persons we encounter are physical, then we should call into question the idea that a personal being (like God) could exist without a body.

Scientism's Problems

Obviously, if God exists, then the range of things we can know will extend well beyond the physical creation. And even when we use the term *science*, this is often a broad, amorphous, catch-all term. It would be clearer to refer to what particular *scientists* say. But scientism, taken on its own merits, shows itself to be overly or unnecessarily restrictive. Let's consider the problems with scientism, especially the strong version. We'll see how it is philosophical, arbitrary, self-refuting, reductionistic, and incomplete.

Philosophical

Strong and weak scientism begin with *philosophical* assumptions. These versions take for granted the authority of science, yet they don't recognize how philosophical their starting point is. In ancient times, the philosopher Plato took for granted the reality of the nonphysical transcendent realm; if you wanted knowledge, the physical world *wasn't* a reliable place to start. By contrast, David Hume and other empiricists have taken the very opposite philosophical stance—namely, starting with the world of sense and physicality in pursuit of knowledge.

In addition, those who consider science authoritative still assume and appropriate a lot of other philosophical ideas and assumptions—ones that can't be scientifically proven. Though they don't always recognize it, scientists will load themselves up philosophically before they engage in their scientific endeavors. So what kinds of philosophical ideas do they take for granted? Here's a start:

Realism: The physical, mind-independent world exists and isn't an illusion, though admittedly some scientists would qualify this.

Logic: Logical laws should be used to guide scientific work and theorizing. As Dallas Willard noted: "Logical results have a universality and necessity to them which no inspection of facts can provide."[9]

Math: Mathematics is important for making sense of the natural world and its processes.

Beauty: Beauty or elegance is a criterion scientists take for granted when assessing scientific theories.

Mental: The mental is required to understand the physical; without the existence of minds, we wouldn't be able to understand our world.

Other minds: We can't prove other minds exist, but we take their existence for granted. Those minds can critically examine and assess the outcomes of scientific studies.

Personal trust: Scientists trust the work of others in the scientific community and build on that research.

Reliable reason: The workings of our minds are generally trustworthy and aren't systematically deceiving us.

Reliable senses: We assume our senses are reliable and not systematically deceiving us.

Natural laws: We count on the consistent natural laws and uniform workings of natural processes.

Mind-world correspondence: The natural world and its workings are capable
of being studied and understood by human minds.

Inferential knowledge: What we observe in nature can provide clues and indicators of *unobservable* processes and patterns (e.g., subatomic particles).

Materialism (for some scientists): Scientism takes for granted the sole reality
of the physical realm. But how can one scientifically prove this? This is
an unverified philosophical assumption.

Again, these ideas are all philosophical, not scientific. Those who advocate
either version of scientism should remember how dependent they are on the
philosophical.

No doubt we've encountered those of a scientistic bent, who demand *scientific* proof to justify belief: "Prove it scientifically." However, we can reply,
"Why must I accept this demand? Science can't prove that science alone can
give us knowledge. That is a *philosophical* assumption. Indeed, we can learn
much from philosophical reasoning apart the scientific realm." In fact, scientific advance often depends on creative philosophical thought. Think of
how early Western (pre-Socratic) philosophers such as Leucippus and his
pupil Democritus used philosophical reasoning—not scientific observation or
experimentation—to come up with the concept of atoms.[10] Science is highly
philosophical, but often the last ones to see this are the scientists.

Arbitrary

To say that only science can give us knowledge is arbitrary. Yes, science can
give us knowledge, but what about other disciplines such as philosophy (as
we've seen), theology, mathematics, aesthetics (beauty), and ethics? They are
a vast storehouse of knowledge.

Besides this, science is incapable of speaking to a lot of things: whether
the soul exists, whether life has meaning, whether we have free will, whether
beauty exists, how consciousness and free will emerged, or what caused the
universe to exist. Why live within the limits of science alone?

Self-Refuting

Scientism, we've seen, is a philosophical claim, not a scientific one. This viewpoint isn't the result of scientific research (a scientific conclusion drawn from
exhaustive research). It's a philosophical assumption—a statement *about* science, not *of* science.

We can't scientifically verify that all knowledge must be scientifically verifiable. The very concept of scientism actually is *self-undermining*. It's like saying "I can't speak a word of English." We can't *validate* science by *appealing to* science. On top of this, the naturalistic scientist can only *assert* that materialism is true and that nature is all there is; she can't *prove* any of it.

Reductionistic

Scientism reduces all reality to the physical, which skews our perspective on reality. Think of metal detectors. They are highly successful in assisting us to find coins and other metal objects. But it would be reductionistic to say that metal detectors therefore reveal all that can be discovered: "If something can't be picked up by metal detectors, it's not discoverable." Likewise, science's great success in giving us knowledge about the natural world doesn't mean that it can therefore give us comprehensive knowledge of all that can be known.[11] That would be reductionistic.

We noted Abraham Maslow's quip: "If you only have a hammer, every problem begins to look like a nail." Likewise, if you look at reality as purely physical, then the only tools to interpret reality will be physical. Scientism must step outside the realm of science in order to claim that you can't step outside science.[12]

Incomplete

We've hinted at the point that *sola scientia*—"science alone"—is false and that it needs other disciplines to broaden our knowledge. Why is science incomplete? We've seen that philosophy is critical to science and that a biblical worldview helped launch modern science. Indeed, if God is in the picture, the natural world—and thus the natural sciences—don't exhaust all that can be known about reality. As we've seen, science can't explain how:

- the universe came into existence a finite time ago;
- natural laws came to be;
- the universe came to be so remarkably finely tuned for life;
- first life emerged;
- consciousness emerged;
- beauty, moral duties, human dignity, free will, and rationality arose.

And as we've already seen, science can't tell us whether something is *actually* designed or only *apparently* designed.

SCIENCE AND SCRIPTURE

A Superficial Conflict

Despite the alleged warfare between science and faith in God, the conflict is only superficial. A lot of these conflict problems arise when we read the early chapters of Genesis as a scientific textbook rather than as a work of ancient Near Eastern literature. Even when the Scriptures give the impression that the earth can't be moved (Pss. 93:1; 96:10), keep in mind that this is poetic language. The psalms are likely presenting a picture of stability—consider the godly psalmist, who won't be "moved"—that is, become unstable (Pss. 17:5; 30:6; cf. Prov. 12:3). Scripture's mention of the sun's rising and setting (Pss. 50:1; 113:3) isn't teaching geocentrism any more than when meteorologists refer to sunrise or sunset on the early evening news. It's merely using the language of appearance and accommodation.[13]

Of course, this fact doesn't mean that Genesis has no bearing on certain scientific discoveries and ways to think about the world: we see biblical indications of creation out of nothing (Gen. 1:1; cf. John 1:1–3) as well as God's ordering of the world as a suitable place for creaturely habitation. As it turns out, these features in Genesis 1 are supported by the scientific discoveries of the big bang and the fine-tuning of the universe.

To focus on whether God created directly or indirectly is not the point. We can look at the entire process and still readily detect God's remarkable care and wisdom displayed in creation. God created Adam from the dust (Gen. 2:7), but Job—who had a normal birth—affirms that God created him from the dust as well (Job 10:9).[14] Also, another of normal birth, the psalmist, said God knit him together in his mother's womb and that he had been "fearfully and wonderfully made" (Ps. 139:13–14). A process doesn't diminish the role or the evidence of divine intelligence. For example, though the mountains were formed over hundreds of millions of years, this doesn't diminish their majesty or beauty; they give clear evidence of divine creativity.

Deep Congruence with Science

The Christian faith is actually deeply *congruent* or *harmonious* with science, as philosopher Alvin Plantinga has argued. If anything, *naturalism* deeply conflicts with naturalism (or scientism) despite superficial harmony. In what way? As we've seen, rationality and knowledge are elusive for the naturalist, since nonrational physical processes—chemical reactions in the brain—produce beliefs over which we have no control, including the belief that naturalism is true.[15]

To insist on the priority of science (scientism) leaves us with "two un-happy results" that can do damage both to faith in God and to the enterprise of science. How so? The question of evidence for biological evolution aside, those who insist that God and evolution are necessarily incompatible (i.e., they equate evolution with naturalism/atheism) make belief in God appear anti-intellectual to those who respect science and reason. This damages faith in God. Yet the claim also *damages science* since it forces people to choose between science and belief in God. It fosters a distrust in the operations and conclusions of science.[16]

A Two-Way Street between Science and Scripture

One mistake some Christians make is to insist that science must always learn from Scripture but not the other way around. Theologians interpret the Scriptures, but not perfectly. That is, while *Scripture* is ultimately authoritative, our *interpretations* of Scripture are not, and we should take care to distinguish between the two.

Scientific work could contribute to our more wisely handling Scripture (e.g., not taking it as a textbook on modern science but as an ancient Near Eastern document). Augustine and John Calvin wrote of those well-meaning but uninformed Christians who used strained interpretations of Scripture to try to teach trained scientists a thing or two. In doing so, they embarrassed themselves and made the Christian faith look foolish.

The lesson from God's two books is that learning should be a two-way street. Through science, we have learned that the earth does move, that the sun doesn't literally rise and set, and that the universe is ancient. Through Scripture, we know that the universe began a finite time ago, although it took science till the twentieth century to produce the empirical evidence for it.

We have good reasons—biblically, philosophically, and empirically—for taking seriously the intersecting of God and science. If the self-revealing, cre-ating, designing triune God exists, then integration of theology and science isn't only possible; it's essential.

METHODOLOGICAL NATURALISM, MIRACLES, AND THE MAKER OF HEAVEN AND EARTH

Practical Atheists in the Lab?

Haldane's earlier statement that doing science is "atheistic" doesn't refer to what we can call *metaphysical* or *philosophical* naturalism (PN). PN would be the view that God doesn't exist, and it would thus rule God out as an explanation for anything. By contrast, methodological atheism or methodological naturalism (MN) is what Haldane has in mind: natural laws and physical explanations can adequately explain physical events without reference to God. In fact, even some believing scientists hold this view: truly scientific observation and analysis of physical processes should be carried out *as though God doesn't exist*. Bringing God in as an explanation confuses things and muddies the waters of acceptable science.

The MN camp wants to protect science from confusion and interference. Leaving open the possibility of God's action would lead to a "God of the gaps" problem. That is, "God explanations" about physical events are an attempt to fill the gaps of our ignorance ("I don't know what caused that chemical reaction in the laboratory. *God* must have done it"). That doesn't help science advance. And the further science does advance, the more irrelevant "God explanations" prove to be, we're told by some MN proponents.

MN is the authoritative position taken by the National Academy of Science: "The statements of science must invoke only natural things and processes."[17] Yet nearly 50 percent of scientists today believe in God or the spiritual realm and are convinced that there is no conflict with how they are doing science.[18] Of course, these scientists don't believe that God or an angel is going to interfere with substances in a chemistry lab or suddenly change the laws of gravity and motion.

Describing Methodological Naturalism

To preserve science, must we really insist that explanations of physical events must *never* depart from the natural realm? Is the assumption that physical events must have physical causes the end of the matter? No and no. For one thing, the task of defining *the physical* or *matter* has become rather messy since the discovery of the bizarre quantum world of subatomic particles and their activity.

Furthermore, let's ask ourselves: If we seek only natural explanations for any physical event, what about the beginning of the universe? Insisting on physical explanations that follow known natural laws isn't going to help us here. Why not? Nature and its laws actually came into existence with the big bang. So to insist on a natural or even physical explanation for this physical event assumes *without argument* that God *couldn't* have caused it. But shouldn't the open-minded scientist seek the *best* explanation of a physical event—not simply the best *physical* explanation?

Christians affirm that God truly acted in the world to raise Jesus from the dead. So we can acknowledge that natural laws can't explain all physical events—just as they do not offer adequate explanations for the very beginning of the universe itself. And if God makes a spectacular universe from nothing, then what's the big deal about God raising the dead (Acts 26:8)?

The skeptic David Hume was committed to empiricism—the idea that all knowledge is derived through sense experience of the physical world. Yet he himself pointed out "the problem of induction": even if humanity has witnessed patterns like "sunrises" and "sunsets" throughout history, it's still possible that tomorrow things may diverge from that pattern. The seeming fixity of the past doesn't guarantee a fixed future. This opens up an interesting consideration: when it comes to God's activity in the physical world, we should follow the evidence where it leads rather than insisting on natural explanations only. Science isn't overthrown. For example, professors may cancel class for a day without throwing the entire academic calendar into confusion. Likewise, a miraculous act by God doesn't destroy the general regularities of natural processes either.

Also, scientists of all stripes can distinguish between natural states of affairs and the actions of intelligent agents. They know how to detect this and incorporate it into their research. The Search for Extra-Terrestrial Intelligence (SETI) program was designed to detect intelligent life elsewhere in the universe via radio frequencies. Neuroscientists require persons to report on their inner experiences since they can't be detected by instruments and mathematical calculations. Archaeologists can distinguish between natural products and processes and agent-designed artifacts like arrowheads and pottery. So if we can detect human agency, intelligence, and intentionality, then why not *divine* agency, intelligence, and intentionality?[19]

Though an atheist, J. L. Mackie was exactly correct when he wrote about divine action: "The laws of nature describe the ways in which the world . . . works when left to itself. . . . A miracle occurs when the world is not left to itself."[20] That is, a miracle can occur if the natural universe is causally *open* (God can act directly in it) rather than *closed* (i.e., no external force can be exerted on it). Science is unable to tell us that the universe is a causally closed system—and thus that God never acts specially in it. Natural processes remain the same even when an external force acts on it.[21]

Responses to Methodological Naturalism

While we can appreciate the scientist's desire for perfect consistency in order to carry out the scientific task, MN isn't the way to deal fairly and openly with the scientific task.

For one thing, modern science took shape largely under the influence of Bible-believing Christians. They believed in a God who not only designed an orderly universe that can be studied; they held that God has specially acted in the world through miracles. Earlier we noted Paul Davies's observation: "Science began as an outgrowth of theology, and all scientists, whether atheists or theists . . . accept an essentially theological worldview."[22] That is, they didn't practice science "atheistically."

So the "warfare" or "conflict" model—"science versus God"—isn't historically true. It's a recent invention from the late 1800s that has been dismissed by contemporary historians of science. Whether we're talking about the Middle Ages, Copernicus, Galileo, the Huxley-Wilberforce debate, Darwin, and so on, cultural myths have grown up around them to discredit the Christian faith's longstanding pursuit of the scientific enterprise.[23]

Second, MN is a kind of methodological straitjacket: it demands that a physical event can be explained *only* by a physical cause and nothing else. But shouldn't we seek the best overall explanation, not simply the most plausible physical explanation? If God exists and acts in the world, then closed-mindedness to the miraculous cuts us off from one set of explanations to physical events. Plenty of philosophical atheists have observed this. Bradley Monton sees MN as a shackle: "Rejection of the supernatural should not be part of scientific methodology. . . . Scientists should be free to pursue hypotheses as they see fit, without being constrained by a particular philosophical account of what science is. If science really is permanently committed to methodological naturalism, it follows that the aim of science is not generating true theories. Instead, the aim of science would be something like: generating the best theories that can be formulated subject to the restriction that the theories are naturalistic."[24]

Atheist thinkers like Philip Kitcher,[25] Keith Parsons,[26] Thomas Nagel,[27] and the notable W. V. O. Quine[28] concur. This is a similar position to Christian philosopher Richard Swinburne's: the case for theism is structured along the same lines as that of "any unobservable entity such as [a subatomic particle like] a quark or neutrino."[29]

Methodological Neutralism and Pluralism

One alternative to methodological naturalism is methodological *neutralism*. This view advocates for openness regarding the *causal*, the *discoverable*, and the *correctable*. First, this view doesn't rule out in advance divine action or *causality* in the world, which often has physical effects (e.g., water turning to wine, Jesus's resurrection). This approach could include well-documented medical cases and testimonies in our day that involve healing in the name of Jesus, such as the aforementioned story of Carl Cocherell.

Second, we are able to *discover* the nature of that cause by following the evidence where it leads us rather than setting conditions in advance about what kinds of causes are permitted. If the former atheist Antony Flew had taken the MN view, he wouldn't have changed his mind about physical evidences for theism—the universe's beginning, fine-tuning, and biological complexity.

Third, by not setting prior conditions through MN, we leave open the possibility of *correcting* our understanding through emerging evidence. If nature had a beginning and thus is not eternal, as a number of indicators support, then it turns out we have evidence pointing toward something nonnatural; why insist the beginning must have a natural cause?[30]

But perhaps neutrality may prove somewhat elusive. We're not always as neutral as we would like to be when it comes to science. So maybe what we need, Robert Larmer suggests, is a methodological *pluralism*. This allows competing worldviews to engage in conversation, to explore the broader framework of those views, and discover which one makes better sense of the overall data.[31]

Further Reading

Copan, Paul, et al., eds. *Dictionary of Christianity and Science*. Grand Rapids: Zondervan, 2017.

Copan, Paul, and Douglas Jacoby. *Origins: Ancient Impact and Modern Implications of Genesis 1–11*. New York: Morgan James Publishers, 2018.

Dennett, Daniel C., and Alvin Plantinga. *Science and Religion: Are They Compatible?* New York: Oxford University Press, 2011.

Hannam, James. *God's Philosophers: How the Medieval World Laid the Foundations of Modern Science*. London: Icon, 2010.

Moreland, J. P. *Scientism and Secularism: Learning to Respond to a Dangerous Ideology*. Wheaton, IL: Crossway, 2018.

Peterson, Michael, and Michael Ruse. *Science, Evolution, and Religion*. New York: Oxford University Press, 2016.

Plantinga, Alvin. *Where the Conflict Really Lies: Science, Religion, and Naturalism*. New York: Oxford University Press, 2011.

Trigg, Roger. *Beyond Matter: Why Science Needs Metaphysics*. West Conshohocken, PA: Templeton, 2015.

> Why is it considered incredible among you people if
> God does raise the dead?
>
> —Acts 26:8

My son Peter was in Delhi, India, during the summer of 2011. He was part of a team from our university, nearly all of whom had been students of mine. It was during this time that they all witnessed a young man being healed from cerebral palsy after being prayed for in the name of Jesus. Immediately after returning to the United States, my wife and I picked up Peter and the India team leader, Ben Greco, and brought them to our home. Ben gave a fresh report of what had happened.

Ben had been asked by an Indian pastor to pray for this young Indian man, whose body was, as Ben described it, "twisted into the shape of a pretzel" and who needed assistance getting from place to place. Ben wondered, *What if nothing happens?* But he sensed God reminding him that this was precisely why he came to India—to see God at work. So he went ahead and prayed, laying his hands on the young man, with the rest of the team at hand.

Ben reported that while he was praying, he could feel the man's bones in his back moving into their proper place. Once the prayer was done, the young man was helped to his feet and, in amazement, started "walking and leaping"— just like the healed lame man in Acts 3:8!

This is just one credible miracle story of many I have gathered over the years.[1] A good number of my students have returned from summer trips abroad, happily—and sanely—reporting various healing miracles in the name of Jesus—and with eyewitnesses to corroborate their stories. Nevertheless, many will challenge the very concept of miracles as unscientific and a belief for gullible, uneducated sorts.

SOME PRELIMINARIES

Deism, Jesus, and the Miraculous

President Thomas Jefferson, a Deist who believed Jesus to be merely a powerful moral teacher of reason, cut up and pasted together portions of the four Gospels that reinforced his belief in a naturalized, nonmiraculous, nonauthoritative Jesus. The result was the severely edited *Life and Morals of Jesus of Nazareth Extracted Textually from the Gospels*—or, *The Jefferson Bible*. In one letter (1819), he claimed that he could easily extract the "lustre" of the real Jesus "from the dross of his biographers, and as separate from that as the diamond from the dung hill."[2]

In an earlier letter to Peter Carr (1757), Jefferson claimed that Jesus was "a man, of illegitimate birth, of a benevolent heart, [and an] enthusiastic mind, who set out without pretensions of divinity, ended in believing them, and was punished capitally for sedition by being gibbeted [i.e., crucified] according to Roman law."[3] Jefferson edited Luke 2:40, "And [Jesus] grew, and waxed strong in spirit, filled with wisdom," omitting, "and the grace of God was upon him." This "Bible" ends with an un-resurrected Jesus: "There they laid Jesus, and rolled a great stone to the door of the sepulchre, and departed"—the end.

Deism's chief motivation for rejecting miracles—along with special revelation—was that they suggested an inept Deity who didn't get everything right at the outset; so he needed to tinker with the world afterwards, adjusting it as necessary. The biblical picture of miracles, though, shows them to be an indication of a ruling God's care for and involvement in the world—indeed, his concern for human salvation. In fact, many across church history and throughout the world in our own day have witnessed specific indicators of direct divine action and answers to prayer.[4]

The Christian faith stands or falls on God's miraculous activity, particularly in Jesus's resurrection (1 Cor. 15)—no resurrection, no Christianity. Scripture readily acknowledges the possibility of miracles in nonbiblical religious settings. It also affirms that demonic powers may "perform great signs" to mimic the signs and wonders performed by God (cf. Rev. 13:13–14).

Even beyond this, we shouldn't rule out God's gracious, miraculous actions even in pagan settings: for example, there's the well-known story of the sixth-century BC Cretan prophet Epimenides (cf. Titus 1:12), who directed the Athenians to sacrifice and pray to the "unknown God"—an act that, as reported by the ancient writer Diogenes Laertius, ended a terrible plague in their city.[5] Nevertheless, we note below that, unlike the many divinely wrought miracles in Scripture, miracle claims in other religions are incidental—not foundational—to the pagan religion's existence.

In earlier chapters, we've looked at plausible reasons for thinking a good, powerful, wise personal God exists. He's not some generic deity, but a covenant-making, initiative-taking God who responds to the human situation of sin, misery, alienation, suffering, and evil. If we're not careful, discussions about God's existence and nature may not go far enough, perhaps ending up with a mere Deism. We must press further to ask: "If God exists, has he done anything to address our desperate human condition?" The Christian story emphatically answers, "Yes!" God's existence and his concern for humanity go hand in hand; he gets his feet dirty and hands bloody in Jesus, bringing creation and redemption together. His ministry and the salvation-event signaled a new exodus and a new creation. His miraculous resurrection from the dead in particular guarantees hope and restoration, and this cornerstone event is accompanied by many publicly accessible reasons—historical, theological, and philosophical.[6]

Miracles in Other Traditional Settings

David Hume has the reputation for having stoked the fires of disbelief about miracles. One of his arguments is that the miraculous claims within the various religions cancel each other out. The Christian claims that Jesus rose from the dead; a Hindu claims that a Ganesh statue is drinking milk.[7] Hume's response would be, "A plague on both your houses!"

However, why *must* this be so? This is the "baby with the bathwater" scenario—the kind of assertion that doesn't want to follow the evidence wherever it leads. Hume's work actually reveals a strong anti-miracle bias such that no evidence, no matter how strong, will actually suffice to overturn that bias. Furthermore, not all worldviews are created equal, and rather than lumping them all together, we should take miracle claims on a principled case-by-case basis, as well as consider the "religious background" or worldview context.

For example, comparing the resurrection of Jesus to the "miracle" of Osiris—the Egyptian lord of the underworld—is all wrong. According to the myth, Osiris's body, cut into fourteen pieces, floats down the Nile. His wife/sister (?) Isis picks up thirteen of the pieces and eventually resuscitates him. The actual point of the myth is Isis's lamentation, *not* Osiris's resuscitation.[8] Closer study of these ancient Mediterranean myths reveals that these gods died but "did not return or rise to live again."[9] In addition, these kinds of ancient myths are part of a cyclical view of history—more specifically, they are connected to seasonal cycles. These aren't actual historical persons, nor is such an alleged "miracle" a datable event of linear history—like Jesus's death on April 3, AD 33 (the fourteenth of Nissan in the Jewish calendar), and resurrection on April 5, AD 33.[10]

In general, miracles are primarily the stuff of the biblical faith; miracles in other traditional religions tend to be incidental and not at all crucial to their validity. Indeed, nontheistic or pantheistic ("God is everything") worldviews have no conceptual room for miracles. Any purported miracles associated with Buddha or Confucius just wouldn't fit within the overall worldview.

Also, historical Jesus scholar Gary Habermas has investigated purported miracle-claims from the ancient world such as the resuscitation ("resurrection") or translation into heaven of great personages. He concludes that the sources are generally late in their "recounting"; they put forth questionable or contradictory accounts; and they are not open to any sort of verification.[11] So not all miracle-claims are created equal. Conflicting miracle-claims between religions don't imply that all of these worldviews are false or that one religion's claims can't be true. If the triune, self-revealing Creator exists, then there's no reason he can't override the natural order he has put in place. He is God, after all.

Miracles and Persuasion

The Scriptures routinely appeal to public miracles to vindicate the teachings of prophets and even of Jesus's ministry. The biblical faith is a public faith, and signs and wonders typically accompany its proclamation.

This doesn't mean that divine miracles *guarantee* belief: "If they do not listen to Moses and the Prophets, they will not be persuaded even if someone rises from the dead" (Luke 16:31). Miracles can be rationalized away (as thunder, in John 12:29) or even suppressed by people who don't want to believe, such as Jesus's enemies seeking to kill miraculous evidence—the resuscitated Lazarus (John 12:1, 10). Miracles don't compel belief, but, for those willing to receive them, they do serve as sufficient indications of God's activity and revelation. John calls them "signs" that point beyond themselves to Jesus's significance: Jesus miraculously feeds bread to a crowd of over five thousand and then declares, "I am the bread of life" (John 6); he says, "I am the light of the world," illustrating it by healing a man born blind (John 8–9); he affirms, "I am the resurrection and the life" and shows it by raising Lazarus (John 11). No wonder Jesus says, "Believe Me that I am in the Father and the Father is in Me; otherwise believe because of the works themselves" (John 14:11). His miracles, revealing God's in-breaking reality in history, are available for public scrutiny.

What Is a Miracle?

Definitions

What *are* miracles? They're not statistically highly improbable or coincidental events—or "an incredible stroke of luck," as Richard Dawkins puts it.[12] A true miracle is an event that couldn't be explained by natural factors or processes.

David Hume calls miracles "violations" of the laws of nature. If loosely understood, perhaps we could allow it, but the trouble with Hume is his circular definition: miracles can't happen because nature's laws can't be violated. But as C. S. Lewis said, if we admit God into the picture, then we have no security against miracles!

The universe isn't "closed" but is open to God's involvement within it. That is, a "natural law" or "the natural order" *describes* how the world generally operates, but it doesn't *control* what happens in it. As noted earlier, a professor's canceling a university class doesn't "violate" the class schedule. In fact, the criterion that all things must conform to prior experience would make scientific progress impossible. If, for instance, the universe came into existence from nothing, how could this event be predicated by natural laws, and on the basis of what prior experience?

Philosopher John Locke recounted the story of the Dutch ambassador who was telling the king of Siam (now Thailand) about life in Holland. He told the king that the weather would get so cold as to make water freeze solid such that an elephant could walk on it. Because of the king's experience of only warm climes, he understandably replied: "Hitherto I have believed the strange things you have told me, because I look upon you as a sober fair man, but now I am sure you lie."[13] In this story of "The King and Ice," frozen water was exhibit A for "Violation of the Laws of Nature"! Indeed, scholars have noted that Hume could never quite get around this objection. The prominent philosopher John Earman—an agnostic—wrote *Hume's Abject Failure* to demonstrate how Hume's arguments against miracles are seriously deficient.[14]

Other definitions of "miracle" may include terms like "suspension of," "exception to," or "nonrepeatable counterinstance to" nature's order and laws. But perhaps something like this will do: miracles are *theologically significant, observable, direct acts of a personal God that can't be predicted or explained by merely natural causes.*

Miracles aren't fluky or contextless (e.g., like Elvis or John Lennon "sightings"). For example, Jesus's resurrection makes sense in light of the Old Testament's theology as well as Jesus's own teaching, ministry, and specific predictions. In general, they can be witnessed (*observable*) so that people can—if they are willing to see it—detect their theological significance.[15]

Ultimately, miracles wouldn't take place if left up to nature. The believer and the skeptic can agree here. *Naturally*, dead people don't live again. However, Jesus's bodily resurrection—impossible according to natural processes—is possible because a personal God exists and can act in the world.

German theologian Ernst Troeltsch claimed we should evaluate any testimony to miracles in light of our own experience. Some analogy must exist between what we've experienced and the miracle-claim itself. But let's say you do witness your first authentic miracle. Given Troeltsch's standard, you'd have to reject it because you hadn't seen anything like it before. In fact, you'd have to reject a whole string of miracles since you'd *never* have a starting point for declaring something miraculous. So it becomes a vicious regress. And what of unique miracles like the incarnation or resurrection? No first miracle could occur since nothing previous compares to it. Furthermore, in some sense *all* events are unique. As Lewis observed, no one sunrise is exactly like another. How much more for miraculous events!

If God Exists, Then Miracles Are Permitted

To claim miracles can't take place assumes that a personal Creator doesn't exist. But, as we've already said, if a God exists who can create a universe from nothing, what's the problem with a virginal conception, resurrection, or physical healing (cf. Acts 26:8)? A miracle-denying worldview like naturalism simply won't be open to whatever evidence there is, since experience by itself is insufficient; a miracle can always be explained away: "If anything extraordinary seems to have happened, we can always say that we have been the victims of an illusion. If we hold a philosophy which excludes the supernatural, this is what we always shall say."[16] Unless God acts, dead people stay dead. Too often philosophical considerations like Hume's overwhelm the historical evidence, no matter how strong. God can't get his foot in the door because a philosophical system has slammed it shut.

The importance of background information or context cannot be overstated. Miracles are probable (or not) relative to the background information or context. If God doesn't exist, miracles aren't just "initially improbable" or "highly improbable." They *can't* happen. All unusual events will be attributed to natural causes. But if God exists, miracles become possible. And if God doesn't act directly in the world, then nature will operate along lawlike, predictable lines.

Providence—Ordinary and Extraordinary

Some Christians claim to have experienced a "miracle"—like finding a perfect parking spot during business hours in New York City. But is that really a miracle? Now, we shouldn't minimize God's concern about the small things in our lives—and we may want to show prudence by taking the train into the city instead. But we must be careful not to trivialize miracles but rather to make proper distinctions about God's working in the world.

God's involvement in the world may be tied to apparently natural events that reveal their supernatural quality by their remarkable *timing*—say, an earthquake causing Jericho to fall at the precisely predicted moment. This would be an example of God's "extraordinary providence."

This kind of working is distinct from God's "ordinary providence," which includes sending sunshine and rain and fruitful seasons (Matt. 5:45; Acts 14:17). In contrast to these two workings of divine providence, true miracles simply can't be predicted or account for by natural processes. God, a personal and willing agent, has freely and directly acted in the world.

Christians, Cretins, and Credulousness

One of Hume's claims is that only gullible and uncivilized ("ignorant and barbarous") people believe in miracles. While not denying plenty of silliness and gullibility about miracle claims, this charge requires a more sober-minded assessment rather than a hand-waving dismissal.

Ironically, modern science was established by intelligent Bible believers who acknowledged the importance of miracles in the Christian story. Also, plenty of academically trained scientists today believe in miracles.

Were people *really* gullible in biblical times? The evidence suggests a ready skepticism about the miraculous—from the elderly Abraham and Sarah laughing at the thought of having their own child to Zacharias doubting the angel Gabriel's message when burning incense in the temple. Even Jesus's own disciples—especially Thomas—refused to believe initial reports that Jesus was raised. They hadn't been expecting an individual's resurrection before the final "day of the Lord." And Joseph, who knew where babies come from, didn't take Mary's word for it; it took an angelic messenger to persuade him. When the disciples heard from the women that Jesus appeared to them, they considered it all nonsense (Luke 24:11). Scripture repeatedly presents miracle-doubters in all their skeptical colors.

Also, what did Hume mean by "ignorant and barbarous people" (who believed or made miracle-claims)? Closer inspection reveals that Hume meant *nonwhites*—people he believed to be of "naturally inferior" intelligence. The implication? Despite having heard reports of exceptions, Hume's experience would have found the existence of an intelligent black person to be just as unreasonable as expecting a miracle. His white European Enlightenment presumption was always against intelligent nonwhites. The point here is simply this: if someone has made up his mind about what is uniform—whether white superiority or the impossibility of miracles—he'll always dismiss any counter-examples (of intelligent blacks or well-attested miracle-claims) as going against probability and reason.[17]

JESUS'S RESURRECTION

The Christian faith's most theologically significant miracle is Jesus's resurrection, and it is a well-supported historical event. Though historical study yields varying levels of probability, we don't have to be mired in historical skepticism. We can still have a high degree of confidence in our historical knowledge as we consider evidence for Jesus's resurrection.

The chief facts surrounding this miracle are these:

- Jesus's burial in Joseph of Arimathea's tomb;
- the discovery of Jesus's empty tomb;
- the postmortem appearances; and
- the origin of the earliest disciples' belief in Jesus's resurrection.

In addition to these are the historically significant conversions of James and Paul. James was Jesus's half-brother, who didn't believe in him before his resurrection (John 7:5; 1 Cor. 15:7) but later became the leader of the Jerusalem church. Paul had been a persecutor of the church but died a Christian martyr.

These are well-established historical facts accepted by the majority of critical biblical scholars—including the most skeptical, who reject Jesus's bodily resurrection.[18] For instance, some scholars may believe the "appearances" were mere hallucinations or psychological/guilt projections, but they do acknowledge that something clearly triggered the disciples' belief in Jesus's postmortem appearances. We should add that Jesus's faithful women followers had no reason to feel guilty; they followed him to the end when the other disciples had fled.

Also, the fact that Jesus appeared to his *female* followers—when women weren't considered reliable witnesses in a law court—adds credibility to the resurrection accounts. This is called the "criterion of embarrassment": Why include material that could detract from your testimony? Inclusion of such materials renders fabrication or falsification far less likely.

This is important: in themselves, these four lines of evidence aren't "miraculous facts" that are somehow beyond historical research; they're available to all students and scholars of history. The point at issue is: Which interpretation or explanation—natural or supernatural—makes the best sense of these facts?

In addition to the ready explanation of God's raising Jesus from the dead, consider also the very low historical probability of available naturalistic explanations of the first Easter—the disciples stole the body; the women went to the wrong tomb; Jesus's followers suffered massive and widespread hallucinations; Jesus didn't really die but swooned and the cool tomb revived him; the common but virtually universally rejected view that the resurrection is just another pagan or "mystery religion" legend.[19] The inadequacy of these naturalistic explanations further reinforces the plausibility of the miraculous explanation.

So while historical facts themselves are not miraculous, an explanation certainly may be. And if God exists, such an explanation is legitimate and theologically warranted. In his massive treatment of the historical evidence, N. T. Wright concludes that the combined historical probability of (a) the empty tomb—something Jesus's enemies assumed (Matt. 28:12–15)—and (b) the postmortem appearances is "virtually certain," being on the level of Caesar Augustus's death in AD 14 or the fall of Jerusalem in AD 70. To have one without the other wouldn't do: just an empty tomb would have been merely a puzzle or a tragedy, and Jesus's postmortem appearances alone could have been chalked up to hallucinations. But taken together, these two matters give the origin of the early church its powerful impetus. Jesus's resurrection isn't "beyond history."[20]

The biblical testimony of (a) *many*, (b) *independent*, and (c) *credible* and *sincere* eyewitnesses should be taken seriously. First Corinthians 15 reports that Jesus appeared to over five hundred, to Peter, to the unbelieving James (Jesus's half-brother), and, though in visionary form, to the hostile persecutor, Paul. John 20 tells us that Jesus showed himself to the skeptic Thomas to examine the wounds on his body. Women as the first witnesses reinforces the strength of the evidence. The basic facts surrounding Jesus's resurrection are consistent in an array of sources—the Gospels, the early Christian sermons in Acts, Paul's epistles, and the very early Jerusalem tradition mentioned in 1 Corinthians 15, which dates to less than two years after Jesus's death.[21]

Furthermore, the Jews of Jesus's day (second-temple Judaism) believed that "resurrection" entailed an empty tomb; a resurrection couldn't take place without a dead body being made gloriously alive again. Naturalistic attempts to explain away the first Easter (hallucination theory, wrong-tomb theory, disciples-stole-the-body theory, swoon theory, and the like) are inadequate and without sufficient explanatory power. The far more probable conclusion for Jesus's empty tomb and for postmortem appearances of an alive-and-well Jesus is that God raised Jesus from the dead.

"Extraordinary Claims Demand Extraordinary Evidence"

The late atheist astronomer Carl Sagan claimed that "extraordinary claims demand extraordinary evidence," a mantra that many a skeptic likes to quote. Doesn't it make sense that a miraculous claim as grand and significant as Jesus's resurrection would require a lot of evidential extras before it can be believed? Though it sounds reasonable, it's actually problematic, which is why John Earman calls such a demand "nonsensical."[22]

For one thing, we're typically not told what "extraordinary" means—perhaps it's an *additional* supporting miracle directly delivered to the person demanding it? To his credit, at least Hume tried to clarify what he meant by "extraordinary." An extraordinary claim is one contradicted by the great weight of existing evidence. Therefore, extraordinary evidence simply means a *large number* of evidences—though not a different *type* of evidence—to support an extraordinary claim.[23] Even so, this demand still ignores the background issue of God's existence and how this fact makes miracles plausible, regardless of the weight of regular natural occurrences.

This brings us to the second point: if God exists, and if we also have an explanatory religious context to make sense of Jesus's bodily resurrection, then we are well on our way to having plausible support for a miracle. For example, this context would include Jesus's ministry, authoritative claims, remarkable signs, and repeated predictions that this would take place.

Beyond this, we may simply then need only *additional* evidence, but not necessarily something *extraordinary* like divine skywriting telling us, "This is a Yahweh-approved miracle." Think of the story of Carl Cocherell in the previous chapter. He had an x-ray taken of a broken bone; then Jesus appeared to him in a vision to tell him he was healed; and then another x-ray was taken to confirm this healing. There's nothing extraordinary about this humble second x-ray.

Finally, this "extraordinary evidence" claim is simply false. Consider the evidence for the resurrection: the empty tomb, the purported appearances of Jesus, the sudden emergence of the church, the early preaching of the resurrection in the early church, the conversions of James and Paul, the sudden boldness of the disciples, their martyr deaths, and so on. Then ask this question: "What is more likely given all of this evidence—that Jesus *did* or *did not* rise from the dead?"

The point is this: we simply wouldn't have this kind of evidence had Jesus's resurrection *not* occurred. The massive pileup of evidence is highly improbable if Jesus *didn't* rise from the dead. That is, you've got a lot more to explain if Jesus didn't rise than if he did. The philosopher John Stuart Mill (1806–1873) comes to our aid on this point: "To know whether a coincidence does or does not require more evidence to render it credible than an ordinary event, we must . . . estimate afresh what is the probability that the given testimony would have been delivered in that instance supposing the fact which it asserts not to be true."[24]

In the end, God's existence makes miracles a genuine possibility. Without God, miracles are a statistical impossibility. Yet the New Testament church was founded on the historical fact of Jesus's bodily resurrection and the empty tomb, which gave sudden rise to the early church, which preached a risen Jesus in the heart of Jerusalem—the very place where an otherwise fabricated miracle story could be most easily refuted. No wonder Peter wrote that he and his fellow apostles hadn't been following "cleverly devised tales," and they even heard the heavenly voice, divinely attesting to Jesus's authority (2 Pet. 1:16). To cite historical theologian Jaroslav Pelikan again, "If Christ is risen, then nothing else matters. And if Christ is not risen, then nothing else matters."[25]

FURTHER READING

Basinger, David. *Miracles*. Cambridge: Cambridge University Press, 2018.

Copan, Paul, and Ronald K. Tacelli. *Jesus' Resurrection: Fact or Figment?* Downers Grove, IL: InterVarsity Press, 2000.

Habermas, Gary, and R. Douglas Geivett, eds. *In Defense of Miracles: A Comprehensive Case for God's Action in History*. Downers Grove, IL: IVP Academic, 1997.

Keener, Craig. *Miracles: The Credibility of the New Testament Accounts*. 2 vols. Grand Rapids: Baker Academic, 2011.

McGrew, Timothy. "Miracles." In *The Stanford Encyclopedia of Philosophy*. Edited by E. Zalta. https://plato.stanford.edu/entries/miracles/ (revised Jan. 23, 2019).

Moreland, J. P. Chapter 7 in *Kingdom Triangle*. Grand Rapids: Zondervan, 2007.

Part III

FALL

How long, O LORD, will I call for help,
And You will not hear?
I cry out to You, "Violence!"
Yet You do not save.
—Habakkuk 1:2

23 | *The Problem of Evil (I): Introductory Matters*

> Unless you repent, you will all likewise perish.
>
> —Luke 13:3, 5

> It is good for me that I was afflicted,
> That I may learn Your statutes.
>
> —Psalm 119:71

EVIL AND GOD'S "VERY GOOD" WORLD

In the beginning, God created all things "very good" (Gen. 1:31) and humans to "rule" with God the world and its creatures (Gen. 1:26). That doesn't mean that this well-watered garden-park in Eden—and especially the world beyond—didn't require human tending and care. As we've noted, the command to "subdue [*kabāsh*]" the land (Gen. 1:28) required exerting force to push back encroaching natural forces rather than being ruled by them; some kind of benign coercion was necessary prior to the fall.[1]

Once ejected from paradise after the fall, life outside the garden-park would mean toil for women in labor and for men in agriculture (Gen. 3:17). To varying degrees this would become unmanageable after the fall. Humans would have to worry about sufficient rain for crops and try to push back the desert and experience challenges to agricultural life. The fall from their former glory would break apart human union with God and inhibit the spread of God's glory throughout the earth.[2]

As we've seen, the fall affected loving relationships—namely, humans' union with *God* and their harmony with *other humans*. And they would become broken, fragmented, and mal-aligned *within themselves*—prideful, rationalizing, self-centered. And their relationship with the *natural world* was impacted; not only did humans become vulnerable to its now-hostile forces from which they had previously been protected by God (tornados, earthquakes, ferocious animals), but also, as we know, humans have misused and brought damage to the creation entrusted to them. In addition, other creatures—fallen angels—had also rebelled against God (Jude 6; cf. 2 Pet. 2:4). They have continued waging a spiritual battle against God's kingdom, partly aimed at bringing harm to humanity and to God's mission in the world (Eph. 6:12).

In reviewing the Christian story, we began with the triune God and then moved to creation. Now we look at various facets of the fall—the next portion of the metanarrative. For starters, we look at the "problem of evil"—a topic that will, for our purposes—require three chapters. This chapter will examine some preliminary questions related to evil. The following longer chapter on evil will address the philosophical problems of evil. The chapter thereafter will look at natural evils, animal pain, and the demonic.

Obvious Evil—Without and Within

During the 1990s war in the former Yugoslavia, atrocities such as this abounded: "A young Muslim mother in Bosnia was repeatedly raped in front of her husband and father, with her baby screaming on the floor beside her. When her tormentors seemed finally tired of her, she begged permission to nurse the child. In response, one of the rapists swiftly decapitated the baby and threw the head in the mother's lap."[3] The philosopher Eleonore Stump observes: "This evil is different, and we feel it immediately. We don't have to reason about it or think it over. As we read the story, we are filled with grief and distress, shaken with revulsion and incomprehension."[4] These—along with child pornography, parental incest, participation in Nazi death camps—are examples of what one philosopher calls "paradigmatic evils." In committing or experiencing these evils, people find "initial reason to doubt the positive meaning of their lives."[5]

We are familiar with such evils *without*, but evils *within* abound as well. When C. S. Lewis first began intentional self-examination, he discovered that the human heart is more deceitful and wicked than we can know (Jer. 17:9; Mark 7:21-23). He wrote: "For the first time I examined myself with a seriously practical purpose. And there I found what appalled me; a zoo of lusts, a bedlam of ambitions, a nursery of fears, a harem of fondled hatreds. My name was legion."[6] Alexandr Solzhenitsyn, who survived his Soviet labor camp experiences, came to realize that "the line separating good and evil passes not through states, nor between classes, nor between political parties either, but right through every human heart, and through all human hearts."[7]

As we look around us and within ourselves, the reality of evil is very apparent to us. This reality is the one thing believer and unbeliever alike tend to agree about. In fact, the unbeliever will use the problem evil to make the strongest available case against God.

Tragically, we've noted that some still deny the obvious. After World War II, Arthur Koestler visited Japan, where a Zen Buddhist scholar told him that

Hitler's gas chambers were "very silly"—not evil. Good and evil, he said, were a Christian invention, and they "exist only a relative scale."[8] The denial of evil is also found in Western philosophies. Richard Dawkins has asserted about our world that "there is, at bottom, no design, no purpose, no evil and no good, nothing but blind pitiless indifference," and we just dance to the music of our unknowing and uncaring DNA.[9] For philosopher Bertrand Russell, all that humans are and have accomplished is the outcome of accidental arrangements of atoms.[10] For the strict naturalist, objective good and evil are just a "corporate illusion fobbed off on us by our genes to get us to cooperate."[11]

We've seen, however, that the burden of proof is on those who deny those unquestionably and obviously horrific, "paradigmatic" evils—something we *just see* and that stares us in the face. Denying the vileness of child abuse and wife-beating is the moral equivalent of denying that 2 + 2 = 4. To do so means tearing apart the very fabric of our humanity and deepest moral understanding that helps us make sense of life. To quote atheist Kai Nielsen again: "Anyone who does not believe [child abuse and wife-beating are evil] cannot have probed deeply enough into the grounds of his moral beliefs."[12]

The Christian faith is realistic, not escapist. It takes evil utterly seriously. Psalmists cry out at evil, and prophets can be perplexed or angry with God because of evil states of affairs (2 Sam. 6:8; Pss. 13:1–2; 35:17–18; Hab. 1:2–3). Indeed, the story of our redemption in Christ both *assumes* and *addresses* the reality of evil.

Despite all the criticism theists receive because of the problem of evil, take note: *every* worldview must grapple with evil. It's not simply a theist's or Christian's problem. What's more, the question is not so much about a worldview *resolving* all the problems related to evil, but rather this: Which worldview offers the *most robust resources* for addressing the problem of evil?

Defining Evil

How should we understand or define evil? For one thing, we should note that biological pain or painful sensation may be beneficial up to a point—perhaps alerting us to some bodily malfunction or a place needing medical attention. But suffering involves a deeper level of pain—an inner pain of the soul. Beyond all this, evil is *a departure from the way things ought to be.* The world is not what it should be.

C. S. Lewis observed that, while an atheist, he railed against God because the universe seemed so cruel, but he assumed a standard of justice by which to judge evil. Judging a stick to be crooked assumes an idea of straightness.[13]

Counterfeit money makes sense only if there's real currency. But if nature is all there is, why think things *ought* to be any different? Things just *are*. Furthermore, why think horrific wickedness could exist in a naturalistic world? There would be no standard from which to deviate, no norm to defy, no duty to which we're obligated.

Some may push back: "We can't know what goodness is unless we know what evil is." But why think this? We know real currency without knowing counterfeits. The standard itself is more fundamental or basic, not the deviation from it. This may raise the question about our first ancestors in the garden: "Didn't they have to know about evil in order to do the good?" Not necessarily. They knew the good, and they should have trusted the God who had cared for them and walked with them (Gen. 3:8). No, the first humans failed in their duty to trust and to listen to their gracious Provider. They took the word of an intruder instead. Only thereafter did they come to *experientially* know the distinction between good and evil.

It turns out that there is an argument *for* God *from* evil: "If you think there really *is* such a thing as horrifying wickedness (that our sense of there being one is not a mere illusion of some sort), and if you also think that the main options are theism and naturalism, then you have a powerful theistic argument from evil."[14]

We could put the argument this way:

- If objective moral values exist, then God (most likely) exists.
- Evil exists.
- Evil is an objective (negative) moral value.
- Therefore God (most likely) exists.

It turns out that the nontheist then has at least *two* major problems that challenge her worldview: not only the problem of *evil*—all worldviews must grapple with this—but also the problem of *goodness*, which is quite at home in the biblical story.

EVIL, REASON, AND EMOTION

How do we address the problem of evil with someone who is dying of cancer or a child whose father or mother just died? What do we say when they ask, "Why?" Such circumstances remind us that evil is more than an *intellectual* problem; there is an *emotional* or *pastoral* problem of evil too. The intellectual or philosophical problem deals with arguments and reasons for and against God's existence, which will be the focus in the present chapter.

The emotional problem addresses the matter of *not liking* a God who permits evil. This means that, more than our rational answers, those who are suffering need our comfort, personal presence, pastoral care, and warm affection. Consider the afflicted Job, whose friends "sat down on the ground with him for seven days and seven nights with no one speaking a word to him, for they saw that his pain was very great" (Job 2:13). In their silence, Job's friends were properly responding to the emotional problem of evil; it was only when they began opening their mouths that the trouble began. That said, even though Job didn't discover any of God's reasons for permitting his suffering, Job was nevertheless content to have God show up to reveal his wisdom and power. God's presence was enough.

C. S. Lewis wrote *A Grief Observed* (1961) after his wife, Joy Davidman, died. But earlier, in his book on the intellectual "problem of pain" (1940), he acknowledged that he was unqualified to write about the emotional problem but urged that, in bearing pain, "a little courage helps more than much knowledge, a little human sympathy more than much courage, and the least tincture of the love of God more than all."[15]

When people ask "Why?" in the midst of mind-baffling suffering, they are asking the wrong question and are setting themselves up for frustration on top of their grief. They assume that they can or should have access to the reason behind this or that particular evil or season of suffering—and they somehow feel justified in turning away from God if the reason hasn't been revealed to them. But Scripture gives no such universal assurances. Despite modern-day pontificators who tell us that this hurricane or that earthquake took place because of God's judgment, Jesus reminds us that we're generally not in a position to know such reasons (Luke 13:1–5). Whether it's moral evils (e.g., Pilate's order to kill Galileans in the temple) or natural evils (e.g., the tower of Siloam's collapse and killing eighteen Israelites), Jesus urges his fellow Jews to be reconciled to God: "Unless you repent, you will all likewise perish" (Luke 13:3, 5; cf. John 9:3).

That is, Jesus suggests that suffering can prompt us to set our hope on the living God rather than trusting in our own resources. In the words of Paul, "we were burdened excessively, beyond our strength, so that we despaired even of life; indeed, we had the sentence of death within ourselves so that we would not trust in ourselves, but in God who raises the dead" (2 Cor. 1:8–9).

Pain often moves people away from God, but it can also prompt them to consider God. Former critic of the Christian faith A. N. Wilson pointed to the reality of death as something of a wake-up call for him, as well as revealing the inadequacy of his atheism: "Watching a whole cluster of friends, and my own mother, die over quite a short space of time convinced me that purely materialist 'explanations' for our mysterious human existence simply won't do—on an intellectual level."[16] With death all around him, Wilson experienced a spiritual wake-up call. He came to realize the intellectual inadequacy of his view and found greater emotional resources in the gospel—a theme we explore more fully in the next chapter.

FURTHER READING

Evans, Jeremy A. *The Problem of Evil: The Challenge to Essential Christian Beliefs.* Nashville: B&H Academic, 2013.

Lewis, C. S. *A Grief Observed.* Various editions.

———. *The Problem of Pain.* Various editions.

Meister, Chad, and James K. Dew Jr. *God and Evil: The Case for God in a World Filled with Pain.* Downers Grove, IL: InterVarsity Press, 2013.

24 | *The Problem of Evil (II):*
Evils Logical and Probabilistic

> "As for you, you meant evil against me, but God meant it
> for good in order to bring about this present result, to
> preserve many people alive."
>
> —Genesis 50:20

EVIL AND LOGIC

As we've seen, the Scriptures take evil very seriously, and they show how God
has acted in the world in order to conquer it. Yet the major complaint about
the Christian faith is not that God allows evil but that their coexistence is
logically contradictory. This is the *logical*—or deductive—problem of evil.

Oxford philosopher J. L. Mackie claimed that the believer both *must* but
cannot hold to the following three statements consistently:[1]

> God is omnipotent.
> God is wholly good God.
> Evil exists.

Give up any *one* of these statements? Fine. But to hold to all *three* of these at
once is logically impossible. The heart of the logical argument is this: If God
could prevent evil, he *would*, and if God *would* prevent evil, he *could*.

The logical problem of evil is a tidy one, but that is its downside. It is a *necessary* argument that allows for no wiggle room whatsoever: it must have no
hidden premises; it doesn't allow us to conclude that "*probably*, God doesn't
exist." If it were a sound argument, the necessary conclusion would be that an
all-good, all-powerful God cannot exist.

We won't devote much space to the logical argument, as it's a massive failure.
Various notable philosophers—including atheists—have acknowledged this:

> WILLIAM ROWE: "Some philosophers have contended that the existence of
> evil is *logically inconsistent* with the existence of the theistic God. No
> one, I think, has succeeded in establishing such an extravagant claim."[2]
> WILLIAM ALSTON: "It is now acknowledged on (almost) all sides that the
> logical argument is bankrupt."[3]

PETER VAN INWAGEN: "It used to be widely held that evil . . . was incompatible with the existence of God; that no possible world contained both God and evil. *So far as I am able to tell, this thesis is no longer defended.*"[4]

So why is it such a bad argument? To see this, we can just add a fourth statement to the other three:

God has morally sufficient reasons for permitting the evils he does.

This simply takes the wind out of the sails of the logical argument.

That's not all. We can add that this argument makes two mistaken assumptions:

Assumption 1: A good being eliminates evil insofar as he can.
Assumption 2: There are no limits to what an omnipotent being can do.

Regarding Assumption 1, a good being will eliminate evils unless he has morally justifiable reasons for permitting them. To be stabbed with a knife would be an evil, yet a surgeon who uses her knife on me in the operating room—a terrible experience though this be—has my overall health in mind.

As for Assumption 2, God has given humans significant free choice regarding what kind of character we will cultivate and how we will set our spiritual compass in life. This freedom is a *great good* worth having—one that even God in his omnipotence won't violate or undermine. It wouldn't be a feasible world if God takes back the dignity of freedom he's bestowed on creatures. So God permits even the abuse of this freedom. Freedom permits us to turn into a Mother Teresa or an Adolf Hitler. If we only had the power to help others but not to harm them, then we wouldn't have any deep or meaningful responsibility for one another.

As Alvin Plantinga has written, "it is possible that God could not have created a universe containing moral good (or as much moral good as this world contains) without creating one that also contained moral evil. And if so, then it is possible that God has a good reason for creating a world containing evil."[5]

Assumption 1: "A good being eliminates evil insofar as he can."	Assumption 2: "There are no limits to what an omnipotent being can do."
It is logically possible that God has **morally sufficient reasons** for permitting evils—reasons that God alone may know but are inaccessible to us.	It is logically possible that God cannot create **significantly free creatures** who never sin, since it is up to creatures to choose.

So the logical problem of evil isn't a problem. Perhaps it might be worth mentioning that J. L. Mackie had earlier written *Inventing Right and Wrong*, which baldly asserts that humans have constructed morality. His book begins: "There are no objective values."[6] Yet here he is, claiming that evil—just a human construction—contradicts God's infinite goodness and power. Thus we have the Mackian problem about the problem of evil: how can there even *be* an argument against God from evil if evil itself is just a human invention?

DEFENSE OR THEODICY?

In light of evil, some philosophers and theologians will take the less-ambitious route of offering a *defense*—simply attempting to show that the coexistence of God and evil is not logically contradictory. Others will go further by offering a *theodicy* (Greek *theos* = God; *dikē* = justice)—positive reasons that justify God's permitting evil. For example, one thoughtful proposal speaks of a "theodicy of love" in which a sovereign, loving, covenant-making God grants robust freedom to human and angelic creatures. In love, God doesn't violate these covenantal relationships by intervening in ways that undermine creaturely freedom, although this means that his creatures can abuse this freedom and do great damage. Yet this God involves humans to do battle in a cosmic conflict against demonic beings, who have limited power and limited time to do their worst. This loving God promises that his good, just kingdom will prevail and that he will vanquish evil.[7]

"Skeptical theists" emphasize how our human cognitive limitations make it unlikely that we'll have robust access to the reasons God has for permitting evil. We aren't well-positioned to make such assessments and should even be skeptical of our capacity to do so since God's thoughts and ways are higher than ours (Isa. 55:9). In the face of criticism, they argue, it's sufficient to give a defense, simply showing that God and evil aren't incompatible, even if we don't know what God's reasons may be. That said, skeptical theists don't rule out that we can know *some* of these reasons—for example, God's using evil redemptively to shape our character ("soul-making").

We'll come back to some of these themes. However, it is probably worth noting these distinctions before further carrying on the conversation about evil.

EVIL AND EVIDENCE

So the tightly structured logical argument from evil is a failure, and what's left for the critic is "something of a comedown" since she will have to use a "much messier and more problematic" argument now.[8] This is the *evidential* or *probabilistic* problem of evil.

The argument here is that, given the vast amount of apparently pointless evils in the world and across the millennia of human history, God's existence—though not illogical—is nevertheless *unlikely*. Think of the horrendous events of the twentieth century alone with over one hundred million deaths, including concentration camps, labor camps, and killing fields. Does the vast amount of evil over the course of history strongly suggest that God most likely doesn't exist?

The question to ask is: "Probable, given what?" If we look *only* at the existence of evil, yes, God's existence seems less likely. But is that the sum of the evidence we should consider? Not at all. Probability takes into account the *entirety* of the relevant background information or context. For example, the problem of evil presupposes the reality of a finely tuned and biofriendly universe as well as the reality of goodness and the value or worth of human beings. But in God-less world, how did such goods emerge from random, valueless, nonconscious processes?

In fact, we've already seen that evil already presupposes a standard or design plan from which it is a deviation. So the full scope of relevant evidence must be considered, not just the specific problem of evil alone. Indeed, we must consider multitudinous factors that are relevant evidence—indicators that must be included in the mix of arguments for and against God, as the following diagram indicates.

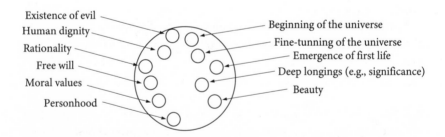

The skeptic's question about God and evil doesn't wipe away the other evidence for God's existence. In fact, the problem of evil is a *secondary* question to evidences such as the beginning of the universe—not to mention the assumption that humans have a dignity that shouldn't be violated by evils. Without the existence of the universe, there would be no human beings to inhabit it and thus no human evils. The question "Why is there anything at all?" is the more fundamental question than "Why is there evil?"

FURTHER THEOLOGICAL CONSIDERATIONS

Moralistic Therapeutic Deism

According to sociologist Christian Smith, we live in a culture that subscribes to "moralistic therapeutic deism": There's a God "out there" who isn't personally involved in our lives ("deism"), but if we live decent lives and are kind to others ("moralistic"), God will guarantee our feeling good and living pain-free, fulfilling lives ("therapeutic").[9] If we encounter gut-wrenching circumstances that disturb our sense of well-being, we take this to be a violation of an implicit divine-human contract.

This doesn't at all resemble the biblical point of view. Knowing that God is the greatest good possible (John 17:3) doesn't exclude a pain-free, trouble-free existence. How many stories do we read by "Christian celebrities" who abandoned their faith after experiencing evil, which they felt contradicted this assumed "happiness contract." But Jesus promised that we will have trouble in this world, yet he also said, "Take courage; I have overcome the world" (John 16:33). Christ promises to keep us *in the midst of* suffering, not to keep us *from* suffering or temptation (John 17:15).

On top of that, our earthly life isn't the only one to consider. Rather, the life to come will put all things in proper perspective. As one who suffered beatings, shipwrecks, imprisonment, stoning, mob attacks, and the like, the apostle Paul wrote that our present sufferings are a "momentary, light affliction" but that the glory we will experience is "beyond all comparison" with the weight of glory that will be revealed (2 Cor. 4:11–18).

Is God a Good Parent?

In response to evil in the world, some will appeal to the "good parent analogy": if it's wrong for a good parent not to intervene to prevent her son from hitting his infant brother with a hammer, why doesn't God, if he exists, intervene when, say, a Holocaust or a Stalin Five-Year Plan is on the horizon? (My own father—born in the Ukraine—lost his father, Andriy, to starvation after Andriy had been sent to a labor camp during Stalin's forced famine.)

We could respond in several ways to point out appropriate *disanalogies*. For one thing, God's goals are broader than that of human parents, and it is quite an ambitious statement to say that God is under obligation to prevent such harms, which means that God would also have to override human freedom and its consequences in every case of potential harm. Further, limited earthly parents, by constantly intervening, may actually damage their children. Also, if God always intervened, then such interventions would actually remove from parents the obligation to prevent these harms: "If a parent didn't feed his child, God would; if a parent pushed his child out a high window, God would catch him."[10] The book of Revelation points out that while God sustains and protects his people *spiritually*, there are no guaranteed protections *physically* (e.g., 2:9–11; 12:13–17). While God sometimes acts to rescue and preserve from harm, God's people are often persecuted and martyred (Heb. 11:32–40).

Evil, Divine Protection, and Illusions

Furthermore, if God were to *remove* pain and suffering so that the consequences of the sin and our alienation from God would be hidden from us, we would live in an illusory world. God would be giving us the impression that we are doing fine without being reconciled to God. What if the prodigal son's father (Luke 15) always intervened in the life of his son so that he never experienced the consequences of sin? Why would he bother looking homeward? Likewise, if we didn't experience the consequences of sin, we would never be dissatisfied in our state of separation from God. If God is to deliver us from our sin and separation from him, he must make us aware of it. As Lewis said, pain is God's megaphone to rouse a deaf world.

Divine Involvement

Beyond this, God is near to the brokenhearted (Ps. 34:18), and he even enters into a world of suffering and injustice. This is particularly evident in the incarnation, life, and death of Jesus Christ, who reveals a God who is *with* us and *for* us and *suffers with* us as well (e.g., Prov. 14:31; Matt. 25:37–40; Acts 9:4). This can truly bring great comfort during our emotional pain. In the words of philosopher Alvin Plantinga, "As the Christian sees things, God does not stand idly by, coolly observing the suffering of his creatures. He enters into and shares our suffering. He endures the anguish of seeing his Son, the second Person of the Trinity, consigned to the bitterly cruel and shameful death of the cross."[11]

MYSTERIOUS VERSUS GRATUITOUS

Paul condemns the flawed theology that claims we can "do evil that good may come" (Rom. 3:8). So it would be incorrect to say that *evil itself* is necessary or essential for God to bring about greater goods for humankind. Rather, we see

God *permitting evil* such that these goods are realized and God's redemptive purposes accomplished. Of course, from one angle, it would have been better had there been no evil at all. But God created free creatures, and, as free agents, it was up to them to sin or to refrain from sinning.

Pointless Evils and Evidence

The critic will challenge belief in God by saying that at least some pointless evils do exist: for example, a baby doe might be burned to death in a forest fire. We may find such scenarios baffling (though see more on animal suffering below). But they don't necessarily show that a good God probably doesn't exist.

Many believers will insist that there are no pointless evils but that there is a divine purpose for every evil. They will also acknowledge that though we don't know all or even most of God's reasons for permitting every evil, there's no reason to think we should: the absence of evidence isn't evidence of absence. For example, as I look through my binoculars into the copse of trees half a mile away, I don't detect the movement of birds, let alone hear any bird sounds. But that doesn't mean they aren't there. I simply may not be well positioned to make this determination.

Likewise, just because we don't know the reason for this or that evil (i.e., it's mysterious or inscrutable), this doesn't mean that that evil must therefore be pointless or gratuitous. It appears that the only evidence for the existence of certain seemingly pointless evils is that it is inscrutable. Yet how can the critic speak with confidence that gratuitous evil therefore exists? All she can say that that this *seems* to be the case. That means that if the strongest position one can take is agnosticism about whether evil is pointless, this significantly tamps down the force of the probabilistic argument.

Some Christian philosophers, however, affirm gratuitous evils *do* exist.[12] But even if we allow that there could be gratuitous evils, this still wouldn't show that God doesn't exist. After all, without a design plan or standard, we have no basis by which to judge anything as evil. To recognize evil is to assume a standard or norm, which points us *toward* God rather than away from him— even if gratuitous evils exist.

That said, if God knows all the details of what humans will freely do in whatever world God places them and can bring about great goods in the wake of those evils, why not think that God can bring about a world without any gratuitous evils at all? So while the atheist can rightly say that *he does not see how a particular evil has a point*, it doesn't follow from this that that evil has no point. Given our cognitive limitations as humans in a fallen world, the critic should be cautious in concluding this.[13]

An Alternative Argument

So instead of seeing gratuitous evil as an argument against God, the argument can be turned on its head:

> If God exists, he does not allow any pointless evil.
> God exists.
> Therefore, there is no utterly pointless evil.[14]

The kind of relationship we have with God depends in part on God's knowing everything and our not knowing everything. This means learning to trust God even when he doesn't explain himself. The problem of evil need not drive us from God but actually can prompt us to trust and hope in him. As the Christian philosopher Peter van Inwagen observes, "I never had the least tendency to react to the evils of the world by saying, 'How could there be a loving God who allows these things?' My immediate emotional reaction has rather been: 'There *must* be a God who will wipe away every tear; there *must* be a God who will repay.'"[15] This brings us to another important consideration.

COSMIC JUSTICE

Imagine a kind, selfless, wealthy woman who gives all she has to help the poor—like the heroine Dorothea Brooke in George Eliot's *Middlemarch*. Just moments prior to her death, her closest relatives find out she is penniless, and they angrily mock and reject her because she is not leaving them anything. Her body is then tossed into a pauper's grave. It seems that all of her saintly behavior was for naught. Why should she have "done the right thing" when all of her life labors led to this kind of unjust outcome? A positive or negative outcome is due to a cosmic accident: what nature gives, nature can take away.[16]

On earth, it would be an utterly intolerable society that fails to hold rapists and murderers to account; likewise, it would be intolerable if no cosmic justice is done—where the wicked get away with murder and the virtuous and loving are humiliated and ostracized in their deaths. This is why a two-worlds view is necessary in attempting to make the best sense of evil and a response to it. This-worldly critiques or attempted resolutions to the problem of evil will inevitably fail.

In essence, we need a narrative explanation for evil—a full picture of how

God is working out his purposes in history from creation to the final eschaton. That is, we need an account that unfolds and develops over time and into the age to come (a *diachronic* view) rather than something of a cost-benefit analysis of evil in the here-and-now (a *synchronic* view).[17]

On a two-worlds view, the existence of God guarantees not only that wrongs will be righted and virtue rewarded in the end. It also guarantees that virtue and happiness will come together. Like Elizabeth Gaskell's poor, weary factory girl in *North and South*, without this hope we would "go mad." The good news is that whatever losses we have experienced for God and others in this life, in Christ God will more than compensate for them in the life to come (2 Cor. 4:17). A God-less universe, however, will inevitably fail to bring about the final justice or ultimate happiness for which we all long.

FURTHER READING

Graham, Gordon. *Evil and Christian Ethics.* Cambridge: Cambridge University Press, 2001.

Lewis, C. S. *The Problem of Pain.* Various editions.

Meister, Chad, and James K. Dew Jr., eds. *God and Evil: The Case for God in a World Filled with Pain.* Downers Grove, IL: InterVarsity Press, 2013.

———. *God and the Problem of Evil: Five Views.* Downers Grove, IL: IVP Academic, 2017.

Peckham, John. *Theodicy of Love: Cosmic Conflict and the Problem of Evil.* Grand Rapids: Baker Academic, 2018.

25 | *The Problem of Evil (III): Evils Natural and Demonic*

> For we know that the whole creation groans and suffers
> the pains of childbirth together until now.
>
> —Romans 8:22

> For our struggle is not against flesh and blood, but
> against the rulers, against the powers, against the world
> forces of this darkness, against the spiritual forces of
> wickedness in the heavenly places.
>
> —Ephesians 6:12

NATURAL EVILS AND ANIMAL PAIN

Natural Evils

While moral evils are carried out by human or fallen angelic agents, *natural* evils involve human suffering and death that come through natural forces such hurricanes, tornadoes, earthquakes, and floods. If we look at the greater picture, these actually serve important functions in maintaining livable conditions on earth.

Hurricanes and tornadoes prevent the oceans from trapping too much of the sun's heat by helping to circulate greenhouse gases globally as they shade the ocean locally, preventing heat from building up too dramatically for the safety of certain sea creatures.[1] Shifting tectonic plates produce earthquakes, which allow for the essential nutrients for life to be recycled back onto the continents. Without earthquakes, "nutrients essential for land life would erode off the continents and accumulate in the oceans. In a relatively brief time, land creatures, at least the advanced species, would starve."[2]

As we noted earlier, once human beings rebelled against God, they become vulnerable to wild animals, hurricanes, tornadoes, earthquakes, thorns, and harmful microbes—from which God had previously protected them. Daniel Howard-Snyder suggests this scenario: "The potentially destructive forces of nature became [Adam's and Eve's and their offspring's] foe since a consequence of separating themselves from God was the loss of special intellectual powers to predict where and when natural disasters would occur and to protect themselves from disease and wild beasts, powers dependent upon their union with God. The result is natural evil."[3]

Yet it is these natural evils that enable us to recognize our own vulnerability and the need for outside assistance. As Eleonore Stump writes:

> Natural evil—the pain of disease, the intermittent and unpredictable destruction of natural disasters, the decay of old age, the imminence of death—takes away a person's satisfaction with himself. It tends to humble him, show him his frailty, make him reflect on the transience of temporal goods, and turn his affections towards other-worldly things, away from the things of this world. No amount of moral or natural evil, of course, can guarantee that a man will seek God's help. If it could, the willing it produced would not be free. But evil of this sort is the best hope, I think, and maybe the only effective means, for bringing men to such a state.[4]

Animal Pain

What of animal pain and suffering? Here we must be brief. God created the food chain in the beginning—before the fall. Psalm 104—a creation psalm—praises the Creator for providing food for animals like lions. As we've noted, this provision for them is "good [*tob*]" (Ps. 104:21, 27–28; cf. 147:9)—the same word used in Genesis 1. God reminds Job of his wisdom in creating certain animals. He mentions that his creatures include predators—like the hawk spying out prey from the rocky crags (Job 39:28–29); its nestlings suck the blood of it, and "where the slain are, there is he."[5]

Some Christian philosophers do not think that animals truly suffer—or suffer as humans do. Richard Swinburne writes: "While the higher animals, at any rate, the vertebrates, suffer, it is most unlikely that they suffer as much as humans do."[6] Peter van Inwagen likewise affirms that "the sufferings of human beings are a much worse evil than the sufferings of beasts . . . even quite large amounts of animal suffering."[7]

Other Christian philosophers will argue that only humans and certain primates have the capacity of suffering through the awareness of their pain states (they have "high-order thoughts"). Invertebrates like insects don't feel pain but have an aversive reaction to "noxious stimuli," and so they pull away from danger. Most vertebrates do experience pain states, but they aren't consciously aware of those pains (low-order thoughts). Their brains just don't have the capacity to consciously access these pain states.

This is analogous to human patients who, because of damage to the brain, experience "blindsight": they report that they cannot see yet are visually able to detect objects in a room and thus successfully avoid bumping into them. That is, they aren't *aware* that they have visual sensory access to the objects around them; they cannot truly suffer, which requires those higher-order thoughts.

Other Christian philosophers insist that animal suffering extends beyond humans and primates to the vast majority of animals. After all, we watch National Geographic specials, and it appears that lion-ravaged gazelles react to pain in the same way that humans do. But others might reply that we cannot be sure this is the case and brain capacity of most vertebrates excludes the possibility of suffering because there is no capacity for high-order thinking.

Evolutionary creationists will affirm that God uses the evolutionary process to bring about his transformative and redemptive purposes for humanity. "Nature red in tooth and claw" involves both animal and human pain; this includes human suffering as well as immense species extinctions (99 percent of all animal species have become extinct). This morally significant outcome of God's forming, redeeming, and transforming humans through suffering and hardship would be sufficient moral justification for permitting so much evil. After all, an environment that involves struggle, death, and the potential for sin and evil allows for the moral and spiritual formation of free human beings; the difficulties of their surroundings require challenging moral decisions, which involve rising above self-centered tendencies and acting in the interests of others. The world is designed in such a way that, by God's grace, good things can be brought about through pain and suffering.

In the end, if we can speak of animal "suffering" as an "evil" (though plenty of Christians would disagree here), we are not restricted to this-worldly solutions to the problem, as the naturalist is. God is able to set matters right in the end. As John Wesley wrote, "The objection vanishes away if we consider that something better remains after death for these creatures also; that these likewise shall one day be delivered from this bondage of corruption, and shall then receive an ample amends for all their present sufferings."[8]

EVIL AND THE DEMONIC

Any treatment of the problem of evil—at least if it is biblical—would be incomplete and inadequate without mentioning the realm of the demonic. John writes that "the whole world lies in the power of the evil one" (1 John 5:19). Christ himself came "to destroy the works of the devil" (1 John 3:8). Historical Jesus scholars have observed that exorcism was inescapably central to his earthly ministry.[9] Unfortunately, many in the West ("global North")—including professing Christians—diminish or deny the reality of the demonic. This isn't the case in the "global South," where the gospel is spreading dramatically, often through healing miracles and "power encounters" with the demonic, as historian Philip Jenkins has documented.[10]

Alvin Plantinga has suggested that demonic beings may be responsible for bringing about what we call "natural evils"—death through famine, earthquakes, hurricanes, and so on. Even if other academics dismiss the demonic in a kind of "we know better now" fashion, the demonic realm is certainly deeply connected to our understanding of the Christian faith, especially as we consider Jesus's view on the matter and his very earthly mission.[11] The cosmic warfare "in the heavenly places" (Eph. 6:12) is taken for granted in the New Testament, in which the gospel advances through displays of Christ's power over demonic forces—for example, with Elymas the sorcerer (Acts 13), the demonized servant girl (Acts 16), and the Ephesians and their magic practices (Acts 19).[12]

Naturalism and other modern philosophical approaches—and most Eastern philosophical traditions—do not have the resources to make sense of horrific evils. Consider the demonic depths of depravity revealed by Ted Bundy, Jeffrey Dahmer, or other serial murderers. We are stunned at how coolly, "rationally," or even gleefully they engaged in the cruel, grisly killing of innocents; indeed, we recognize that a greater evil power has gained entrance into their hearts—something otherworldly and devilish (cf. Luke 22:3).

Philosopher Gordon Graham affirms that in the face of such evils, calling on and seeking out for God is utterly appropriate: "We need the help of God . . . because the other world we have encountered has brought us face to face with Satan."[13] It is as though such killers are "depending for [their] activity on the presence of visible, tangible agents."[14]

The modern impulse is to treat the deeply flawed and sinful condition of humanity with an unconstrained, "enlightened" utopian optimism. According to this idea, humans are naturally malleable and perfectible. Through education, social engineering, redistributing wealth, and getting the right people into positions of power, humans can be reshaped to eliminate their flaws and eliminate "root causes" of poverty and crime. Thus did the Romantic poet Friedrich Hölderlin rightly say: "What has always made the state a hell on earth has been precisely that man has tried to make it his heaven."[15]

By contrast, the more realistic and biblical understanding is the restrained or "tragic" vision; it recognizes deep human depravity and flaws, and that the depths of our evil condition cannot be readily reshaped by external forces—as though humans were just a blank slate. No, evil resides in even the best of human beings, and certain problems will never be eradicated in this life—and the attempt to do so will only perpetuate more serious evils. Thus, for properly functioning societies, various checks and balances are needed to curb these self-centered tendencies and flaws. But again, we cannot eliminate all evil.[16]

Ultimately, the transforming message of the gospel addresses our deepest problem—namely, alienation with God—and through the power of Christ confronts and breaks the stranglehold created by sin, self-centeredness, societal structures, and the dominion of Satan himself.

Though it is unfashionable to speak of demonic powers in the West (or "global North"), the presence and power of these evil supernatural agents are taken for granted in the global South. As historian Philip Jenkins observes:

> Yet a Christian worldview that acknowledges supernatural evil does not disqualify itself from participation in worldly struggles, including movements for far-reaching social and economic transformation. Whatever their spiritual truth—whatever their fidelity to Christian tradition—supernatural approaches can be valuable in moving societies away from pernicious traditional superstitions. For instance, offering distinctively Christian solutions to witchcraft helps disarm the sometimes bloody practices of anti-witchcraft rituals. In a relatively short time, the new Christian emphasis on prayer and Bible reading defuses the fatalism inherent in a traditional system based on such notions as witchcraft, curses, and the power of ancestors. Instead, Christians are taught to rely on faith and on the role of the individual, who is no longer a slave to destiny or fate. By treating older notions of spiritual evil seriously, Christians are leading an epochal cultural revolution.[17]

In contrast to this-worldly efforts to understand and respond to evil, the fuller Christian story provides not only a context but also a confident hope that evil will not have the last word. Indeed, God has already made clear that in Christ's death and resurrection, evil powers have been vanquished (Col. 2:13–15), death has lost its sting (1 Cor. 15:54–58), and that Christ—not sin—is our new Master (Rom. 6:14).

Further Reading

Jamison, Wes, and Paul Copan, eds. *What Would Jesus Really Eat? The Biblical Case for Eating Meat.* Pickering, ON: Castle Quay, 2019.

Lewis, C. S. *The Problem of Pain*. Various editions.

Meister, Chad, and James K. Dew Jr., eds. *God and Evil: The Case for God in a World Filled with Pain*. Downers Grove, IL: IVP Academic, 2013.

———. *God and the Problem of Evil: Five Views*. Downers Grove, IL: IVP Academic, 2017.

Peckham, John. *Theodicy of Love: Cosmic Conflict and the Problem of Evil*. Grand Rapids: Baker Academic, 2018.

> All of us like sheep have gone astray,
> Each of us has turned to his own way.
>
> —Isaiah 53:6

> If you then, who are evil, know how to give good gifts to
> your children, how much more will your Father who is
> in heaven give good things to those who ask him!
>
> —Matthew 7:11 ESV

> Every good gift and every perfect gift is from above,
> coming down from the Father of lights, with whom
> there is no variation or shadow due to change.
>
> —James 1:17 ESV

Is God the Author of Evil?

How did evil originate in a "very good" world (Gen. 1:31)?[1] Some have been troubled by the conclusion—albeit faulty—that God, who created everything, must therefore be the author of evil. This is an incorrect inference to draw. But if God isn't the author of evil, where else could it come from?

One Christian theologian has concluded that, no, God is indeed the "culprit"—the "author" of evil and the creator of sin—who "introduced evil into this world."[2] This theologian wouldn't say God is evil in his character, but he "introduced evil into this world."[3] Why would he do that? The theologian states that God *has to* create evil so that he can exercise his eternal attribute of wrath to display his glory. God had no choice in the matter.[4]

To add to the confusion, the King James Version of the Bible appears to support this in places: "I [God] form the light, and create darkness: I make peace, and create evil: I the LORD do all these things" (Isa. 45:7). Don't both "evil and good" proceed from God (Lam. 3:37–38)? If there's "evil in a city," then hasn't the Lord done it (Amos 3:6)?

The problem here is both theological and translational. On the theological level, God is the joyful Creator who creates freely rather than out of compulsion. No, God doesn't *have* to create—let alone create certain persons just to damn them. Creatures damn themselves by resisting the grace of God (Acts 7:51). Wrath isn't an "eternal attribute." As we've seen, wrath is an expression of divine love, but divine wrath arises when creatures defy him. If God had chosen not to create, then God would never have been wrathful.

Furthermore, God is not the source of evil. James reminds us that God gives what is good and isn't the source of evil. *Every good thing* comes from God (Acts 1:13, 17). Indeed, "everything God created is good" (1 Tim. 4:4 NIV). Jesus affirms the goodness of our heavenly Father, which is greater than that of sinful, earthly parents who nevertheless give good gifts to their children (Matt. 7:11).

Evil then originates with creatures (whether angelic or human) whom God created good. And while God created all *things*, evil isn't a "thing." As we've seen, evil is a deviation from the way things ought to be.

Another theological problem with the perspective we've been discussing is that a needy God is a contradiction in terms. God is self-sufficient and does not have to create. He needs nothing outside himself: "If I were hungry I would not tell you, For the world is Mine, and all it contains" (Ps. 50:12).

As for the translation problem in the King James Version, the word "evil" or "wickedness" (Hebrew: *ra'ah*) can also be translated "trouble," "disaster," or "calamity." Yes, God sends *calamity*, but God is too pure to do evil (Hab. 1:13; cf. Jer. 19:4–5). He doesn't "create evil."

THE EMERGENCE OF EVIL

Having looked at some of these preliminaries, how can we make sense of (a) a moral creature in a "very good" environment who (b) comes to be the originator of evil? One successful account of primal sin—or primeval evil—can be found in *On the Free Choice of the Will* by the notable theologian Augustine (AD 354–430). As we track his reflections on the early chapters of Genesis, we can readily see how his view upholds both God's goodness and genuine creaturely freedom.[5]

Freedom

By freedom, we mean that our actions are *up to us*; the moral buck stops with the agent. The agent's environment or emotions or moods are *influences*, but they don't *cause* our actions. No wonder God tells Cain: "Sin is crouching at the door; and its desire is for you, but you must master it" (Gen. 4:7). *We* are responsible for our actions, and we can't blame God or someone else for our wrongdoing. No temptation comes to us from which we can't find a way of escape, with God's help (1 Cor. 10:13). As we saw with Kant, *ought* implies *can*, though with the ever-available grace of God. That is, if I have a duty to do something, then this entails that I would be able to carry it out. For a paraplegic confined to a wheelchair, someone's demand to make me run or dance—barring a miracle—would be not only cruel but also impossible to carry out.

Sin doesn't originate in God, although he can permit creaturely evil and failure, and he can use it to bring about redemptive goods (e.g., Gen. 50:20; Acts 2:23–24; 3:15; Rom. 8:28).[6] The devil, not God, is the beginning of sin—a "murderer from the beginning" and "the father of lies" (John 8:44). The Creator of free moral agents is no more the author of sin than the Wright brothers are the authors of airplane crashes.

Sin as Deviation from the Good

As we've seen, evil isn't a *thing*. Evil arises when an act, motive, or character deviates from the way things ought to be. Our first ancestors were created good—*without* moral defect. But their choice to disobey was the result of misusing the good gift of creaturely freedom.

The First Sin as Voluntary

Sin begins with the free moral creatures God has made. Though created without moral defect, creatures can become sinners by freely resisting God's commands or design. If creatures were sinners by nature, they couldn't have resisted doing evil. But God isn't blameworthy for a morally deficient creation. It was up to his creatures to choose. In creating, God didn't rig the system against them. And importantly, by the free choice of the will, something new and radical broke into God's good created order.

Turning from God to the Creaturely

The present point is crucial. Sin arose from the creature turning attention away from the ultimate, unchanging Good (God) and focused on a lesser, created good. This began with certain good angelic beings, who turned their focus away from God and onto themselves. Then human beings came to focus on the creaturely—the tree of the knowledge of good and evil—which became a fixation to them.

Evil invaded creation because agents with free will turned from the highest, unchangeable, and ultimate Good to lesser, changeable, finite goods. Creatures that fell away from God didn't turn to evil things. Rather, their love became disordered. In the hierarchy of loves, they set their affection and focus on the finite rather than the Infinite. Rather than fixing their eyes on God's uncreated goodness and beauty, they latched on to lesser goods and beauties.

So the first sin was a failure of focus: creatures failed to pay attention to God as the highest Good, and they failed to attend to the reasons for loving God supremely—reasons they should readily have recognized. It wasn't the result of a weak will or irrationality or mistaken thinking; it wasn't some blunder or oversight. Rather than focusing on the eternal, they focused on the temporal.

Human creatures ignored God in their rationalizations. They focused on certain *aspects* of God: his prohibition, his threat of death, his talk of good and evil. The tree of the knowledge of good and evil was part of God's good creation, yet it became a focal point for the first humans: it was "good for food," "a delight to the eyes," and "desirable to make one wise" (Gen. 3:6). The first couple had come to love the finite over the Infinite and so became guilty for ignoring reasons for considering God the highest good. They ignored positive aspects of God's care for them: his love, his friendship, his kind intentions, his gracious provision.

The walking and talking serpent—a symbol of evil in the ancient Near East—attempted to distract Eve from certain truths about God. He tried to drive in a wedge between humans and God by pointing out God's prohibition: "Indeed, has God said, 'You shall not eat from any tree of the garden'?" (Gen. 3:1). Eve *was* thinking about God: "God has said, 'You shall not eat from it'" (v. 3). Yet, in all of this, she failed to focus her thoughts on God as the highest good. What's more, she even went *beyond* God's explicit command by highlighting the fruit's untouchability—something God *hadn't* mentioned (v. 3). She displayed a thought pattern that was fixated on God's prohibition, but she overlooked God's goodness and bountiful care.

So this first sin was no irrational slip-up. It was a conscious choice, but not one rooted in some preexisting moral defect or character state or the external environment. Because angels and humans were ultimately created out of nothing by the power of God's word, they are finite, changeable, and utterly dependent on God. That's just the condition of all creatures. By contrast, God is self-sufficient, necessarily good, incorruptible, and infinite. But our inherent creaturely limitations aren't the same thing as moral flaws or deficiencies that inevitably lead to sin.

A Gradual Process

While the early chapters of Genesis give us a condensed version of primeval history, we should be careful about reading it like a newspaper or a history book, especially given its rich symbolism—for example, God breathing, Adam made from the dust, Eve made from a rib, a serpent talking, two trees in the garden.[7]

We should be careful not to draw from the biblical text more than is warranted. But we have indications that Adam and Eve didn't suddenly turn away from God. As we saw in the previous point, Eve's exaggerated addition—"or touch it"—to God's original prohibition (Gen. 3:3) gives a hint of something more gradual. Genesis 1–3 provides us with a kind of telescoping of events. In the case of humans falling away from God, we see that a gradual separateness between creatures and God climaxed in an intentional, thought-out choice to turn away from God. It serves as a reminder that giving attention to where we set our minds (Col. 3:1) and what we treasure or value (Matt. 6:21) sets the trajectory of our lives—and our ultimate destinies.

Being careless about our duties is truly a moral failure. What if you promise your children to take them on an outing on the weekend, but then spontaneously decide that attending a conference might be good for you professionally, thus ignoring the earlier promise? We intuitively recognize this decision to be wrong—even we can't cite reasons or motives for breaking our promise.

Similarly, Adam and Eve failed to focus on the most crucial reasons (which is a defect) and volitionally acted (an effect of the failure). Both of these were completely up to our first parents, and they could have chosen otherwise. Their choice was free, not necessary. As one philosopher notes, "The evil angels and the first human beings will have introduced genuine and deep evil into creation only when their irrationality has solidified into a decisive and enduring state of will—that is, only when they have finally and utterly turned away from God."[8]

No, God isn't the source of evil, but rather moral creatures were. The first sinners didn't just make some sudden choice without any motive whatsoever. Their sin was *voluntary*, *culpable*, and *avoidable*.

Further Reading

MacDonald, Scott. "Primal Sin." Pages 110–39 in *The Augustinian Tradition*, edited by Gareth B. Matthews. Berkeley: University of California Press, 1999.

Meister, Chad, and James K. Dew Jr., eds. *God and Evil: The Case for God in a World Filled with Pain*. Downers Grove, IL: InterVarsity Press, 2013.

27 | *Original Sin*

> Therefore, just as sin came into the world through one
> man, and death through sin, and so death spread to all
> men because all sinned.
>
> —Romans 5:12 ESV

> For as in Adam all die, so also in Christ all will be made
> alive.
>
> —1 Corinthians 15:22

A common complaint against the Christian faith is the doctrine of original sin. The Enlightenment thinker Jean-Jacques Rousseau called Adam's sin a "fatal accident," and he dismissed this doctrine because it didn't have much explanatory power. Through no fault of our own, the *primal* sin of Adam and Eve we noted in the previous chapter has led to *original* sin—namely, the spread of a spiritual and moral disease to the entire human race.

We come into this world as bent, misshapen creatures. Everyone of us is a human turned or curved in on oneself (*homo incurvatus in se*) as Martin Luther affirmed, following Augustine. Although the Reformer loved children, he called them "little heathens."[1] So here we are today, utterly removed from our theological ancestors circumstantially, chronologically, and personally. That is, the act of someone else, ages ago, and in a completely different setting profoundly affects us today.

What adds interest—and complication—are recent lively discussions about the genetic or ancestral (hominin) predecessors to Adam and Eve. Christians may accept or reject the notion of a common ancestor to human beings—or simply remain agnostic on the matter. Some Christians will argue that evolutionary creationism doesn't rule out a historical couple from whom all God's image-bearers descended, a historical falling away from God, or damage that comes to humanity as a result.[2] We'll come back to this later on.

VARYING VIEWS: NO OFFICIAL POSITION

The British monk Pelagius (c. 360–418) claimed that each of us is as Adam was in the garden of Eden and that each of us is born morally neutral, with the capacity to do right or go wrong. We don't need divine assistance. Adam's fall didn't bring to us any debilitating consequences, such as our self-centered orientation. This view has come to be known as Pelagianism, and it has been roundly condemned by the church, beginning with Augustine's forceful resistance.[3]

The church has also stood against semi-Pelagianism at the Council of Orange (AD 529); this was the error that we humans have the capacity to initiate the first steps toward God, who then in response can supply whatever grace we may lack. In both cases, these views deny the depths of our own self-orientation that, without God's grace, doesn't seek after God (Rom. 3:11). God, who is not far from each human being, commands every human to repent (Acts 17:27, 30). This means that he must supply the necessary grace for us to carry out this command. If we are to see our deep sinfulness and turn to God, he must open our eyes to enlighten us lest we continue in the sleep of spiritual death (John 1:9; Heb. 6:4; 10:32; cf. Ps. 13:3). This illumination, however, can be resisted or rejected (Ps. 81:10–16; Acts 7:51).

That we come into the world morally and spiritually damaged is clear. The nature of "original sin," however, is murkier. Centuries of theologizing have brought an array of perspectives. One view claims that each of us was somehow "present" with Adam when he sinned. We sinned "in him," as though we were with him in the garden. Another view affirms that Adam stands in as our legal human representative, our "federal head." Not only do the consequences of his action fall to us but we also share in his guilt. In addition, another approach—one that I favor—emphasizes that we are guilty before God because of our *own* sin—that spiritual death came to us "because all sinned," not because Adam sinned (cf. Rom. 5:12). Adam's own death ("in the day that you eat from it you will surely die" [Gen. 2:17]) must refer to a relational or spiritual death—obviously not physical death.

This view of original sin emphasizes the consequences of Adam's sin, but not his guilt. We are punished for our own sins, not the sins of others (e.g., 2 Chron. 25:4; Jer. 31:29–30; Ezek. 18:4). This view is also the one adopted by Eastern Orthodoxy, although Christians outside this tradition also hold it.

Four Affirmations about Original Sin

We can affirm at least four things about original sin. First, we've seen that it is *contingent*; it is not part of the order of creation but alien to it. When we say "contingent," we mean that this sinful state isn't necessary or inevitable. That's why it's confusing to speak of a "sinful nature." This sounds like it defines our humanity (a "nature" is something that makes a thing what it is). This term "sinful nature" (e.g., Rom. 7:5, 18, etc., NIV) is a poor translation of the Greek word "flesh [*sarx*]."[4] According to Paul, we are no longer in the flesh but in the Spirit (Rom. 8:9); "in the flesh" has to do with our former status in the unfolding of salvation history. What was part of the old era "in Adam" is over, and the new creation "in Christ" has come.

Second, it is *universal*—what we could call the ubiquity of iniquity. Sin affects each of us, and none of us can escape its deep influence. We earlier cited the late Russian writer Alexandr Solzhenitsyn, who reflected on life in Soviet labor camps: "Gradually it was disclosed to me that the line separating good and evil passes not through states, nor between classes, nor between political parties either, but right through every human heart, and through all human hearts." Indeed, this line shifts during our lifetimes, and the heart "overwhelmed by evil" still retains some goodness, and in the best of hearts yet "there remains . . . an unuprooted small corner of evil."[5]

Third, it is *radical*. Sin isn't simply a "mistake" or "deviation." The solution to this radical problem requires redemption and transformation. We need serious rescue from a Savior, not simply therapy. The problem runs deep, and attempts to treat it with superficial measures such as social, governmental, or educational structures are fraudulent or naive. We must always guard our hearts with all diligence (Prov. 4:23)—indeed, to flee from ourselves and to cast ourselves upon the Lord's grace: "God, be merciful to me, a sinner" (Luke 18:13 ESV).

Finally, it is *communicable*; it is somehow passed on to us from our forebears. How so? Some have assumed that it is communicated to our newly originated souls at conception (the "creationist" view). Others claim that we should view our souls as being more closely tied to our parents. This more organic view sees the soul, though unique to each person, as being part of a spiritual "plant"—coming from a root that grows and builds on previous growth as it branches out. This has been called the "traducian" view (*tradux* is the Latin for "root").[6]

While the doctrine of original sin raises perplexing questions, we can breathe a momentary sigh of relief. For one thing, we can readily exclude certain views as unorthodox—like Pelagianism and semi-Pelagianism. We can affirm that several original sin perspectives fall within the range of orthodoxy and that there is no one "official" Christian position on this doctrine. While sin and depravity are obvious and universal, the relationship between our first ancestors and us is difficult to discern.

Guilt versus Damage

Did we inherit Adam's *guilt*—or just the damaging *consequences* of his actions? Did our mothers conceive us with the stamp of guilt on us (cf. Ps. 51:5), or do we all simply enter into a fallen and broken world through Adam's sin? Some claim we're guilty because we are united to Adam ("in Adam"); others say we're damaged or corrupted but that by itself doesn't render us guilty.

The view that we inherit Adam's guilt is implied in the Westminster Confession of Faith (1647): "Elect infants, dying in infancy, are regenerated, and saved by Christ, through the Spirit, who works when, and where, and how He pleases." It was through the influence of Augustine (AD 354–430) that this doctrine became pronounced. However, it's widely agreed that Augustine mistranslated Romans 5:12—a key text for those who take the guilt view—that "death spread to all men *in whom* all sinned." He took it that we somehow mysteriously sinned "in Adam." The New Testament phrase *'eph hō* ("because") was translated as into the Latin as *in quod* ("in whom")—"in whom all sinned"—rather than "because all sinned." This Augustinian idea is reflected in the old Puritan *New England Primer*: "In Adam's fall, we sinned all." This is something of a backdrop to the "guilt" view.

As we saw in the last chapter, sin is something alien to creation. Those who proclaim human beings to be "worthless sinners" are reading Genesis incorrectly, beginning with Genesis 3 rather than starting with Genesis 1–2. God created all things "very good" (Gen. 1:31), including human nature. We have been made "a little lower than God" (Ps. 8:5). So sin or evil is *foreign* to God's creation. We are made in God's image, which gives to us special status and dignity as God's representatives in this world (James 3:9). As we've observed, God's "very good" creation doesn't mean that it was "perfect" but rather that we have many good things to work with as stewards of the earth. Nevertheless, humans, though created innocent, were not morally mature or developed; the church father Irenaeus said that humans were created to grow and develop morally and spiritually, which comes over time and life and through human experience.

What's more, God didn't create human beings with immortal resurrection bodies, but rather with mortal ones. These bodies God graciously sustained in life until they rebelled against God. God withdrew his life-sustaining grace, and this inherent mortality would become apparent. Our first ancestors no longer had access to the tree of life—immortality (Gen. 3:22). Humans would then become vulnerable to all the forces—predatory animals, earthquakes, hurricanes—from which God had earlier protected them.

Did we inherit Adam's *guilt*? If so, infants and those with mental limitations are guilty as well. But this can't be right. God's judgment of us isn't based on our being the offspring of Adam. All humans will be judged according to deeds "done in the body" (2 Cor. 5:10 ESV; cf. Rom. 2:6; Col. 3:25); all mouths will be silenced and the world held accountable to God (Rom. 3:19). But infants and the mentally limited don't do anything blameworthy, and the Scriptures routinely reject the punishment of the innocent with the guilty.[7]

By contrast, when parents make choices, *consequences* for their children follow, but not their parents' *guilt*. The consequences can be positive, neutral, or negative—whether from taking on a new job, moving out of the country, or abusing drugs and alcohol. And as Adam's children, certain damaging effects—not guilt—come to us. We come into this world with a spiritual disease that is pervasive and deep. Our souls are mal-aligned with disordered desires and loves, often focused more on our own interests than those of others (Phil. 2:4, 21). So our guilt is *conditional*; we *become* guilty once we side with sin against God.

This raises another problem. If we can't help sinning, how can we be condemned? Are we simply doomed because we come into life with a self-centered tendency?

Sorting through the Damage

Let's unpack the implications of this doctrine a bit more.

First, this doctrine points to an inescapable reality—namely, deep human depravity and evil in our hearts (Jer. 17:9). Scripture takes seriously the breadth and depth of sin and evil. Something is profoundly wrong with us, and this can't be explained merely by one's social or cultural environment—nor can it be fixed through education and self-realization. Such "solutions" are just too shallow. Even the agnostic philosopher Michael Ruse acknowledges original sin's explanatory power: "I think Christianity is spot on about original sin— how could one think otherwise, when the world's most civilized and advanced people (the people of Beethoven, Goethe, Kant) embraced that slime-ball Hitler and participated in the Holocaust? I think Saint Paul and the great Christian philosophers had real insights into sin and freedom and responsibility, and I want to build on this rather than turn from it."[8]

Likewise, G. K. Chesterton said that the doctrine of original sin is the only Christian doctrine that could be empirically verified. It's a fact "as plain as potatoes."[9] Of course, we can't ignore the fact that evil spiritual forces are actively contributing to further dehumanization and corruption of our condition through deceptive ideologies, false doctrine, pornography, and the like (cf. 2 Cor. 4:4; Eph. 2:1–3; 1 Tim. 4:1–5).

Second, the *inevitability* of sin is not the same as its *necessity*. A common criticism of original sin is that a cosmic moral system is rigged against us. How can I be held responsible? Well, we should note the important fact that we do make choices—including mental ones—and we are responsible for these. These include actions (deeds of *commission*) and inactions (deeds of *omission*). Cain was told that he should "master" sin "crouching at the door" (Gen. 4:7). Giving in to sin is not necessary: "No temptation has overtaken you but such as is common to man; and God is faithful, who will not allow you to be tempted beyond what you are able, but with the temptation will provide the way of escape also, so that you will be able to endure it" (1 Cor. 10:13).

Philosopher Alvin Plantinga distinguishes between *necessity* and *inevitability*. We don't sin *necessarily*; that is, it's not assured that we *must* commit this or that particular sin. Or as another philosopher notes: "bad desires incline," but "they do not (as such) necessitate."[10] However, we do sin *inevitably*; that is, in addition to our inclination to sin, given the vast array of opportunities to sin, we eventually do sin at some point.

Keith Wyma offers the helpful analogy from the sports world.

> As I write this, my beloved Indiana Pacers have just lost to the boorish Miami Heat. The loss snapped a twenty-five home-game winning streak. Could the Pacers have won the game? Yes. For each of the particular home games remaining this season, can the Pacers win it? Yes. Could the team then have won a home-streak stretching from November of '99 (when the actual streak started) through the end of the '00 season? Regretfully, I think not. In general, it is within the team's power to win *in each* game they play, but it's beyond their ability to win *all* their games.[11]

Our self-centered propensity doesn't condemn us, but we are blameworthy when we break God's commands. God will hold us accountable for our *deeds*, not our propensities.

Third, our deep sinfulness isn't the whole story; recognizing this points us toward the solution. The Canadian artist Douglas Coupland poignantly acknowledged: "My secret is that I need God—that I am sick and can no longer make it alone. I need God to help me give, because I no longer seem to be capable of giving; to help me be kind, as I no longer seem capable of kindness; to help me love, as I seem beyond being able to love."[12] God is not far from each one of us and is near to the brokenhearted and crushed in spirit (Acts 17:27; Ps. 34:18). In fact, those who appear free from anxiety and conflict and think they have it all together "may be only a well-adjusted sinner who is dangerously maladjusted to God; and it is infinitely better to be a neurotic saint than a healthy-minded sinner."[13]

Fourth, the meaning of Adam's primal sin can't be isolated from the second Adam's saving act and the new creation he brought into being through his resurrection. If we focus on our personal narrative of proneness to sin and other damage wrought by the first Adam, we must step into the larger story of God's redemptive activity through the Christ who gave his own life to undo that damage and to remake creation into something glorious. We may feel condemned, doomed as "vessels of wrath" (Rom. 9:22, a reference to ethnic Jews who are unrepentant). But, through Christ's Spirit, we who have been "vessels of . . . dishonor" can repent so that we may become "a vessel for honor, sanctified, useful to the Master, prepared for every good work" (2 Tim. 2:20–21). Sin doesn't have to be the total picture in anyone's biography.

We've referred to the "moral gap" between the ideal and our own failing performance. We need divine grace to bridge that gap. Only God "is able to keep you from stumbling, and to make you stand in the presence of His glory blameless with great joy" (Jude 24).

Fifth, perhaps it's as if we were with Adam in the garden: it could be that God in his omniscience was aware that any one of us would have made the same choice Adam did. What if Adam's story is the same story as any of ours? What if Adam is the "Everyman" or "Human"—the one who portrays each of us? Perhaps it's the case that we would have done what Adam did. Given God's awareness of the range of possible worlds and what humans in those worlds would have done, this scenario isn't far-fetched. This point, of course, doesn't address the connection between Adam and the rest of the human race and how moral corruption is transmitted.

In the end, the doctrine of original sin—with all of its puzzles and mysteries—makes better sense of our human condition than do alternative worldviews that bypass or minimize the problem of embedded human sinfulness. And original sin is not the last word; through the second Adam's death and resurrection, he has secured a new creation and wrought our redemption to reverse the curse.

Given the lengths to which the triune God has gone to go secure our reconciliation with him, we can surely leave in God's hands such difficult questions as original sin.

WHAT ABOUT ORIGINAL SIN AND SOME QUESTIONS FROM CURRENT UNDERSTANDINGS OF SCIENCE?

Some (though not all) Christian scholars who embrace evolutionary creationism think that this doctrine can't be squared with the historicity of Adam and Eve—the primal couple. Maybe Adam is solely archetypal or literary—an "everyman" figure who typifies the human experience.[14] Like Adam, we too are vulnerable to temptation, quick to blame others, and capable of rationalizing away our sin. Not only is the historical couple called into question; so is the historical fall. What we call "original sin" is, they claim, simply the residual, untamed beastly or animal nature we inherited from our primate ancestors.

This, however, isn't the impression we get as we read the Scriptures, though. Even in the time of Second Temple Judaism (530 BC–AD 70), the general assumption was that Adam was a historical person. One sample second-century text reads, "O Adam, what have you done? For though it was you who sinned, the fall was not yours alone, but ours also who are your descendants" (2 Esd. 7:118 NRSV).

Others will argue that God selected a pair of hominids and "refurbished" them with rational and moral capacities that set them apart from their predecessors and made them capable of union with God and loving others. This view has been held by notable theologians such as B. B. Warfield, John Stott, and N. T. Wright. One Christian philosopher, Peter van Inwagen, suggests this scenario:

> For millions of years, perhaps for thousands of millions of years, God guided the course of evolution so as eventually to produce certain very clever primates, the immediate predecessors of *Homo sapiens*. At some time in the last few thousand years, the whole population of our pre-human ancestors formed as a small breeding community—a few thousand or a few hundred or even a few score. That is to say, there was a time when every ancestor of modern human beings who was then alive was a member of this tiny, geographically tightly knit group of primates. In the fullness of time, God took the members of this breeding group and miraculously raised them to rationality. That is, he gave them the gifts of language, abstract thought, and disinterested love—and, of course, the gift of free will. Perhaps we cannot understand *all* his reasons for giving humans beings free will, but here is one very important one we *can* understand: He gave them the gift of free will because free will is necessary for Love. Love, and not only erotic love, implies free will.[15]

It is quite evident that animal death took place before the appearance of humans on the scene—and, thus, before the fall. We can add that while questions remain, nothing we know today undermines a bottleneck of a primal human pair as the ancestors for all humanity or a historical fall.

Some scientists in the Christian community have argued that, based on what we know of genetics and ancestry, it's possible to have an originating human pair—a "bottleneck" in our ancestry—from whom all present-day humans have come. Some look to a unique starting point around 200,000 years ago with the rise of *Homo sapiens*. Even before this, the six-foot tall *Homo erectus* showed rational capabilities—evidenced by careful toolmaking—around 750,000 years ago. Genetically speaking, we don't need more than a single pair to account for the wide array of human variation.

The discussions on these matters continue, and we continue to learn and process the expanding information on these topics. So perhaps we should leave things here while remaining attuned to the conversations that informed, faithful Christians are having.[16]

FURTHER READING

Blocher, Henri. *Original Sin: Illuminating the Riddle.* Downers Grove, IL: InterVarsity Press, 1997.

Copan, Paul, et al., eds. *Dictionary of Christianity and Science.* Grand Rapids: Zondervan, 2017.

McFarland, Ian T. *In Adam's Fall: A Meditation on the Doctrine of Original Sin.* Oxford: Wiley-Blackwell, 2010.

Meister, Chad, and Jamie Dew. *God and Evil.* Downers Grove, IL: IVP Academic, 2017.

Swamidass, S. Joshua. *The Genealogical Adam and Eve: The Surprising Science of Universal Ancestry.* Downers Grove, IL: IVP Academic, 2019.

> These will pay the penalty of eternal destruction, away
> from the presence of the Lord and from the glory of
> His power.
>
> —2 Thessalonians 1:9

The doctrine of hell has troubled both believers and unbelievers alike. C. S. Lewis wrote with his usual frankness: "There is no doctrine which I would more willingly remove from Christianity than this, if it lay in my power. But it has the full support of Scripture and, specially, of Our Lord's own words; it has always been held by Christendom; and it has the support of reason."[1]

Various unbelievers have denounced the doctrine of hell, insisting that hell looks like a "divine torture chamber." Even within the Christian tradition, some have insisted that hell is ultimately the extinction of the unredeemed person—a view called "conditional immortality": one receives immortality *only if* one has repented and received God's forgiveness made available through Christ's sacrificial death. Others have argued for *universalism*—that eventually all will be saved, but through Christ rather than through some other pathway; Jesus is still the only door to salvation (John 10:7-9). And even if people reject him in this life, they will eventually enjoy the presence of God in the next, perhaps after a period of punishment (what has been called "purgationism").

LITERAL OR FIGURATIVE?

The Scriptures present various pictures or images concerning the destiny of the unrepentant—language referring to "death" or "the second death" (Rev. 2:11; 20:14), "destruction" (Matt. 7:13) or "eternal destruction" (2 Thess. 1:9). A key image of hell or separation from God is that of flame—"unquenchable fire" (Matt. 3:12). In Luke 16, Jesus tells of the rich man, who ignored the poor, pious Lazarus (whose Hebrew name *Eliezer* means "God is my help"). In the throes of judgment, the rich man cries out, "I am in agony in this flame" (Luke 16:24). He is in Hades—the realm of the dead. That realm includes not only the unrighteous dead (Luke 16:23) but also the righteous dead who enter Paradise (Acts 2:27, 31; cf. Luke 23:43). This realm of death will eventually be thrown into "the lake of fire" (Rev. 20:14).

Despite the Bible's mention of flame, separation from God also includes "outer darkness," which involves "weeping and gnashing of teeth" (Matt. 8:12; 22:13; 25:30). Now if both *flame* and *darkness* were literal, they would cancel each other out. Even the Reformers Martin Luther and John Calvin held that these "fiery" passages are metaphorical. Likewise, we shouldn't view the "worm" that "does not die" as living everlastingly, devouring decaying bodies in the afterlife (Isa. 66:24; cf. Mark 9:48). Extrabiblical Jewish literature also assumes this figurative picture, linking, say, "black fire" with "cold ice" (2 Enoch 10:2).

In other words, we shouldn't think of hell as a place of high thermal output; rather, the Bible uses figures and images to depict the terrible tragedy of life apart from God. "Fire" presents a serious—even dreadful—picture of divine judgment or of life without God (Deut. 4:24; Rev. 1:14).

Another reason to view this figuratively is that hell was created for the devil and his angels (Matt. 25:41)—spirit-beings. Literal fire affects physical bodies with nerve endings, not spirit-beings that can't be physically pained.[2] As one philosopher wrote: "The damned in hell do not suffer bodily fires or tortures. Their punishment is pain of loss, not of sense."[3]

Revelation 14:10 refers to the unredeemed as "tormented"? Does this suggest a "divine torture chamber" image? No, it doesn't. While "torture" is imposed from without, "torment" is an internal and ultimately self-inflicted condition. The wailing and gnashing of teeth imagery primarily emphasizes spiritual misery, not agonizing physical suffering.

Christian philosopher Jerry Walls suggests that while hell is a realm of misery, it is not necessarily unbearable. Hell may have its own deformed satisfactions through pursuing miserable pleasures—though not pure joy.[4]

THE ESSENCE OF HELL

Absent from the Lord

The intermediate state of "heaven" is to be present with the Lord—even the soul is temporarily "absent from the body" (2 Cor. 5:6, 8). No wonder Paul said that to live is Christ but to die is gain (Phil. 1:21). And at the final resurrection when Jesus returns, the new earth and heaven will be filled with God's glorious presence; God will dwell in the midst of his people (2 Pet. 3:13; Rev. 21:1–4).

By contrast, the essence of hell is to be absent from the Lord. One is removed from God's presence—cut off from the source of life and joy. It is "the great divorce"—one's separation from God. This is to be "away from the presence of the Lord" (2 Thess. 1:9)—the greatest loss possible. God, of course, will be *aware* of those separated from him; they will still be "tormented . . . in the presence of the holy angels and *in the presence of the Lamb*" (Rev. 14:10). The point here is that Christ/God is obviously aware of those who experience this separation ("in the presence of the Lamb"). Nevertheless, the emphasis in 2 Thess. 1:9 is that unbelievers are cut off from his blessing as the source of hope and joy ("away from the presence of the Lord").

Proportionality Problem

This raises the "proportionality question": Isn't it unjust for God to punish persons *everlastingly* for sins committed during a *limited* period of time on earth? This is a fair question. One response is that discrete, individual sinful acts aren't the issue, but rather a life directed away from God. That is, hell isn't a surprise outcome but naturally flows from how one lived and operated on earth.[5] If one steadfastly refuses God's influence while on earth, why think this will change in the afterlife? We ultimately get what we want in the afterlife. In fact, God's presence would be torment for those who don't desire it, and the absence of God is precisely what hell is.

Hell is the best God can do for those who want to avoid God.[6] Dallas Willard writes: "The greatest thing about heaven is going to be the presence of God. He has allowed us to avoid him here on earth in some measure if we want to, but if you go to heaven, God's the biggest thing on the horizon. You're no longer going to be able to avoid him. And that would be supreme torture if you haven't gotten over thinking of *yourself* as God."[7] Willard adds that "the fires of heaven burn hotter than the fires of hell."[8] Think of how the sun can bring warmth and cause plants to grow and bear fruit—and also how it can produce intensely hot, desertlike conditions inhospitable to most plants.

While hell is punishment, it is also the fruit of one's earthly life. Hell is actually a provision for what people ultimately want; as we pointed out, it's the best God can do for some people.[9] When people freely resist the grace of God, they permanently separate themselves from God.

Sending People to Hell?

When critics ask why a "good God would send people to hell," they frame the question incorrectly. God desires for all to be saved (2 Pet. 3:9), and his grace is available to all persons so that they can repent (Acts 17:30). So, no, he doesn't *send* persons to hell. Because they have spent a lifetime resisting God's grace (Acts 7:51), they condemn themselves. With each choice we make, we further reinforce the direction of our lives, whether toward or away from God. As Lewis wrote, the doors of hell are locked from the *inside*. So in the end, there are only two kinds of people: those who say to God, "Thy will be done," and those to whom God says, "Thy will be done."[10] Hell is the only safe place for those who want their own way. Indeed, the human will that defies the grace of God is the sole reason that universal salvation is not achieved.

Another point of response. Hell is the result of committing the ultimate sin—rejecting God himself. That is, the "finite" sins of the unredeemed are simply a manifestation of the "infinite" sin—turning away from the infinite, gracious, self-giving God. Hell is having my own way forever. God, in the end, leaves the unrepentant alone.

Universalism, Conditionalism, and "Corrosivism"

As Christian theologians have wrestled with the doctrine of hell, some have claimed that no one will ultimately be separated from the love of God (universalism). Others have claimed that, unless one trusts in Christ, the ultimate fate of the unrepentant is personal extinction or destruction—not conscious everlasting torment. Immortality is not intrinsic to humans but conditional (conditionalism). Perhaps there are other ways of piecing together what hell involves; we'll take a look at one of these ("corrosivism").

Universalism

Some theologians have claimed that the traditional doctrine of hell is incompatible with the love and the justice of God. What's more, hell presents an "untidy" end of the biblical story: the unredeemed continue living but removed from God while the redeemed enjoy God's company. Christian universalists such as Thomas Talbott, Marilyn Adams, and Robin Parry have claimed that the love of God will ultimately prove successful and that all will find salvation. God may have to repair one's damaged capacity for making free choices and help all who lack it move toward rational clarity. Once this happens—after some restorative, refining, or curative punishment after death—they can freely receive God's love.

Divine judgment will not have the final word. And Scripture, in some texts, seems to affirm that Adam's one act brought condemnation to "all," but this was reversed by Christ's, who brought "justification to all men" and full "reconciliation" as well (Rom. 5:18–19; Col. 1:20). God will successfully save everyone. While we can appreciate the desire to emphasize the infinite love of God, it presents a lopsided picture: it goes against the teachings of Scripture and also presents some philosophical problems.

Scriptural Challenges

For one thing, we simply do not see any of this "salvation for all" message in the Old Testament (e.g., Ps. 1), and this pattern is followed in the New. For example, consider the judgment of the sheep and the goats (Matt. 25) or the simple contrast in John 3:16 of those who "perish" and on whom the wrath of God remains (John 3:36)—as opposed to those who "have eternal life." And, without undermining human free choice in response to God's grace, Revelation 13:8 indicates something non-universalistic: a limited, non-expanding number of names written in the Lamb's "book of life"—names written "from the foundation of the world" (Rev. 13:8; 17:8)—without which one cannot be in the presence of God (Rev. 20:15).

Further, why would Paul wish he could be condemned so that his Israelite brothers and sisters could be saved (Rom. 9:3)? Paul himself insisted that those who preach a false gospel are accursed (Gal. 1:8–9). As for Romans 5, typically universalists detach this text from the rest of Paul's writings (e.g., 2 Thess. 1:9—"eternal destruction") and even the context of Romans 5:1, where believers have been "justified by faith." Moreover, the "all" in Adam aren't the "all" in Christ. Christ, the second Adam, is the founder of a new, redeemed humanity. Or perhaps the "all" could refer to people from "all nations" (gentiles) rather than merely Jews alone (cf. Rom. 1:16; 2:28–29; 9:6). In fact, in 1 Corinthians 15:22–23 (ESV), the "all" who are "made alive" are "in Christ" and "belong to Christ."

Then what about the apparent universal reconciliation in Colossians 1:20, where God has worked "to reconcile all things to Himself" through Christ's cross? However, Paul adds that "*He has now reconciled you*" (v. 22) but he adds this conditional: "*if indeed you continue in the faith* firmly established and steadfast" (v. 23). This suggests that the extent of Christ's reconciliation isn't *that* universal after all. Another concern about universalism is its practical outworking: why bother living an upright life if the moral corrosion of one's character ultimately doesn't matter; one can live for self or for God, but it will all somehow be patched up in the end.[11]

Furthermore, it is true that salvation is *potentially* offered to all, but not all *actually* freely accept it (1 Tim. 2:4; 2 Pet. 3:9). There are those who ultimately deny "the Master who bought them" (2 Pet. 2:1). So, while salvation is *universal in intent* (God's *desired* will), this is not achieved *in fact* (God's *permissive* will).

The universalist may point out that all will bow and acknowledge Christ's lordship (Phil. 2:10; cf. Rev. 15:4). Perhaps at first glance—however, a closer look reveals that not all gladly and willingly will bend the knee. Here Paul cites Isaiah 45:23, but we have indications from the Old Testament—including Isaiah—that not all bowing is positive. Indeed, it may involve a humiliated, shameful acknowledgment (Isa. 49:23; Zeph. 2:11). In Revelation 3:9, hostile Jews will be made to "come and bow down at your feet."

In addition, Jesus spoke of an *unpardonable* sin that won't be forgiven even in the life to come (Matt. 12:31–32). When asked whether only a few would be saved, Jesus replied, "Strive to enter through the narrow door; for many, I tell you, will seek to enter and will not be able" (Luke 13:23–24). And what of Revelation 14:11, which seems a problem for this view: "And the smoke of their torment goes up forever and ever; they have no rest day and night, those who worship the beast and his image, and whoever receives the mark of his name."

Philosophical Concerns

Philosophically, universalism fails to take genuine creaturely freedom seriously. Consider Satan's words in John Milton's *Paradise Lost*: "Better to reign in hell than serve in Heaven."[12] Universalists assume that when God more fully reveals himself to creatures, they will inevitably—and freely—take the rational course of eventually repenting and submitting to God. But universalists fail to understand the nature of robust libertarian freedom, in which it is up to the agent to choose.

Universalists will have to opt for a kind of "freedom" that is compatible with determinism, in which God creates the conditions that guarantee humans will choose to love God. But this ignores that very point of human freedom to either love God or to turn away from his initiating grace—without any divine "rigging" of that choice. What's more, although some universalists deny any punishment at all, we have no assurance that temporary punishment will truly restore human beings to God and turn them into virtuous beings.[13]

However, sin is not rational, and despite the best conditions and clearest explanations, some will steadfastly refuse the gracious rule of God over them. Satan and his minions once served in the presence of God; they were all very well-informed and fully rational before turning away from their good Creator. Why think that fallen human beings—once placed in the presence of God—would inevitably (eventually) embrace God?

There are places in Scripture where God is "exasperated" and can do no more than what he has done: "Judge between Me and My vineyard. What more was there to do for My vineyard that I have not done in it?" (Isa. 5:3–4). For stubborn rebels, it could well be the case that the clearer God's revelation and the more he pours out his grace, the more strongly they want to flee and the more they hate him. They want to try to find happiness on their terms.

So while the unredeemed don't choose hell or enjoy its conditions—as with the rich man in Luke 16—they may prefer happiness their way rather than God's. As we've seen, Michael Ruse writes about the afterlife: "What I dread is that God might give me what I need rather than what I want."[14] No wonder C. S. Lewis responded to the claim "All will be saved" with the reply, "Without their will or with it?" If *without* their will, "I at once perceive a contradiction; how can the supreme voluntary act of self-surrender be involuntary?" But if *with* their will, Lewis responded: "How if they *will not* give in?"[15] Those in hell, he said, are successful rebels to the end.

No wonder D. A. Carson writes that "there is no hint in the Bible that there is any repentance in hell. . . . Perhaps we should think of hell as a place where people continue to rebel, continue to insist on their own way, continue societal structures of prejudice and hate, continue to defy the living God. And as they continue to defy God, so he continues to punish them. And the cycle goes on and on and on."[16]

People in hell don't sin for just a *finite* earthly time, but they *continue* to sin and defy God in their perpetual refusal to repent.

Conditionalism

A growing number of theologians have argued that since humans are not intrinsically immortal, then we have grounds for thinking that immortality is a gift of God for those who put their trust in God and in his Son's saving work. Those who refuse God's grace to the very end will cease to exist—though after a period of punishment. This position has been called "conditionalism," "conditional immorality," "terminal punishment," and "annihilationism."

This view is based on biblical language such as "destruction," "perish," and "death"—along with other images such as trees being cut down (Matt. 7:27) or chaff and branches being burned up (Matt. 3:12; John 15:6). God's judgment of "raging fire" will "consume the enemies of God" (Heb. 10:26–29 NIV). Sometimes the New Testament (Jude 7) will refer back to the destruction of Sodom and Gomorrah (Gen. 19) as "an example in undergoing the punishment of eternal fire" (Jude 7). If these cities were incinerated, shouldn't this inform our picture of final judgment? Second Peter 2:6 suggests this—these cities were burned "to ashes," making them "an example of what is going to happen to the ungodly" (NIV).

In addition to having significant biblical support, it does have the benefit of tidiness (evil will eventually be destroyed, not simply quarantined in the realms of hell). In addition, some theologians such as John Stott argue that the doctrine of conditional immortality diminishes the "intolerable" emotional strain produced by the idea of everlasting conscious torment. However, as Stott rightly acknowledges, God's Word, not our emotions, should govern this question.[17]

In response, we can acknowledge that a number of biblical texts appear to support this position. Of course, the images of final judgment are often mixed, and so we must take care not to quote a set of texts in isolation. Yet, to my mind at least, the evidence for conditionalism doesn't overturn the traditional interpretation of ongoing conscious torment. We can disagree here too for reasons related to Scripture, philosophical reasoning, and the Christian tradition.

Scriptural Challenges

As we consider Scripture, we can agree that "eternal life" (John 17:3) can refer to a *quality* of life—life in the sphere of the triune God—and that this doesn't necessarily focus on everlastingness. However, in the sheep-goats judgment, we have what appears a natural parallel of some going to "eternal life" and others to "eternal punishment," and they seem to experience ongoing conscious awareness (Matt. 25:46).

This is reinforced by the picture of the unredeemed going to realms of weeping and gnashing of teeth (Matt. 8:12; 13:42, 50; 22:13; 24:51; 25:30); this would be strange if the unredeemed ceased to exist. Also, while the language of fire can suggest the finality of existence, it is curious that Jesus refers to the worm not dying or fire not going out if cessation of existence is in view (Mark 9:48). Furthermore, if we don't exist prior to our life on earth, then what is the point of Jesus saying about his betrayer Judas Iscariot that it would have been better if he hadn't been born (Matt. 26:24)? If Judas simply went from nonexistence to existence back to nonexistence again, this doesn't carry the weight Jesus assigns to Judas's fate.

As for the Sodom and Gomorrah references from Jude and 2 Peter, they seem to move from the lesser to the greater (Jude 7, 13)—that is, from earthly fiery judgment to lasting "eternal fire" and permanent darkness ("reserved forever"). Moreover, the book of Revelation seems to reinforce this theme. The redeemed enter their rest while the unrepentant are restless or "tormented"—the opposite of rest (Rev. 9:5; 11:10; 12:2; 18:7, 10, 15; 20:20; cf. Matt. 4:24 ["pains"]). Those who worship the beast and his image, "will be tormented with burning sulfur in the presence of the holy angels and of the Lamb. And the smoke of their torment will rise for ever and ever." Now this is not simply a picture of cessation of existence. The text adds: "There will be no rest day or night for those who worship the beast and its image, or for anyone who receives the mark of its name" (Rev. 14:9–11 ESV).

Conditionalists may respond that the "beast" is judged and "tormented day and night forever and ever" (Rev. 20:10). Yet the beast symbolizes an evil, anti-Christian empire (cf. Dan. 7), but how can an empire be tormented? Aren't individual persons tormented? Yes, but empires are comprised of individuals, who can be judged. Consider how "all the nations" will be gathered before Christ, and he himself will "separate the people one from another" (Matt. 25:32–33 NIV). And we shouldn't overlook the fact that those involved in opposing the people of God—whether individuals or "beastly" empires (which are made up of individuals)—will still be "tormented," along with the devil, a personal being (Rev. 14:11; 20:10).

Furthermore, that which is "destroyed" doesn't necessarily cease to exist—for example, the world during the time of Noah (2 Pet. 3:6). A coin may be "lost" (*apollymi*—the word for "destroy" [Luke 15:9]). Also, the "second death" doesn't necessarily suggest being extinguished; after all, we were once spiritually "dead in [our] trespasses and sins," though physically alive (Eph. 2:1).

We commonly hear people say that they have "gone through hell," by which they often mean experiencing deeply trying or agonizing circumstances. While they aren't necessarily making a theological point, they remind us that the life to come is a continuation of the present: the redeemed begin to experience eternal life now (1 John 5:12–13), and those who will be separated from God "are perishing" (1 Cor. 1:18). The redeemed who have found rest in Christ (Matt. 11:28) will finally enter their rest with God (Rev. 14:13) while the unredeemed will "have no rest" (Rev. 14:11). The choices we make in this life carry over into the next. In this life, we receive either a foretaste of glory divine or of separation from the divine.

Philosophical Concerns
As for philosophical questions, we can say first that our intuitions about the "more morally tolerable" position of conditionalism may not be as apparent. Jerry Walls suggests: "Capital punishment is widely believed to be a more severe punishment than life in prison. Annihilation is seemingly the ultimate form of capital punishment, the metaphysical death penalty."[18] Some may argue that the person in hell experiences no goods, while a prisoner for life might receive some. However, the traditional understanding of hell doesn't require maximal misery. It could be that hell affords its citizens "the limited, twisted pleasures involved in holding on to one's coveted sins and rebellion

against God."[19] The damned—who prefer darkness to light (John 3:19)—would prefer these measly, fleeting pleasures in their misery rather than being extinguished. And they would prefer this even though genuine happiness continually eludes them.

The Christian Tradition

In terms of the Christian tradition, conditionalism goes against the received understanding of hell within Eastern Orthodoxy, Roman Catholicism, and Protestantism. And this testimony goes back to the earliest church fathers. For example, the apostle John's disciple Polycarp experienced a fiery martyrdom at age eighty-six. Before he perished, he replied to the threat that he would be burned with fire: "You threaten me with fire which burns for an hour, and is then extinguished, but you know nothing of the fire of the coming judgment and eternal punishment, reserved for the ungodly. Why are you waiting? Bring on whatever you want."[20]

Though reasonably strong, the case for conditional immortality is not, to my mind, persuasive in the end.

Corrosivism

Perhaps the experience of hell is something akin to J. R. R. Tolkien's hobbit Sméagol, who became so enamored of the magical, powerful, corrupting ring that he not only killed to obtain it but eventually turned into the diminished, corroded, wisp-like creature Gollum. He became less and less recognizable as a hobbit because his own character had become corrupted and twisted.

Could it be that in the afterlife, the unredeemed find themselves increasingly diminished in their humanity? In *The Great Divorce*, C. S. Lewis describes a grumbling woman who eventually comes to more strongly resemble a grumble than she does a woman. She simply fades over time and turns into something machinelike.

The New Testament scholar N. T. Wright puts it this way:

> It seems . . . it is possible . . . for human beings to choose to live more and more out of tune with the divine intention, to reflect the image of God less and less, [such that] there is nothing to stop them finally ceasing to bear that image, and so to be, as it were, beings who were once human but are not now. Those who persistently refuse to follow Jesus, the true Image of God, will by their own choice become less and less like him, that is, less

and less truly human. We sometimes say, even of living people, that they have become inhuman. . . . I see nothing in the New Testament to make me reject the possibility that some, perhaps many, of God's human creatures do choose, and will choose, to dehumanize themselves completely.[21]

Since we become like what we worship, we may—through our own choices—continue so far down this road that we move toward becoming less and less human, to the point of entering an "ex-human state."[22]

Concluding Remarks

Some have claimed that it is unsettling to think that God could somehow allow people to continue to exist apart from his presence and apart from the company of the redeemed. While this seems "untidy," God's cordoning off sin from himself makes sense. He creates people with the capacity to know and love God, but this capacity can be turned toward self-centered ends. For those who freely refuse to repent in response to God's grace, what alternative is there? Remember the older brother in the parable of the prodigal son (Luke 15:11–32)? After the younger brother left home, squandered his inheritance, and came back to his senses, his father called for a hearty celebration of his return. Nevertheless, his brother refused to come inside while the lost son was being feted.

Why did God create a world, knowing that many people would reject him forever? Some complain that they weren't consulted about the matter before they were born. Of course, how *could* they be consulted if they didn't even exist? But who is ultimately to blame? Humans engage in self-separation from God by resisting his initiating grace.

Also, what if it's the case no possible world would contain persons who always freely choose to do what is good? What if certain persons would never freely embrace God, no matter what world God placed them in? This condition has been called "transworld depravity," and it includes persons who may have come very close in the actual world—perhaps even having apostatized from the Christian faith—but in the end ultimately decide against God. What if God arranges the world in such a way that those who would desire salvation ultimately receive it, and those who desire autonomy from God end up getting what they want in the end?

What more can God do for those who refuse to come in to celebrate? He has made redemption available to all and fully given himself for us and our salvation. God isn't going to be held captive by those who haven't abandoned their pride to accept God's gracious forgiveness. The spoilsports and grouches have a right to sit out, but they don't have the right to hold up the party that revels and rejoices in God's redeeming us from captivity. Why should the saints' celebration stop simply because some refuse to enter the banquet hall?[23] A victorious army—whether physical or spiritual—that has fought in a just cause properly rejoices that justice has been done; they enjoy the results of that victory, even if that means the losing side gets what it deserves (Rev. 18:20; cf. 6:9–10). In the end, evil will be quarantined, kept away from God's good renewed creation (Rev. 22:14–15).

This world, though laden with trouble and sorrow, is the pathway to the best kind of world in the future—a life enjoying God's immediate presence. It is a world in which we set our spiritual compass toward or away from God so that in the end, we get what we most desire. We are sealed in the choices we have made all along. Or we could approach this matter another way: in the afterlife, those who have been redeemed and have seen the irrationality of sin and the damage it brings will have no desire to go back to that way of life; that would be like poking out our eyes or cutting off our fingers. So while it would be theoretically possible to freely do these things in our redeemed state, we would never seriously consider going back to it.

FURTHER READING

Lewis, C. S. *The Great Divorce*. Various editions.

———. *The Problem of Pain*. Various editions.

McClymond, Michael. *The Devil's Redemption: A New History and Interpretation of Christian Universalism*. Grand Rapids: Baker Academic, 2018.

Sprinkle, Preston, ed. *Four Views on Hell*. 2nd ed. Grand Rapids: Zondervan, 2016.

Part IV

REDEMPTION AND RE-CREATION

In Him we have redemption through His blood, the forgiveness of our trespasses, according to the riches of His grace which He lavished on us.
—Ephesians 1:7–8a

So if anyone is in Christ, there is a new creation: everything old has passed away; see, everything has become new!
—2 Corinthians 5:17 NRSV

For behold, I create new heavens and a new earth;
And the former things will not be remembered or come to mind.
—Isaiah 65:17

> The Word became flesh, and dwelt among us.
>
> —John 1:14

> . . . Christ Jesus who, although He existed in the form
> of God, did not regard equality with God a thing to
> be grasped, but emptied Himself, taking the form of a
> bond-servant, and being made in the likeness of men.
>
> —Philippians 2:5–7

DID GOD BECOME A JEW?

The triune God created, but the very creatures meant for relationship with God went their own way and sought satisfactions elsewhere.[1] God does something new—though not a switch to plan B because plan A had failed. No, God's redemptive purposes were in view from the beginning (1 Pet. 1:17–20). What was foreshadowed in the first creation and first exodus find fulfillment in a new creation and new exodus. Through the second Adam and the true Son of God, deity takes on human form to identify with us in our weaknesses, experiencing hostility and injustice and rejection.

God became a first-century Jew in Jesus of Nazareth (John 1:1, 14). As typified in the best sort of fairy tales, God sent forth a *champion* or *hero* (*archēgos*) of our faith (Heb. 12:2; cf. 2:10) to rescue the helpless, ungodly, sinners, and enemies of God (Rom. 5:6–10).[2] This divine hero came to redeem those from "the lost sheep of the house of Israel" (Matt. 15:24; cf. John 1:11–12). In giving his life as a ransom for many (Mark 10:45), he would fulfill the promise to Abraham, whose offspring would one day bring blessing to those not part of God's covenant with Israel. He took "strangers" and "aliens" and made them "fellow citizens" and members of "God's household" (Eph. 2:19). This momentous event of history was accomplished through the incarnation of the Son of God.

Since Jesus shares in the divine of the identity of God, the incarnation is something of a gateway into understanding and clarifying the doctrine of the Trinity. Both doctrines have mystery about them, but the incarnation—the "enfleshment of God"—appears to be more than a theological perplexity; it seems self-contradictory. Orthodox Christianity affirms that the *one person* of Jesus of Nazareth possessed *two natures*—divine and human: "perfect God, perfect man subsisting of a reasoning soul and human flesh," according to the sixth-century Athanasian Creed. The Son of God is *homoousios*—of the same substance or being—with the Father (Council of Nicea, AD 325); he is "truly God and truly man"—two natures preserved without confusion, change, division, or separation (Council of Chalcedon, AD 451).

Yet how could God become human without contradiction? Perhaps Jesus simply possessed a profound, intense consciousness of God's presence, as philosopher John Hick argued. Clearly, Jesus was human (1 Cor. 15:21, 47–49; 1 Tim. 2:5; 3:16), but perhaps Jesus's well-meaning followers eventually came to deify a mere human who never made any of the lofty claims ascribed to him.

In a seriously monotheistic, anti-idolatrous culture, the elevated claims of Jesus and the worship of Jesus as presented in the New Testament are shocking and sudden. The Word who was "with God" and "was God" becomes human (John 1:1). What would lead an orthodox Jew to affirm this? Jesus's claim to forgive sins rendered the temple superfluous (Mark 2:5, 7); he insisted that he was the judge of the world (Matt. 7:22–23; 25:31–46; cf. 2 Cor. 5:10); his followers prayed to him (Acts 7:59–60; 1 Cor. 16:22; 2 Cor. 12:9); he is not only "God with us" (Matt. 1:23) but is specifically called "God" (John 1:1, 18; 20:28; Acts 20:28; Rom. 9:5; Titus 2:13; Heb. 1:8; 2 Pet. 1:1; 1 John 5:20). The list goes on.

Some might attribute such claims or events in the Gospels to legend, not history. But legend expert C. S. Lewis was critical of such critics: "I distrust them as critics. They seem to me to lack literary judgment, to be imperceptive about the very quality of the texts they are reading." Though studying the New Testament from their youth up, they lack the needed literary experience and so miss "the obvious things" about these texts: "If he tells me that something in a Gospel is legend or romance, I want to know how many legends and romances he has read, how well his palate is trained in detecting them by flavour; not how many years he has spent on that Gospel."[3]

Even so, this leaves us with theological questions, including Jesus's not knowing the time of his return (Matt. 24:36). But isn't God necessarily omniscient? And was Jesus really holding the universe together and answering prayers while in utero or as an infant? Given such questions, should we conclude that Jesus wasn't really divine?

SELF-EMPTYING (*KENOSIS*)

Some theologians have proposed a *kenosis* theory—a term that comes from Philippians 2:7: the Son, equal with God, "emptied [*ekenōsen*] himself" by taking on the form of a human being. And, beyond that, he descended even further to a death by crucifixion, reserved for runaway slaves and criminals (v. 8). According to one version of the kenosis view, the Son sheds divine properties like omniscience and omnipotence. Since he, say, doesn't know the date of his own return (Matt. 24:36), perhaps omniscience isn't a *necessary* divine property.

This version of kenoticism, however, would undermine the affirmation of Jesus's divinity while on earth—he forgives sins (Mark 2:1–12), is Lord of the Sabbath (Mark 2:28), will be the final judge (Matt. 7:21–23), and makes claims that his detractors view as making himself equal to God (John 5:18; 10:23). Yet on this view, Jesus needn't be any more powerful or knowledgeable than any other human being. But this seemingly small-potatoes view of the incarnation fails to take seriously what the Scriptures themselves affirm is required of divinity.

Now what if Jesus is only *temporarily* without omniscience or omnipotence but can recover them once his earthly mission is completed? In this case, we can rightly wonder whether he ever gave them up in the first place. But if he *permanently* gave them up, then we're talking about a diminished deity—if even that—rather than the incomparable God.

Some suggest that this seeming loss of the "omni" attributes is a kind of simulation—that the Son merely *appeared* to lack them. But this would be a divinely engineered false impression. This is like the Gnostic heresy of Docetism (from the Greek word *dokeō*—"to appear, seem"): the Son of God *seemed* to have been physical and to have experienced death. On the other hand, a kenotic view that affirms that the Son of God simply *limited* the exercise of his undiminished, divinely necessary powers presents no theological problem. Here the Son of God doesn't give up knowledge or forget things. Rather, he merely gives up having *access* to that knowledge—or to the full use of his power. In this case, the emptying has do to with *function*, not *being* or *nature*.[4] It's like an athletic parent holding back from exerting full strength and technical prowess while teaching a sport to a child. "Going easy" on a child should be taken to be not a lack of strength or ability but merely an exercise in restraint.

JESUS'S TWO LEVELS OF AWARENESS—DIVINE AND HUMAN

The incarnation was possible precisely because human beings have been made *in God's image* (Gen. 1:26–27; Ps. 8, esp. v. 5: "a little lower than God"). What is essential to humanness is derived from God's nature; thus the incarnate Christ is the truest or archetypal human—"*the* image of God" (Col. 1:15; 2 Cor. 3:18; Heb. 1:3): "It is because man in the creative order bears the image of his Creator that it was possible for the Son of God to become incarnate as man and in His humanity to display the glory of the invisible God."[5]

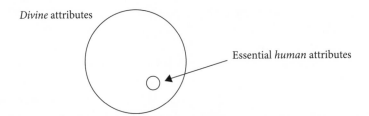

How do we work out the divine-human interrelationship? Scripture doesn't offer a philosophical resolution for us. The theologian Dietrich Bonhoeffer claimed that because the incarnation is a mystery, it doesn't require a philosophical defense. However, various theologically minded philosophers have taken a crack at it; they present incarnation models or scenarios that attempt to be (a) *faithful to Scripture* and (b) *logically coherent*, though without removing its mystery. So long as the model meets both of these criteria, then this is all that is required, even if the model in the end turns out not to be true. Now, one leading model puts forward the idea of Jesus having two "minds" or levels of awareness. That is, the divine awareness of Jesus of Nazareth contains—but isn't contained by—Jesus's first-century, Jewish human awareness.[6] This model is, in my view, very much worth exploring.

THREE IMPORTANT DISTINCTIONS

To unpack this, consider three crucial distinctions.

1. *Nature* and *person*: A thing's *nature* or *essence* makes it what it is; without essential properties, necessarily that thing would not exist. You and I are *persons*—that is, *centers of (self-)consciousness, will, action, and responsibility*. We *have* a *nature*. Those who qualify as persons include humans, angels, and members of the triune Godhead. Jesus of Nazareth is one *person* who shares our human nature while still possessing the divine nature.
2. *Fully* (or *essentially*) versus *merely* human: Although humans *commonly* sin, have four limbs, and die, these are *merely*—not *fully* or *essentially*—human characteristics. For example, while sin is a universal condition,

redeemed humans will be sinless in the afterlife, and Jesus himself was sinless. And although we humans inevitably die, this isn't *necessarily* so: Enoch and Elijah didn't die. *Being essentially/fully human doesn't exclude the possibility of being fully divine.* We are essentially—not merely—God's image-bearers with rational, relational, creative, spiritual, and moral capacities to carry out our function as God's representative king-priests on earth. These qualities derive *from God*—a finite subset of infinite divine qualities. But doesn't Jesus die? Yes, but his death pertains to his *mere* humanity, not his *essential* humanity. And it certainly isn't *God* who dies—since God is necessarily immortal. Jesus did not die with respect to his *divinity* or divine nature.

3. *Divine awareness* and *human awareness*: This is comparable to our *two levels of "consciousness"*—conscious and preconscious—working in tandem. We know about the operations of the conscious mind—a direct awareness. By contrast, the *preconscious* is an accessible, "ready to hand" level of awareness. It is like having calculus or algebraic formulas thoroughly embedded in our minds, which we can draw on at will at any time, although we aren't consciously thinking about them as we go about our day.[7] Similarly, the voluntarily restrained powers of, say, divine omniscience and omnipotence in Jesus of Nazareth would be located and readily accessible in this preconscious awareness of his mind.

    What is the difference between the *pre*conscious and the *sub*conscious? The philosopher Andrew Loke offers this explanation: "Now, the *preconscious* is different from the shadowy *subconscious*, to which we don't typically have ready access. More often than not, it is impenetrable and hidden from us." He adds that the analogy of the *preconscious* helps preserve the unity of Christ's mind whereas using the analogy of the *subconscious* could resemble two persons rather than one: "So the idea of Christ's divine awareness as akin to the subconscious could undermine 'I' thoughts and function more like two persons rather than one."[8]

In the incarnation, the Son of God fully identifies with the human situation without loss of any divine attributes. His *conscious* mind is that of a first-century, Aramaic-speaking Nazarene who grew in virtue (Luke 2:52; Heb. 2:18; 5:8) and in the understanding of his mission as he read the Hebrew Scriptures. All the while he possessed the eternal, divine *preconscious*, drawing on this divine knowledge as necessary in order to accomplish his triunely predetermined task on earth (cf. John 17:5, 22–6; Phil. 2:6–11).

IF JESUS WAS GOD, HOW COULD HE BE TEMPTED?

James 1:13 affirms that it is impossible for God to tempt anyone to sin—or to be tempted himself. This is the doctrine of divine *impeccability*: God cannot go wrong, since this would imply that God's goodness isn't a necessary goodness, that something could potentially overcome God, and that God would have to display ignorance so as to be led astray. But what then are we to make of Jesus's temptation? As God, how could he truly experience temptation if he couldn't sin? And, being God, surely he wouldn't be ignorant about this basic truth, would he?

In response, we could say that Jesus's mission included living with human weakness as well as growing to maturity and into a deepened obedience to his Father's will through struggle and suffering (Luke 2:52; Heb. 2:18; 5:8). By reading the Scriptures, he came to see with increasing clarity his messianic status. As our high priestly mediator, Jesus shows sympathy toward us in our weakness, since he "has been tempted in all things as we are, yet without sin" (Heb. 4:15).

This mission also involved *self-restricted access* to knowing consciously—though not preconsciously—that it was impossible for him to sin or what the timing of his return would be (Matt. 24:36). As one theologian put it, the "divine reality was not fully and comprehensively present to the [human] mind of Jesus."[9] While Jesus *could have* had conscious access to knowing these matters, he voluntarily gave this up in order to live out faithfully Adam's (humanity's) and Israel's story and calling.

The Scriptures clearly present Jesus as really struggling in the face of temptation. Jesus didn't engage in playacting, as though being tested by Satan was trivial. And yet, because of his divinity, sinning was impossible. Some might think that this is a bizarre kind of temptation—there is apparently nothing all that tempting about it. In his temptation, Jesus was God after all, wasn't he?

Admittedly, God's identification with humans is a unique situation. His facing temptation without being able to sin is unusual, but not self-contradictory. Indeed, genuine temptation without the possibility of sinning is still conceivable and quite reasonable. Imagine entering a room and, unbeknownst to you, the glass door has an automatic two-hour time lock. You consider leaving once or twice. Perhaps friends pass by and motion to you to come out and join them, but you politely decline because you freely decide to catch up on some reading for the full two hours, after which time you leave the room to enjoy their company. While you, in fact, would not have been able to leave the room during that two-hour timeframe, you didn't even bother to move toward the door to try getting out because you freely decided to stay put.

Or consider a spy who goes on a dangerous mission. In case he's tortured and thus more likely to divulge top-secret information, he takes along with him a limited-amnesia-producing pill with an antidote for later use. Though under the effects of the amnesia pill if captured, he still possesses this vital information in his mind but has chosen this self-limitation for a short time and a specific purpose.[10]

Likewise, Jesus didn't lose certain divine attributes; rather, he voluntarily, temporarily suppressed or gave up immediate access to certain divine capacities and powers he possessed all along. Again, remember the parent holding back rather than exerting the full force of his powers while playing soccer or baseball with his kids. Likewise, prior to his to his mission to earth, the Son of God—in concert with Father and Spirit—determined to restrain his divine capacities in order to complete his redemptive task as a human being so that he could be genuinely tempted and endure human weakness like us, yet without sin (Heb. 4:15).[11]

Even though through this divine self-restraint Jesus gave up having access to the knowledge that he couldn't sin, he is still presented in the Gospels as being omniscient. His disciples acknowledged, "Now we know that you know all things and do not need anyone to question you; this is why we believe that you came from God" (John 16:30 ESV). Peter later confessed: "Lord, you know everything" (John 21:17 ESV)—the same word used in Matthew 24:36 about Jesus not knowing the time of his return (*oiden*). Thus, "the notion that Jesus was not consciously aware of all things . . . and the notion that he knew all truths . . . are both consistent with the use of this word."[12]

The three distinctions noted above provide a helpful framework for addressing questions such as: (a) If Jesus was God, who was running the universe when he was a baby or on the cross? (b) How could God die? (c) If God "so loved the world," why did he send his Son rather than come himself? This two-levels-of-awareness incarnational model helps us see that Jesus experienced the ongoing mutually indwelling Trinitarian life—still governing the universe as a baby and while dying on the cross. And he died as a mere—not essentially—human being; the divine nature wasn't crucified, but the divine person, who is also human. The mutual life of the Trinity suggests that each divine person experienced pain at the crucifixion; Jesus didn't suffer alone: "God was in Christ reconciling the world to Himself" (2 Cor. 5:19).

MISCELLANEOUS QUESTIONS

Jesus Christ is one subject who bears both essentially divine and human properties. Some are *merely* human properties (death, weakness) while others are *essentially* or *fully* human. These kinds of distinctions give us some insight in responding to common questions raised about the incarnation.

Question: Did God die on the cross?

Response: No. Jesus, as one personal subject, could be immortal with respect to his divine nature but not by virtue of his *mere* human condition. God, who is essentially immortal, did not die. Rather, Jesus died with respect to his mere humanness.[13]

Question: Doesn't God know all truths consciously and immediately—in one intuition? Wouldn't Jesus's preconscious (non-immediate) knowledge contradict this, though?

Response: While knowing all truths is necessary for divinity, *how* these truths are known isn't necessary for divinity. For example, one could have conscious (or "occurrent") knowledge of all truths—or preconscious (or "dispositional") knowledge of those truths. We could compare this to viewing information on a computer screen—in contrast to the information readily available in the computer's memory on a hard drive. Likewise, we could say during his earthly ministry, Jesus of Nazareth intentionally focused only on what he consciously thought about; this is why he wasn't immediately aware of the day or the hour of his return. If it were necessary, Jesus could have directed his attention to this dispositional (preconscious) knowledge of the day and the hour; he could have drawn on that knowledge. Indeed, Jesus drew on his divine preconsciousness *only as needed* in order to faithfully fulfill his mission. So then, why couldn't God—in order to accomplish a self-humbling act of incarnation—freely choose to maintain full knowledge in a preconscious rather than a conscious state?[14]

Question: Did Jesus have false beliefs as a child?

Response: Making errors is *common* to humans, but it isn't *essential* to being human. So the triune God could have arranged circumstances such that the incarnate Christ wouldn't possess false beliefs or commit errors.[15]

Question: Who was running the universe while Jesus was in the womb, was a small child, or was in a state of sleep? After all, the keeper of Israel "will neither slumber nor sleep" (Ps. 121:4).

Response: We could speak of the Son of God preprograming "his preconscious according to his infallible omniscience what actions would activate in any situation throughout the universe during those moments when his consciousness was limited, such that his preconscious functioned as an infallible 'autopilot' when Jesus was an embryo and while he slept."[16] Or what if it was the case that the triune God arranged that Jesus would never be fully unconscious and that his divine preconscious would always be sustained?[17]

Question: If Jesus cried out "My God, my God" from the cross, doesn't this imply that Jesus wasn't divine after all?

Response: No, the members of the Trinity can fittingly appropriate terminology like "God" and "Lord" of one another. In the book of Hebrews, the *Father* says to the Son, "Your throne, O God, is forever and ever" (1:8). The Father also calls the Son "Lord": "You, *Lord*, in the beginning laid the foundation of the earth" (1:10). So for Jesus to call the Father "God" doesn't diminish his own deity, since the Father calls his son *God* and *Lord*.

FINAL THOUGHT

In my favorite Christmas carol, "Hark! the Herald Angels Sing," Charles Wesley wrote:

> Veiled in flesh the Godhead see.
> Hail th' incarnate Deity!
> Pleased, as man, with men to dwell,
> Jesus, our Emmanuel!

Truly, "great is the mystery of godliness"—that the Son of God was "revealed in the flesh" (1 Tim. 3:16)—"Mild he lays his glory by." While we have good reasons for affirming "the logic of God incarnate," this doesn't diminish its mystery, beauty, and power.

FURTHER READING

Loke, Andrew Ter Ern. *A Kryptic Model of the Incarnation*. Burlington, VT: Ashgate, 2014.

Moreland, J. P., and William Lane Craig. *Philosophical Foundations for a Christian Worldview*. 2nd ed. Downers Grove, IL: IVP Academic, 2017.

Morris, Thomas V. *Our Idea of God*. Downers Grove, IL: InterVarsity Press, 1990.

> I have been crucified with Christ; and it is no longer I
> who live, but Christ lives in me; and the life which I now
> live in the flesh I live by faith in the Son of God, who
> loved me and gave Himself up for me.
> —Galatians 2:20

> For what the Law could not do, weak as it was through
> the flesh, God did: sending His own Son in the likeness
> of sinful flesh and as an offering for sin, He condemned
> sin in the flesh, so that the requirement of the Law might
> be fulfilled in us, who do not walk according to the flesh
> but according to the Spirit.
> —Romans 8:3–4

Jesus's Death in the Greco-Roman World

Historian Tom Holland discovered that the Greco-Roman world he had praised—the world of classical antiquity—was quite "alien and unsettling" upon closer inspection. He was shocked to learn about its pervasive calloused spirit and its view of the poor or weak as having no intrinsic value. He realized that it was the Christian faith that left its mark on this world by bringing a radically new mind-set shaped by the historic events of Jesus's death and resurrection. This new, transforming vision was inspired by the blameless and just Messiah pouring out his life in self-giving love to rescue the helpless, ungodly enemies, and sinners (Rom. 5:6–10). In the first-century Mediterranean world, worshiping a Master who died naked on a Roman cross was considered madness or insanity (*moria*) to gentiles and offensive to Jews (1 Cor. 1:18). This would have been considered an embarrassment—never the talk of polite company.

Holland continues: "Nothing could have run more counter to the most profoundly held assumptions of Paul's contemporaries—Jews, or Greeks, or Romans. The notion that a god might have suffered torture and death on a cross was so shocking as to appear repulsive. Familiarity with the biblical narrative of the Crucifixion has dulled our sense of just how completely novel a deity Christ was. In the ancient world, it was the role of gods who laid claim to ruling the universe to uphold its order by inflicting punishment—not to suffer it themselves."[1]

Perhaps the most famous painting of the crucifixion is Mattias Grünewald's Isenheim altarpiece—now at the Unterlinden Museum in the Alsacian town of Colmar, France. Back in July 2017, my wife and I had the privilege of studying up close this long-standing favorite work of art. The painting was specially made for a monastic hospital for syphilis patients. The artist intentionally depicted the crucified Jesus as having not only a twisted, mangled body but also the marks of syphilis all over it. It is a picture of Jesus not only as the sacrificial "Lamb of God" to whom John the Baptist is awkwardly pointing, but also as the one who identifies with us in the depths of our broken and afflicted humanity.

WHAT JESUS'S DEATH ACCOMPLISHED: PICTURES OF THE ATONEMENT

Hymn writer Isaac Watts wrote of Christ's death, "Love so amazing, so divine, demands my soul, my life, my all." Was Jesus's death, then, something that merely inspires love and self-sacrifice—but accomplishes nothing more than this? Scripture does indicate that this personal moral influence is one of the biblical pictures of what happens through the atonement.

This doctrine refers to how sinful humans could be reconciled to—or find "at-one-ment" with—God, and to how the disparity between a righteous God and unrighteous humans is rectified. First Peter 2:21–25 affirms that Christ's death serves as "an example" to follow. Yes, the death of Christ stirs us *within* and inspires us to lay down our lives for others (1 John 3:16; cf. Phil. 2:3–8)—a *subjective* view represented in Scripture. (This view emphasized by the medieval theologian Peter Abelard.) But this isn't all. In this same passage, Jesus accomplishes something *objective*: he suffered "for you" and "bore our sins in His body on the cross." Paul writes about the Son of God, who "loved me and gave Himself up for [*hyper*] me" (Gal. 2:20).

While theologians may speak of "theories of the atonement," it is better to speak of biblical "pictures of the atonement" instead. "Theory" often implies a human construct that may go well beyond what Scripture indicates, and it may also suggest that one view ("*the* theory") is true and the others are false—rather than being complementary and mutually reinforcing.

Routing the Powers

One picture reminds us of Christ's victory over Satan and his forces, evil, the powers of sin, the law, and death (*Christus victor*): "Now judgment is upon this world; now the ruler of this world will be cast out" (John 12:31). As Paul wrote, "He had disarmed the rulers and authorities" and "made a public display of them, having triumphed over them through Him" (Col. 2:14–15). We see that the impact of Christ's death is not simply personal (Gal. 2:20) but also cosmic. As biblically important as this victory over these dehumanizing, oppressive, evil powers is, it doesn't get to the heart of how Christ's death covers or atones for our sin—or how he is our substitute.

Ransoming the Captives

Another picture is that Christ paid a ransom (Mark 10:45). Theologians like Irenaeus (second century) said that this payment must have been *to* someone, and the candidate he and other church fathers came up with is Satan. However, Satan isn't owed anything by us or by God. Rather, *God* is owed something—our faithful and righteous obedience.

Recapitulating/Reversing the Effects of Adam

Another perspective—most notably connected to Irenaeus—is that Jesus, as the second Adam, recapitulates the first Adam's story by living a life of faithful obedience and undoing or reversing the curse that Adam brought. For example, Jesus takes on our curse by hanging on the tree (Gal. 3:13). In his death, Christ reestablishes us as God's image-bearers through his death. While Jesus being the second Adam ("the new man") is a key theme in the New Testament—and one we have repeatedly emphasized in this book—recapitulation doesn't actually inform us about how the penalty for sin is paid and guilt removed.

Restoring Honor

Likewise, another view of the atonement is that of satisfaction. In his book *Cur Deus Homo* (*Why God Became Man*), the eleventh-century theologian Anselm attempted to use a purely philosophical argument for the incarnation—without appealing to biblical texts—to show the logic of the atonement. He claimed that our sin offends God and that God's honor must be restored or satisfied. While only humans must pay what they owe God, only God can pay it. This is why the Son of God becomes human—so that as a man he pays what humans owe but as God he makes satisfaction possible. God acts to satisfy the divine requirements.

Critics have claimed that this imagery borrows from a medieval feudal system: the lord of the manor has been offended, and honor must be restored. True, Anselm is reflecting familiar cultural themes of his day, but it's indeed the case that we have dishonored God. Anselm helpfully sheds light on the need for God to act on humanity's behalf in the God-man, Jesus Christ. But even so, *more* than satisfaction is needed in this salvific transaction.

Removing Sin: Penal Substitution as the Heart of the Atonement

Central to the atonement is substitution to remove sin because we failed to live up to God's righteous demands. Because "God so loved the world" (John 3:16), Jesus died "for [*hyper*] us" (Rom. 5:8; 8:32; 2 Cor. 5:21)—on our behalf. In doing so, he pays the just legal penalty "for our sins" (1 Cor. 15:3). The just character of the triune God demands we unjust humans pay—"the wages of sin is death" (Rom. 6:23)—which we cannot do.

However, the gracious triune God makes a startling provision—"the just for the unjust" (1 Pet. 3:18). Of course, Jesus's own death was *unjust*—utterly undeserved: he was blameless and was put to death by sinners (John 19:11). Indeed, it was not just first-century sinners who crucified Jesus. *Our* sins—yours and mine—put him there. The artist Rembrandt van Rijn's *Raising of the Cross* portrays that reality. In this painting, Rembrandt includes himself, wearing his artist's beret, in the mob putting Jesus on the cross.

Jesus laid down his life as our substitute so that the just penalty could be paid to render us not guilty (Rom. 8:33–34). While we can be grateful that Christ has come to identify with us by stepping into this sinful world, this *identification* by itself is insufficient to remove sin. It is meager comfort that someone incapable of swimming jumps in to keep us company in the water but drowns in the process. We need someone who capable of pulling us out of the water.

But beyond this, being *rescued* from sin isn't sufficient either. Sin needs to be *removed*. As the second Adam and the true Israel, Jesus is not only our representative before God—much like an elected government official who represents our interests. Jesus is also our *substitute*: what happens to him is legally applied to us. As Simon Gathercole points out, "Christ's death for our sins *in our place, instead of us,* is in fact, a vital ingredient in the biblical understanding of the atonement. . . . Jesus . . . did something, underwent something, so that we did not and would never have to do so."[2] To specify further, "the God of Israel [takes] his own eschatological judgment on himself in the form of his Son, Jesus of Nazareth."[3]

God's justice is satisfied through this substitutionary act: God is not only "the just" (the standard of justice) but also "the justifier," who graciously makes provision for us to be declared "not guilty" (Rom. 3:26).

Romans 5:6–10 tells us just how great an act of love Christ's sacrifice was: "For while we were still helpless, at the right time Christ died for the ungodly. For one will hardly die for a righteous man; though perhaps for the good man someone would dare even to die. But God demonstrates His own love toward us, in that while we were yet sinners, Christ died for us. . . . For if while we were enemies we were reconciled to God through the death of His Son, much more, having been reconciled, we shall be saved by His life."

The likely backdrop to this text of Jesus as our champion or hero is that of well-known Greco-Roman heroes who die for good or righteous men and women. These heroes die for their friends or family or those with whom they have a relationship. One noted pagan account is given by Euripides.[4] He writes of the vicarious or substitutionary death of Alcestis, who dies for her husband, Admetus. Here there is something of a parallel with Jesus's death: "The sacrificial death of the one aims at rescuing the other from death." What is stunning in Romans 5 is that God's agent, Jesus of Nazareth, dies for the *enemies* of God, and this act *turns the enemies of God into friends of God.*[5]

The reason that we need a champion is this: God alone is fully qualified to pay the price we humans must pay but can't. So God graciously steps into our world as a human being—God in the flesh in Jesus of Nazareth. He gets his feet dirty and hands bloody so that he, as God's Son, can pay the price that humans cannot. As theologian John Stott affirmed, *the essence of sin is humans substituting themselves for God, and the essence of salvation is God substituting himself for humans.*[6]

SOME OBJECTIONS AND QUESTIONS

"The Crucifixion Is Divine Child Abuse"

There are plenty of popular, though misguided, atonement analogies that suggest God the Father engaged in "divine child abuse" toward his Son. According to one fictitious story, a train switchman hears a train coming, only to see that his very young son has wandered off to play on those very tracks. There is no time for warning or rescue. To hit the switch and alter the train's course would save his son but kill many passengers, who would be struck by an oncoming train from the opposite direction. So he chooses to keep the train on course and "sacrifices" his own son in the process.

Some critics of penal substitution pounce on these bad analogies. They will claim that the crucifixion of the Son of God as divine judgment on sin is nothing more than divine child abuse. God is angry with sinners, but a hapless Jesus is "left on the tracks," taking the "hit" from the "wrath train" to take what we deserve.

This is a distorted picture of actual penal substitution in Scripture, however. Nor does it reflect what scholarly defenders of this view have written. For one thing, the Son is not going to his death against his will; rather, he *voluntarily* gives his life, and no one takes it from him: "I [Jesus] lay down My life for the sheep. . . . For this reason the Father loves Me, because I lay down My life so that I may take it again. No one has taken it away from Me, but I lay it down on My own initiative. I have authority to lay it down, and I have authority to take it up again" (John 10:15–18). Second, we don't have three parties involved—God the Father, Jesus, and sinful humanity; rather, we have just two—the perfectly loving and just triune God and sinful humanity. This means keeping in mind that the Father loves the world (John 3:16) and does not desire that any perish (2 Pet. 3:9). The Father also deeply loves his Son (John 3:35; 5:20); he does not act independently of the agreement and purposes of the entire Trinity—a plan devised from eternity. Furthermore, not only is the *Father* wrathful against sin, but the *Son* is himself wrathful against sin, as evidenced by Jesus's temple cleansing (John 2) and "the wrath of the Lamb" against sin (Rev. 6:16; cf. 14:10).

Despite prevalent false analogies, we can affirm a more biblical picture. The atonement involves *divine self-substitution*: a loving and just God himself (2 Cor. 5:19) takes initiative on our behalf through Christ, who freely, voluntarily lays down his life for us (John 10:15, 17).

"The Father and Son Were Separated at the Cross"

Some might reply: "But aren't God the Father and the Son separated from each other rather than united?" After all, Jesus's "cry of dereliction" from the cross appears to indicate this: "My God . . . why have you forsaken Me?" (Mark 15:34, citing Ps. 22:1). One theologian, Jürgen Moltmann, claims that we actually have a splitting of the Trinity, in which the Son and Father are pitted against each other because the Son became sin for us (2 Cor. 5:21). As it turns out, this Trinity-splitting idea—a recent theological innovation—reads too much into an isolated text. Let's look at this a bit more closely.

For one thing, the biblical text indicates the unity of the Trinity at the cross; Father and Son are not pitted against each other. Just before his crucifixion, Jesus said: "You [disciples will] be scattered, each to his own home, and to leave Me alone; and yet I am not alone, because the Father is with Me" (John 16:32). Furthermore, on the cross itself, Jesus says, "*Father*, forgive them," and, "*Father*, into your hands I commit my spirit" (Luke 23:34, 46). Paul affirms that, at the cross, "God was in Christ reconciling the world to Himself" (2 Cor. 5:19). Second, Psalm 22 indicates God's nearness despite the psalmist's (or Jesus's) feeling abandoned. At the cross, Jesus is quoting the afflicted David, who felt the absence of God—even though God is with him! Verse 22 indicates:

> I will tell of Your name to my brethren;
> In the midst of the assembly I will praise You.

This is followed by verse 24:

> For He has not despised nor abhorred the affliction of the afflicted;
> Nor has He hidden His face from him;
> But when he cried to Him for help, He heard.

The psalm ends:

> They will come and will declare His righteousness
> To a people who will be born, that He has performed it. (v. 31)

This sounds much like Jesus's final words, "It is finished!" (John 19:30).

Third, it is impossible for the Son to be literally (metaphysically) separated from Father and Spirit, since relations within the Trinity are unbreakable. Even so, the Son could *feel* the depths of alienation, exile, and abandonment in a number of ways: seeing his closest friends forsaking him; experiencing the shame and humiliation in the barbarism of crucifixion—reserved for criminals and runaway slaves—while hanging naked for all to see; facing and feeling the forces of deep evil from Satan and from his hostile earthly opponents, though Jesus himself is blameless and pure; experiencing the assault of evil in his spirit—even though the love and presence of God are clearly displayed at the cross (2 Cor. 5:21).

While Christ takes our exile on himself, paying the legal penalty for our sins, he still feels the weight of our sin on himself—the assault of evil in his spirit—without himself *being* sinful or guilty. Consider the following analogy.

In Tolkien's *Lord of the Rings*, the naive hobbit Pippin was curious about the glowing Palantir—the crystal ball that exposed him to the evil eye of Sauron. Though not acting with evil intent, he foolishly gazed into it, only to feel its overwhelming power and traumatizing effect.[7] Similarly, though Jesus was morally pure, he inwardly felt the weight of sin as he directly confronted it so that he could ultimately defeat it. He feels the evil without becoming corrupted by it.

The cross is the place where Jesus was "lifted up" (John 12:32, 34)—literally and figuratively. This is the point of God's great achievement—when he and the Father are "glorified" in his self-sacrifice (John 12:23–24, 28; 13:31). This language is taken from Isaiah 52:13, where the suffering servant is "lifted up" and "highly exalted" (NIV).

"The Cross Was a Miscarriage of Justice"

A common objection to the penal substitution is: "How can the blameless Jesus take our guilt/blameworthiness on himself? Isn't this utterly unjust? For an innocent person to die for the guilty is a corruption of justice." A few fitting responses are in order.

First, we are aware of legal scenarios in which innocent persons pay the penalty for the guilty without violating standards of justice. Consider the following scenarios in which *innocent* persons take legal liability for another's misdeed or failure:

- Auto insurance policies require payment by an insurance holder, even if another party was driving the car and damaged another car. Another (the car owner) assumes the payment for one who actually did the damage (car borrower).
- Perfectly upright parents will be held liable for damages for (minor) children who ruin the property of a neighbor's house or injure someone.
- An honorable, respected CEO will "assume full responsibility" for someone else's mismanagement of funds within the company and seek to make matters right.
- A prosperous company might voluntarily buy up a lesser, failing company and pay all of its debts in order to subsume that smaller company within its operations.

Second, Jesus does not *become* a sinner but pays the legal penalty demanded by the just triune God. Penal substitution is a legal or forensic transaction. It is not a moral one—as though an innocent person *becomes* a wrongdoer or *becomes* guilty for another person's sin. If Jesus became a sinner, he would not be a perfect sacrifice (cf. 1 Pet. 1:19). As our substitute and proxy, Christ did not become an immoral sinner by taking on our sin. But doesn't Paul say that Jesus became sin for us (2 Cor. 5:21)? Remember, if Jesus "became sin" in the sense of becoming immoral—as a rapist or a murderer, say—then he wouldn't be the perfect substitutionary sacrifice as the spotless Lamb of God. As we just saw, the Son of God could experience the weight of evil without becoming evil himself.

The essential idea behind the atonement is *sacrifice*, and the central text to understanding Christ's atonement is Isaiah 53 with its picture of sacrifice. There the suffering servant "will justify many" (v. 11 NIV; cf. Mark 10:45: "a ransom for many"). This Servant becomes "an offering for sin" (NIV) or "a guilt offering" (v. 10). So 2 Corinthians 5:21 could be rendered "he became a sin offering for us."

So we are pardoned in this legal or forensic sense. Jesus takes the punishment we deserve. The declaration that we are not guilty is the result of Christ's fully paying the penalty for our sins. This payment is not automatic. Forgiveness comes to us only if we accept this offer.

Third, as the God-man, Jesus's sacrifice is deemed perfect and acceptable according to the triune God's just standards. We need not look for further justification than God's seal of approval. We are familiar with the insanity defense in law courts. A person can be declared "not guilty by reason of insanity." So why couldn't it be that—despite our misdeeds—we sinful agents are declared not guilty "by reason of" a just God's taking merciful action on our behalf?

Finally, because just punishment is directed at wrongs deserving punishment and because God has made gracious provision to bridge the moral and spiritual gap between us and God, then it would be folly to reject such an offer. Just punishment must always be directed toward wrongs deserving punishment. However, no injustice exists if the following demands be met: (a) a moral authority and perfectly qualified person (b) acts voluntarily to (c) meet the required legal demands that I as a guilty sinner cannot; (d) that person's merits can be transferred to me to provide for a new legal standing ("not guilty"); and (e) I as the guilty party accept this substitution that removes my legal debt. As we have seen, all kinds of legal provisions in our society reveal that such a legal transfer is appropriate and not far-fetched at all. In such scenarios, the innocent party will often pay the debt of those who are guilty or liable.

In human societies, we have no solid guarantee that such a transfer will yield important goods. We don't make this kind of transfer for serious crimes because we typically do not have any good reasons—and usually have no reasons—for transferring punishment. Not so with Jesus's act of self-sacrifice, which "justifies the ungodly" (Rom. 4:5)—we certainly do have good reasons! Isaiah 53 indicates that the suffering servant "shall see his offspring; he shall prolong his days; the will of the LORD shall prosper in his hand. . . . Out of the anguish of his soul he shall see and be satisfied" (Isa. 53:10–11 ESV).[8]

"It's God's Job Simply to Forgive"

A common question critics raise is: "Why can't God just forgive? Isn't that his job?" In Islam, Allah can simply declare one forgiven—or damned—and it is so by sheer force of Allah's will. In Scripture, we see another picture. Atonement is anchored in the coming together of God's love and justice. To simply forgive without addressing the violation of justice first of all undermines God's perfect justice. For the same reason, good judges don't let murderers and rapists back out on the street. In addition, such an act of "just forgiving someone" undermines human responsibility; humans are not held accountable for their actions if they can sin with impunity or are simply let off the hook.

This misguided view of God "doing his job" ignores the costly gift of forgiveness. Forgiveness is not a right but an act of grace. Think of how ugly it is to see a wrongdoer demanding or assuming forgiveness. We all recognize that when a wound is deep, forgiveness is all the more difficult rather than automatic. Only an act of grace can break the stranglehold to move us from *hurt* and then *hate* to *healing*. Even in Jesus's parable of the unforgiving servant (Matt. 18:23–35), the king who forgives a great debt—around 160,000 years of daily wages—isn't "just forgiving." He feels the loss in parting with a huge sum of money.

Once again, even if provision is made for our pardon, this doesn't guarantee that the transaction will be completed. Pardon is conditional on our acceptance of it. In our legal system, if we refuse the gift of pardon, we remain liable for the wrongdoing. Accepting it means that the act of pardon can be applied. The same is true in the biblical story. Pardon is potentially ours, but it becomes actually ours when we receive God's gracious offer in Christ. This in turn means that privilege entails responsibility.

It's been said that the Christian faith is a religion of gratitude. To receive God's grace overflows into a life of thanks and a zeal to obey. God's grace instructs us "to deny ungodliness and worldly desires and to live sensibly, righteously and godly in the present age, looking for the blessed hope and the appearing of the glory of our great God and Savior, Christ Jesus, who gave

Himself for us to redeem us from every lawless deed, and to purify for Himself a people for His own possession, zealous for good deeds" (Titus 2:12–14).

If our essential starting point is a just and merciful God who humbles himself to enter our broken world, suffer with us, and lovingly pour out his life for his enemies in order to turn them into friends, this message has the power to transform us. Our lives will increasingly become personifying displays of the divine reality.

FURTHER READING

Craig, William Lane. *Atonement*. Cambridge: Cambridge University Press, 2018.
Gathercole, Simon. *Defending Substitution: An Essay on Atonement in Paul*. Grand Rapids: Baker Academic, 2015.
McCall, Thomas. *Forsaken: The Trinity, the Cross, and Why It Matters*. Downers Grove, IL: IVP Academic, 2012.

31 | *Jesus's Uniqueness and the Plurality of Religions*

> And there is salvation in no one else; for there is no
> other name under heaven that has been given among
> men by which we must be saved.
>
> —Acts 4:12

> So Paul, standing in the midst of the Areopagus, said:
> "Men of Athens, I perceive that in every way you are very
> religious. For as I passed along and observed the objects
> of your worship, I found also an altar with this inscrip-
> tion, 'To the unknown god.' What therefore you worship
> as unknown, this I proclaim to you."
>
> —Acts 17:22–23

> How will we escape if we neglect so great a salvation?
>
> —Hebrews 2:3

Our era's definition of "tolerance" isn't the classic, robust view, which allows people to think differently—to put up with error, falsehood, or whatever else they may find disagreeable. We don't *tolerate* things we *enjoy*—like chocolate or Johann Sebastian Bach's music. Rather, today's flawed view of tolerance calls for "accepting," even "embracing" or "celebrating," differences—*until* someone starts making exclusive truth-claims or, worse, evangelizing! The "tolerant" won't accept or celebrate "narrow" claims. Persuading people about faith is "arrogant" and upsetting. So people write books to persuade people that it's wrong to persuade others! Educator Allan Bloom described this mind-set well: "Conflict is the evil we most want to avoid."[1]

Christians claiming that Jesus is "the only way" or "the unique Savior" are often perceived to be arrogant, imperialistic, harmful, and insensitive. Why just *one* way of salvation, which appears to leave untold millions, through no fault of their own, cut off from salvation in their ignorance? Does religious pluralism offer a genuine solution?

Understanding Religious Pluralism

The Gospel, Religious Pluralism, and the West

The gospel is no stranger to religiously pluralistic environments; it was first proclaimed throughout the religiously mixed Mediterranean world with its many gods and temples, Greek philosophies, and emperor worship. Today's religious pluralism, however, offers an appealing approach for liberal democratic Western societies: all religions are equally capable of salvation or liberation, none being superior to another. Some pluralists view the different religions as different manifestations of the Ultimate Reality or the Transcendent—*God*, *Brahman*, the *Tao*, *Nothingness*. Like a three-dimensional hologram, just one film or picture underneath projects a different image depending on the angle and distance from which one observes it. So, one person might view the same underlying Ultimate Reality differently than another person. Or the religions could be likened to gold or silver (representing the underlying Ultimate Reality). These metals can be (a) solid, shaped, and polished; (b) a molten liquid; or (c) a rough, unrefined ore (which represents the various world religions, each of which purportedly contains precious metal).

"All roads lead to the top of the mountain" is a common pluralist affirmation. One pluralistic analogy handed down to us is that of six Indian blind men before an observer: each touches a different part of the elephant, drawing dogmatic conclusions about the elephant based on his limited experience. Of course, the observer thinks such rigid beliefs rather comical. Applying this scene to "theologic wars," poet John Godfrey Saxe (1816–1887) writes of religious disputants with their exclusivistic claims: they "rail on in utter ignorance" and "prate about an elephant not one of them has seen!"[2]

The late pluralist John Hick called for a "Copernican revolution of religions." Cosmology has shifted from a *Ptolemaic* geocentric (earth-centered) view of the universe to a *Copernican* heliocentric (sun-centered) one. Similarly, Hick said, we must replace a Christocentric view with a God-centered or Reality-centered view. That is, we must get rid of the biblical understanding of Jesus as God's unique, saving revelation as central, with all other religions revolving or orienting themselves around it. And we must adopt a new model in which all the religions, including Christianity, "revolve" around "God" or the Ultimate Reality. Hick said we need to accept that there are "different ways of experiencing, conceiving, and living in relation to the ultimate divine Reality which transcends all our varied versions of it."[3]

Hick knew better than to naively insist that "all religions are basically the same." They can't all be true in what they affirm, since their fundamental differences are *massive*. Buddhism's Dalai Lama puts it plainly: "Among spiritual faiths, there are many different philosophies, some just opposite to each other on certain points. Buddhists do not accept a creator; Christians base their philosophy on that theory."[4] The Dalai Lama accepts the binary nature of truth: by definition, truth excludes something—namely, error or falsehood. Some in the Buddhist tradition like the late Alan Watts reject the validity of necessary logical laws—they repudiate the either-or "Western logic" in favor of a both-and "Eastern logic."[5] The problem, though, is that Watts assumed the inescapable and necessary "either-or" logic that is fundamental to all thought: it's *either* Western *or* Eastern logic, not both! Indeed, Christians *and* Buddhists can't both be right on this matter; either God exists or he doesn't. Muslims and Christians can't both be right about Jesus's death. Muslims reject his death on a cross (Surah 4:157–58); if correct, then the Christian faith crumbles (1 Cor. 15:13–19).

The Dogmas of Religious Pluralism

All the world's religions differ significantly about the nature of *Ultimate Reality* (a personal God; an impersonal, undifferentiated consciousness; or nothingness), the *human condition* (sin, ignorance, or craving/desire), its *solution* (salvation, enlightenment, or the elimination of desire), and the *afterlife* (personal enjoyment of/separation from God or reincarnations or rebirths followed by personal extinction). Except for these massive differences, sure, all religions are "basically the same"! While *naive* pluralists will claim this, *sophisticated* pluralists recognize that there are (a) genuine, significant irreconcilable differences. This is the first key tenet of religious pluralism.

Further, for Hick and his ilk, (b) religious belief is the result of culturally conditioned attempts to get at the Ultimate Reality. The nomadic Muslim Tuareg or the Krishna devotee will be oriented to "the Real" through the filter or "baggage" of his particular religious and cultural background. Religious beliefs are *true* in the sense that they're oriented toward the Ultimate Reality, but *false* in another, due to cultural conditioning. There are different ways of conceiving, experiencing, and responding to this Ultimate Reality. Its *reality* is different from the *experience* of it. This resembles what the philosopher Kant asserted: we can't have direct access to the *noumenal* realm (the thing in itself), only to the *phenomenal* realm (as it appears to us). This position itself, however, raises questions about how Kant or Hick could *know* that this thing-in-itself or the Real is *unknowable*.

So perhaps traditional religious belief is like the famous duck-rabbit and young woman–crone illustrations. Different religionists around the world will see different things, and the pluralist thinks she is helpfully pointing out what the traditional religionist doesn't see. So when we say "Jesus is Lord," the pluralist Paul Knitter tells us that the earliest Christians were only speaking "confessionally" about how much love they had for Jesus; this is much like when husbands and wives say to each other, "You're the best!" But they weren't making absolute statements about reality—that is, speaking "ontologically."[6] If we understand this confessional-ontological distinction, we will enhance mutual understanding in our interreligious dialogue, Knitter claims.

Another affirmation of religious pluralism is that (c) all the world's religions are equally capable of bringing salvation or liberation. Salvation is the transformation from *self*-centeredness to *reality*-centeredness, and no particular religion has a monopoly on such a transformation.

Religious pluralists typically claim that (d) the realization of liberation is evidenced by the producing of morally upright "saints" in different religions. The major world religions produce moral fruits in their devotees—in particular, treating others as they want to be treated. Christians have Jesus or Mother Teresa; Hindus, Mahatma Gandhi; and Buddhists, the Dalai Lama. No religion has the moral high ground over another.

Responses to Religious Pluralism

The Christian maintains that the Christian faith is true and that the sacrificial death of Jesus is the basis of genuine salvation, whereas other religions are not savingly effective. Where other religions disagree with the Christian revelation, *at that point* they would be in error. This view is *particularlistic* or *exclusivistic*, but, as we'll see, *all* religious truth-claims are exclusionary. Before addressing problems with religious pluralism, we ought to keep four things in mind.

First, all truth is God's truth—whether within the Christian faith or outside it. In Acts 17, Paul cited pagan (Stoic) thinkers who spoke of God as the Creator and Sustainer who isn't contained by human temples. We likewise should pay attention to commonalities and bridges with other religionists, affirming the God-originated truth where we come across it. Buddhists or Confucians believe in honoring parents or in religious freedom; Muslims maintain that an eternally existent God created the universe. Because all humans are God's image-bearers, Christians can affirm that the poor or illiterate should be helped without making basic aid or education contingent on receiving the gospel.

Second, non-Christians who consider Christians "narrow-minded" for believing in Jesus's uniqueness should remember that Christ spoke of it first and that Christians are simply trying to faithfully follow him. Christians aren't making this up (e.g., John 14:6; cf. Acts 4:12). The critic must ultimately contend with the authoritative and staggering identity claims of Jesus himself.

Third, religious dialogue requires equal respect, not equality of belief. Here's a common "interfaith" scenario: Christians are invited to prayer breakfasts, dialogues, and panel discussions. But then they're told they can't pray in Jesus's name or mention Jesus's uniqueness—this might "offend" Jews or Muslims. But isn't *that* restriction offensive to *Christians*? Why is it all right to offend Christians but not Jews and Muslims? After all, Christians don't know how to pray *except* in the name of Jesus. So the Christian invited to such events should be allowed to pray *as a Christian*, not as a Deist to some generic deity. In dialogue, one should graciously speak *as a Christian* rather than accept a lowest-common-denominator approach in discussion.

While Christians, Jews, and Muslims share an "Abrahamic faith," this doesn't mean they're equally capable of bringing salvation. So if any discussants approach the religious roundtable assuming religions are equally legitimate and true, they're not doing so *as* Christians, Muslims, or Hindus. Religious dialogue must begin with the equality of *persons,* not *belief.* All participants can discuss their particular convictions and experiences openly, and all sides can benefit from empathetically listening to clarify views and prevent the creation of caricatures and stereotypes (James 1:19). So when Paul Knitter claims that traditional Christian language about Jesus prevents genuine religious dialogue, Knitter is actually setting *his own* pluralistic ground rules for this dialogue: if we accept *his* starting points—and thus reject Jesus's fundamental uniqueness—only then can we engage in real dialogue!

Fourth, religion—including idolatrous conceptions of God within "Christendom"—may actually prevent people from knowing the living God. As with many religious leaders in Jesus's day, "religiosity" may hinder people from truly and savingly encountering God. Rather than being "happy as they are," many live in fear of evil spirits, oppressed by karma, bound by superstition, burdened by severe ascetic practices, and paralyzed by the fear of death. This is the spirit of slavery leading to fear. This is vastly different from the Spirit of adoption we receive through Christ so that we may cry out, "Abba! Father!" (Rom. 8:15; Gal. 4:6). As we study the world's religions in light of the human condition, the beauty of Jesus becomes increasingly evident.

RELIGIOUS PLURALISM'S PROBLEMS

With these preliminaries in mind, let's consider some problems with religious pluralism.

Presuming Non-uniqueness

Religious pluralism eliminates the possibility of specific, historical divine revelation. Religious pluralism seeks to begin "from the ground up" by observing what goes on in mosques, church buildings, synagogues, temples, and Sikh gurdwaras. Many pluralists believe Jesus was just a God-conscious human being, not God incarnate; he didn't die for the sins of the world; and his body did not rise from the grave. His later followers would *ascribe* divinity to him, as some of the Buddha's followers did to him. The pluralist, if correct, ultimately undermines the historic Christian faith; Christianity cannot be just one of many legitimate ways of finding salvation or liberation.

The pluralist resists the particularity of the Christian faith in favor of the universal. Yet, while God begins with the particularities of Abraham or the incarnation, he has the *universal* in mind—to bless *all* the families of the earth (Gen. 12:1–3). Like ripples from a particular stone tossed into a pond, so Christian mission to the world flows from the incarnation; it offers salvation through a singular person but offers it to all persons through God's enabling Spirit (Acts 17:30). Pluralism, however, leaves us with a propertyless, contentless Ultimate Reality—and it undermines the unique, historical features of the Christian faith.

The Exclusivity and Arrogance of Pluralism?

Logically, religious pluralism is just as exclusivistic as the Christian—or any other—traditional religion. It *takes an authoritative stance*, just as any traditional religionist does. The pluralistic-sounding Dalai Lama has declared that Tibetan Buddhism is "the highest and complete form of Buddhism";[7] indeed, "only Buddhists can accomplish" what's necessary for liberation.[8] One orthodox Jewish rabbi claims to be "absolutely against any religion that says that one faith is superior to another"—something he considers to be spiritual racism ("we are closer to God than you"), which leads to hatred.[9] But isn't orthodox Judaism itself uncompromisingly monotheistic?

More generally, religious pluralism itself is just as non-neutral and exclusivistic regarding the status of religious truth-claims. The religious pluralist believes that her view is true and that the exclusivist—Christian, Muslim, Buddhist—is wrong or misguided in rejecting her view. She believes she has a virtue the Christian or Muslim doesn't.

Pluralism actually implies that Christians ought to abandon belief in Jesus's deity, atoning death, and resurrection—beliefs pluralism takes to be literally false and more like mere inspiring metaphors. Though the Christian faith is a *particular* exclusivism, however, religious pluralism turns out to be a *generic* exclusivism. Ironically, Hick claims that "natural pride" can lead to the "harmful" elevation of belief to the level of "dogma," "implying an exclusive or a decisively superior access to the truth or the power to save." But Hick is creating his own pluralistic dogma, and he seems to assume his own "superior access to the truth."[10]

Another pluralist philosopher, Joseph Runzo, claims that religious exclusivism has "the morally repugnant result of making those who have privileged knowledge . . . a religious elite" over against those who "have no access to the putatively correct religious view." This is "neither tolerable nor any longer intellectually honest" in light of what we know of other faiths today.[11] But this sounds just like what the pluralist claims the traditional religionist does: the pluralist is claiming to have "privileged knowledge" and appears to be part of the "religious elite," over against those who "have no access" to the correct religious view.

While pluralists may appeal to those "all roads lead to the top of the mountain" or elephant analogies, we could ask how they *know* that all religions' roads lead to the top and why those who disagree are *wrong*. How is it that *they* have the correct vantage point? Besides, such analogies don't actually *prove* a point; they only *illustrate* it. So perhaps Christians can just *change the analogy* to something more appropriate: perhaps religions are like a labyrinth or a maze with only one way out.[12] Here Jesus proves to be an advantageous starting point: What do we do with Jesus, who—unlike other world religious leaders—claims to reveal God to us and to share in that divine identity, calling every human to personally embrace him?

What's more, pluralists engage in a kind of radical pluralistic revisionism: they don't allow for doctrinal distinctives in traditional religions to retain their significance. After all, the founders of various traditional religions held to views they deemed essential to salvation or liberation—Muhammad's monotheism, Buddha's no-soul doctrine (*anatman*), and so on. Keith Ward wryly comments on this drastic modern-day pluralistic revisionism: "If a Buddhist is prepared to regard belief in reincarnation as a myth, a Christian thinks of the Incarnation as a mistaken fourth-century doctrine, and a Muslim agrees that the Koran is a fallible and morally imperfect document, they might well be able to agree much more than they used to."[13]

The power and heart of the Christian faith are removed if purported historical events like Jesus's resurrection never took place. This in turn would undermine our devotion to Christ. Paul says that instead of believing lies like "the Christian faith gives me purpose, even though Jesus didn't really rise from the dead," we should just get real by becoming party animals because we have no hope without Jesus's resurrection (1 Cor. 15:32).

The Geography Objection

Pluralists typically raise the geography objection: "If you'd been born in Saudi Arabia, you'd likely be a Muslim—or if in India, a Hindu." Though statistically true, this statement doesn't tell us very much, let alone establish the truth of religious pluralism. The geography of a belief neither confirms nor neutralizes its truth. We could apply this pluralistic line to a Marxist, monarchist, conservative Republican, or progressive Democrat: "If you grew up in Nazi Germany, you would likely have joined the Hitler Youth." Even if statistically true, we don't conclude that all political systems are equally legitimate. Independent reasons exist for defending certain forms of government over others.[14]

The same applies to beliefs about Ultimate Reality and the human condition: we rightly reject profoundly incoherent beliefs; we correctly question claims that depend heavily on phony or forged documents or on the character of a charismatic, womanizing charlatan who founds a religion—*even if* his followers turn out to be morally decent people. Indeed, if the Christian faith more readily explains many features of the universe and of the human condition than, say, various Eastern religions or other secular alternatives, then its greater plausibility shouldn't be trumped by the geography objection. Pluralists who reject Jesus's bodily resurrection or his remarkable authority claims as historically unreliable are hardly neutral observers of the religious landscape. And they are taking quite a gamble: Jesus's radical uniqueness and resurrection completely undermine pluralism, and these Christian affirmations are buttressed by very strong historical support.

In addition, we can turn the tables on the pluralist: If *he* had been born in Madagascar or medieval France, *he probably wouldn't have been a pluralist!*[15] If all religions are "culturally conditioned attempts" to get at the Ultimate Reality, then pluralism is *just as culturally conditioned* as Christian or Hindu beliefs. How has the pluralist risen above his cultural conditioning to see things more clearly than the rest of us? Does the religious pluralist think that *he's* just another blind man touching *his* part of the elephant? No, he takes the view of the *onlooker* who sees the whole elephant and thinks the blind men to be foolish for their narrow-minded dogmatism!

The Moral Fruits Argument

A religion's moral fruitfulness isn't necessarily the ultimate test of its legitimacy. "Moral atheists" may help their neighbors but reject the transcendent realm as delusional and full of false promises. Does their rejection of the transcendent matter at all? Or what of religions that include ritual human sacrifice or racist beliefs? Are these also legitimate, culturally conditioned attempts to get at the Ultimate Reality?[16]

Furthermore, as we observe the same cultural conditioning that the pluralist does, why not conclude that "religion" is completely natural, cultural, and human—and not divine at all? To start from the ground up and then conclude that "all the great religions are equally capable of saving" isn't more obvious than the conclusion that "it isn't the case that all these religions are equally capable of saving." So perhaps the more reasonable position is the agnostic one: we have no idea whether all religions are or aren't equally capable of saving.[17]

Undermining Religious Pluralism

Despite the above points, pluralism of some sort could logically still be true. But if Jesus truly is God's incarnate Son and the Savior of the world, this effectively renders religious pluralism false. Jesus wasn't merely "another great religious teacher." Rather, he was and is savingly unique for a number of reasons.

> Jesus made radical claims that world religious leaders didn't make—authority to forgive sins, to be the full revelation of God, to hear and answer prayers, to be the final judge, and so on. Muhammad would have considered these claims blasphemous, and Buddha—a nontheist—made no such assertions.
>
> Jesus's strongly monotheistic followers were persuaded that he shared in the identity of God, and they worshiped him.
>
> Jesus's bodily resurrection vindicated his identity claims; no other world religious leader rose from the dead.

In Jesus, God sacrifices himself for us—to the point of dying a death of shame, nakedness, and degradation for his own enemies. The God of the Christian faith has scars to prove his love for humanity (Rom. 5:6).

On top of this, many traditional religions and worldviews highly respect Jesus and want to claim him, quote him, and highlight him as a moral example. Unlike other world religious leaders, he carries near-universal clout—a remarkable testament to the spiritual authority of Jesus.

The Christian faith uniquely emphasizes grace—unmerited favor by which God "justifies the ungodly" (Rom. 4:5)—namely, his own enemies (Rom. 5:10). Rather than our earning divine favor and acceptance, Christ does this on our behalf.

Unlike other traditional religions, the Christian faith is checkable; it opens itself up to scrutiny, examination, and even falsifiability. At a number of points, it is in principle falsifiable—for example, the bodily resurrection.

If there is salvation outside of Christ, then Jesus's coming to be a ransom for many (Mark 10:45) was an ultimately misguided failure: if so, contrary to Jesus's Gethsemane impressions, the bitter cup *could have* been removed from him *and* humans could somehow be saved.

In the end, religious pluralism won't let Jesus be Jesus. If it did, it would undermine itself.

THE QUESTION OF THE UNEVANGELIZED

Agnosticism on the Question

If Jesus is the unique Savior, what of those who've never heard of him? A simple response is that our good and wise God has the question of the unevangelized figured out and won't act unjustly. If Jesus is truly God's incarnate Son, the "question of the heathen" is secondary; we should begin with what is clear and then work out the implications from there. So if Jesus has reliably revealed God to us, we can even take an agnostic position: "I don't know what the answer is to this challenging question of the unevangelized, but I do know a trustworthy God who has acted dramatically and remarkably in Christ, and this true, life-changing message must be proclaimed! Presumably this God isn't caught off guard on such matters." Also, no one will be condemned for never having heard of Christ; the more relevant question is: How do the unevangelized respond to pervasive Spirit-promptings and divine clues? God won't judge unjustly (Gen. 18:25).

Alternative Views

Besides the agnostic and "exclusivist" or "particularist" views,[18] consider some of the following variants.[19]

Inclusivism (Wider-Hope View)

While God's grace in Christ is the *actual* (ontological) basis for *every* person's forgiveness, inclusivists insist that *knowing* about Jesus of Nazareth (epistemological) isn't necessary to be saved: Christ's death is *ontologically* (actually) but not *epistemologically* necessary for salvation. Those dying as infants and those with mental limitations haven't done anything to incur God's judgment and thus, many Christians agree, would still be saved. And Old Testament saints like Abraham and David who cast themselves on God's mercy were saved by what Christ would one day accomplish (Heb. 10:4; cf. 9:13–14)—though they didn't know about Jesus of Nazareth.

Despite its merits, inclusivism has its critics. For one thing, its overoptimism about untold multitudes who cast themselves on God's mercy seems to go against the negative assessment of Romans 1–3. Also, inclusivism doesn't really deal with the problem that many people don't respond to general revelation yet do respond to the preaching of the gospel—which isn't surprising since the gospel is the power of God for salvation (Rom. 1:16). Third, inclusivism still has its own question of "injustice" to deal with: many could complain that they were "born in the wrong place at the wrong time," having only the dim light of natural revelation, while others no more worthy were fortunate enough to be born in a time and place where they were able to hear the gospel and be saved. That's the problem inclusivism has been trying to solve in the first place.

Postmortem Evangelism

Some Christians believe the unevangelized—and even those with mental limitations and those who died as infants—will have a postmortem opportunity to personally encounter Jesus, hear the gospel, and either embrace it and enjoy God's presence or reject it and be removed from God's presence. The offer of salvation isn't limited to an earthly existence. While an intriguing possibility, this view is sometimes based on highly disputed biblical passages (e.g., 1 Pet. 3:18–22).

Accessibilism (Middle-Knowledge View)

Building on the earlier discussion of divine foreknowledge and human freedom, I'll summarize a view I detail elsewhere.[20] We can safely assume that our good, wise God is willing that none perish but rather all find salvation (2 Pet. 3:9) and that he makes provision for everyone without exception to heed his command to repent (Acts 17:30). We can infer that ours is a world in which no person is born at the wrong place or time. Salvation is accessible through God's pervasive grace to whoever would want it. Though most reject the light of God's general revelation (Rom. 1–3), this graciously given knowledge is adequate for people to turn to God and be saved—based on Christ's redemptive work (as with Old Testament saints): God's "righteous judgment" will give to each person according to his deeds—"to those who by perseverance in doing good seek for glory and honor and immortality, eternal life" (Rom. 2:5–7).

A good argument is on offer that God knows what free creatures would do in an array of possible worlds he could create and that he has brought about a world in which the maximal number of persons is saved and the minimal number of persons condemned. Despite the workings and wooings of God's gracious Spirit, many will freely resist God in *any* world God placed them—*whether or not* they would hear the gospel. Those who are lost in *actuality* are those who would be lost in *any* world in which God placed them. Despite God's grace toward them, their freely self-created condition of *transworld depravity* prevents them from embracing God. Their resistance to God isn't the result of a defective design; God simply knows that these humans would freely resist his initiating grace in any feasible world in which they happen to be placed, and it's up to human agents to accept or resist this grace.

So why should God refrain from bringing many into his family simply because others, like the prodigal's older brother, refuse to enjoy the feasting and festivities? God isn't unjust or unkind if people he creates freely refuse his grace; so why should he be blamed? What if, in the end, there is just no person who, having rejected the light of revelation that he does have, would have believed had he received more? An unevangelized person is (justly) condemned, not because he would freely reject God's salvation no matter what possible world he might be placed in, but because he *does* reject God's saving grace in his actual circumstances.

While accessibilism, the middle knowledge view, may not be the precise resolution to our problem and another view on the unevangelized may well be true, its very logical possibility suggests the defensibility of God's just, merciful character toward all. Our topic ultimately goes beyond making inferences from scattered biblical verses and themes to *trusting in a good God to do no wrong*. Can the covenant-making, salvation-desiring God, whose self-expression—Jesus of Nazareth—died for the sins of the world, be trusted with such perplexing questions? Can't we trust God, who loves all without exception and desires their salvation, to do his utmost so that none is prevented from experiencing salvation who truly desires it? We shouldn't think about the unevangelized apart from *God's character, motives, and good purposes.*[21]

Beyond this, God has ways of revealing himself to Cornelius-like figures (Acts 10) who haven't yet heard the gospel. In a remarkable affirmation of Yahweh's working among the nations, Yahweh asks Israel, "Are you not as the sons of Ethiopia to Me, O sons of Israel?" and, "Have I not brought up Israel from the land of Egypt, And the Philistines from Caphtor and the Arameans from Kir?" (Amos 9:7). Angelic messengers might appear to inform people about Jesus. Also, Jesus himself shows up in the dreams of Muslims, and reports continue to come in about Muslim-background believers who had experienced a vision of Jesus.[22] (I myself have met a number of these former Muslims, who have told me their stories.) God is able to do far more than we can ask or imagine—even when it comes to the unevangelized. They're in good hands with him.

FURTHER READING

Copan, Paul. Part 5 of *"True for You, but Not for Me": Overcoming Objections to Christian Faith.* 2nd ed. Minneapolis: Bethany House, 2009.

Netland, Harold. *Encountering Religious Pluralism: The Challenge to Christian Faith and Mission.* Downers Grove, IL: IVP Academic, 2001.

Stewart, Robert, ed. *Can Only One Religion Be True? Paul Knitter and Harold Netland in Dialogue.* Minneapolis: Augsburg Fortress, 2013.

Tennent, Timothy C. *Christianity at the Religious Roundtable.* Grand Rapids: Baker Academic, 2002.

> Truly I say to you, today you shall be with Me in
> Paradise.
>
> —Luke 23:43

> For this perishable must put on the imperishable, and
> this mortal must put on immortality.
>
> —1 Corinthians 15:53

The Apostles' Creed affirms, "I believe in the resurrection of the body and the life everlasting." The creed does not talk about dying and going to heaven as our final state, yet in the minds of many believers, this is the presumed destiny of the redeemed. What's worse, at a broader cultural level, many people hold sentimentalized views of the afterlife: getting wings, sitting on clouds, playing harps. Others have speculated that immortality will be tedious and boring. The *Makropulos Affair* opera (by the Czech composer Leos Capek) is about Elina Makropulos, forty-two, who is offered an elixir by her father to grant her life in three-hundred-year increments. If she wants to live another three hundred years after the first one, she can elect to do so. But at age 342, she is bored with life and so chooses to die rather than extend her life another three hundred years.

Reflecting on this opera, the philosopher Bernard Williams examined the topic of "the tedium of immortality."[1] He believed that immortality would be an intolerable state of boredom. If things remain "stable" as they are, and I continue as I am without alteration, then boredom would readily set in.

The chief consideration to bear in mind is this: the heart of the believer's immortal life is communion and delight in the presence of the infinitely fascinating, inexhaustible God. This fact itself challenges philosophical dismissals of immortality as "boring." The Fourth Evangelist wrote about Jesus's "mere" three-year ministry, stating that the world couldn't contain all the books that could be written about Jesus (John 21:25). Furthermore, God would grant his redeemed, resurrected people the ever-expanding capacity to deepen in their love and enjoyment of God. As Paul reminds us, we simply can't imagine what God has prepared for those of us who love him (1 Cor. 2:9). Immortality with God will be glorious, not tedious.

SOME THEOLOGICAL CONSIDERATIONS

Afterlife: The Greek versus the Biblical

The view that we die and "go to heaven" and permanently live in a disembodied state is a Platonic or Gnostic idea; it privileges the soul and discounts the body as having any significance. Yet Christ "the first fruits"—the first of the harvest (cf. Lev. 23:10)—has been *bodily* raised. This event guarantees that the bodies of us who are redeemed—the rest of the resurrection harvest to come—will be "raised . . . immortal" (1 Cor. 15:42 GNB). Resurrection of the body (*sōma*) is what Scripture means by "immortality," whereas the immortality of the soul (*psychē*) is a Greek philosophical view.

True *immortality* (Greek: *aphtharsia, athanasia*) is immunity from decay and death because of our participation in the new creation and the eternal life of the triune God. Let's explore the nature of the resurrection body more carefully.

A Transformed Physicality

Orthodox Christianity rejects the soul's permanent disembodiment but affirms a transformed physicality. Theologian Oscar Cullmann once said that if the soul is immortal, Easter is rendered unnecessary and isn't a revolutionary event at all.[2] Just "going to heaven" at death implies there's no new creation; death hasn't been defeated after all. But this is precisely the point of Jesus's bodily resurrection. Our resurrection bodies will be part of the new heavens and earth—God's perfected re-creation (Rev. 21:1-4). Christ won't return to take us away from earth but will establish us on the new earth. Rather than abandoning creation, God renews it, affirming the goodness of the material world—a point reinforced by Christ's own incarnate body made permanent by resurrection.[3]

God will be "making all things new" (Rev. 21:5)—not "making new things." And the apocalyptic language of 2 Peter 3 of "fire" and "destruction" can be understood a refining fire of purification, transformation, and renovation. This is comparable to the Noahic deluge that flooded and purged the earth without literally destroying it (2 Pet. 2:5).[4] The renovated earth indicates a transformed physicality from things transitory that are purified or renewed and made permanent.

The immortal resurrection body reinforces this theme of transformed physicality: even though we have newness, we also have historical continuity between the mortal and the immortal, as exemplified in Jesus's own bodily resurrection. It is like a seed that is sown perishable—in dishonor and weakness—but raised imperishable, glorious, and powerful (1 Cor. 15:42–44). This continuity doesn't require atom-for-atom replacement, which might present problems for bodies of missionary-eating cannibals who later become Christians! God is able to use whatever bodily matter remains. And even if a saint's body is, say, vaporized in an explosion, God is able to create an immortal body suitable to that particular believer.

Some raise the question: In 1 Corinthians 15:44–46, doesn't Paul refer to a "spiritual body" as opposed to a "physical body" (RSV, NRSV)? Actually, "physical body" is a bad translation. It should be rendered "natural body"— literally, a "soul-animated [*psychikon*] body." This is indeed physical, but so is the transformed immortal body with its new capacities. This is the "spiritual [*pneumatikon*] body"—that is, a body animated by the Holy Spirit. This is much like the "natural person" and the "spiritual person" mentioned earlier in Paul's letter (1 Cor. 2:14–15): the spiritual (or, Spirit-animated or Spirit-indwelt) person is still in a physical body but is able to understand spiritual realities that the natural person without the Spirit cannot.

So Paul isn't contrasting the physical and the immaterial. The first-century Jew understood resurrection to involve physical bodies. Rather, it is two types of physical body—one naturally animated by the human soul and the other supernaturally animated by God's Spirit. That's why Paul declares elsewhere that we long for "the redemption of our body" (Rom. 8:23), and that Christ "will transform the body of our humble state into conformity with the body of His glory" (Phil. 3:21)—a transformed physicality.

BODY AND SOUL

Scriptural Support for the Soul

Scripture affirms a deep body-soul integration; they function as an organic whole from conception onward ("functional holism"). Sometimes the soul represents the whole person in her totality: "Bless the LORD, O my soul," which is parallel to "and all that is within me, bless His holy name" (Ps. 103:1). But the Scriptures also indicate that the soul or self is a distinct substance from the body and that it can survive bodily death ("substance dualism"). Yet the soul's survival of bodily death—the "intermediate state"—is a period of incompleteness; it is a parenthesis between this life and the final state of transformed physicality at the future resurrection when Christ returns.

After the prophet Samuel had died and his body was buried in Ramah, he presented himself to Saul at the conjuring of the spiritist of Endor (1 Sam. 28:3, 13–15); clearly, he didn't need his body to make an appearance. The very prohibition to avoid necromancers and spiritists to make contact with the dead suggests a postmortem disembodied existence (e.g., Isa. 8:19; Lev. 19:31; 20:6; Deut. 18:11).

The soul's separability from the body is implied when Jesus tells the criminal on the cross: *"Today* you will be with me *in paradise"* (Luke 23:43 ESV).[5] After Lazarus's death, Jesus declares that everyone "who believes in Me will live even if he dies" (John 11:25; cf. 8:51). Though we may experience bodily death, we can survive bodily death and continually experience spiritual life. Jesus corrects the resurrection-denying Sadducees: the God of the patriarchs is the God of the living; though their bodies be dust and bones, they "live to Him" (Luke 20:38). Paul desires to depart—at death—and be "with Christ" (Phil. 1:23–24). In the intermediate state (2 Cor. 5:3–8), death brings an unnatural, temporary "naked" state with the "unclothed" soul apart from the body; then we "put on" or are "clothed" with a resurrection body—"life after life-after-death," as someone has said. Death, the soul's absence from the body, brings the soul into Christ's heavenly presence. The "souls" of martyred saints in heaven haven't yet received resurrection bodies (Rev. 6:9–10), and the new Jerusalem is presently inhabited by the "spirits" of humans made perfect (Heb. 12:22).[6]

Over the past decades, an emergent phenomenon has been that of "Christian materialism." Human beings are material or physical only—not material and spiritual or soulish. Some from this persuasion will appeal to Scripture to show how this is so. Others, like Kevin Corcoran, readily acknowledge that the consistent teaching of the Scriptures and the early church fathers affirms a human body-soul duality. Corcoran says that Jesus and Paul were "substance dualists," though he disagrees with their metaphysical outlook.[7] We can ask: Why wouldn't the authority of Jesus—not to mention Paul—be sufficient to ground our belief in the soul's existence and to reject materialism?

What Is the Soul?

Imagine yourself walking into a large room. You see many things around you, but you carefully focus on—you direct your attention to—a painting on the wall or the intricate pattern on the Persian rug beneath your feet. What is directing the focused attention? Why aren't your eyes simply looking at the panorama as you walk in? Your intentionality is due to the fact that your soul is directing your eyes to focus.

We've seen that the reality of consciousness serves as a powerful pointer to a supremely self-aware spirit-being, which we call "God." This reality also brings to the fore the question of the soul—the center of consciousness or awareness. We've seen that a good case for the soul can be made from Scripture. But a philosophical case can be made as well.

For starters, consider how the body (matter) and the soul or mind have radically different properties. I am *not* my body. I *just see* or *immediately know* that I am distinct from my body. The "I" is the soul or self. It is *who I am*. My *soul* is a substance with characteristics that just can't be physical: thoughts, feelings, intentionality, the "first-person" experience. I have that certain "inner feel" of own unique experience that an outsider can't access. My body is a *physical* substance; it has its own distinct physical properties like texture, color, being spatially extended, and so on. Body and soul can't be identical to each other. The philosopher Leibniz's "principle of the identity of indiscernibles" emphasizes that if Thing 1 and Thing 2 are truly identical, then anything that's true of Thing 1 will apply to Thing 2. It's quite clear that the mental and physical have distinct properties.

Body-Soul Interaction

Furthermore, the soul and the body are capable of interacting with each other as an organic whole. A physical pain affects my soul, and worry in my immaterial soul or mind will cause my body to break out into a sweat or cause my stomach to churn. The soul uses the brain, but it isn't the same as the brain. Indeed, the soul is "present" at every point in the human body, directing it to grow and develop from conception to adulthood and "informing" it to carry out actions determined by the soul, the "I."

What happens in the body can certainly impact the soul. This means that some of the soul's capacities may not be realized due to a physical limitation like Alzheimer's disease, a stroke, or Down syndrome; such physical limitations—not to mention mind-altering drugs taken into the body—block or prevent the soul from thinking clearly or operating as it was designed. But if that blockage were to be removed or one stopped using those drugs, then the soul's capacities or potentialities could be realized. So while there is a correlation between body and soul, this isn't a reduction—that is, the soul's functions can't simply be reduced to bodily functions.

How then do body and soul even interact? For starters, we have direct self-awareness; the belief that I am a soul is basic and central to my belief structure; to give up this idea means surrendering my belief structure and what it means to be human.[8] Furthermore, the soul is simple—it is not comprised of parts—and it acts immediately and directly on the body without any intermediate mechanism. I choose to move my arm, and it moves; I feel a pain in my foot, and I feel it directly. This is just a commonsensical operation.

A common objection to this soul-body interaction is this: How can something immaterial interact with something material? An indirect response is that God's existence actually furnishes us with a context for soul-matter interaction. After all, the spirit-being God created a material world, and he sustains that physical world in being and also acts within it by, say, turning water into wine. Also, the Scriptures speak of demonic spirit-beings who can physically oppress people (e.g., Mark 5:1–20).

Various naturalistic philosophers of mind—Jaegwon Kim, Ned Block, Colin McGinn, John Searle—admit they haven't a clue about these two crucial items: (a) how consciousness and technicolor subjective experience could emerge from the brain's soggy grey matter; and (b) how the mental and physical can interact—which, ironically, is one of their stated reasons for rejecting substance dualism! They have their own "interaction problem." Jaegwon Kim challenges substance dualism by questioning how an immaterial entity could influence even *one* molecule. Yet he admits to "our seeming inability to understand the phenomenon of consciousness as part of a world that is essentially physical" and to not knowing how we would even achieve such an understanding.[9]

WHY THE SOUL MAKES SENSE

As the body's cells are entirely replenished every seven years, the soul or self is the preferred candidate to ground personal identity over time. Consider too that if my body perishes in an explosion, and this body is immediately replaced by another (resurrection) body from God, what justifies the idea that the two utterly distinct, sequential bodies are the same person? What gives continuity from body A to body B—just identical *physical* properties? This doesn't make sense. In the switch from one body to another, the "I" is lost in the transfer. The enduring soul allows for the continuity between the two body-possessions.

The materialist—Christian or otherwise—might say that he sees no use for the nonphysical soul: "It doesn't explain anything about consciousness that cannot be explained without it."[10] Actually, it seems the existence of a soul or a self makes better sense of a number of things than the materialist position does.

Volition

If we are completely composed of matter, how do we account for free choices and personal responsibility? The existence of the soul makes it far easier to avoid the implications of determinism than if we are material beings.

Identity

We intuitively recognize personal continuity or identity over time. From childhood onward, I have an immediate awareness of my decades-long lived past. I am the same person as the one represented in my boyhood fishing and salamander-hunting photos. Yet my body has completely changed a number of times since then. According to the materialist view of persons, I don't have a proper basis for thinking I am the same person throughout. And why should I fear a future of living in a nursing home or of having dementia if I'll get a complete physical changeover several times before then?

Personal identity over time also relates to moral responsibility: Why think someone is guilty of a crime committed decades ago if the person's physical parts have been entirely overhauled? And why not save all of those cold-case detectives a lot of time and money by informing them that the persons who committed those murders no longer exist and thus can't be held responsible for their actions?

Imagination

If bodily matter is the basis for the mental life, and if the activity of that very matter has been determined by previous states of matter, it's hard to see what gives rise to the imagination. After all, one material state deterministically depends on the material state preceding it, but imagination is a break from any preset pattern. As C. S. Lewis argued, we are at perfect liberty to imagine a tower was produced by a magician's wave of the wand and "is supported by four hundred jinns."[11] A soul or self readily makes ample room for the imagination, since it isn't constrained by prior physical processes.

Near-Death Experiences (NDEs)

Woody Allen has said, "If you can survive death, you can survive just about anything." As it turns out, we have many examples of those who have indeed survived death—at least for the short term. Atheist philosopher A. J. Ayer, while temporarily dead, saw a red light that was painful to experience. This event led him to believe that death isn't necessarily the end of consciousness. Others who were temporarily clinically dead have reported in vivid, accurate detail what has gone on elsewhere in the hospital or even a distance away. Medical doctor Michael Sabom reports that, despite his initial skepticism, he encountered numerous people who had such out-of-body experiences; their testimonies were sane, well-documented, and rock-solid. This persuaded him that a person can have lucid sensory experiences while her body lies lifeless on an operating room table or hospital bed.[12]

Integration

What unifies my multisensory experiences when I simultaneously hear the mild sounds of the palm warbler outside, read a book by historian David Mc-Cullough, and taste Earl Grey tea? One integrating, unified, and unifying self has greater—and simpler—explanatory power than to attribute this to multiple selves or to just a bundle of sensory experiences, as David Hume claimed.

THE SOUL AND THE INCARNATION

I have heard some Christian materialists claim that they can't imagine themselves without their bodies—that this is so basic as to be fundamentally persuasive for them. Yet most of humanity over the millennia have readily assumed that they could exist without their body. That is, they have believed their soul would exist in the afterlife without a body. Further, spirit-beings like God or angels not only exist but also think without a body. And while Jesus was on earth, he could recall thinking about living without a body when he referred to the glory he had prior to the world's beginning (John 17:5, 24).

We saw earlier that in the incarnation, God—a spirit-being—took on a human body and a human nature. However, the Christian materialist philosopher Trenton Merricks argues that the Son of God is now identical with Jesus's body and that, in becoming human, the Son of God became a body. But how can something immaterial (the eternal Son of God) turn into a material object (a physical body) and thus become an object that *began* to exist? In this case, it's hard to see how the Son of God could still retain his divinity. It does seem that this idea is a non-starter.[13]

Here's something else: What happened to Jesus between his crucifixion and resurrection? According to physicalism, a person can't exist without his body. What happened after Jesus committed his spirit to his Father (Luke 23:46)? If the Son of God became a body, and if a person can't exist without his body, then the Trinity didn't exist while Jesus's body was in the tomb. Yet Jesus told the criminal on the cross that both of them would be in paradise *that day*. But Jesus's body was placed in the tomb *that day*, and that body was only raised immortal on the *third day*. So if the Son of God is identical to his body during the incarnation and beyond, he apparently ceases to exist for a short time. In fact, Jesus's entering paradise signals his own "intermediate state," which suggests the soul's existence.[14]

Thoughts on Hylomania and Pneumatophobia

David Hume denied that a self exists. What we might call the "self" or "soul" was simply a bundle of properties for Hume. His philosophical critic Thomas Reid sarcastically remarked: "It is certainly a most amazing discovery, that thought and ideas may be without any thinking being." Presumably, then, Hume's *Treatise of Human Nature* had no author after all! The book is only a set of ideas that came together and "arranged themselves by certain associations and attractions"![15] In our day, the same sorts of denials exist. We saw how Daniel Dennett called consciousness an "illusion," yet to experience an illusion requires consciousness or awareness.

Christian philosopher J. P. Moreland has noted two related phenomena in the relevant philosophical literature: *hylomania* (a fixation on matter) and *pneumatophobia* (fear of spirit or soul). He observes that many academic treatments of the mind-body issue are overly dismissive of (body-soul) substance dualism. This shouldn't be surprising, since naturalism has no room for a soul or self.

Moreland notes that these critics typically follow the pattern of interacting with René Descartes's more compartmentalized, nonintegrated version of dualism; they simply reject it and assume they've done away with dualism. However, they usually ignore or refuse to address more sophisticated treatments of this view.[16]

Concluding Remarks

If an embodied soul exists and is capable of surviving physical death, this would present a good support for theism over against naturalism. It would point to a nonphysical source of reality capable of creating and engaging with the physical world.

Furthermore, the existence of the soul is a commonsensical view that is both biblically and philosophically supportable. The notion of "substance dualism" isn't a Greek doctrine—but is a view commonly held over time and across civilizations.

Even so, the postmortem disembodiment of the soul isn't the final state. We eagerly await a new heavens and earth (2 Pet. 3:13), at which time the one "who raised Christ Jesus from the dead will also give life to your mortal bodies through His Spirit who dwells in you" (Rom. 8:11)—so, life after life-after-death. This physical resurrection is part of the finalized new creation, which began at Jesus's resurrection and will be completed at his return.

FURTHER READING

Goetz, Stewart C., and Charles Taliaferro. *A Brief History of the Soul.* Oxford: Wiley-Blackwell, 2011.

Green, Joel B., ed. *In Search of the Soul: Perspectives on the Mind-Body Problem.* 2nd ed. Eugene, OR: Wipf & Stock, 2013.

Loose, Jonathan, et al., eds. *The Blackwell Companion to Substance Dualism.* Oxford: Wiley-Blackwell, 2018.

Moreland, J. P. *The Soul: How We Know It's Real and Why It Matters.* Chicago: Moody Press, 2014.

Afterword

> And I heard a loud voice from the throne saying, "Behold, the dwelling place of God is with man. He will dwell with them, and they will be his people, and God himself will be with them as their God."
>   —Revelation 21:3 ESV

Now we have reviewed the Christian story—beginning with the triune God through creation, fall, redemption, and then finally re-creation. We've seen that Jesus of Nazareth is "myth became fact"—the historical embodiment of humanity's best epic stories and myths, its loftiest philosophies, and its highest ethical ideals and powerful virtues. He is the very wisdom of God (1 Cor. 1:24) and the one in whom are hidden all the treasures of wisdom and knowledge (Col. 2:3). This biblical story—the essence of all fairy stories, as Tolkien said— is historically rooted, philosophically sound, and existentially relevant without losing its mystery and power or its capacity to capture our imagination.

In life we will experience doubts and find our faith challenged by evil and other unsettling matters. Yet we must consider how God's revelation in Christ nevertheless speaks with clarity and force in the following ways:

- the *beauty* and *power* of Jesus's life and ministry and teaching;
- his *identification* with the human condition—his becoming weak and poor for our sakes;
- his facing *temptation* squarely; his experiencing injustice, cruelty, rejection, and misunderstanding;
- his self-sacrificial, humiliating *death* to redeem us, the enemies of God; and
- his glorious bodily *resurrection*, which reminds us that sin and death do not have the final word and that in Christ the promises of God are confident and sure.

As we wrestle with our questions and deal with conundrums and perplexity, this arresting revelation of God in Christ nevertheless leaves us with questions we must answer and with a choice we must inescapably make.

Will we privilege our doubts or skepticism over against what God has done for us in Christ?

Will we give priority to the problem of evil or our own distressing experiences with evil over against a God who loves us and suffers with us—and who himself faces evil and the cruelty of an unjust and humiliating crucifixion?

Will we place our trust in lesser, contingent things as opposed to God, who is our only hope to secure cosmic justice and to set right all of the world's wrongs, richly compensating those who love God far beyond anything they may have suffered and endured in this life?

Will we place greater weight on philosophies that cannot assuage our guilt or shame, help us overcome our fear of death, or give a stable purpose and meaning to our lives, or will we trust in the all-sufficient Christ, who is the hope and desire of the nations and who guarantees that all sorrows, tears, and pain will be replaced by unspeakable joy and peace?

If we take leave of Christ, what are the alternatives to give more robust explanations, more solid foundations, and more powerful resolutions to the human condition? As the former atheist C. S. Lewis discovered, the Christian faith is not only true; it also provides the light by which to make sense of everything else. Or as Christ's own disciple Peter put it, "Lord, to whom shall we go? You have words of eternal life" (John 6:68).

Discussion Questions

CHAPTER 1: THE BLESSINGS OF PHILOSOPHY

1. Why do you think there is often skepticism about philosophy among Christians?
2. How would you describe the task of *doing* philosophy?
3. Can you think of a few philosophical principles that have guided big decisions in your own life?
4. How could "right thinking" enhance our worship of God?
5. Can you recall a conversation with a friend who has wrestled with doubt? Did you feel capable of engaging with these doubts and to help process them in a useful way?
6. At present, how comfortable do you feel in sharing your faith with those who deem Christianity illogical or a "psychological crutch" for the weak?
7. What examples do we have of Jesus engaging in philosophical conversation? How about Paul (e.g., at Athens in Acts 17:16–31)? Is there a noticeable difference in their approach to the "wisdom" of those opposing them?
8. Are there any issues others may see as obstacles to studying or engaging with philosophy? Given its demonstrated importance, how might we help others overcome these obstacles?

CHAPTER 2: PHILOSOPHY AND SCRIPTURE

1. Is there a real conflict in the "faith versus reason" dichotomy? In your previous experience, has your faith, as you've understood it, somehow "required" you to sacrifice rationality?
2. How can we simultaneously do *hard thinking about things* while also *fearing the Lord*?
3. Why do you think philosophy is often perceived as a lofty or abstract exercise?
4. Despite the history of philosophical thought covering a whole range of beliefs in or about God, philosophy today is often associated with an atheistic worldview. Why might this be the case?

5. We've seen that Paul himself engaged in philosophical discussion. What, then, might he have been warning against when he called the world's wisdom "foolish"?

6. If we appropriate the tools of philosophy as we think about and communicate the gospel, how can we protect against arrogance and the neglect of God's grace?

7. Can you think of ways in which the study of philosophy might enhance your study of Scripture and doing theology?

CHAPTER 3: FAITH AND RELIGION

1. What is a helpful definition of biblical faith we could offer in response to Mark Twain's definition of faith?

2. Do you see a difference in Mortimer Adler's use of the phrase "leap of faith" as opposed to its popular understanding? How is Adler's experience illuminating for you?

3. Think of a few examples of influential artists or thinkers who were inspired by their Christian faith. Can you see how their belief in God may have had this impact?

4. Why do you think religion is often seen as an intellectual "straitjacket" and naturalism considered free from such constraints?

5. If we are all, like Darwin, bound to place certain aspects of our experience over others, how might we know which ones deserve to be prioritized?

6. What do you think of Thomas Nagel's confession? Do you think this attitude is held by many "nonreligious" people you know?

7. Why is defining "religion" problematic?

8. How might we define "worldview"?

9. Using the definition of religion at the end of this chapter, can you think of other, "nonreligious" beliefs that would equally be *comprehensive*, *incapable of abandonment*, and *of central importance* to a person's form of life?

CHAPTER 4: KINGS AND PRIESTS

1. How might Chesterton's idea of Christianity as a "perfect coat" be applied when comparing different worldviews?

2. Think of your favorite fairy tale or sci-fi or fantasy story—can you pick

out themes of redemption and/or reconciliation? Why do you think these themes are so pervasive?

3. How does the life and death of Jesus change our understanding of who God is and what it means to worship him? Does this worship seem contrary to human dignity?

4. Aside from the anthropologies mentioned in the chapter, how else might our culture attempt to define a human being?

5. What is the twofold task of those made in the image of God? How does this translate in your daily life?

6. Why do both Deism and pantheism fail to describe God's relationship with his creation?

7. What is the significance of Jesus presenting himself as the "true Israel"? Does this change how you look at the Old Testament narrative at all?

8. How can we understand the gospel as a correction of our failure to live out our vocation as human beings?

CHAPTER 5: THE NEED FOR GOD

1. Consider the "four longings" that N. T. Wright sees as being satisfied in God. If not in relationship with God, where else do people go to fulfill these longings?

2. Would you say that the decline in belief in God is the result of people finding other ways to satisfy their basic longings? If not, what do you think might be the reason for it?

3. Francis Spufford speaks of having a new perspective on Christianity versus the one he had as a child. What unhelpful teaching about God may have left people feeling alienated from him, and how would you approach a conversation with someone who has experienced this?

4. How might you explain the problem of assuming a secular worldview for people who claim to be uninterested in discussions of God and religion?

5. Do you find the "common sense" argument a convincing one for the Christian faith?

6. According to an atheistic or naturalistic worldview, what is its explanation for the search for meaning that seems to be intrinsic to our human nature? How does the Christian worldview respond to this explanation?

7. How does the pursuit of pleasure and happiness differ within an atheistic worldview as opposed to one in which eternal happiness is considered possible?

8. At the end of this chapter, we noted C. S. Lewis's argument from desire. Do you find his argument persuasive? Why or why not?

CHAPTER 6: WIRED FOR GOD

1. What is the "psychological crutch" argument? Have you ever heard someone use a version of this?
2. What is the "genetic fallacy"? How does this fallacy apply to the crutch argument?
3. Why is it important to differentiate between the rationality of belief and the psychology of belief?
4. What does this need for a psychological crutch, in one form or another, reveal about us as human beings? How can we turn this argument on its head?
5. Is the skepticism about the natural human inclination toward belief in God promoted by "neurotheology" consistent with how we view other natural inclinations—for example, toward friendship or pleasure? If not, why do you think this inconsistency exists?
6. In your own experience or in that of Christians you know well, has living as a follower of Jesus been the easy route?
7. Why do you think many of us automatically see our dependence on something external as a negative trait?

CHAPTER 7: THE TRIUNE GOD

1. The doctrine of the Trinity is central to the Christian faith yet ignored by many Christians. Why is the doctrine of the Trinity so important?
2. What are the three "corners" of Trinitarian theology, and why are they important to our understanding of the Triune God?
3. What is the doctrine of the Trinity? Try to describe it accurately. Note the distinction between the "is" of identity and the "is" of predication (the Mark Twain analogy).
4. What do you think of the Cerberus analogy? Is it helpful?
5. In what ways is God one? What is the doctrine of *perichoresis*?
6. How does the doctrine of the Trinity address concerns raised by philosophers who are religious pluralists, feminists, or pantheists?
7. If relational human beings exist because of a relational God, what model of relationship and community might we draw from the doctrine of the Trinity?
8. Does the doctrine of the Trinity currently shape your devotional life?

What might change about your prayer, worship, relating to others, work, and so on with a greater appreciation of the Triune God?

CHAPTER 8: TALKING ABOUT GOD AND KNOWING GOD

1. What is "the problem of religious language," according to some atheists?
2. What are some suitable responses to this alleged problem?
3. What is the difference between cataphatic and apophatic theology?
4. Historically, what motivated apophatic theology? What are the benefits and drawbacks of apophatic theology's emphases?
5. Does "negative theology" seem to fit what the Scriptures teach? Why or why not?
6. In what ways might our understanding of various doctrines be impacted by an unwillingness to move beyond apophatic theology?
7. How might we discern the difference between humility in understanding the mystery of God and a disobedient resistance to his self-revelation?
8. The Westminster Confession says that our chief end or goal is to "glorify God and enjoy him forever." How do we move beyond knowing about God to knowing and enjoying him?

CHAPTER 9: THE ATTRIBUTES OF GOD (I)

1. What is the difference between God's being *necessary* and *everlasting*? What is the significance of this distinction?
2. How might the Greek classical philosophical categories help us to consider questions about God's nature? How might they be a hindrance?
3. Can you define "cognitive idolatry"? What do you think might help prevent this for you personally?
4. Why is it misguided to deny a human capacity to know anything truly about the attributes of God?
5. How would you explain "perfect being theology" to a friend?
6. What does it mean to say that God is a necessary, self-sufficient being? How would you answer someone's question, "If God made the universe, who made God?"

CHAPTER 10: THE ATTRIBUTES OF GOD (II)

1. What is time? What do you think about the statement "God is outside of time"? Do you think it is accurate?

2. What are the A- and B-theories of time? Why do some people perceive this as posing a challenge to the idea of an omniscient God?

3. Has our discussion of God's relationship to time given any insights or raised any questions for you?

4. What does it mean that God is all-knowing (omniscient)? What are some misunderstandings about omniscience? How does God's omniscience influence the way we live?

5. Why is it metaphysically absurd to claim that God must have an experiential knowledge identical to that of humans in order to be divinely omniscient?

6. What is the relationship of God's foreknowledge to human free choices? Can we affirm both of these without contradiction? How does this have a bearing on prayer or the question of the unevangelized?

7. Are there any other helpful illustrations of God's relationship to time that you might use to explain this concept to someone?

CHAPTER 11: THE ATTRIBUTES OF GOD (III)

1. Read Psalm 139:1–18. What does the psalmist have to say about God's omnipresence? How would you articulate what omnipresence is?

2. Why is it significant that God is "spirit"? What are your thoughts on the discussion of divine incorporeality?

3. Have you ever considered the existence of beauty as an argument for God's existence? Do you find it persuasive? Why or why not?

4. When we hear that God is all-powerful (omnipotent), what does that mean? What does it *not* mean? Can God do *literally* everything? Is it a problem if he can't?

5. Why is it nonsensical to say that God should be able to undo the past?

6. What is Anselm's answer to the challenge that God cannot sin and therefore cannot be all-powerful? Do you find this convincing?

CHAPTER 12: THE ATTRIBUTES OF GOD (IV)

1. How does God's immutability give focus to your life? What does it mean for God to be unchanging? How has this doctrine been misunderstood? In what ways does God repent, and in what ways does he not repent?

2. What does it mean that God suffers? What scriptural instances of divine suffering stand out to you?

3. What were your impressions on the topic of divine humility? What are

the implications of divine humility for your daily life, your relationships, and communicating the gospel?

4. Summarize the doctrine of divine simplicity. What are its merits and/or shortcomings?

CHAPTERS 13 AND 14: THE GOD OF TRUTH

1. What are the key differences between premodernism, modernism, and postmodernism? What is the appeal—right or wrong—of postmodernism? What lessons can postmodernism teach us? What are some problems with it?
2. What is wrong with defining knowledge as having 100 percent certainty? Why is important to think in terms of *degrees* of knowledge?
3. Why are (a) truth denial, (b) knowledge denial, and (c) total (global) skepticism impossible positions to take? What does this reveal about how we are designed/"wired"?
4. Can you explain the *coherence* and *pragmatic* views of truth? What are the problems with these views? Why should we seek truth as *correspondence*?
5. How would you address the concerns that a relativist has over the dangers of metanarratives, as proven by historic regimes such as Communism and Nazism?
6. What are some other factors that might incline someone to adopt a relativistic worldview? Can you think of effective ways of uncovering these motivations and ways in which you might address them?
7. What does it mean that Jesus is "the truth" (John 14:6)? How can we be people of truth? What does this encompass?
8. How can we illustrate the difference between objective "truth" as an oppressive metanarrative and God's liberating truth (John 8:32)?

CHAPTER 15: MOVING TOWARD GOD

1. In what two major ways does God reveal himself? Why should Christians keep this in mind when talking to their non-Christian friends?
2. Why might God choose not to reveal himself in an undeniable way?
3. What do people mean when they say the world is "religiously ambiguous"? How do you respond to such a claim?
4. What is natural theology? Is this a valuable endeavor to undertake? Why or why not?

5. What is the problem with giving "proofs" to "demonstrate" God's existence? What is a wiser and more fruitful approach?

6. How might you respond the next time you are asked to give evidence for God's existence?

7. What is the difference between "thin" theism and "thick/robust" theism? Why is it important to go beyond thin theism? How do we do so?

8. Reflecting on your own testimony, how far has evidence for God's existence brought you in growing in a loving relationship with him? What have been the other important factors?

Chapters 16 and 17: God—The Best Explanation

1. When people say, "There isn't enough evidence for God," how do you respond? What do people need to consider besides "evidence"?

2. How might we distinguish "broad naturalism" from the stricter naturalism? What are the issues with taking such a worldview?

3. Why is the "inference to the best explanation" so important in discussing God's existence and attributes?

4. Describe the approach taken in the naturalism-theism chart. Do you find this more helpful than simply looking at individual arguments for God? Why or why not?

5. Which of the phenomena from the chart are to you most strikingly explained within a theistic context? How would you explain this to a friend in your own words?

6. Outline the components of the TULIP method for assessing worldviews. How might you apply this model in conversations you have with people who are working through their own questions about God and reality?

7. How do admitted problems (to account for consciousness, beauty, human rights, and the universe's beginning and fine-tuning) cited by naturalists offer assistance to the believer in God?

8. Despite offering supporting arguments for a theistic worldview, many atheists remain firm in their skepticism. What does this tell us about the role of argument in people coming to see the truth of the gospel? What must we remember when having discussions of a philosophical nature?

Chapter 18: The Reasons for God (I)

1. How will we know if we are acting as "armchair theologians" as opposed to truly seeking God?

2. What is a cosmological argument for the existence of God?

3. What does it mean to "beg the question"? Why is the question "who created God?" an example of this?

4. How do we distinguish between necessary and contingent beings?

5. What are the issues with arguing that the universe exists necessarily?

6. Peter Atkins has openly admitted his unwillingness to be persuaded of the falsehood of his atheistic worldview. How might you respond to someone who takes a similar position?

7. Our instinct to search for meaning manifests itself in many ways, including the search for meaning in our personal lives. How can this serve as a further pointer to God?

Chapter 19: The Reasons for God (II)

1. What are some aspects of creation that cause you to marvel at the intricate design of the natural world?

2. How might you respond to someone who sees the apparently "cruel" order of nature as a barrier to belief in a loving God as designer of the universe?

3. Why does Darwin's challenge to divine design not put an end to the discussion over an intelligent Designer?

4. What is the significance of some of the probabilities given in the table on pp. 161–62 for the existence of a universe that is life-permitting, life-producing, and life-sustaining?

5. What is the "many worlds" hypothesis? What are some of the issues with using this as an argument against God as Designer of the universe?

6. Why is the "Who designed the Designer?" line of reasoning not a valuable one in this discussion?

7. How can Paul Davies assert that all scientists essentially accept a theological worldview?

8. What kind of response would you offer to someone who claims that we shouldn't be surprised at the biofriendly order of the universe?

Chapter 20: The Reasons for God (III)

1. What is a properly basic moral belief?

2. How would you explain the moral argument for God's existence?

3. What is the Euthyphro dilemma, and why is it really a non-dilemma?

4. Why do you think naturalists strive to make a case for the existence of a morality, even when it is not consistent with the nihilistic outworking of such a worldview?

5. What are some of the dangers of removing God from our ethical framework? What problems does this pose on a personal and societal level?

6. How might you respond to someone who claims that morality is simply an illusion that has sprung from evolutionary processes?

7. Why does a naturalistic worldview not allow for moral duties to exist?

8. Do you think the moral argument is a convincing one? Why or why not?

CHAPTER 21: SCIENCE, NATURE, AND GOD

1. What is the difference between science and scientism?

2. What's wrong with the demand to "prove that scientifically"?

3. What philosophical assumptions do scientists begin with? Why should we keep this in mind?

4. What is the "God of the gaps" problem? Does it have any merits?

5. How do you respond to this charge when people talk about the "warfare" between science and religion?

CHAPTER 22: MIRACLES

1. What are miracles? Are they "violations" of natural laws? Do you find helpful the distinction between (a) ordinary providence, (b) extraordinary providence, and (c) miracles? How does this discussion help us understand Scripture's emphasis on prayer's effectiveness?

2. Have you ever encountered any miraculous events? Why do you think it is more common to hear accounts of miracles from people who have ministered in different (non-Western) cultural contexts?

3. What do we make of miracle claims in other religions? What about JFK or Elvis "sightings"?

4. How would you respond to someone using Hume's line of reasoning that miracles are impossible because they are a violation of the natural laws?

5. What are some other arguments used to undermine miracles, and how do you answer them?

6. Why is it problematic to separate the life and wisdom of Jesus from the miraculous? Why might Jefferson have been tempted to do this?

7. If it is true that "extraordinary claims demand extraordinary evidence," what kind of evidence would you deem sufficient for the extraordinary claim of Jesus's bodily resurrection?

8. What significance does it have that the entire Christian faith is rooted in belief in the miraculous? How does this shape your view of God's relationship with those who choose to follow him?

CHAPTER 23: THE PROBLEM OF EVIL (I)

1. How would you outline the theological explanation for evil in the world?
2. What is a paradigmatic evil? How can this be a starting point in conversation with a person who denies objective morality?
3. Why is the problem of evil not a unique one for the theist to grapple with?
4. How did C. S. Lewis's reflection on injustice lead him to admit the need for God to support those convictions?
5. What is Alvin Plantinga's argument from evil? Do you find this a helpful argument?
6. Can you think of any ways in which times of suffering in your own life have more clearly highlighted the truth of the Christian faith to you? Or perhaps obscured it? In either case, why so?
7. Why do we often find it difficult to avoid falling into the same trap as Job's friends when it comes to helping others in their suffering?
8. How would you go beyond trying, like Job's friends, to give an intellectual justification for a person's suffering?

CHAPTERS 24 AND 25: THE PROBLEM OF EVIL (II AND III)

1. What is the logical problem of evil? Why has it been largely dismissed in philosophy?
2. What is the difference between a defense and a theodicy? Which of the two seems more suitable to the problem of evil? Why?
3. Do you see evidence in your community of the "moralistic therapeutic deism" that Christian Smith speaks of? How might we challenge such an attitude?
4. How might the reality that God allows certain kinds of evil in the world reorient our thinking about the purposes he has for creation?
5. How is the argument from gratuitous evil used as evidence against the existence of God? How might the argument be reversed?
6. What aspect of the question of evil has been most prominent in your own walk with God? Which of the arguments discussed in these two chapters are most helpful in addressing those concerns?
7. Why do you think there is a tendency to ignore the Bible's emphasis on the demonic? What might it look like for us to take a healthy, intellectually rigorous approach to understanding these powers?
8. How would you explain to someone the significance of your hope that Christ has ultimate victory over evil?

CHAPTER 26: PRIMAL SIN

1. Why is understanding God's role in the origin of evil both a theological and a translational problem?
2. What is the significance of human freedom to the question of primal sin?
3. What do we mean when we say that sin isn't a *thing*?
4. How can we understand the first sin as a "failure of focus"?
5. What are some important considerations to bear in mind when we read and seek to understand the creation narrative in Genesis?

CHAPTER 27: ORIGINAL SIN

1. What is original sin? What are some different ways in which it has been understood within the church?
2. What is Pelagianism, and why has it been deemed heretical in its various forms?
3. Explain why Aleksandr Solzhenitsyn concluded that the line separating good and evil runs through every human heart. In what way is this reality true in your own life?
4. What is the difference between the "guilt" and "damage" interpretations of original sin? What are the implications of each? Which do you find more satisfying morally and biblically?
5. Why does original sin *not* mean that we are born into a "rigged system"?
6. We noted that our fallenness doesn't give a complete picture of who we are. How does the second Adam inform our understanding of the first Adam?
7. What is "the moral gap," and how may original sin be a kind of grace to us?
8. How does recent scientific discussion raise new questions in our understanding of original sin?

CHAPTER 28: HELL

1. Before reading this chapter, how would you have explained the concept of hell to someone?
2. Explain the key tenets of—and differences between—universalism, conditionalism, and corrosivism.
3. What are the challenges raised by each of these different theories?
4. What are some reasons for taking hell's fire and darkness to be figurative?

5. How can the doctrine of hell be squared with the character of God? Is the punishment disproportionate to the crime?

6. Why is the freedom of the will so crucial in coming to terms with hell?

7. Which objection to the doctrine of hell do you find most challenging? How do you respond to it?

8. Which of the explanations offered in this chapter might be helpful in future conversations you have with others struggling with the idea of hell?

CHAPTER 29: THE INCARNATION

1. What does the doctrine of the incarnation affirm? Why is this so crucial for our salvation?

2. How does Scripture affirm both Jesus's divinity and humanity? How does the image of God help our understanding of the coherence of the incarnation?

3. We noted three important distinctions to better understand the reasonableness of the incarnation: (a) Jesus's *person* and *nature*; (b) being *fully* versus *merely* human; (c) Jesus's *human* and *divine* awareness/consciousness. Explain each distinction. Did you observe any helpful analogies to better understand the incarnation?

4. If Jesus is God, how could he be tempted? What do you think of the claim that the Son of God temporarily surrendered having access to certain capabilities—including knowledge that it was impossible to deviate from the Father's will—in order to accomplish his mission?

5. Why was Jesus not play-acting in his temptation? How does Jesus's weakness and temptation encourage you in your own struggle against sin and learning submission to God?

6. How does the idea of God voluntarily limiting his divinity as he took on human nature shape your understanding of him? How might it inform the way you share the gospel with others?

7. What are some questions that have troubled you or others close to you surrounding the simultaneous divinity and humanity of Christ? How might you begin to form a response?

8. What do you make of Bonhoeffer's claim that we needn't try to philosophize about the incarnation?

CHAPTER 30: THE CROSS OF CHRIST

1. What is the difference between *objective* and *subjective* theories of the atonement? Which should receive priority and why?

2. What did the atonement achieve *corporately*—not simply *individually*? (Keep in mind Jesus's representative exile for Israel, as the true Son of God, and for humanity, as the second Adam.)
3. What did the atonement achieve *cosmically*?
4. Which of the theories of atonement best encapsulates how you have—up to this point—personally understood what Christ achieved on the cross?
5. Why is it important to reflect on our understanding of the atonement? How might it influence your personal worship?
6. What are some helpful or unhelpful illustrations you've heard used to explain atonement?
7. Is there something morally problematic with an innocent person's taking a guilty person's punishment?
8. Is the charge of "divine child abuse" (God's sending Christ to die on the cross for us) a fair one? How do you respond to this assertion?
9. Can you think of ways in which the biblical pictures of the atonement might work together to develop our understanding of what Christ came to accomplish?

Chapter 31: Jesus's Uniqueness and the Plurality of Religions

1. What is "tolerance," and how has the definition changed? What is the problem with the current understanding of tolerance?
2. Can you think of particular contexts you may find yourself in where there is a flawed understanding of tolerance? How might you challenge this idea?
3. Define "religious pluralism." What are its main features? Have you talked with religious pluralists about their views? What have your conversations been like?
4. Can all religions be "basically the same"? Why or why not?
5. How should Christians engage in religious dialogue? What guidelines should all parties set down from the outset before engaging in dialogue?
6. Why is the pluralist's certainty of the pluralist view problematic?
7. In what ways do the main world religions look alike? What are their fundamental differences?
8. How do you answer the question of the unevangelized? What should we keep in mind as we try to think through this issue?

CHAPTER 32: BODY, SOUL, AND IMMORTALITY

1. Compare the Greek doctrine of immortality with the Christian view. What are the significant differences?

2. What are the biblical and theological supports for the soul's surviving death before the final resurrection (i.e., the intermediate state)?

3. Why does it make better sense to say that the soul—not the body—gives a person her ongoing identity?

4. What are some philosophical reasons for believing that a soul exists? Which do you find most persuasive, and why? Why does naturalism fail to account for important "soulish" capabilities of humans?

5. What is the issue with asserting that consciousness is merely an illusion?

6. In what way is the existence of the soul a pointer to the truth of God's existence?

7. What is the theological significance of bodily resurrection? Would it make a difference if our bodies died and our souls just "went to heaven" (end of story)?

8. What does the robust physicality of the new heavens and new earth suggest? Do many Christians need to revise their understanding of the afterlife?

Notes

Preface

1. Charles Taliaferro states: "the roots of what we call philosophy of religion stretch back to the earliest forms of philosophy." "Philosophy of Religion" (2019), in the *Stanford Encyclopedia of Philosophy*, https://plato.stanford.edu/entries/philosophy-religion/.

2. Incidentally, see a similar approach to ethics in Robertson McQuilkin and Paul Copan, *Introduction to Biblical Ethics: Walking in the Way of Wisdom* (Downers Grove, IL: IVP Academic, 2014).

3. Taken from Alvin Plantinga, "Twenty Years' Worth of the SCP," *Faith and Philosophy* 15 (April 1998): 153; Alvin Plantinga, "Advice to Christian Philosophers," *Faith and Philosophy* 1 (July 1984): 255.

4. To use the words of Francis Schaeffer.

5. Jonathan Merritt, "It's Getting Harder to Talk about God," *New York Times*, Oct. 13, 2018, https://www.nytimes.com/2018/10/13/opinion/sunday/talk-god-sprituality-christian.html.

6. For an articulation of what Protestant evangelicalism is (and many of the misperceptions and mischaracterizations about Protestantism more particularly), see Kevin J. Vanhoozer, *Biblical Authority after Babel* (Grand Rapids: Baker Academic, 2016). See also Vanhoozer's "Response" in Matthew Levering, *Was the Reformation a Mistake?* (Grand Rapids: Zondervan, 2017).

7. That is, the seventeenth-century Lutheran theologian Rupertus Meldenius.

8. For example, see Peter M. Head, "The More Difficult Reading," *Evangelical Textual Criticism*, Feb. 6, 2009, http://evangelicaltextualcriticism.blogspot.com/2009/02/more-difficult-reading.html; also, "Prefer the Shorter Reading?," *New Testament Textual Criticism: Theory and Research*, http://www.nttext.com/newcms/index.php/scribal-habits/the-shorter-reading.

Chapter 1

1. Diogenes Allen and E. O. Springsted, *Philosophy for Understanding Theology*, 2nd ed. (Louisville: Westminster John Knox Press, 2007), ix–x.

2. Richard Bauckham, *God Crucified: Monotheism and Christology in the New Testament* (Grand Rapids: Eerdmans, 1998), 78–79.

3. Stephen Hawking and Leonard Mlodinow, *The Grand Design* (New York: Bantam, 2012), 5.

4. Alvin Plantinga, *God, Freedom, and Evil* (Grand Rapids: Eerdmans, 1977), 1.

5. Abraham Maslow, *The Psychology of Science: A Reconnaissance* (New York: Harper & Row, 1966), 15.

6. "Learning in War-Time," in *The Weight of Glory* (New York: Macmillan, 1965), 28.

7. D. A. Carson makes this statement in his book *Exegetical Fallacies* (Grand Rapids: Baker, 1996).

8. The video and text of Conan O'Brien's June 12, 2011, address can be found here: http://www.dartmouth.edu/~commence/news/speeches/2011/obrien-speech.html.

9. See Bruce Ellis Benson, "Christian Philosophy as a Way of Life," *Andrews University Seminary Studies* 50, no. 2 (2012): 149.

10. Plato, *Phaedo* 64A.

11. See Tremper Longman III, *The Fear of the Lord Is Wisdom* (Grand Rapids: Baker Academic, 2017).

12. Martin Luther, *Letters of Spiritual Counsel*, trans. and ed. Theodore G. Tappert (1960; (Vancouver, BC: Regent College Publishing, 2003), 86–87.

13. Brian Leftow, "From Jerusalem to Athens," in *God and the Philosophers: The Reconciliation of Faith and Reason*, ed. Thomas V. Morris (New York: Oxford University Press, 1994), 193.

14. On Jesus as a philosopher, see Douglas Groothuis, *On Jesus*, Wadsworth Philosophers Series (Belmont, CA: Wadsworth, 2003).

15. Ben Witherington III, *Paul's Narrative Thought World* (Louisville: Westminster John Knox, 1994), 216.

16. N. T. Wright, *Paul and the Faithfulness of God* (Minneapolis: Fortress, 2013), 203.

17. For further discussion of Paul's Mars Hill speech and its relevance for Christians today, see Paul Copan and Kenneth Litwak, *The Gospel in the Marketplace of Ideas* (Downers Grove, IL: IVP Academic, 2014).

18. These descriptions are found in Antony Flew, *There Is a God* (New York: HarperOne, 2009), 185–86; Antony Flew with Gary Habermas, "My Pilgrimage from Atheism to Theism," *Philosophia Christi* 6, no. 2 (2004): 208; Antony Flew in *Did the Resurrection Happen?*, ed. David Baggett (Downers Grove, IL: InterVarsity Press, 2009), 57.

Chapter 2

1. Some material from this chapter is summarized from portions of my book *A Little Book for New Philosophers: Why and How to Study Philosophy* (Downers Grove, IL: IVP Academic, 2016).

2. Tremper Longman III, *The Fear of the Lord Is Wisdom* (Grand Rapids: Baker Academic, 2017), 11–13.

3. Cited in Tom Morris, *Philosophy for Dummies* (New York: IDG Books, 1999).

4. Luc Ferry, *A Brief History of Thought: A Philosophical Guide to Living* (New York: Harper Perennial, 2011), 72–73.

5. Cited in Preserved Smith, *The Life and Letters of Martin Luther* (Boston: Houghton Mifflin, 1911), 342.

6. John Calvin, *Paul's Epistles to the Galatians, Ephesians, Philippians, and Colossians*, ed. David W. Torrance and Thomas F. Torrance, trans. T. H. L. Parker (Grand Rapids: Eerdmans, 1965), 329 (my emphasis).

7. Justin Martyr, *Second Apology* 8. In *The Writings of Justin Martyr and Athenagoras*, vol. 2 of *The Ante-Nicene Christian Library*, ed. Alexander Roberts and James Donaldson (Edinburgh: T&T Clark, 1886), 96.

Chapter 3

1. See Matthew Bates, *Salvation by Allegiance Alone* (Grand Rapids: Baker Academic, 2017).

2. *Mishnah Pesahim* 10 (my emphasis).

3. Quoted in Martin E. Marty, "Professor Pelikan," *Christian Century* 123 (June 13, 2006): 47.

4. Mortimer Adler, "A Philosopher's Religious Faith," in *Philosophers Who Believe*, ed. Kelly James Clark (Downers Grove, IL: InterVarsity Press, 1993), 209, 215.

5. C. S. Lewis, "Is Theology Poetry?," in *The Weight of Glory and Other Addresses* (New York: Macmillan, 1965), 140.

6. Michael F. Bird, "How God Became Jesus—and How I Came to Faith in Him," April 16, 2014, http://www.christianitytoday.com/ct/2014/april-web-only/how-god-became-jesus -and-how-i-came-to-faith-in-him.html.

7. Anthony Kenny, *Faith and Philosophy* (New York: Columbia University Press, 1983), 59.

8. This letter can be found at the Darwin Correspondence Project (Cambridge University), https://www.darwinproject.ac.uk/letter/DCP-LETT-2814.xml.

9. R. W. L. Moberly, *The Bible in a Disenchanted Age: The Enduring Possibility of Christian Faith* (Grand Rapids: Baker Academic, 2018), 92. This point is drawn from chapter 3 in Moberly.

10. See Charles Taliaferro's treatment of this topic in *Evidence and Faith: Philosophy and Religion Since the Seventeenth Century* (Cambridge: Cambridge University Press, 2005).

11. Thomas Nagel, *The Last Word* (New York: Oxford University Press, 1997), 130–31.

12. Ninian Smart, "Towards a Definition of Religion" (unpublished paper, Lancaster University, 1970); Ninian Smart, *The World's Religions* (Englewood Cliffs, NJ: Prentice-Hall, 1989), 10–21.

13. Martin E. Marty with Jonathan Moore, *Politics, Religion, and the Common Good* (San Francisco: Jossey-Bass, 2000), 10.

14. N. T. Wright, *Paul and the Faithfulness of God* (Minneapolis: Fortress, 2013), 203.

15. Paul J. Griffiths, *Problems of Religious Diversity* (Oxford: Blackwell, 2001), 2–12.

16. Bertrand Russell, *The Basic Writings of Bertrand Russell, 1903–1959*, ed. Robert E. Egher and Lester E. Denonn (New York: Simon & Schuster, 1963), 191.

17. Some themes in this chapter can be found in Paul Copan, *A Little Book for New Philosophers: Why and How to Study Philosophy* (Downers Grove, IL: IVP Academic, 2016).

Chapter 4

1. See Greg Koukl, *The Story of Reality: How the World Began, How It Ends, and Everything Important That Happens in Between* (Grand Rapids: Zondervan, 2017).

2. C. S. Lewis, "Is Theology Poetry?," in *The Weight of Glory and Other Addresses* (New York: Macmillan, 1965), 140.

3. G. K. Chesterton, "The Return of the Angels," *Daily News*, March 14, 1903.

4. J. R. R. Tolkien, "On Fairy Stories," available at various places on the internet. Originally published in *Essays Presented to Charles Williams*, ed. C. S. Lewis (Oxford: Oxford University Press, 1947), 38–89.

5. This analogy is taken from N. T. Wright, "On What It Means to Be an Image-Bearer,"

BioLogos, June 16, 2010, https://biologos.org/resources/audio-visual/nt-wright-on-being
-an-image-bearer.

Chapter 5

1. N. T. Wright, *Simply Christian: Why Christianity Makes Sense* (New York: Harper-
SanFrancisco, 2006), x.

2. Noted by Michael Peterson in Michael Peterson and Michael Ruse, *Science, Evolution,
and Religion: A Debate about Atheism and Theism* (Oxford: Oxford University Press, 2017),
12. See Howard Mumma, *Albert Camus and the Minister* (Brewster, MA: Paraclete Press,
2000).

3. So begins the book by Julian Barnes, *Nothing to Be Frightened Of* (Boston: Alfred A.
Knopf, 2008).

4. Roger Scruton, *The Face of God* (New York: Bloomsbury, 2012), 155, 177–78.

5. Francis Spufford, *Unapologetic* (New York: HarperOne, 2012).

6. Luis Rivas with Francis Spufford, "Q&A on 'Impenitente [*Unapologetic*]),'" Oct.
11, 2014, http://unapologetic-book.tumblr.com/post/99715799639/qa-about-impenitente
-english-version.

7. See Jonathan Rauch, "Let It Be," *Atlantic Monthly,* May 2003, https://www.theatlan
tic.com/magazine/archive/2003/05/let-it-be/302726/34. Some thoughts in this section are
taken from K. Robert Beshears, "Apatheism: Engaging the Western Pantheon of Spiritual
Indifference," April 2016, https://hcommons.org/deposits/objects/hc:11094/datastreams
/CONTENT/content.

8. See this documentation in Robert Woodberry, "The Missionary Roots of Liberal
Democracy," *American Political Science Review* 106, no. 2 (2012): 244–74.

9. Thomas Sowell (a conservative economist) speaks of ideas that have never been put
to the test beyond the university's paneled walls—an "unDarwinian" environment "where
ideas do not have to work in order to survive." Indeed, except in some fields, the "academic
world is the natural habitat of half-baked ideas." He concludes, "Just as you don't find eagles
living in the ocean or fish living on mountain tops, so you don't find leftists concentrated
where their ideas have to stand the test of performance." Thomas Sowell, "The Survival
of the Left," *Forbes* (Sept. 10, 1997), https://www.forbes.com/forbes/1997/0908/6005128a
.html#634ba999c4c3.

10. Paul Moser, "Agapeic Theism: Personfying Evidence and Moral Struggle," *European
Journal for Philosophy of Religion* 2 (2010): 1–18.

11. Augustine, *Confessions* 1.1.

12. Some thoughts here are taken from Gregory E. Ganssle, *Our Deepest Desires: How
the Christian Story Fulfills Human Aspirations* (Downers Grove, IL: IVP Academic, 2017);
and especially from Stewart Goetz, *The Purpose of Life: A Theistic Perspective* (New York:
Bloomsbury, 2012); Stewart Goetz, *C. S. Lewis* (Oxford: Blackwell, 2018).

13. C. S. Lewis, *The Screwtape Letters* (New York: Macmillan, 1950), 112–13.

14. See book 2, part 2 ("The Invasion") in C. S. Lewis's *Mere Christianity,* various editions.

15. See Wes Jamison and Paul Copan, eds., *What Would Jesus Really Eat? The Biblical
Case for Eating Meat* (Pickering, ON: Castle Quay, 2019), especially chapters 5 and 6 written
by Timothy Hsiao.

16. Elizabeth Cleghorn Gaskell, *North and South* (Cambridge: Putnam, 1906), 117–18.

17. See letter 21 in C. S. Lewis, *Letters to Malcolm, Chiefly on Prayer* (various editions).

Chapter 6

1. Ludwig Feuerbach, *The Essence of Christianity*, trans. George Eliot (New York: Harper & Brothers, 1957), xxxix.

2. Pascal Boyer, *Religion Explained: The Evolutionary Origins of Religious Thought* (New York: Basic Books, 2001), 298.

3. Richard Dawkins, *The God Delusion* (Boston: Houghton Mifflin, 2006), 184.

4. Justin Barrett, *Born Believers: The Science of Children's Religious Belief* (New York: Atria Books/Free Press, 2012).

5. See John Goldingay, *Psalms*, vol. 1, *Psalms 1–41* (Grand Rapids: Baker Academic, 2002), 212–13; and his *Psalms*, vol. 2, *Psalms 42–89* (Grand Rapids: Baker Academic, 2007), 151.

6. C. S. Lewis, "The Weight of Glory," in *The Weight of Glory and Other Addresses* (New York: Macmillan, 1965), 6–7.

7. Lewis, "The Weight of Glory," 7.

8. See Paul C. Vitz, "The Psychology of Atheism: From Defective Fathers to Autism to Professional Socialization and Personal Convenience," in *The Naturalness of Belief: New Essays on Theism's Rationality*, ed. Paul Copan and Charles Taliaferro (Lanham, MD: Lexington Books/Rowman & Littlefield, 2019), 175–95; and Paul C. Vitz, *Faith of the Fatherless: The Psychology of Atheism*, 2nd ed. (San Francisco: Ignatius, 2013). Key ideas in this section are taken from these works.

9. Sigmund Freud, *Leonardo da Vinci* (New York: Vintage/Random House, 1947), 98.

10. Peter van Inwagen, "Explaining Belief in the Supernatural," in *The Believing Primate: Scientific, Philosophical, and Theological Reflections on the Origin of Religion*, ed. Jeffrey Schloss and Michael J. Murray (Oxford: Oxford University Press, 2009), 136.

11. Deborah Kelemen, "Are Children 'Intuitive Theists'? Reasoning about Purpose and Design in Nature," *Psychological Science* 15, no. 5 (2004): 295–301.

12. Scott Atran, *In Gods We Trust: The Evolutionary Landscape of Religion* (Oxford: Oxford University Press, 2002), 57.

13. Timothy Lenoir, *The Strategy of Life* (Chicago: University of Chicago Press, 1992), ix.

14. Francis Crick, *What Mad Pursuit* (New York: Basic Books, 1988), 138.

15. Christian Smith, *Moral, Believing Animals: Human Personhood and Culture* (New York: Oxford University Press, 2003), 110, 122. Some comments here are found in expanded form in Paul Copan, "Does Religion Originate in the Brain?," *Christian Research Journal* 31, no. 2 (2008): 32–40.

Chapter 7

1. N. T. Wright, "Jesus and the Identity of God," *Ex Auditu* 14 (1998): 44.

2. Gk.: *ousia*; Lat.: *substantia*.

3. Gk. (pl.): *hypostaseis*; Lat. (pl.): *personae*.

4. See chapter 6 on the question of "eternal functional subordination" in Thomas H. McCall, *Which Trinity? Whose Monotheism?* (Grand Rapids: Eerdmans, 2010).

5. Roger Nicole, "The Meaning of the Trinity," in *One God in Trinity*, ed. Peter Toon and James D. Spiceland (Westchester, IL: Cornerstone, 1980), 1–4.

6. See Jeffrey E. Brower and Michael C. Rea, "Understanding the Trinity," *Logos: A Journal of Catholic Thought and Culture* 8, no. 1 (2005): 147–57.

7. Jeremy Begbie, "Hearing God in C Major," in *Beholding the Glory: Incarnation through the Arts* (Grand Rapids: Baker, 2000). A summary is available in Gordon College's *Stillpoint* (Summer 2005), www.gordon.edu/download/galleries/Summer2005Stillpoint1.pdf.

8. "Mark Twain's Cigars Were His Muse," Corona Cigar Co., June 23, 2015, https://www.coronacigar.com/Mark-Twain%27s-Cigars-Were-His-Muse/3621/.

9. Cornelius Plantinga, "The Perfect Family," *Christianity Today* 28 (March 4, 1988): 27.

10. Colin Gunton, *The One, the Three, and the Many* (Cambridge: Cambridge University Press, 1993).

Chapter 8

1. *Harvey*, written by Mary Chase, directed by Henry Koster (Universal Studios, 1950).

2. Lewis Carroll, *Alice in Wonderland and Through the Looking Glass* (Kingsport, TN: Grosset & Dunlap, 1946), 240.

3. David Hume, *An Enquiry Concerning Human Understanding* (New York: Liberal Arts Press, 1955), 173.

4. J. L. Mackie, *The Miracle of Theism* (Oxford: Clarendon, 1982), 1–4.

5. Carl Sagan, *Cosmos* (New York: Random House, 1980), 4.

6. Antony Flew with Roy Abraham Varghese, *There Is a God: How the World's Most Notorious Atheist Changed His Mind* (New York: Harper, 2007).

7. William Alston, "Referring to God," *Philosophy of Religion* 24 (1988): 116, 120; cf. 113.

8. Thomas Aquinas, *Summa Theologica*, 1a.3.

9. From Charles Wesley's hymn "Love Divine, All Loves Excelling."

10. Some comments here are taken from Colin E. Gunton, *Act and Being: Towards a Theology of the Divine Attributes* (Grand Rapids: Eerdmans, 2003).

11. Richard Cross, "Problems in Religious Language," in *Philosophy: Religion*, Macmillan Interdisciplinary Handbooks: Philosophy Series, ed. Donald M. Borchart (Farmington Hills, MI: Macmillan Reference USA/Gale, 2017), 255–56.

Chapter 9

1. Jaroslav Pelikan, *The Christian Tradition*, vol. 1, *The Emergence of the Catholic Tradition: 100–600* (Chicago: University of Chicago Press, 1971), 52–53.

2. Thomas H. McCall, *An Invitation to Analytic Christian Philosophy* (Downers Grove, IL: IVP Academic, 2015), 32–35.

3. McCall, 5, 45–51.

4. Robert Audi, "Intuition and Its Place in Ethics," *Journal of the American Philosophical Association* 1, no. 1 (2015): 57–77.

5. See Stephen T. Davis's defense of the ontological argument in *The Rationality of Theism*, ed. Paul Copan and Paul K. Moser (London: Routledge, 2003), 93–111.

6. Panentheism takes a variety of forms. See John W. Cooper, *Panentheism: The Other God of the Philosophers—From Plato to the Present* (Grand Rapids: Baker Academic, 2006).

7. Paul Davies, "The Birth of the Cosmos," in *God, Cosmos, Nature and Creativity*, ed. Jill Gready (Edinburgh: Scottish Academic Press, 1995), 8–9.

8. Paul Copan and William Lane Craig, *Creation out of Nothing: A Biblical, Philosophical, and Scientific Exploration* (Grand Rapids: Baker Academic, 2004).

Chapter 10

1. See Greg Ganssle, ed., *God and Time: Four Views* (Downers Grove, IL: InterVarsity Press, 2001); William Lane Craig, *Time and Eternity* (Wheaton, IL: Crossway, 2001).

2. Augustine, *Confessions* 11.15.

3. James Barr, *Biblical Words for Time* (London: SCM Press, 1962), 80.

4. Jay Wesley Richards, *The Untamed God* (Downers Grove, IL: InterVarsity Press, 2003), 202–7.

5. God could have created angels prior to the space-time universe, and this event would have marked the beginning of time. Or God, anticipating creation, could have counted down in his mind, "Three, two, one . . . let there be light!" Again, this change or happening would be sufficient to ground time as well.

6. Doesn't God's "foreknowledge" of the creation or redemption of humans suggest a future for God without creation? Scripture uses this term non-technically/non-philosophically. It would be more precise to say that upon creation, God's tenseless knowledge of all truths would then become "indexed"—ordered according to his awareness of tensed truths. With creation, God becomes aware of future-tensed truths and thus has foreknowledge. William Lane Craig, "Response to Critics" in *God and Time*, ed. Gregory Ganssle, 175–86; William Craig, *God, Time, and Eternity* (Dordrecht: Kluwer, 2001), 271–75.

7. Daniel Dennett, "Conditions of Personhood," in *The Identities of Persons*, ed. Amelie Oksenberg Rorty (Berkeley: University of California Press, 1976), 175–96. I'm following William Craig's analysis in *God, Time, and Eternity*, 43–55.

8. E.g., Michael Martin, "A Disproof of God's Existence," *Darshana* 10 (1970): 22–24.

9. Michael Martin and Ricki Monnier, eds., *The Impossibility of God* (Amherst, NY: Prometheus, 2003), 234.

10. Patrick Grim, "Some Neglected Problems of Omniscience," *American Philosophical Quarterly* 20, no. 3 (1983): 272.

11. Linda Zagzebski, *Omnisubjectivity: A Defense of a Divine Attribute* (Milwaukee: Marquette University Press, 2013).

12. Exod. 13:17–18; 19:21; 1 Sam. 16:2–3; 2 Kings 21:8; Jer. 18:7–10.

13. Aquinas, *Summa Theologica*, 1.14.13, ad 3.

14. William Craig notes: "I should go so far as to say that the implicit assumption of the perceptual model underlies virtually all contemporary denials of the possibility of divine foreknowledge of free acts." *The Only Wise God* (Grand Rapids: Baker, 1987), 121. (This volume is now available through Wipf & Stock [2000]).

15. This scenario is something akin to the demonized Philippian slave-girl who could accurately predict the future (Acts 16:16).

16. Augustine, *On the Free Choice of the Will* 3.3.6.

17. Even if, say, backward causation is possible, the past is still unchangeable. Changing the past is different from causing the past. If a person prays about an event that has already taken place without knowing the outcome, it could be that his prayers to a foreknowing God *causally effect* what has already taken place. Craig, *The Only Wise God*, 76–77.

18. This perspective of divine foreknowledge and human freedom is, I believe, well-

rooted in Scripture. It has been called the "middle knowledge" view or "Molinism"—named after the Spanish Jesuit theologian Luis de Molina (1535–1600). Thomas Flint sees the alternatives to this view as being open theism and Thomism/Calvinism. For a response to recent philosophical criticisms of this view by Dean Zimmerman and others, see Thomas P. Flint, "Molinism," *Philosophy/Philosophy of Religion*, Oxford Handbooks Online, February 2015, doi: 10.1093/oxfordhb/9780199935314.013.29.

Chapter 11

1. See chapter 10 in William Lane Craig, *Time and the Metaphysics of Relativity* (Dordrecht: Kluwer Academic Publishers, 2001).

2. John Hick, "God and Christianity according to Swinburne," *European Journal of Philosophy of Religion* 2, no. 1 (Spring 2010): 27.

3. Jaegwon Kim, "Epiphenomenal and Supervenient Causation," in *Midwest Studies in Philosophy*, vol. 9, ed. P. A. French, T. E. Uehing, and H. Wettstein (Minneapolis: University of Minnesota Press, 1984), 266.

4. See Roger Scruton, *Beauty: A Short Introduction* (Oxford: Oxford University Press, 2009); and Roger Scruton, *Modern Culture* (New York: Bloomsbury, 1997).

5. Scruton, *Modern Culture*, 31.

6. J. R. R. Tolkien, "On Fairy Stories," available at various places on the internet. Originally published in *Essays Presented to Charles Williams*, ed. C. S. Lewis (Oxford: Oxford University Press, 1947), 38–89.

7. See David Bentley Hart, *The Beauty of the Infinite* (Grand Rapids: Eerdmans, 2003).

8. This connection is noted in *Philokalia*, the famous collection of Eastern Orthodox spiritual authorities.

9. Thanks to Ravi Zacharias, who has mentioned this person on occasion.

10. C. S. Lewis, *The Problem of Pain* (New York: Macmillan, 1962), 27–28.

11. Anselm, *Proslogion* 7. In *A Scholastic Miscellany: Anselm to Ockham*, ed. Eugene R. Fairweather (Louisville: Westminster John Knox, 1958), 77.

12. Anselm, *Why God Became Man* 2.10. In *A Scholastic Miscellany*, 156. Thomas Morris writes that God's inability to sin "only indicates a necessarily firm directedness in the way in which God will *use* his unlimited power." See *Our Idea of God* (Downers Grove, IL: InterVarsity Press, 1991), 80.

13. Aquinas, *Summa Theologica*, I.25.3 ad 2.

14. Michael Martin, *Atheism* (Philadelphia: Temple University Press, 1990), 309.

15. Charles Taliaferro, *Contemporary Philosophy of Religion* (Malden, MA: Blackwell, 1998), 80–81.

16. The following list is from Thomas P. Flint and Alfred J. Freddoso, "Maximal Power," in *The Existence and Nature of God* (Notre Dame, IN: University of Notre Dame Press, 1983), 81–113.

17. Taliaferro, *Contemporary Philosophy of Religion*, 75.

Chapter 12

1. Colin E. Gunton, *Act and Being: Towards a Theology of the Divine Attributes* (Grand Rapids: Eerdmans, 2003), 126.

2. Jay Wesley Richards, *The Untamed God* (Downers Grove, IL: InterVarsity Press, 2003), 196. See Richards's more detailed discussion of immutability.

3. Jaroslav Pelikan, *The Christian Tradition*, vol. 1, *The Emergence of the Catholic Tradition: 100–600* (Chicago: University of Chicago Press, 1971), 52–53.

4. This meaning of "repent" (*nacham*) in the Niphal is found in Exod. 32:12, 14; 1 Sam. 15:29; Ps. 110:4; Isa. 57:6; Jer. 4:28; 15:6; 18:8, 10; 26:3, 13, 19; Ezek. 24:14; Joel 2:13–14; Amos 7:3, 6; Jon. 3:9–10; 4:2; Zech. 8:14.

5. H. Van Dyke Parunak, "A Semantic Survey of NHM," *Biblica* 56 (1975): 512–32; R. B. Chisholm, "Does God 'Change His Mind'?," *Bibliotheca Sacra* 152 (Oct.–Dec. 1995): 387–99.

6. D. A. Carson, *How Long, O Lord?* (Grand Rapids: Baker, 1990), 186, 187–88.

7. Pelikan, *Emergence of the Catholic Tradition*, 52–53.

8. Richard Creel, "Immutability and Impassibility," in *A Companion to Philosophy of Religion*, ed. Charles Taliaferro, Paul Draper, and Philip L. Quinn, 2nd ed. (Oxford: Wiley-Blackwell, 2010), 326. Incidentally, Creel once adhered to divine impassibility but was persuaded that God's being touched by human suffering or success is an indication of divine perfection.

9. Alvin Plantinga, "A Christian Life Partly Lived," in *Philosophers Who Believe*, ed. Kelly James Clark (Downers Grove, IL: InterVarsity Press, 1993), 71.

10. Gunton, *Act and Being*, 128–29.

11. Jay Wesley Richards, *The Untamed God* (chapter 9) gives a nicely nuanced presentation and assessment of these versions. I borrow from some of his insights. See also Alvin Plantinga, *Does God Have a Nature?* (Milwaukee: Marquette University Press, 1980); for another view, see Eleonore Stump, *The God of the Bible and the God of the Philosophers* (Milwaukee: Marquette University Press, 2016).

12. Though we may not accept the traditional understanding of divine simplicity as espoused by, say, Aquinas, we can speak of, say, God's *knowledge* as being simple. Cf. William Alston, "Does God Have Beliefs?," *Religious Studies* 22 (1986): 287–306.

13. Though *not* in the Aristotelian (or Thomistic) sense, which sees potency and actuality as creaturely.

14. See Paul Copan and William Lane Craig, *Creation out of Nothing: A Biblical, Philosophical, and Scientific Exploration* (Grand Rapids: Baker Academic, 2004), 173–80.

15. Bede Rundle, *Why Is There Something Rather Than Nothing?* (Oxford: Oxford University Press, 2004), 18 (citing Hume's Dialogue Concerning Natural Religion).

16. I draw from C. S. Lewis, *Reflections on the Psalms* (New York: Harcourt Brace, 1958); Lewis, "The Weight of Glory," in *The Weight of Glory and Other Addresses* (New York: Macmillan, 1965); and Lewis, "The Great Sin," in book 3, chapter 8 of *Mere Christianity* (New York: Macmillan, 1952); Charles Taliaferro, "The Vanity of God," *Faith and Philosophy* 6 (April 1989): 140–54.

17. N. T. Wright, *For All God's Worth: True Worship and the Calling of the Church* (Grand Rapids: Eerdmans, 1997), 7.

18. Richard Bauckham, *Bible and Mission: Christian Witness in a Postmodern World* (Grand Rapids: Baker Academic, 2004), 37.

19. E.g., Exod. 20:5; 34:14; Deut. 4:24; 6:15; 29:20; 32:16, 21; Josh. 24:19; 1 Kings 14:22; Ezek. 8:3 (a graven "image of jealousy" ESV); 16:38, 42–43; 39:25; Joel 2:18; Nah. 1:2; Zeph. 1:18; 3:8; Zech. 1:14; 8:2; 1 Cor. 10:22.

20. C. S. Lewis, *Reflections on the Psalms*, 94–95.

21. Colin E. Gunton, *The Christian Faith: An Introduction to Christian Doctrine* (Oxford: Blackwell, 2002), 181.

Chapter 13

1. Dallas Willard, *The Allure of Gentleness* (New York: HarperOne, 2015), 81.

2. For a defense of the Protestant Reformation against charges that it led to pluralism, secularism, and the like, see Kevin Vanhoozer, *Biblical Authority after Babel: Retrieving the Solas in the Spirit of Mere Protestant Christianity* (Grand Rapids: Zondervan, 2016); in reply to this charge, see also Vanhoozer's "Response" at the end of Matthew Levering's book, *Was the Reformation a Mistake?* (Grand Rapids: Zondervan, 2017).

3. See the comments of Brendan Sweetman (a Catholic philosopher) in "Introduction: The Failure of Modernism," in *The Failure of Modernism: The Cartesian Legacy and Contemporary Pluralism*, ed. Brendan Sweetman (Mishawaka, IN: American Maritain Association, 1999), 1–3.

4. Jean-François Lyotard, *The Postmodern Condition*, trans. Geoff Bennington and Brian Massumi (Minneapolis: University of Minnesota Press, 1984), xxiv.

5. Paul Elie, *The Life You Save May Be Your Own* (New York: Farrar, Straus & Giroux, 2003), 427.

6. Craig M. Gay, *The Way of the (Modern) World: Or, Why It's Tempting to Live as If God Doesn't Exist* (Grand Rapids: Eerdmans, 1998), 5.

Chapter 14

1. Dallas Willard, "Toward a Phenomenology for the Correspondence Theory of Truth," *Discipline filosofiche* 1 (1991): 125–47. Found online at www.dallaswillard.com.

2. R. W. L. Moberly, *The Bible in a Disenchanted Age* (Grand Rapids: Baker Academic, 2018), 92.

3. William Alston, "Religious Experience Justifies Religious Belief," in *Contemporary Debates in Philosophy of Religion*, ed. Michael L. Peterson and Raymond J. Vanarragon (Oxford: Blackwell, 2004), 138.

4. Alvin Plantinga in Alvin Plantinga and Michael Tooley, *Knowledge of God* (Oxford: Blackwell, 2008), 175.

5. Roger Scruton, *Modern Philosophy* (London: Pimlico, 2004), 6.

6. John R. Searle, *Mind, Language and Society: Philosophy in the Real World* (New York: Basic Books, 1998), 17.

7. See Don Everts and Doug Schaupp, *I Once Was Lost: What Postmodern Skeptics Taught Us about Their Path to Jesus* (Downers Grove, IL: InterVarsity Press, 2008).

Chapter 15

1. For a response to Hick, see Paul Copan, "Why the World Is Not Religiously Ambiguous: A Critique of Religious Pluralism," in *Can Only One Religion Be True?*, ed. Robert Stewart (Minneapolis: Fortress, 2013), 139–62.

2. These two principles are mentioned in C. Stephen Evans, *Natural Signs and the Knowledge of God: A New Look at Theistic Arguments* (Oxford: Oxford University Press, 2010).

3. *Pensées* (in English: *Thoughts*), #430.

4. Keith Green, "Soften Your Heart," on *No Compromise*, Sparrow Records, 1978.

5. In Michael Ruse and Michael Peterson, *Science, Evolution, and Religion* (New York: Oxford University Press, 2016), 22.

6. See Paul K. Moser, *The Elusive God: Reorienting Religious Epistemology* (Cambridge: Cambridge University Press, 2008). Though I would disagree with Moser's assessment of natural theology, he highlights the inescapability of personal knowledge of God.

7. Moser, *The Elusive God*, 161.

8. M. Scott Peck, *The Road Less Traveled* (New York: Simon & Schuster, 1978), 45.

9. Anthony Kenny, *The God of the Philosophers* (Oxford: Clarendon, 1979), 129.

10. Stephen T. Davis, *God, Reason, and Theistic Proofs* (Grand Rapids: Eerdmans, 1997), 4.

11. "A Debate on the Existence of God," in *The Existence of God*, ed. John Hick (New York: Macmillan, 1964), 167.

12. Thomas Aquinas, *Summa Theologica*, I.2.3.

13. See Paul Copan, ed., *The Kalām Cosmological Argument: Philosophical Arguments for the Finitude of the Past* (New York: Bloomsbury, 2018), as well as *The Kalām Cosmological Argument: Scientific Evidence for the Beginning of the Universe* (New York: Bloomsbury, 2018).

14. Dallas Willard, "Language, Being, God, and the Three Stages of Theistic Evidence," in J. P. Moreland and Kai Nielsen, *Does God Exist? The Great Debate* (Nashville: Thomas Nelson, 1990), 207.

15. Peck, *The Road Less Traveled*, 241.

16. Eric Reitan, *Is God a Delusion? A Reply to Religion's Cultured Despisers* (Oxford: Blackwell, 2009), 83–84.

17. Alvin Plantinga in Alvin Plantinga and Daniel Dennett, *Science and Religion: Are They Compatible?* (Oxford: Blackwell, 2011), 58–59.

18. Plantinga in Plantinga and Dennett, *Science and Religion*, 59.

19. Louise Cowan, "The Importance of the Classics," in *Invitation to the Classics* (Grand Rapids: Baker, 1998), 19–24.

20. See C. S. Lewis, "On Stories" in *On Stories and Other Essays*, ed. Walter Hooper, available in many editions. Also, Michael Ward, "The Good Serves the Better and Both the Best: C. S. Lewis on Imagination and Reason in Christian Apologetics" (three parts), *Knowing & Doing* (C. S. Lewis Institute), http://www.cslewisinstitute.org /The_Good_Serves_the_Better_and_Both_the_Best_Part_1_Full_Article.

21. On this, see Paul Gould, *Cultural Apologetics: Renewing the Christian Voice, Conscience, and Imagination in a Disenchanted World* (Grand Rapids: Zondervan, 2019).

22. Alvin Plantinga, "Advice to Christian Philosophers," *Faith and Philosophy* 1, no. 3 (July 1984): 255.

Chapter 16

1. Thomas Nagel, *The Last Word* (New York: Oxford University Press, 1997), 130–31.

2. See Quentin Smith, "The Metaphilosophy of Naturalism," *Philo* 4, no. 2 (2001).

3. Edward O. Wilson, *Consilience: The Unity of Knowledge* (New York: Knopf, 1998), 266.

4. Bertrand Russell, "Science and Ethics," in *Religion and Science* (Oxford: Oxford University Press, 1961).

5. Kai Nielsen, "Naturalistic Explanations for Theistic Belief," in *The Blackwell Companion to Philosophy of Religion*, ed. Charles Taliaferro, Paul Draper, and Philip Quinn (Oxford: Blackwell, 2009), 519.

6. Thanks to Charles Taliaferro on this point.

7. Jaegwon Kim, "Mental Causation and Two Conceptions of Mental Properties" (paper presented at the American Philosophical Association Eastern Division Meeting, Dec. 1993), 22–23.

8. John R. Searle, *Freedom and Neurobiology* (New York: Columbia University Press, 2007), 4.

9. Huw Price, "Naturalism and the Fate of the M-Worlds," *Proceedings of the Aristotelian Society*, supp. vol. 71 (1997): 247.

10. John Searle, *The Mystery of Consciousness* (New York: New York Review of Books, 1997), 154.

11. Michael Ruse and E. O. Wilson, "The Evolution of Ethics," in *Religion and the Natural Sciences*, ed. J. E. Huchingson (Orlando: Harcourt Brace, 1993), 310–11. For discussion on this, see Matthew H. Nitecki and Doris V. Nitecki, *Evolutionary Ethics* (Albany: State University of New York Press, 1993), 8.

12. Francis Crick, *The Astonishing Hypothesis: The Scientific Search for the Soul* (New York: Charles Scribner's Sons, 1994), 3.

13. Anthony O'Hear, *Beyond Evolution: Human Nature and the Limits of Evolutionary Explanation* (Oxford: Oxford, 1997), 195, 199.

14. Richard Dawkins, *A Devil's Chaplain: Reflections on Hope, Lies, Science, and Love* (New York: Houghton Mifflin, 2003), 10–11.

15. Richard Lewontin, "Billions and Billions of Demons," *New York Review of Books*, Jan. 9, 1997, 28–32.

16. Alvin Plantinga, *Warranted Christian Belief* (New York: Oxford University Press, 2000), 218.

17. Thomas Nagel, "Is Consciousness an Illusion?," review of *From Bacteria to Bach and Back Again* by Daniel Dennett, *New York Review of Books*, March 9, 2017, http://www.nybooks.com/articles/2017/03/09/is-consciousness-an-illusion-dennett-evolution/.

18. Richard Fumerton, *Knowledge, Thought, and the Case for Dualism* (Cambridge: Cambridge University Press, 2013), 233.

19. See Wielenberg's *Value and Virtue in a Godless Universe* (Cambridge: Cambridge University Press, 2005); and *Robust Ethics: The Metaphysics and Epistemology of Godless Normative Realism* (Oxford: Oxford University Press, 2014).

Chapter 17

1. Erik J. Wielenberg, "A Defense of Moral Realism," *Faith and Philosophy* 25 (2009): 40n.

2. Cited in *The Existence of God*, ed. John Hick (New York: Collier, 1964), 175.

3. Huston Smith, "The Religious Significance of Postmodernism: A Rejoinder," *Faith and Philosophy* 12 (July 1995): 415.

4. Paul Copan, "Ethics Needs God," in *Debating Christian Theism*, ed. J. P. Moreland, Chad V. Meister, and Khaldoun Sweis (Oxford: Oxford University Press, 2013), 85–100; and Paul Copan, "The Naturalists Are Declaring the Glory of God: Discovering Natural Theology in the Unlikeliest Places," in *Philosophy and the Christian Worldview: Analysis, Assessment and Development*, ed. David Werther and Mark D. Linville (New York: Continuum, 2012), 50–70.

5. Cited in Norman Malcolm, *Ludwig Wittgenstein: A Memoir* (London: Oxford University Press, 1958), 70.

6. Michael Ruse, "Why God Is a Moral Issue," *New York Times*, March 23, 2015, "The Stone" section.

7. John D. Barrow and Joseph Silk, *The Left Hand of Creation*, 2nd ed. (New York: Oxford University Press, 1993), 38.

8. Barrow and Silk, *The Left Hand of Creation*, 209.

9. "Cosmological Argument," in *William L. Rowe on Philosophy of Religion: Selected Writings*, ed. Nick Trakakis (Burlington, VT: Ashgate, 2007), 349.

10. Stephen Hawking and Leonard Mlodinow, *The Grand Design* (New York: Bantam, 2012), 160–62.

11. Timothy Lenoir, *The Strategy of Life* (Chicago: University of Chicago Press, 1992), ix.

12. Richard Dawkins, *River out of Eden* (New York: Basic Books, 1993), 17–18.

13. Francis Crick, *Life Itself: Its Nature and Origin* (New York: Simon & Schuster, 1981), 88.

14. Alfonso Ricardo and Jack W. Szostak, "Life on Earth," *Scientific American* (Sept. 2009): 54.

15. Colin McGinn, *The Mysterious Flame: Consciousness Minds in a Material World* (New York: Basic Books, 1999), 13–14.

16. Geoffrey Maddell, *Mind and Materialism* (Edinburgh: Edinburgh University Press, 1988), 141. David Papineau likewise notes that "to this question [of consciousness's origin] physicalists' 'theories of consciousness' seem to provide no answer." *Philosophical Naturalism* (Oxford: Blackwell, 1993), 119.

17. Michael Lockwood, "Consciousness and the Quantum World," in *Consciousness: New Philosophical Perspectives*, ed. Quentin Smith and Aleksandar Jokic (Oxford: Oxford University Press, 2003), 447.

18. Lockwood, "Consciousness and the Quantum World."

19. William Provine, "Evolution and the Foundation of Ethics," *Marine Biological Laboratory Science* 3 (1988): 27–28.

20. Thomas Nagel, *The View from Nowhere* (New York: Oxford University Press, 1986), 111, 113.

21. Noam Chomsky, *Language and the Problems of Knowledge: The Managua Lectures* (Cambridge, MA: MIT Press, 1988), 157–58.

22. Richard Rorty, *Philosophy and the Mirror of Nature* (Princeton NJ: Princeton University Press, 1979), 387.

23. Taken from Douglas Geivett and James Spiegel, "Beauty: A Troubling Reality for the Scientific Naturalist," in *The Naturalness of Belief*, ed. Paul Copan and Charles Taliaferro (Lanham, MD: Lexington, 2018), 141–57.

24. Steven Weinberg, *Dreams of a Final Theory* (New York: Vintage Books, 1992), 250.

25. Anthony O'Hear, *Beyond Evolution: Human Nature and the Limits of Evolutionary Explanation* (Oxford: Oxford University Press, 1997), 195.

26. O'Hear, *Beyond Evolution*, 199.

27. Paul Draper, "Seeking but Not Believing," in *Divine Hiddenness: New Essays*, ed. Daniel Howard-Snyder and Paul K. Moser (Cambridge: Cambridge University Press, 2002), 204.

28. Joel Marks, "An Amoral Manifesto (Part 1)," *Philosophy Now* 80 (Feb./Mar. 2015), https://philosophynow.org/issues/80/An_Amoral_Manifesto_Part_I.

29. J. L. Mackie, *The Miracle of Theism* (Oxford: Clarendon, 1982), 115.

30. Richard Dawkins, *The Selfish Gene*, 2nd ed. (New York: Houghton Mifflin, 2006), 200–201.

31. Daniel Dennett, *Breaking the Spell: Religion as a Natural Phenomenon* (New York: Viking, 2006), 4.

Chapter 18

1. J. I. Packer, *Knowing God* (London: Hodder & Stoughton, 1973), 5–6.

2. See Justin Brierley's *Unbelievable!* interview with Peter Atkins and Hugh Ross, "Debating the Origins of the Laws of Nature," Aug. 10, 2018, https://www.youtube.com /watch?v=hVCVt-dvVOc.

3. Richard Taylor, *Metaphysics*, 3rd ed. (Englewood Cliffs, NJ: Prentice-Hall, 1974), 103–4.

4. Michael Martin, *Atheism* (Philadelphia: Temple University Press, 1990), 106.

5. John Polkinghorne, *One World* (Princeton, NJ: Princeton University Press, 1986), 67.

6. Hume wrote this in a letter to John Stewart (Feb. 1754). See *The Letters of David Hume*, 2 vols., ed. J. Y. T. Greig (Oxford: Clarendon, 1932), 1:187.

7. Taylor, *Metaphysics*, 103–4.

8. In Bertrand Russell, "Why I Am Not a Christian," in *Why I Am Not a Christian and Other Essays on Religion and Related Topics* (New York: Simon & Schuster, 1957), 6.

9. Daniel C. Dennett, "Atheism and Evolution," in *The Cambridge Companion to Atheism*, ed. Michael Martin (Cambridge: Cambridge University Press, 2007), 143.

10. Paul Davies, "The Birth of the Cosmos," in *God, Cosmos, Nature and Creativity*, ed. Jill Gready (Edinburgh: Scottish Academic Press, 1995), 8–9.

11. See Stephen Hawking and Leonard Mlodinow, *The Grand Design* (New York: Bantam, 2012).

12. See Alexander Vilenkin, "The Beginning of the Universe," in *The* Kalām *Cosmological Argument: Scientific Evidence for the Beginning of the Universe*, ed. Paul Copan (New York: Bloomsbury, 2018), 155.

13. Stephen T. Davis, "The Cosmological Argument and the Epistemic Status of Belief in God," *Philosophia Christi* 1 (1999): 5–15.

14. Paul Williams, *The Unexpected Way: On Converting from Buddhism to Catholicism* (Edinburgh: T&T Clark, 2002), 27–30.

15. Paul Williams, "On Converting from Buddhism to Catholicism: One Convert's Story," http://whyimcatholic.com/index.php/conversion-stories/buddhist-converts/65-buddhist -convert-paul-williams.

Chapter 19

1. Charlotte Brontë, *Jane Eyre*, III.28.9.

2. Paul Davies, *The Mind of God* (New York: Simon & Schuster, 1992), 169.

3. James Rachels, *Created from Animals: The Moral Implications of Darwinism* (New York: Oxford University Press, 1990), 110.

4. John Henry Newman, *The Grammar of Assent*, in *The Letters and Diaries of John Henry Newman*, vol. 25, ed. C. S. Dessain and T. Gornall (Oxford: Clarendon, 1973), 97.

5. Stephen Hawking, *A Brief History of Time* (New York: Bantam, 1988), 121–22.

6. Fred Hoyle, *The Intelligent Universe* (London: Michael Joseph, 1983), 220.

7. Dennett, "Atheism and Evolution," in Martin, *Companion to Atheism*, 144.

8. Roger Penrose, *The Emperor's New Mind* (New York: Bantam, 1991), 344.

9. Penrose, *The Emperor's New Mind*, 344.

10. Mentioned in Stephen Meyer, *Signature in the Cell* (New York: HarperOne, 2009). For documentation of other biologists' calculations, see Meyer's peer-reviewed essay, "Intelligent Design: The Origin of Biological Information and the Higher Taxonomic Categories," in *Proceedings of the Biological Society of Washington* 117, no. 2 (2004): 213–39. For a brief video on the intricacies of the cell, see "Journey Inside the Cell," http://www.uncommondescent.com/intelligent-design/more-on-id-at-justin-brierleys-unbelievable/.

11. John Barrow and Frank Tipler, *The Anthropic Cosmological Principle* (New York: Oxford University Press, 1986), 557–66.

12. Noted in Frank J. Tipler, "Intelligent Life in Cosmology," *International Journal of Astrobiology* 2 (2003): 142.

13. R. E. Michod and D. Roze, "Cooperation and Conflict in the Evolution of Multicellularity," *Heredity* 86 (2003): 2.

14. Michael Polanyi, "Life's Irreducible Structure," *Science* 160 (1968): 1311. Some material here taken from Jeff Schloss, "'Lions and Tigers and Bears, Oh My!': Evolution's Big Three Challenges to Theism?" (paper, Dabar Conference, Trinity Seminary, Deerfield, IL, June 2016).

15. N. T. Wright, *After You Believe* (New York: HarperOne, 2010), 74.

16. Wright, *After You Believe*, 75.

17. Taken from Hugh Ross, *Improbable Planet* (Grand Rapids: Baker Books, 2016), 24.

18. Richard Dawkins, *The Blind Watchmaker* (New York: Norton, 1986), 1.

19. Richard Dawkins, "Big Ideas: Evolution," *New Scientist*, Sept. 17, 2005, 33.

20. Eugene P. Wigner, "The Unreasonable Effectiveness of Mathematics in the Natural Sciences," *Communications in Pure and Applied Mathematics* 13, no. 1 (Feb. 1960), http://www.dartmouth.edu/~matc/MathDrama/reading/Wigner.html.

21. Bertrand Russell, "A Free Man's Worship," in *Mysticism and Logic and Other Essays* (London: Longmans, Green, 1919), 48.

22. Richard Dawkins, *The Blind Watchmaker* (New York: Norton, 1986), 6.

23. Antony Flew, "Letter from Antony Flew on Darwin and Theology," *Philosophy Now* 47 (August/September 2004), https://philosophynow.org/issues/47/Letter_from_Antony_Flew_on_Darwinism_and_Theology.

24. Antony Flew, *There Is a God* (New York: HarperOne, 2008).

25. John Leslie, *Universes*, 14 (London: Routledge, 1989), 14.

26. Leslie, *Universes*, 14 (my emphasis).

27. Richard Dawkins, *The God Delusion* (Boston: Houghton Mifflin, 2006), 157–58.

28. See Del Ratzsch, *Nature, Design, and Science: The Status of Design in Natural Science* (Albany: SUNY Press, 2001), 24.

29. Paul Davies, Are We Alone? (New York: Basic Books, 1995), 96.

30. Immanuel Kant, *The Critique of Pure Reason*, 2nd ed., trans. Norman Kemp Smith (New York: St. Martin's Press, 1929), 521 (A 625–26/B 653–54).

31. Paul Davies, "Physics and the Mind of God," *First Things* (Aug./Sept. 1995): 34.

32. Aristotle, *On the Soul* (De Anima). Note chapter 3 ("Freedom, Human and Nonhuman") in James Reichmann, *Evolution, Animal "Rights," and the Environment* (Washington, DC: Catholic University Press of America, 2000).

Chapter 20

1. Leonard Cohen and Sharon Robinson, "Everybody Knows," on *I'm Your Man*, Sony/ATV Music, 1988.

2. Francis Schaeffer, *The Church at the End of the Twentieth Century*, 2nd ed. (Wheaton, IL: Crossway, 1985), 49–50.

3. Kai Nielsen, *Ethics without God* (Buffalo, NY: Prometheus, 1990), 10–11.

4. *Thomas Reid's Inquiry and Essays*, ed. Keith Lehrer and Ronald E. Beanblossom (Indianapolis: Bobbs-Merrill, 1975), 84–85.

5. C. S. Lewis, *Mere Christianity* (New York: Macmillan, 1943), 17.

6. Michael Martin, "Atheism, Christian Theism, and Rape," *Internet Infidels* (website), http://www.infidels.org/library/modern/michael_martin/rape.html.

7. See Paul Copan, "Is Michael Martin a Moral Realist? *Sic et Non*," *Philosophia Christi* n.s. 1, no. 2 (1999): 45–72; Paul Copan, "Atheistic Goodness Revisited: A Personal Reply to Michael Martin," *Philosophia Christi* 2, no. 1 (2000): 91–104.

8. John E. Hare, *God and Morality: A Philosophical History* (Oxford: Blackwell, 2007).

9. Alex Rosenberg, *An Atheist's Guide to Living* (New York: Norton & Norton, 2012), 286.

10. Cited in Greg Ganssle, "Necessary Moral Truths," *Philosophia Christi* 2, no. 1 (2000): 111.

11. Christian Smith, "Does Naturalism Warrant a Moral Belief in Universal Benevolence and Human Rights?," in *The Believing Primate: Scientific, Philosophical, and Theological Reflections on the Origin of Religion*, ed. J. Schloss and M. J. Murray (Oxford: Oxford University Press, 2009). The idea of "supervenience" is more an assertion than a genuine explanation. On the problems with naturalistic accounts of supervenience, see Alvin Plantinga, "Naturalism, Theism, Obligation, and Supervenience," *Faith and Philosophy* 27 (2010): 247–72.

12. Robert Pirsig, *Zen and the Art of Motorcycle Maintenance* (New York: Bantam, 1976), 143–44.

13. Michael Ruse, *The Darwinian Paradigm* (London: Routledge, 1989), 262.

14. Michael Ruse, "Evolutionary Ethics: A Phoenix Arisen," in *Issues in Evolutionary Ethics*, ed. Paul Thompson (Albany: SUNY Press, 1995), 236.

15. Ruse, "Evolutionary Ethics," 235.

16. Michael Ruse and E. O. Wilson, "The Evolution of Ethics," in *Religion and the Natural Sciences*, ed. J. E. Huchingson (Orlando: Harcourt Brace, 1993), 310–11. For discussion on this, see Matthew H. Nitecki and Doris V. Nitecki, *Evolutionary Ethics* (Albany: SUNY Press, 1993), 8.

17. Charles Darwin to Wm. G. Down, July 3, 1881, in *The Life and Letters of Charles Darwin*, ed. Francis Darwin (London: John Murray, Abermarle Street, 1887), 1:315–16.

18. For example, Erik J. Wielenberg claims that humans "can reason, suffer, fall in love, set goals for themselves" and "experience happiness and tell the difference between right and wrong," which presumably gives them value. Erik J. Wielenberg, "In Defense of Non-Natural, Non-Theistic Moral Realism," *Faith and Philosophy* 26, no. 1 (January 2009): 40.

19. Michael Shermer, *The Science of Good and Evil: Why People Cheat, Gossip, Care, Share, and Follow the Golden Rule* (New York: Henry Holt, 2004), 57.

20. C. S. Lewis, *Miracles* (New York: Macmillan, 1960), 37.

21. Lewis, *Miracles*, 38, 37.

22. John Hick, *Arguments for the Existence of God* (London: Macmillan, 1970), 63.

23. Ruse and Wilson, "The Evolution of Ethics," 311.

24. Michael Ruse, *The Darwinian Paradigm* (London: Routledge, 1989), 262, 268.

25. Randy Thornhill and Craig T. Palmer, *A Natural History of Rape: Biological Bases of Sexual Coercion* (Cambridge, MA: MIT Press, 2000).

26. John Hare, *The Moral Gap: Kantian Ethics, Human Limits, and God's Assistance* (Oxford: Clarendon, 1996).

27. John Rist, *Real Ethics* (Cambridge: Cambridge University Press, 2001), 1.

28. Plato, *Euthyphro* 10a.

29. See Louise Antony, "Atheism as Perfect Piety," in I*s Goodness without God Good Enough? A Debate on Faith, Secularism, and Ethics*, ed. Robert K. Garcia and Nathan L. King (Lanham, MD: Rowman & Littlefield, 2009), 70.

30. For example, William P. Alston, "Some Suggestions for Divine Command Theorists," in Christian Theism and the Problems of Philosophy, ed. Michael D. Beaty (Notre Dame, IN: University of Notre Dame Press, 1990); Thomas V. Morris, "Duty and Divine Goodness" and "The Necessity of God's Goodness," in Anselmian Explorations (Notre Dame, IN: University of Notre Dame Press, 1987); Thomas V. Morris, Our Idea of God (Downers Grove, IL: InterVarsity Press, 1991); etc.

31. Wes Morriston, "What If God Commanded Something Terrible? A Worry for Divine-Command Meta-ethics," *Religious Studies* 45 (2009): 249–67.

32. David Baggett and Jerry Walls, *Good God: The Theistic Foundations of Morality* (New York: Oxford University Press, 2011), 47.

33. For example, Keith Yandell, Richard Swinburne, and Stephen Layman.

34. See William Lane Craig in *Does God Exist?*, ed. Stan W. Wallace (Burlington, VT: Ashgate, 2003), 168–73. Yandell and Swinburne don't believe that God exists in every possible world yet objective moral values exist in all possible worlds.

35. William Lane Craig, "The Most Gruesome of Guests," in Garcia and King, *Is Goodness without God Good Enough?*, 170.

Chapter 21

1. For example, a quick check on the internet brings us to "Obsolete scientific theories" at Wikipedia—and there are many: https://en.wikipedia.org/wiki/Category: Obsolete_scientific_theories.

2. Ian Barbour, *Religion and Science*, rev. ed. (New York: HarperOne, 1997); Mikael Stenmark presents various categories and subcategories in "Ways of Relating Science and Religion," in *The Cambridge Companion to Science and Religion*, ed. Peter Harrison (Cambridge: Cambridge University Press, 2010), 278–95.

3. Stephen J. Gould, *Rocks of Ages: Science and Religion in the Fullness of Life* (New York: Ballantine, 1999).

4. Richard Lewontin, "Billions and Billions of Demons," *New York Review of Books*, Jan. 9, 1997, 28–32.

5. Cited in Lawrence M. Krauss, "God and Science Don't Mix," *Wall Street Journal*, June 2009, http://online.wsj.com/article/SB124597314928257169.html.

6. Alvin Plantinga, "Naturalism against Science," in Daniel C. Dennett and Alvin Plantinga, *Science and Religion* (New York: Oxford University Press, 2011), 64.

7. Craig Keener, *Miracles*, 2 vols. (Grand Rapids: Baker Academic, 2011), 1:439–40. See Keener's documentation and credible reportage of hundreds of such cases.

8. Stephen Hawking, *A Brief History of Time* (New York: Bantam, 1988), 13.

9. Dallas Willard, "Space, Color, Sense Perception and the Epistemology of Logic," *Monist* 72 (Jan. 1989): 122.

10. Roger Trigg, *Beyond Matter: Why Science Needs Metaphysics* (West Conshohocken, PA: Templeton, 2015), 13.

11. Edward Feser, "Nagel and His Critics, Part 2," Oct. 27, 2012, http://edwardfeser.blog spot.com/2012/10/nagel-and-his-critics-part-ii.html.

12. Gerard M. Verschuurren, *What Makes You Tick? A New Paradigm for Neuroscience* (Antioch, CA: Solas Press, 2012), viii.

13. See John J. Collins, *Reading Genesis Well* (Grand Rapids: Zondervan, 2018).

14. Some evangelical scholars (e.g., Tremper Longman III and John Walton), however, see Job as literary rather than historical.

15. See Alvin Plantinga, *Where the Conflict Really Lies* (New York: Oxford University Press, 2012).

16. Plantinga, *Where the Conflict Really Lies*, 34.

17. In chapter 3 of the NAS book *Teaching Evolution and the Nature of Science* (1998), https://www.nap.edu/read/5787/chapter/4#42.

18. Elaine Howard Ecklund, "Religious Scientists: Faith in the American University," *Huffington Post*, May 25, 2011, http://www.huffingtonpost.com/elaine-howard-ecklund-phd /what-is-keeping-universit_b_839161.html.

19. Various naturalistic scientists *assume* a certain conception of God when critiquing theism. For example, an intelligent Designer would apparently have to create organisms with maximum efficiency. Why are some things in nature seemingly "inefficient"—like the clumsy function of a panda's thumb when peeling bamboo or the injury-prone human back? Why not perfect function? As indicated earlier, "inefficiency" or "wastefulness" doesn't seem to bother biblical writers (e.g., Job 39:13–17; Jer. 17:11), for whom efficiency wasn't a central concern. On the one hand, such scientists won't allow for evidence of divine design, but, on the other hand, they'll allow for evidence of divine inefficiency.

20. J. L. Mackie, *The Miracle of Theism* (Oxford: Clarendon, 1982), 19–20.

21. Alvin Plantinga, "Divine Action in the World," in *The Meaning of Theism*, ed. John Cottingham (Oxford: Blackwell, 2007), 116.

22. Paul Davies, *Are We Alone?* (New York: Basic Books, 1995), 96.

23. See Ronald L. Numbers, ed., *Galileo Goes to Jail and Other Myths about Science and Religion* (Cambridge, MA: Harvard University Press, 2012); for a brief overview, see chapter 3 in Alister McGrath, *The Twilight of Atheism: The Rise and Fall of Disbelief in the Modern World* (New York: Doubleday, 2004). See also James Hannam, *God's Philosophers: How the Medieval World Laid the Foundations of Modern Science* (London: Icon, 2010).

24. Bradley Monton, "Is Intelligent Design Science?," Jan. 3, 2006, http://www.arn.org /docs/monton/is_intelligent_design_science.pdf, 2, 9–10.

25. Kitcher says that positing an unobserved Creator doesn't have to be any more unscientific than unobservable particles. *Abusing Science* (Cambridge, MA: MIT Press, 1983), 125.

26. Parsons sees no reason "why, in principle, supernatural hypotheses might not be rigorously tested vis-à-vis natural ones." Keith M. Parsons, "Review of Michael Ruse's *Can a*

Darwinian Be a Christian? (2001)," at https://infidels.org/library/modern/keith_parsons /darwinian.html.

27. Thomas Nagel observes that the definitional limits set by MN on what does or doesn't belong to science "is of limited interest to someone who wants to know whether the hypothesis is true or false." See "Public Education and Intelligent Design," *Philosophy & Public Affairs* 36, no. 2 (2008): 195.

28. W. V. O. Quine said, "I would joyfully accord [spirits or a Creator] scientific status" on par with black holes and quarks if they had "indirect explanatory benefit." See "Naturalism; Or, Living within One's Means," *Dialectica* (June 1995): 252.

29. Swinburne, *The Existence of God* (Oxford: Oxford University Press, 1979), 3.

30. Robert Delfino, "Replacing Methodological Naturalism," *Global Spiral* (May 2007), http://www.metanexus.net/Magazine/tabid/68/id/10028/Default.aspx.

31. Robert Larmer, *Water into Wine?* (Montreal: McGill-Queen's, 1996), 75–92.

Chapter 22

1. I could add that besides Keener's two-volume *Miracles* (Grand Rapids: Baker Academic, 2011), we have J. P. Moreland, *Kingdom Triangle* (Grand Rapids: Zondervan, 2007), chapter 7; and J. P. Moreland, *The God Question* (Eugene, OR: Harvest House, 2009), 138–47, 209–27.

2. Thomas Jefferson, "Letter to William Short" (Oct. 31, 1819), https://founders.archives .gov/documents/Jefferson/98-01-02-0850.

3. Thomas Jefferson, "Letter to Peter Carr, with Enclosure" (Aug. 10, 1787), https://found ers.archives.gov/documents/Jefferson/01-12-02-0021.

4. Again, see Craig Keener, *Miracles*, esp. vol. 1.

5. Diogenes Laertius, *Lives of Eminent Philosophers*, "Epimenides," 10.110, trans. R. D. Hicks, Loeb Classics (Cambridge, MA: Harvard University Press, 1925), 114–15.

6. Keener, *Miracles*.

7. "The 'Milk Miracle' That Brought India to a Standstill," *BBC News*, Dec. 17, 1996, https://www.youtube.com/watch?v=2MG64rk6qkg. Although the Scriptures recognize demonic powers (Rev. 13:13–15; cf. Exod. 7:11, 22; 8:7), see also attempted explanations of the "Hindu Milk Miracle" at https://en.wikipedia.org/wiki/Hindu_milk_miracle.

8. Even Harvard scholar Helmut Koester notes that it is never claimed that Osiris rose from the dead. *Introduction to the New Testament*, vol. 1, *History, Culture, and Religion of the Hellenistic Age* (Philadelphia: Fortress, 1982), 190.

9. Tryggve N. D. Mettinger, *The Riddle of Resurrection: "Dying and Rising Gods" in the Ancient Near East* (Stockholm: Almquist & Wiksell, 2001), 4.

10. These dates are defended by Andreas J. Köstenberger and Justin Taylor in *The Final Days of Jesus: The Most Important Week of the Most Important Person Who Ever Lived* (Wheaton, IL: Crossway, 2014).

11. Gary Habermas, "Resurrection Claims in Non-Christian Religions," *Religious Studies* 25 (1989): 167–77.

12. Richard Dawkins, *The Blind Watchmaker* (New York: Norton, 1986), 139.

13. John Locke, *An Essay Concerning Human Understanding*, XV.5.

14. John Earman, *Hume's Abject Failure: The Argument against Miracles* (Oxford: Oxford University Press, 2000).

15. See David Basinger, *Miracles* (Cambridge: Cambridge University Press, 2018), 18–28.

16. C. S. Lewis, *Miracles* (New York: Macmillan, 1960), 3.

17. See Charles Taliaferro and Anders Hendrickson, "Hume's Racism and His Case against the Miraculous," *Philosophia Christi* 4 (2002): 427–41.

18. See Gary R. Habermas, "Resurrection Research from 1975 to the Present: What Are Critical Scholars Saying?," *Journal for the Study of the Historical Jesus* 3, no. 2 (2005): 135–53.

19. Efforts to find parallels between Christianity and these mystery religions "have failed, as virtually all Pauline scholars now recognize," and to do so "is an attempt to turn the clock back in a way now forbidden by the most massive and learned studies on the subject." N. T. Wright, *What Saint Paul Really Said* (Grand Rapids: Eerdmans, 1997), 172, 173. Historian Michael Grant makes clear that no dying-and-rising-god cults existed in first-century Palestine. *Jesus: An Historian's Review of the Gospels* (New York: Scribner's, 1992), 199.

20. N. T. Wright, *The Resurrection of the Son of God* (Minneapolis: Fortress, 2003), 710.

21. E.g., Jesus's feeding miracle to show he's the bread of life (John 6).

22. Earman, *Hume's Abject Failure*, 43.

23. David Deming, "Do Extraordinary Claims Require Extraordinary Evidence?," *Philosophia* 44, no. 4 (Dec. 2016): 1319–31.

24. J. S. Mill, *A System of Logic: Ratiocinative and Inductive*, 8th ed. (London: Harper and Brothers, 1904), 448.

25. Quoted in Martin E. Marty, "Professor Pelikan," *Christian Century* 123 (June 13, 2006): 47.

Chapter 23

1. R. L. Harris, G. L. Archer, and B. K. Waltke, *Theological Wordbook of the Old Testament* (Chicago: Moody Press, 1980), 430, 951.

2. John Goldingay, *Old Testament Theology*, vol. 1, *Israel's Story* (Downers Grove, IL: InterVarsity Press, 2003), 143–44, 146, 148.

3. Eleonore Stump, "The Mirror of Evil," in *God and the Philosophers*, ed. Thomas V. Morris (New York: Oxford University Press, 1994), 239.

4. Stump, "The Mirror of Evil," 239.

5. See Marilyn M. Adams, "Horrendous Evils," in *Readings in Philosophy of Religion*, ed. Linda Zagzebski and Timothy D. Miller (Oxford: Wiley, 2009).

6. C. S. Lewis, *Surprised by Joy* (New York: Harcourt Brace, 1956), 219.

7. Alexandr I. Solzhenitsyn, *The Gulag Archipelago: 1918–1956*, vol. 2, trans. Thomas P. Whitney (New York: HarperCollins, 2007), 312.

8. Arthur Koestler, *The Lotus and the Robot* (New York: Macmillan, 1961), 273–74.

9. Richard Dawkins, *River out of Eden: A Darwinian View of Life* (New York: Basic Books/HarperCollins, 1995), 132–33.

10. Bertrand Russell, "A Free Man's Worship," in *Mysticism and Logic and Other Essays* (London: Allen & Unwin, 1963), 41.

11. Michael Ruse and E. O. Wilson, "The Evolution of Ethics," in *Religion and the Natural Sciences*, ed. J. E. Huchingson (Orlando: Harcourt Brace, 1993), 310–11.

12. Kai Nielsen, *Ethics without God*, rev. ed. (Buffalo: Prometheus, 1990), 10–11.

13. C. S. Lewis, *Mere Christianity* (New York: Macmillan, 1952), 45–46.

14. Alvin Plantinga, "A Christian Life Partly Lived," in *Philosophers Who Believe*, ed. Kelly James Clark (Downers Grove, IL: InterVarsity Press, 1993), 73.

15. C. S. Lewis, *The Problem of Pain* (New York: Macmillan, 1962), 10.

16. A. N. Wilson, "Why I Believe Again," *The New Statesman*, April 2, 2009, http://www.newstatesman.com/religion/2009/04/conversion-experience-atheism.

Chapter 24

1. J. L. Mackie, "Evil and Omnipotence," in *Readings in the Philosophy of Religion: An Analytic Approach*, ed. Baruch Brody (Englewood Cliffs, NJ: Prentice-Hall, 1974), 157.

2. William L. Rowe, "The Problem of Evil and Some Varieties of Atheism," *American Philosophical Quarterly* 16 (Oct. 1979): 41n. William Alston writes, "It is now acknowledged on (almost) all sides that the logical argument is bankrupt." "The Inductive Problem of Evil and the Human Cognitive Condition," *Philosophical Perspectives* 5 (1991): 29.

3. Alston, "The Inductive Problem of Evil and the Human Cognitive Condition," 29.

4. Peter van Inwagen, "The Problem of Evil, the Problem of Air, and the Problem of Silence," in *The Evidential Problem from Evil*, ed. Daniel Howard-Snyder (Bloomington: Indiana University Press, 1996), 150.

5. Alvin Plantinga, *God, Freedom, and Evil* (Grand Rapids: Eerdmans, 1997), 31. We must distinguish between *logically possible* worlds and *feasible* worlds for God to create. While a sin-free human world is *logically/theoretically* possible, it may not be *feasible* for God to create it since it is up to humans to respond to God's grace and love.

6. J. L. Mackie, *Inventing Right and Wrong* (New York: Penguin, 1977), 15.

7. John Peckham, *Theodicy of Love: Cosmic Conflict and the Problem of Evil* (Grand Rapids: Baker Academic, 2018).

8. Alvin Plantinga in Alvin Plantinga and Michael Tooley, *Knowledge of God* (Oxford: Blackwell, 2008), 152.

9. Christian Smith and Melina L. Denton, *Soul Searching: The Religious and Spiritual Lives of American Teenagers* (New York: Oxford University Press, 2005).

10. David Baggett and Jerry Walls, *Good God: The Theistic Foundations of Morality* (New York: Oxford University Press, 2011), 155.

11. Alvin Plantinga, "A Christian Life Partly Lived," in *Philosophers Who Believe*, ed. Kelly James Clark (Downers Grove, IL: InterVarsity Press, 1993), 71.

12. See, for example, Bruce Little, *God, Why This Evil?* (Lanham, MD: Hamilton, 2010).

13. See Stephen Wykstra, "A Skeptical Theist View," in *God and the Problem of Evil: Five Views*, ed. Chad Meister and James K. Dew (Downers Grove, IL: IVP Academic, 2017), 99–127.

14. C. Stephen Evans, *Philosophy of Religion* (Downers Grove, IL: InterVarsity Press, 1985), 138–39.

15. Peter van Inwagen, "Quam Dilecta," in *God and the Philosophers*, ed. Thomas V. Morris (New York: Oxford University Press, 1994), 47.

16. This portion is taken from David Oderberg, "Morality, Religion, and Cosmic Justice," *Philosophical Investigations* 34, no. 2 (April 2011): 189–213.

17. See chapter 5 in Gordon Graham's important *Evil and Christian Ethics* (Cambridge: Cambridge University Press, 2001).

Chapter 25

1. Hugh Ross, "Hurricanes Bring More than Destruction," *Facts and Faith* 12, no. 4 (1998): 4–5.

2. Hugh Ross, "Tremors Touch Off Questions," *Facts and Faith* 6, no. 3 (1992): 2–3.

3. Daniel Howard-Snyder, "God, Evil, and Suffering," in *Reason for the Hope Within*, ed. Michael Murray (Grand Rapids: Eerdmans, 1999), 93.

4. Eleonore Stump, "The Problem of Evil," *Faith and Philosophy* 2, no. 4 (1985): 409.

5. For one biblical perspective on animal pain and death, see Wes Jamison and Paul Copan, eds., *What Would Jesus Really Eat? The Biblical Case for Eating Meat* (Pickering, ON: Castle Quay, 2019).

6. Richard Swinburne, *Is There a God?* (New York: Oxford University Press, 1996), 110.

7. Peter van Inwagen, *The Problem of Evil* (New York: Oxford University Press, 2006), 127.

8. John Wesley, "The General Deliverance," in *The Works of John Wesley*, 3rd ed. (Grand Rapids: Baker, 1998), 251.

9. See Graham Twelftree, *Jesus the Exorcist*, reprint ed. (Eugene, OR: Wipf & Stock, 2011).

10. Philip Jenkins, *The Next Christendom: The Coming of Global Christianity*, 3rd ed. (New York: Oxford University Press, 2011).

11. Alvin Plantinga, "Supralapsarianism or 'O Felix Culpa,'" in *Christian Faith and the Problem of Evil*, ed. Peter van Inwagen (Grand Rapids: Eerdmans, 2004), 1–25.

12. See, for example, Craig S. Keener, "Paul and Spiritual Warfare," in *Paul's Missionary Methods: In His Time and Ours* (Downers Grove, IL: InterVarsity Press, 2012), 107–23.

13. Gordon Graham, *Evil and Christian Ethics* (Cambridge: Cambridge University Press, 2001), 153.

14. Graham, *Evil and Christian Ethics*, 191–92.

15. Friedrich Hölderlin, *Hyperion*, chapter 10: "Immerhin hat das den Staat zur Hölle gemacht, daß ihn der Mensch zu seinem Himmel machen wollte," at https://gutenberg .spiegel.de/buch/hyperion-264/10.

16. See Thomas Sowell, *A Conflict of Visions* (New York: Basic Books, 2007); also, Steven Pinker, *The Blank Slate: The Modern Denial of Human Nature*, reprint ed. (New York: Penguin, 2003).

17. Philip Jenkins, "Believing in the Global South," *First Things* (Dec. 2006), https://www .firstthings.com/article/2006/12/believing-in-the-global-south.

Chapter 26

1. This draws on themes from "Evil and Primeval Sin," in *God and Evil: The Case for God in a World Filled with Pain*, ed. Chad V. Meister and Jamie K. Dew Jr. (Downers Grove, IL: InterVarsity Press, 2013). See http://www.ivpress.com/cgi-ivpress/book.pl/code=3784.

2. R. C. Sproul Jr., *Almighty over All* (Grand Rapids: Baker, 1999), 51.

3. Sproul, *Almighty over All*, 51.

4. Sproul, *Almighty over All*, 52–53.

5. I follow Augustine's "On Free Will," trans. J. H. S. Burleigh, in *Augustine: Earlier Writings* (Philadelphia: Westminster, 1953). I borrow a good deal from Scott MacDonald's interpretation of Augustine in his essay "Primal Sin," in *The Augustinian Tradition*, ed. Gareth B. Matthews (Berkeley: University of California Press, 1999), 110–39.

6. See William Lane Craig, *The Only Wise God* (Eugene, OR: Wipf & Stock, 1999); Ken-

neth Keathley, *Salvation and Sovereignty: A Molinist Approach* (Nashville: B&H Academic, 2009).

7. For discussions of these Genesis-related topics, see Paul Copan et al., eds., *The Dictionary of Christianity and Science* (Grand Rapids: Zondervan, 2017).

8. MacDonald, "Primal Sin," 130.

Chapter 27

1. Martin Luther, "Admonition to Peace," in *Luther's Works*, vol. 25, ed. Jaroslav Pelikan and Walter Hansen (St. Louis: Concordia, 1975), 345. The "little heathens" remark is noted in Steven Ozment, *Protestants: Birth of a Revolution* (New York: Doubleday, 1991), 165; cf. 168.

2. For example, Christian philosopher Michael Murray and biologist Joshua Swamidass (www.peacefulscience.org) would take this view. We could add others like evangelical theologians John Stott, J. I. Packer, and Henri Blocher.

3. Thanks to Thomas McCall for some of his insights on this topic presented at the Dabar Conference at Trinity Seminary, Deerfield, IL, in June 2018.

4. Thomas R. Schreiner points out that the term *sinful nature* "introduces ontological categories precipitously" into Paul's writings. Believers are no longer "in Adam" (or "in the flesh"); they are "in Christ" and thus "in the Spirit" (Rom. 8:9). See *Paul, Apostle of God's Glory in Christ: A Pauline Theology* (Downers Grove, IL: InterVarsity Press, 2001), 143.

5. Alexandr I. Solzhenitsyn, *The Gulag Archipelago: 1918–1956*, vol. 2, trans. Thomas P. Whitney (New York: HarperCollins, 2007), 312.

6. See Alistaire McFayden, *Bound to Sin: Abuse, Holocaust, and the Christian Doctrine of Sin* (Cambridge: Cambridge University Press, 2006), 16–18.

7. A deep remedy is necessary to remove the stain of original sin in each of us—from conception onward. Even those who die in infancy and have done nothing worthy of judgment still need the death of Christ to remove that lingering corruption that came through Adam's disobedience.

8. Michael Ruse, "Darwinism and Christianity Redux: A Response to My Critics," *Philosophia Christi* 4 no. 1 (2002): 192.

9. G. K. Chesterton, *Orthodoxy*, reprint ed. (Garden City, NY: Image/Doubleday, 1959), 15.

10. Richard Swinburne, *Responsibility and Atonement* (Oxford: Clarendon, 1989), 138.

11. Keith D. Wyma, "Innocent Sinfulness, Guilty Sin: Original Sin and Divine Justice," in *A Reader in Contemporary Philosophical Theology*, ed. Oliver D. Crisp (Edinburgh: T&T Clark, 2009), 288.

12. Douglas Coupland, *Life after God* (New York: Simon & Schuster, 1994), 359.

13. Vernon Grounds, "Called to Be Saints—Not Well-Adjusted Sinners," *Christianity Today*, Jan. 17, 1986, 28.

14. In the previous section, we noted how Adam's actions could represent what we would have done had we been in the same setting—an archetypal or "everyman" perspective on this particular point. That, however, should not be viewed as the entire picture, as though Adam and Eve were not historical.

15. Peter van Inwagen, *The Problem of Evil* (Oxford: Oxford University Press, 2008), 85.

16. On the question of Scripture and science, see the work of Dr. Joshua Swamidass, www.peacefulscience.org; Ann Gauger and Douglas Axe at BioLogic, http://www.biologic institute.org/; Hugh Ross and Fazale Rana at Reasons to Believe, www.reasons.org; and the

organization BioLogos, www.biologos.org. These Christians holding a range of views are engaging in fruitful conversation. Some of those discussions take place through the Creation Project at Trinity Seminary's Henry Center and sponsored by the Templeton Foundation, http://henrycenter.tiu.edu/evangelical-theology-and-the-doctrine-of-creation/.

Chapter 28

1. C. S. Lewis, *The Problem of Pain* (New York: Macmillan, 1962), 118.
2. William V. Crockett, "The Metaphorical View," in *Four Views on Hell*, ed. William V. Crockett (Grand Rapids: Zondervan, 1996), 61.
3. Mortimer Adler, "A Philosopher's Religious Faith," in *Philosophers Who Believe*, ed. Kelly James Clark (Downers Grove, IL: InterVarsity Press, 1993), 222.
4. Jerry Walls, *Heaven, Hell, and Purgatory* (Grand Rapids: Brazos, 2015), 84.
5. What of Matt. 7:21–23, where professing believers seem surprised at Christ's final pronouncement? In response, we should note that they are called "workers of lawlessness" (ESV), which indicates that they wouldn't at all be at home in Christ's presence.
6. Michael J. Murray, "Heaven and Hell," in *Reason for the Hope Within*, ed. Michael J. Murray (Grand Rapids: Eerdmans, 2000), 296.
7. Dallas Willard, *The Allure of Gentleness* (New York: HarperOne, 2015), 67.
8. Willard, *The Allure of Gentleness*, 67.
9. Willard, *The Allure of Gentleness*, 69–70.
10. C. S. Lewis, *The Screwtape Letters* (New York: Touchstone, 1946), 72.
11. See Michael McClymond, *The Devil's Redemption: A New History and Interpretation of Christian Universalism* (Grand Rapids: Baker Academic, 2018), 960–65.
12. *Paradise Lost*, book 1, line 263.
13. Some thoughts here taken from Ioanna-Maria Patsalidou, "Against Universalism" (PhD thesis, University of Glasgow, Scotland, 2011).
14. Michael Ruse in Michael Peterson and Michael Ruse, *Science, Evolution, and Religion* (New York: Oxford University Press, 2016), 22.
15. C. S. Lewis, *The Problem of Pain* (New York: Macmillan, 1962), 118–19.
16. D. A. Carson, *How Long, O Lord?* (Grand Rapids: Baker, 1990), 102. What of the rich man and Lazarus (Luke 16)? The rich man doesn't prefer a God-centered existence but simply wants relief. He (like Judas Iscariot after betraying Jesus) is remorseful, not repentant. He wouldn't have preferred a God-centered existence in paradise.
17. See John Stott's discussion of this in his book (with David Edwards) *Evangelical Essentials: A Liberal-Evangelical Dialogue* (Downers Grove, IL: InterVarsity Press, 1989), 312–29.
18. Jerry Walls, "God and Hell Reconciled," in *God and Evil: The Case for God in a World Filled with Pain*, ed. Chad Meister and James K. Dew Jr. (Downers Grove, IL: InterVarsity Press, 2013), 256.
19. Walls, "God and Hell Reconciled," 256.
20. The account of Polycarp's martyrdom can be found at http://www.earlychristian writings.com/text/martyrdompolycarp-lightfoot.html.
21. N. T. Wright, *Following Jesus* (Grand Rapids: Eerdmans, 1995), 100.
22. N. T. Wright, *Surprised by Hope* (New York: HarperOne, 1998), 183.
23. N. T. Wright, *Evil and the Justice of God* (Downers Grove, IL: InterVarsity Press, 2006), 92, 96.

Chapter 29

1. This chapter in part summarizes ideas taken from Paul Copan, "Incarnation," in *The Dictionary of Christianity and Science*, ed. Paul Copan et al. (Grand Rapids: Zondervan, 2017); and Paul Copan, "Did God Become a Jew?," in *Contending with Christianity's Critics*, ed. Paul Copan and William Lane Craig (Nashville: B&H Academic, 2007), 218–32.

2. The author of Hebrews uses this word *champion*, which was used for the legendary Hercules, who wrestled with and conquered the dark lord of death in order to rescue Alcestis. As William Lane puts it, the author of Hebrews "intended to present Jesus to his hearers in the language that drew freely upon the Hercules tradition in popular Hellenism." William L. Lane, *Hebrews 1–8*, Word Biblical Commentary 47A (Dallas: Word, 1991), 57.

3. C. S. Lewis, "Fern Seed and Elephants," in *Fern-Seed and Elephants and Other Essays on Christianity*, ed. Walter Hooper (London: Collins, 1975), 106–7.

4. C. Stephen Evans, *Exploring Kenotic Christology: The Self-Emptying of God* (Oxford: Oxford University Press, 2006); Stephen T. Davis et al., eds., *The Incarnation: An Interdisciplinary Symposium on the Incarnation of the Son of God* (Oxford: Oxford University Press, 2004).

5. F. F. Bruce and E. K. Simpson, *The Epistles of Paul to the Ephesians and to the Colossians* (Grand Rapids: Eerdmans, 1957), 194.

6. See Thomas V. Morris, *The Logic of God Incarnate* (Ithaca, NY: Cornell University Press, 1986); Thomas V. Morris, *Our Idea of God* (Downers Grove, IL: InterVarsity Press, 1990); Garrett DeWeese, "One Person, Two Natures: Two Metaphysical Models of the Incarnation," in *Jesus in Trinitarian Perspective*, ed. Fred Sanders and Klaus Issler (Nashville: B&H Academic, 2007), 114–53. For a view that challenges and modifies this perspective, see Andrew Ter Ern Loke, *A Kryptic Model of the Incarnation* (Burlington, VT: Ashgate, 2014).

7. Thanks to Andrew Loke for this insight.

8. Loke, *Kryptic Model*, 47–48.

9. Gerald O'Collins, *Interpreting Jesus* (Ramsey, NJ: Paulist, 1983), 186.

10. I borrow these images from Morris, *The Logic of God Incarnate*, 91, 149–50.

11. Gerald Hawthorne, *The Presence and the Power* (Dallas: Word, 1991), 218.

12. Loke, *Kryptic Model*, 148.

13. Loke, *Kryptic Model*, 98.

14. Loke, *Kryptic Model*, 114–15, 117.

15. Loke, *Kryptic Model*, 122.

16. Loke, *Kryptic Model*, 128.

17. Loke, *Kryptic Model*, 132.

Chapter 30

1. Tom Holland, "Why I Was Wrong about Christianity," *New Statesman*, Sept. 14, 2016, http://www.newstatesman.com/politics/religion/2016/09/tom-holland-why-i-was-wrong-about-christianity.

2. Simon Gathercole, *Defending Substitution: An Essay on Atonement in Paul* (Grand Rapids: Baker Academic, 2015), 13–14, 15.

3. Neil B. MacDonald, *Metaphysics and the God of Israel: Systematic Theology of the Old and New Testaments* (Grand Rapids: Baker Academic, 2006), 232.

4. See Euripides, *Alcestis*.

5. MacDonald, *Metaphysics and the God of Israel*, 104.

6. John Stott, *The Cross of Christ* (Downers Grove, IL: InterVarsity Press, 1986), 160.

7. Thanks to Eleonore Stump for this analogy.

8. See Steven Porter, "Rethinking the Logic of Penal Substitution," in *Philosophy of Religion: A Reader and Guide*, ed. William Lane Craig (New Brunswick, NJ: Rutgers University Press, 2002), 596–608.

Chapter 31

1. Allan Bloom, *The Closing of the American Mind* (New York: Simon & Schuster, 1987), 228. For a helpful overview on religious pluralism, see David Basinger, *Religious Diversity: A Philosophical Assessment* (Burlington, VT: Ashgate, 2002).

2. See Subhamay Das, "The Parable of Six Blind Men and the Elephant," *Learn Religions*, https://www.learnreligions.com/six-blind-men-and-the-elephant-1770380.

3. John Hick, *An Interpretation of Religion*, 2nd ed. (London: Macmillan, 2004), 235–36.

4. Dalai Lama, *Kindness, Clarity and Insight* (New York: Snow Lion, 1984), 45.

5. For example, see the quotes at https://pantheism.com/about/luminaries/alan-watts/. For a response, see David K. Clark, *The Pantheism of Alan Watts* (Downers Grove, IL: InterVarsity Press, 1978).

6. See Paul Knitter's discussion in *Can Only One Religion Be True? Paul Knitter and Harold Netland in Dialogue*, ed. Robert B. Stewart (Minneapolis: Augsburg Fortress, 2013).

7. Dalai Lama, *Kindness, Clarity and Insight*, 51.

8. In José Ignacio Cabezón, ed., *The Bodhgaya Interviews* (New York: Snow Lion, 1988), 22.

9. Schmuley Boteach, "Should Christians Stop Trying to Convert Jews?," *Larry King Live*, Jan. 12, 2000, http://www.cnn.com/TRANSCRIPTS/0001/12/lkl.00.html.

10. John Hick, "Religious Pluralism and Absolute Claims," in *Religious Pluralism*, ed. Leroy Rounder (Notre Dame, IN: University of Notre Dame Press, 1984), 197.

11. Joseph Runzo, "God, Commitment, and Other Faiths," *Faith and Philosophy* 5 (1988): 348, 357.

12. Thanks to Alister McGrath on this point.

13. Keith Ward, "Truth and the Diversity of Religions," in *The Philosophical Challenge of Religious Diversity*, ed. Philip L. Quinn and Kevin Meeker (Oxford: Oxford University Press, 1999), 124.

14. Peter van Inwagen, "Non Est Hick," in *God, Knowledge, and Mystery* (Ithaca, NY: Cornell University Press, 1995), 213–14.

15. Alvin Plantinga, "Ad Hick," *Faith and Philosophy* 14 (July 1997): 295–302.

16. Roger Trigg, *Rationality and Religion* (Oxford: Blackwell, 1998), 56–57.

17. Paul Griffiths, *Problems of Religious Diversity* (Oxford: Blackwell, 2001), 149.

18. *Exclusivist, inclusivist,* and *pluralist* are three standard categorizations that aren't always helpful and can overlap. Depending on the context, these terms need further nuancing. For example, a Christian exclusivist shouldn't hold that truth can't be found outside the Christian revelation, and a Christian inclusivist believes that Christ alone is the basis of anyone's salvation. Harold Netland, *Encountering Religious Pluralism* (Downers Grove, IL: InterVarsity Press, 2001).

19. See John Sanders, ed., *What about Those Who Have Never Heard?* (Downers Grove,

IL: InterVarsity Press, 1995); Veli-Matti Kärkkäinen, *An Introduction to the Theology of Religions* (Downers Grove, IL: InterVarsity Press, 2003).

20. See part 5 in Paul Copan, *"True for You, but Not for Me": Overcoming Objections to Christian Faith*, 2nd ed. (Minneapolis: Bethany House, 2009). On this, I follow the work of William Craig.

21. William Lane Craig, "Is 'Craig's Contentious Suggestion' Really So Implausible?," *Faith and Philosophy* 22, no. 3 (July 2005): 361.

22. For example, see Darren Carlson, "When Muslims Dream of Jesus," *The Gospel Coalition*, May 31, 2018, https://www.thegospelcoalition.org/article/muslims-dream-jesus/.

Chapter 32

1. Bernard Williams, "The Makropulos Case: Reflections on the Tedium of Immortality," in *Problems of the Self* (Cambridge: Cambridge University Press, 1973), 82–100.

2. Oscar Cullmann, *Immortality and Resurrection: Four Essays by O. Cullmann*, ed. H. Wolfson, K. Sendahl et al. (New York: Macmillan, 1965).

3. See N. T. Wright, *For All the Saints: Remembering the Christian Departed* (Harrisburg, PA: Morehouse, 2003).

4. See Douglas J. Moo, "Nature in the New Creation: New Testament Eschatology and the Environment," *Journal for the Evangelical Theological Society* 49, no. 3 (2006): 449–88.

5. Some claim that when Jesus says, "Truly I say to you, today you will be with me in Paradise," the comma could be placed after "today": "Truly I say to you today, you will be with me . . ." As it turns out, we only have Jesus using his standard "Truly I say to you" (or "Truly, truly" in John's Gospel)—but never with "today."

6. Some confusion has come from N. T. Wright, who, on the one hand, had previously affirmed as biblical a position strongly resembling substance dualism, but, on the other, came to distance himself from this philosophical position. For a review and critique, see Brandon Rickabaugh, "Responding to N. T. Wright's Rejection of the Soul," *Heythrop Journal* 59 (2018): 201–20. Available at https://www.brandonrickabaugh.com /nt-wright-rejection-of-the-soul.

7. Kevin Corcoran, "Dualism, Materialism, and the Problem of Post Mortem Survival," *Philosophia Christi* 4, no. 2 (2002): 395–409. I was present when Corcoran plainly acknowledged that Jesus and Paul were both substance (body-soul) dualists at the annual American Academy of Religion meeting, San Francisco, CA (Nov. 19, 2011).

8. Stewart C. Goetz, "Human Persons Are Material and Immaterial (Body and Soul)," in *Debating Christian Theism*, ed. J. P. Moreland et al. (New York: Oxford University Press, 2013), 264.

9. Jaegwon Kim, "Mind, Problems of the Philosophy of," in *The Oxford Companion to Philosophy*, ed. Ted Honderich (New York: Oxford University Press, 1995), 578.

10. Kevin Corcoran, "Human Persons Are Material Only," in Moreland et al., *Debating Christian Theism*, 270.

11. C. S. Lewis, *Image and Imagination* (Cambridge: Cambridge University Press, 2013), 47.

12. A. J. Ayer, "What I Saw When I Was Dead," an appendix in Terry Meithe and Antony Flew, *Does God Exist?* (San Francisco: HarperCollins, 1991), 225. See J. P. Moreland and Gary Habermas, *Beyond Death: Exploring the Case for Immortality* (Eugene, OR: Wipf & Stock,

2004); Michael B. Sabom, MD, FACC, *Recollections of Death: A Medical Investigation* (New York: Harper & Row, 1982).

13. See Trenton Merricks, "The Resurrection of the Body and the Life Everlasting," in *Reason for the Hope Within*, ed. Michael Murray (Grand Rapids: Eerdmans, 1999), 261–86. See also comments by Thomas McCall, *An Invitation to Analytic Christian Theology* (Downers Grove, IL: IVP Academic, 2015), 114–21.

14. McCall, *An Invitation to Analytic Christian Theology*, 11–21.

15. Thomas Reid, *An Inquiry into the Human Mind: On the Principles of Common Sense*, ed. Derek R. Brookes, 4th ed. (Edinburgh: University of Edinburgh Press, 1997), 35 (2.6.13–14).

16. See the last chapter of J. P. Moreland, *Consciousness and the Existence of God: A Theistic Argument* (London: Routledge, 2008).

Index